SOCIETY FOR NEW TESTAMENT STUDIES
MONOGRAPH SERIES

MATTHEW BLACK, D.D., F.B.A.

13

JOHANNINE CHRISTOLOGY
AND THE EARLY CHURCH

JOHANNINE CHRISTOLOGY
AND THE
EARLY CHURCH

T. E. POLLARD

Professor of New Testament Studies
in the Theological Hall, Knox College, Dunedin

CAMBRIDGE
AT THE UNIVERSITY PRESS
1970

Published by the Syndics of the Cambridge University Press
Bentley House, 200 Euston Road, London N.W.1
American Branch: 32 East 57th Street, New York, N.Y.10022

© Cambridge University Press 1970

Standard Book Number: 521 07767 2

Printed in Great Britain
at the University Printing House, Cambridge
(Brooke Crutchley, University Printer)

CONTENTS

To Noela

PREFACE

The research on which this work is based was commenced in the Faculty of Divinity of the University of St Andrews under the supervision of Professors J. H. Baxter and E. P. Dickie. Principal Matthew Black and Dr R. McL. Wilson also gave me considerable encouragement and advice. The period of study in St Andrews was made possible by a generous research grant made to me by the late A. Thyne Reid through the Council of St Andrew's College, Sydney. More recently a research grant from the University Grants Committee of New Zealand has enabled me to bring the research up to date. To all of these my deepest gratitude is due.

My thanks are due also to the following:

The Librarians and their assistants in the Libraries of the University of St Andrews, the University of Otago, and Knox College, Dunedin, for helping me to locate important material; the isolation of Australasia and the lack of adequate patristic collections in this part of the world have made research in this field difficult and often frustrating, and I am aware of several *lacunae*, e.g. H. de Riedmatten's collection of the fragments of Paul of Samosata in *Les actes du procès de Paul de Samosate*, and M. Spanneut's collection of fragments of Eustathius of Antioch in *Recherches sur les écrits d'Eustathe d'Antioche*, neither of which was procurable.

My colleague, Professor Ian Breward who has read much of the manuscript and made valuable suggestions, and my former student, the Rev. K. N. Booth, for help with proof-reading and preparation of indices.

Mrs Anne Harvey who has painstakingly typed the manuscript.

The Editors of *The Scottish Journal of Theology* and *New Testament Studies* for permission to use material already published in articles in their Journals.

Lastly, to my wife who bore more than the usual share of family duties in caring for a young family while I carried out my research.

ABBREVIATIONS

ABR	*Australian Biblical Review.*
ACW	*Ancient Christian Writers.*
ANCL	*Ante-Nicene Christian Library.*
Ang	*Angelicum.*
BA	*Biblical Archaeologist.*
BASOR	*Bulletin of the American Schools of Oriental Research.*
BJRL	*Bulletin of the John Rylands Library.*
BullSNTS	*Bulletin of Studiorum Novi Testamenti Societas.*
CBQ	*Catholic Biblical Quarterly.*
CH	*Church History.*
CPT	*Cambridge Patristic Texts.*
CQR	*Church Quarterly Review.*
CTM	*Concordia Theological Monthly.*
DCB	*Dictionary of Christian Biography.*
DOP	*Dumbarton Oaks Papers.*
DTC	*Dictionnaire de théologie catholique.*
ECQ	*Eastern Churches Quarterly.*
ERE	*Encyclopaedia of Religion and Ethics.*
ExpT	*Expository Times.*
GCS	*Die griechischen christlichen Schriftsteller der ersten drei Jahrhunderte.*
Greg	*Gregorianum.*
HJ	*Hibbert Journal.*
HTR	*Harvard Theological Review.*
JBL	*Journal of Biblical Literature.*
JEH	*Journal of Ecclesiastical History.*
JES	*Journal of Ecumenical Studies.*
JRH	*Journal of Religious History.*
JTS	*Journal of Theological Studies.*
LCC	*Library of Christian Classics.*
LCL	*Loeb Classical Library.*
LTQ	*Lexington Theological Quarterly.*
MSR	*Mélanges de science religieuse.*
NovT	*Novum Testamentum.*
NPNF	*Nicene and Post-Nicene Fathers.*
NTS	*New Testament Studies.*
PG	*Patrologiae cursus completus, series graeca* (ed. J. P. Migne).
PL	*Patrologiae cursus completus, series latina* (ed. J. P. Migne).
RAM	*Revue d'Ascétique et Mystique.*

RB	*Revue Biblique.*
RE	*Realencyclopädie für protestantische Theologie und Kirche.*
RGG	*Religion in Geschichte und Gegenwart.*
RHE	*Revue d'histoire ecclésiastique.*
RHPR	*Revue d'histoire et de philosophie religieuses.*
RPh	*Revue de philologie.*
RechSR	*Recherches de science religieuse.*
RevSR	*Revue des sciences religieuses.*
RTP	*Revue de théologie et de philosophie.*
SAB	*Sitzungsberichte der deutschen Akademie der Wissenschaften zu Berlin.*
SC	*Sources chrétiennes.*
SD	*Studies and Documents.*
SE	*Studia Evangelica* (*TU*).
SEÅ	*Svensk exegetisk årsbok.*
SJT	*Scottish Journal of Theology.*
SO	*Symbolae Osloenses.*
SP	*Studia Patristica* (*TU*).
StC	*Studia Catholica.*
ST	*Studia Theologica.*
TCL	*Translations of Christian Literature.*
TDNT	*Theological Dictionary of the New Testament* (tr. G. W. Bromiley).
ThS	*Theological Studies.*
TLZ	*Theologische Literaturzeitung.*
TS	*Texts and Studies.*
TU	*Texte und Untersuchungen zur Geschichte der altchristlichen Literatur.*
TWNT	*Theologische Wörterbuch zum Neuen Testament.*
TZ	*Theologische Zeitschrift.*
VC	*Vigiliae Christianae.*
ZKG	*Zeitschrift für Kirchengeschichte.*
ZNTW	*Zeitschrift für die neutestamentliche Wissenschaft und die Kunde der älteren Kirche.*
ZRGG	*Zeitschrift für Religions- und Geistesgeschichte.*
ZST	*Zeitschrift für systematische Theologie.*
ZTK	*Zeitschrift für Theologie und Kirche.*

INTRODUCTION

The revival of interest in patristic exegesis during the past twenty years has opened up many exciting avenues of study, and is contributing in no small measure to the increasing co-operation and mutual understanding of scholars from the different Christian traditions. Through the study of the way in which the early church used and interpreted scripture, fresh insight is being gained into the way in which doctrine developed in the church.

While this present work concentrates on the way in which the Fathers interpreted St John's Gospel, I am not unaware that other books and key passages of scripture (e.g. Philippians ii. 6 ff., Colossians i. 15 ff., Proverbs viii. 22 ff.) also played an important role. Nevertheless I believe that it was St John's Gospel, with its Logos-concept in the Prologue and its emphasis on the Father–Son relationship, that raised in a most acute way the problems which led the church to formulate her doctrines of the trinity and of the person of Christ.

In this study attention is fixed mainly on the trinitarian problem, although it has been necessary at many points to look at the strictly christological problem as well. Naturally whatever we may say about the relationship between Jesus Christ and God has implications for our doctrine of the person of Christ. In this regard I have found it necessary to modify the *schemata* which have now become familiar in christological discussion since A. Grillmeier's work on early christology in *Das Konzil von Chalkedon*, vol. I, and *Christ in Christian Tradition*. Grillmeier has distinguished between the *Logos–sarx* schema, in which the *Logos* is a divine hypostasis and *sarx* is less than full manhood, and the *Word–man* schema, in which the *Word* is not fully hypostatised and therefore rather an attribute or power of God, and *man* is fully personal manhood. I believe that to complete the picture it is necessary to add a third schema, *God–man*, in which both the divinity and the humanity are seen to be complete.

Any discussion of the development of doctrine in the early church involves semantic difficulties. This is particularly true of the word *Logos*, whose exact meaning in a particular context is frequently very difficult to define. Is it to be translated as 'reason', or 'word', or 'speech', or should it simply be transliterated as 'Logos'? Similar difficulty attends the cognate words λογικός and ἄλογος. I have tried wherever possible to indicate which meaning I believe these words to have, even to the extent of giving translations which may appear to be clumsy and ugly.

In chapter 2 I have avoided any detailed discussion of the relationship between gnosticism and St John's Gospel. My lack of any knowledge of Coptic has prevented me from studying the Nag-Hammadi texts in any detail, and my poor knowledge of Spanish has precluded any assessment of the work of A. Orbe. Readers are referred to the chapter on gnosticism and St John in M. F. Wiles, *The Spiritual Gospel*, and to R. McL. Wilson's recently published *Gnosis and the New Testament*.

In order to complete the study of the influence of St John's Gospel on the development of the doctrine of the person of Christ it would be necessary to go beyond the point at which the trinitarian question is settled to the strictly christological controversies of the end of the fourth and the beginning of the fifth centuries. That, however, is beyond the scope of the present work.

PART I
JOHANNINE CHRISTOLOGY AND THE ANTE-NICENE CHURCH

CHAPTER I

THE CHRISTOLOGY OF ST JOHN

At the turn of this century, F. C. Conybeare, in a review of Alfred Loisy's *Le quatrième évangile*, wrote: 'If Athanasius had not had the Fourth Gospel to draw texts from, Arius would never have been confuted.'[1] That is however only part of the truth, for it would also be true to say that if Arius had not had the Fourth Gospel to draw texts from, he would not have needed confuting. Without in any way diminishing the importance of other biblical writings in the development of the church's doctrine, it is St John's Gospel—and the First Epistle of St John—that brings into sharpest focus the problems which created doctrinal controversy in the early church and which indeed still perplex the church today.

Recent study has made it impossible to draw a hard and fast distinction between the Synoptic gospels as basically historical accounts of the life of Jesus and the Fourth Gospel as basically a theological interpretation of the significance of Jesus, a distinction which appears to have originated as early as the end of the second century when Clement of Alexandria wrote: 'But last of all John, perceiving that the external facts (τὰ σωματικά) had been made plain in the gospel, composed a spiritual (πνευματικόν) gospel.'[2]

The distinction was revived by Baur and the Tübingen school during the first half of the nineteenth century,[3] and became axiomatic for nineteenth-century study of the gospels. In *The Quest of the Historical Jesus*, A. Schweitzer scarcely mentions the Fourth Gospel. In 1904 A. von Harnack could say dogmatically: 'The Fourth Gospel cannot be used as a historical source... (it) can hardly at any point be taken into account as a source for the history of Jesus.'[4] Indeed, almost until the present this radical distinction has been a basic presupposition

[1] *HJ*, VII (1903), 620.
[2] Quoted by Eusebius, *Hist. Eccl.* VI, 14, 7.
[3] A. Schweitzer, *The Quest of the Historical Jesus*, London, 1911, pp. 139 f.
[4] *What is Christianity?*, London, 1904, p. 13.

1-2

of what J. A. T. Robinson has called 'critical orthodoxy',[1] and still appears to be a basic presupposition of the post-Bultmannian scholars engaged in 'the new quest of the historical Jesus'.[2] Recent form- and redaction-criticism of the Synoptic gospels has demonstrated that they are themselves theological interpretations of the Christ-event,[3] while on the other hand, in British scholarship at least, increasing emphasis is being placed on the historical element in St John's Gospel.[4] Nevertheless the closing of the gap between the Synoptics and St John must not be allowed to obscure the fact that however close they may be brought to each other, striking differences will always remain: in St John's Gospel the work of theological reflection and interpretation has been carried to a greater depth than in the Synoptics, or indeed in any other New Testament writing.[5]

Recently John Knox has shown[6] that within the New Testament three distinct types of christology can be seen, sometimes standing in isolation, often standing side by side in the writings

[1] 'The New Look on the Fourth Gospel', SE, I (1959), 338–50, reprinted in Twelve New Testament Studies, London, 1962, pp. 94–106.

[2] Cf. R. E. Brown, 'After Bultmann, What?', CBQ, XXVI (1964), 1–30; especially pp. 28 ff.: 'A third reason for the meagre results of the new quest is the failure to take the Fourth Gospel seriously. The post-Bultmannians take for granted that in John we have the Kerygma so superimposed upon Jesus that very little of what Jesus says or does in John can be taken as historical. Bornkamm (Jesus of Nazareth, London, 1960, p. 14) says flatly that "John is to such a degree the product of theological reflection that it can be treated only as a secondary source".'

[3] E.g. R. H. Lightfoot, The Gospel Message of St Mark, Oxford, 1950; G. Bornkamm, G. Barth and H. J. Held, Tradition and Interpretation in St Matthew, London, 1963; H. Conzelmann, The Theology of St Luke, London, 1960.

[4] Cf. A. J. B. Higgins, The Historicity of the Fourth Gospel, London, 1960; T. W. Manson, Studies in the Gospels and Epistles, Manchester, 1962, ch. 6; C. H. Dodd, Historical Tradition and the Fourth Gospel, Cambridge, 1963. In America, Raymond E. Brown is making a valuable contribution to the study of the historical element in St John; cf. his 'The Problem of Historicity in John', CBQ, XXIV (1962), 1–14 (= New Testament Essays, London, 1965, ch. 9).

[5] This difference is dealt with in a remarkable way by Franz Mussner, The Historical Jesus in the Gospel of St John, London, 1967. One way in which he states the difference is: 'The Johannine Christ speaks differently from the Christ of the synoptics; he speaks John's language' (p. 7).

[6] The Humanity and Divinity of Christ, Cambridge, 1967. Cf. also R. E. Brown, 'How much did Jesus know?', CBQ, XXIX (1967), 26.

4

of the same author and, indeed, intertwined with each other, even though ultimately they may be irreconcilable. The first type, for which evidence may be found in the Petrine speeches in Acts (e.g. ii. 22; iii. 13, 19 ff.; v. 31; x. 38 f.), in the Synoptic accounts of the baptism of Jesus (especially in the Western variant reading of Luke iii. 22), and in Paul's letters (e.g. Rom. i. 4), may be called 'adoptionism', although care must be taken not to read into these passages the developed adoptionist christologies of the dynamic monarchians[1] and of Paul of Samosata.[2] The second type, most clearly discernible in Paul and Hebrews, ascribes pre-existence to Christ and results in a 'kenotic' view of his person during his historical existence, the view that the pre-existent divine being 'emptied himself' (ἐκένωσεν, Phil. ii. 7) in order to become man.[3] The third type of christology, which Knox calls 'incarnationism', is that expressed most explicitly in the Gospel and First Letter of St John, the view that God became man in Jesus, in whose earthly existence the divinity is fully present in, with and under the humanity. Knox points out that 'incarnationism' is always in danger of passing over into 'docetism' in which the divinity is so strongly emphasised that the humanity is evaporated into mere appearance or fantasy. Yet in both Gospel and Letter, St John[4] opposes docetism which was already being suggested as a christology in the church or churches for which he wrote. Aware of the dangers of docetism, he strives to hold in balance the divinity and humanity of Jesus.

St John's 'incarnationism' raises, in a way that 'adoptionism' and 'kenoticism' do not, the problems of christology. It may be debated whether it was necessary for the church to go beyond either of the latter to the deeper insight of 'incarnationism', but the fact quite simply is that in the Johannine writings the church did penetrate to this christological depth, and in doing so found itself forced, during the next four centuries, to explicate the double problem posed by the Johannine christology:

[1] See below, pp. 51 ff.   [2] See below, pp. 113 ff.

[3] There is wide agreement that this idea is pre-Pauline, finding its most explicit expression in the hymn, Phil. ii. 6–11. Cf. R. P. Martin, *Carmen Christi*, Cambridge, 1967, for the most recent exhaustive study of this hymn.

[4] The question of identity of authorship for Gospel and Epistle is still an open one. If they are not from the same hand, they are certainly from the same school.

(i) the relationship between the pre-existent Logos–Son and the godhead, and

(ii) the relationship between the divine and the human in Jesus Christ.

'Church teaching had to develop trinitarian and christological dogma side by side if it was to maintain the divine Sonship of Christ in any true sense.'[1]

A. THE PROLOGUE AND THE LOGOS-CONCEPT[2]

The importance of the Logos-concept, which St John uses in the Prologue of his Gospel (i. 1–18), for later christological formulation can hardly be over-estimated, yet, as G. L. Prestige[3] says, 'the doctrine of the Logos, great as was its importance for theology, harboured deadly perils in its bosom'. What these perils were will become clear in the course of this study; at this stage it must be asked whether, in fact, St John had 'a doctrine of the Logos', what content the Logos-concept had for him and why he chose it as a means of introducing his readers to the Gospel of Jesus Christ.

Commentators are unanimous in emphasising that the concept of the Logos, or rather a variety of concepts of Logos, was current in the Graeco-Roman world of the first century A.D. Therefore it would make a suitable point of contact for the evangelist as he sought to commend his gospel. That he uses it primarily—we may almost say solely—as a point of contact should be evident from the fact that, having used the concept in the Prologue, he does not use it again, and that in his closing words he says that the purpose of his Gospel is 'that you may believe that Jesus is the Christ, the Son of God, and that believing you may have life in his name' (xx. 31).[4] The regulative christological concept of the Gospel is not *Logos*, but *the Christ*,

---

[1] A. Grillmeier, *Christ in Christian Tradition*, London, 1965, p. 93.

[2] The amount of literature on the Prologue and Logos-concept is vast. For a good select bibliography see R. E. Brown, *The Gospel according to St John*, New York, 1966, I, appendix II. Cf. also Arndt–Gingrich, *Lexicon*, λόγος.

[3] *God in Patristic Thought*, London, 1952, p. 129.

[4] It is generally agreed that chap. 21 is an epilogue added by the final redactor of the Gospel. Cf. R. E. Brown, *The Gospel according to St John*, I, xxxvi.

the Son of God. 'The historical redemptive role of the incarnate Son has a full-bodied vitality which the Logos-concept is hardly fitted to express, and the fact that the author drops the term before the Prologue is concluded makes it clear that it is not capable of expressing adequately what he wants to say about Jesus.'[1]

The prevalence of a variety of Logos-concepts in the first-century Hellenistic world, together with the variety of interpretations given to the concept by the gnostics and the early Fathers, makes it important to investigate the meaning which the term had for St John himself, who as far as we know was the first to apply it as a title to Jesus Christ. In Johannine research in the past century the roots of St John's Logos-concept have been found in every type of Logos-speculation that was current in the first Christian centuries and even in later centuries.[2] For a long time it was widely assumed that the Fourth Gospel was the most 'hellenistic' writing in the New Testament, with little or no contact with the Palestine in which the Gospel events took place.[3] Recently, mainly due to the discovery of the Dead Sea Scrolls and their remarkable parallels with the Fourth Gospel, increasing emphasis has been placed on the Palestinian-Jewish milieu of Johannine thought and the Palestinian-Jewish tradition on which the Gospel rests.[4] If Johannine thought has

---

[1] F. V. Filson, 'The Gospel of Life', in *Current Issues in New Testament Interpretation* (ed. W. Klassen and G. F. Snyder), London, 1962, pp. 111 ff.

[2] Cf. P. H. Menoud, *L'évangile de Jean d'après recherches récentes*, Neuchâtel and Paris, 1947; W. F. Howard, *The Fourth Gospel in Recent Criticism* (4th edn. revised by C. K. Barrett), London, 1955.

[3] Another of 'the presuppositions of critical orthodoxy' which J. A. T. Robinson, 'The New Look on the Fourth Gospel', calls in question.

[4] It would not be possible to give a complete bibliography on this point. The following is merely a representative sample: R. E. Brown, *The Gospel according to St John*, i, lix ff.; 'The Qumran Scrolls and the Johannine Gospels and Epistles', *CBQ*, XVII (1955), 559 ff., reprinted in K. Stendahl (ed.), *The Scrolls and the New Testament*, New York, 1957, pp. 183 ff.; 'Second Thoughts: the Dead Sea Scrolls and the New Testament', *ExpT*, LXXVIII (1966–7), 21 ff.; K. G. Kuhn, 'Johannesevangelium und Qumrantexte', in *Neotestamentica et Patristica* (Supplement to *NovT*, VI), pp. 111 ff.; 'Die in Palästina gefundenen hebräischen Texte und das N.T.', *ZTK*, XLVII (1950), 192 ff.; L. Mowry, 'The Dead Sea Scrolls and the Background for the Gospel of John', *BA*, XVII (1954), 78 ff.; W. H. Brownlee, 'A Comparison of the Covenanters of the D.S.S. with pre-Christian Jewish Sects', *BA*, XIII (1950), 71 ff.; F. M. Braun, 'L'arrière-fond judaïque du quatrième

its roots in Palestinian soil and rests on a Palestinian-Jewish tradition which originated before the fall of Jerusalem in A.D. 70,[1] it would appear reasonable that the first place to look for the content of St John's Logos-concept would be this same milieu.

A considerable number of scholars have emphasised that 'the roots of the doctrine are in the Old Testament and that its main stem is the *d⁰bhar Yahweh*, the creative and revealing Word of God, by which the heavens and the earth were made and the prophets inspired'.[2] Pedersen emphasised that the Hebraic *dabhar*-concept is dynamic rather than static,[3] and his insight has been developed by Boman,[4] Macnicol,[5] and Knight[6] amongst others. Macnicol says that in Hebrew thought 'a true word is both speech and action';[7] the Word of God 'is God Himself in action', an effective word 'which is powerful in proportion as this word is the Word of God Himself, uttered by the Almighty, and therefore certain to accomplish that which He pleases'.[8]

évangile et la Communauté d'Alliance', *RB*, LXI (1955), 5 ff.; *Jean le théologien*, Paris, 1959, I, 226 ff.; Millar Burrows, *The Dead Sea Scrolls*, London, 1955, pp. 338 ff.; *More Light on the Dead Sea Scrolls*, London, 1958, pp. 123 ff.; M. Black, 'Theological Conceptions in the Dead Sea Scrolls', *SEA*, XVII–XIX (1953–4), 80 ff.; W. Grossouw, 'The Dead Sea Scrolls and the New Testament: a Preliminary Survey', *StC*, XXVI (1951), 289 ff.; XXVII (1952), 1 ff.; W. F. Albright, 'Recent Discoveries in Palestine and the Gospel of John', in *The Background of the N.T. and its Eschatology* (ed. W. D. Davies and D. Daube), Cambridge, 1956, pp. 153 ff.

[1] Cf. J. A. T. Robinson, 'New Look'; R. D. Potter, 'Topography and Archaeology in the Fourth Gospel', *SE*, I (1959), 329 ff.; W. F. Albright, 'Recent Discoveries'; A. M. Hunter, 'Recent Trends in Johannine Studies', *ExpT*, LXXI (1959–60), 164 ff.; C. H. Dodd, *Historical Tradition*.

[2] T. W. Manson, *Studies in the Gospels and Epistles*, p. 118; cf. E. Stauffer, *New Testament Theology*, London, 1955, pp. 55 ff.

[3] J. Pedersen, *Israel, its Life and Culture*, I–II, Oxford, 1926.

[4] *Hebrew Thought compared with Greek*, London, 1960, pp. 58 ff.

[5] 'Word and Deed in the N.T.', *SJT*, V (1952), 237 f.

[6] *A Biblical Approach to the Doctrine of the Trinity* (*SJT* Occasional Paper 1), Edinburgh, 1953; *From Moses to Paul*, London, 1949.

[7] 'Word and Deed', p. 240.

[8] P. 247. Cf. Boman, p. 67. James Barr (*The Semantics of Biblical Language*, Oxford, 1961, pp. 129 ff.) criticises Pedersen and Macnicol for their treatment of the semantics of *dabhar*. This criticism does not appear to apply to Macnicol's study of *d⁰bhar Yahweh*, which appears to be valid even if his treatment of *dabhar* taken by itself is open to criticism.

Grillmeier[1] and Dodd,[2] as well as others before them,[3] have correctly pointed out that along with this Old Testament idea of 'the Word of Yahweh', another Old Testament concept closely related to it must be taken into account—the concept of Wisdom (חכמה–σοφία)—even though 'Wisdom' is never directly said to be 'the Word of Yahweh'.[4]

The Wisdom of the Old Testament and the Logos of St John have many features in common. Both exist from the beginning (Prov. viii. 22; Ecclus. xxiv; John i. 1; cf. Gen. i. 1),[5] and dwell with God (Ecclus. xxiv. 4 LXX; Prov. viii. 23–5, 30). Common to both is their work in the world, though this is emphasised more strongly in Proverbs and Ecclesiasticus than, for example, in John i. 3, 10. Wisdom and Logos come to men (Ecclus. xxiv. 7–22 LXX; Prov. viii. 31) and 'tabernacle' with them (Ecclus. xxiv. 8 LXX—John i. 14). So strong is the similarity between the Johannine Prologue and Proverbs viii and Ecclesiasticus xxiv that we can speak of a literary dependence.[6]

Grillmeier suggests that St John avoided using the word 'Wisdom' on purpose because in both its Greek and Hebrew forms (σοφία–חכמה) it is feminine, and as such would lend itself to gnostic speculation, although there is no evidence that by the end of the first century (the latest possible date for the composition of the Gospel) proto-gnostic speculation had begun to elaborate the system of male–female syzygies which were to be a prominent feature of the more sophisticated gnostic systems which Irenaeus, Hippolytus and Tertullian were to attack a century later.

Some attempt has been made to link the Johannine Logos-concept with the Rabbinic concept of *memra* (מימרא),[7] which

[1] *Christ in Christian Tradition*, pp. 30 f.

[2] *The Interpretation of the Fourth Gospel*, Cambridge, 1953, pp. 273 ff.

[3] E.g. J. Rendell Harris, *The Origin of the Prologue to St John's Gospel*, Cambridge, 1917. Cf. also P. Bonnard, *La Sagesse en Personne, annoncée et venue: Jésus-Christ*, Paris, 1966, pp. 123 ff.

[4] However, in Ecclus. xxiv. 3 Wisdom says, 'From the mouth of the Most High I came forth'.

[5] Cf. *Rashi's Commentary on the O.T.* (ed. A. M. Silbermann, London, 1946) at Genesis i. 1.

[6] Grillmeier, pp. 30 f.

[7] Cf. Strack and Billerbeck, *Kommentar zum N.T. aus Talmud und Midrasch*, Munich, 1924, II, 302–33; C. K. Barrett, *The Gospel according to St John*, London, 1955, p. 128; R. E. Brown, *The Gospel according to St John*, I, pp. 523 f.

was used as a reverential periphrasis for the name of God. While it must not be entirely discounted as an illuminating parallel in Jewish thought, the lack of evidence for its use in Judaism contemporary with St John's Gospel makes any argument for dependence of St John upon it exceedingly tenuous.

Passing reference has already been made to the close parallels in terminology and thought-forms between the Dead Sea Scrolls and the Johannine writings; these parallels have led many scholars to see in Essene Judaism the 'genuine old Jewish milieu'[1] and 'ideological atmosphere'[2] of Johannine thought. Of particular interest for our present purpose is the remarkable parallel between John i. 3 and *The Manual of Discipline* xi. 11, a passage which is echoed elsewhere in the *Manual* and in the *Hymns of Thanksgiving*:[3]

'All things come to pass by his (God's) knowledge;
He establishes all things by his design
and without him nothing is done.'[4]

Brownlee declares this to be 'an approach to the doctrine of the Logos';[5] Cullmann says that here 'the divine thought appears as mediator of creation';[6] while Reicke says that 'what the Qumran text calls "the knowledge" or "the thought" of God is actually his creative intellect or very much the same as what the Fourth Gospel calls the Logos of God'.[7] The parallel is too close to be accidental, and if it is legitimate to speak, as Grillmeier does,[8] of 'a literary dependence' of the Prologue on Prov. viii and Ecclus. xxiv, there appears to be even more justification for speaking of a literary dependence of John i. 3 on this hymn which forms the concluding section of *The Manual*

---

[1] Grossouw, 'D.S.S. and N.T.', p. 289 (see p. 7, n. 4 above).

[2] O. Cullmann, 'The Significance of the Qumran Texts for Research into the Beginnings of Christianity', *JBL*, LXXIV (1955), 216, reprinted in K. Stendahl (ed.), *The Scrolls and the N.T.*, p. 20.

[3] *Manual* iii. 15; xi. 17 f.; *Hymns* i; x; xiv. 27.

[4] G. Vermes' translation in *The Dead Sea Scrolls in English*, London, 1962, p. 93. It should be noted that the context of this passage and of all the echoes of it is not cosmological but ethical; cf. my article 'Cosmology and the Prologue of the Fourth Gospel', *VC*, XII (1958), 147–53.

[5] 'Comparison of the Covenanters of the Dead Sea Scrolls', pp. 71 ff. (p. 7, n. 4 above).

[6] 'Significance of the Qumran Texts', p. 216.

[7] 'Traces of Gnosticism in the D.S.S.?', *NTS*, I (1954–5), 140.

[8] *Christ in Christian Tradition*, pp. 30 f.; cf. p. 9, n. 6 above.

of Discipline. Furthermore, if, as Grillmeier suggests,[1] St John intentionally avoided using the Greek word σοφία (Wisdom), so also it is possible that he intentionally avoided the Greek equivalent of the Hebrew דעת (γνῶσις–knowledge) because it was already being used in gnostic circles. That this avoidance is intentional is made almost certain by the fact that while St John uses the verb γινώσκειν more frequently than any other New Testament writer, he never uses the noun γνῶσις.

In any investigation of the background and roots of St John's Logos-concept, the possible influence of 'New Testament formulas and ideas which had taken shape before him'[2] must not be overlooked. Elsewhere in the New Testament, particularly in Acts and the Pauline letters, λόγος frequently bears the meaning 'message', i.e. the message of the Gospel (Acts viii. 25; I Thess. i. 6 and elsewhere).[3] For St John the central content of the message is Jesus Christ himself; he, himself, is *the message*, the message made flesh. It is possible to see in the prologue to the First Letter of John an intermediate stage between this extra-Johannine usage of λόγος and the Johannine designation of Christ himself as the λόγος; I John i. 1: τοῦ λόγου τῆς ζωῆς —'the word of life' which 'we have looked on...and touched' (i. 1); it 'has been made visible' and 'we have seen it' (i. 2). In i. 5 this λόγος τῆς ζωῆς is equated with ἡ ἀγγελία (= 'message').

None of these concepts—Word, Wisdom, Knowledge—in its pre-Johannine usage has been hypostasised or personalised, although in the Wisdom Literature Wisdom is frequently personified (Prov. viii; Ecclus. xxiv), as also is Logos in the Wisdom of Solomon (xviii. 15).[4] C. H. Dodd attempts to 'account for the whole of the doctrine of the Prologue',[5] arguing that it is necessary to look beyond the concepts of the Word of Yahweh and of Wisdom to the Logos-concept found in the syncretistic Jewish philosophy of Philo of Alexandria.

---

[1] P. 31.

[2] Grillmeier, p. 31. He cites Paul's description of Christ as 'the wisdom of God' (I Cor. i. 24), as 'the image of the invisible God, the first-born of all creation' (Col. i. 15).

[3] Cf. Brown, *Gospel according to St John*, I, appendix II.

[4] Cf. R. E. Murphy, 'Assumptions and Problems in O.T. Wisdom Research', *CBQ* XXIX (1967), 109 ff.

[5] *Interpretation of the Fourth Gospel*, p. 273.

He concludes that 'the substance of a Logos-doctrine similar to that of Philo is present all through the Gospel...with and in the Hebraic conception of the Word of God'.[1] Few commentators would now be prepared to follow Dodd's emphasis on 'Philonic' background of the Gospel, while most would feel that to attempt to account for the whole of John's doctrine of the Logos in terms of extra-Johannine thought implies, at least, that the evangelist lacks any originality. St John must be recognised as 'a thinker *sui generis*. He stands unique and alone not only in the ancient world, but also in the primitive church.'[2] He is 'a figure with his own originality'.[3] No one familiar with Philo's writings can fail to notice the parallels with the Johannine Prologue, but these parallels can be accounted for by the view that they are due to common dependence on the Old Testament. 'In the concept of the *Logos* they both draw on the Wisdom Literature of the Old Testament.'[4]

St John's use of the Logos-concept in the Prologue has points of contact with many forms of contemporary thought, but clearly he 'does not seek to bring himself into line with the surrounding world, but to make the world understand, and in speaking to the world the language it can understand, the very person of Jesus'.[5] He uses the Logos-concept, whatever it meant for him, only in order to establish contact with his readers, whoever they were. Once he has identified the Logos (made

[1] *Ibid.* p. 279. For a detailed criticism of Dodd's argument see my article, 'The Background of the Fourth Gospel and its Early Interpretation', *ABR*, VII (1959), 41 ff.; there I was over-critical of Dodd's insistence on Johannine dependence on the Wisdom-concept. Dodd's use of the Philonic Logos-concept to illuminate the Gospel is paralleled by H. A. Wolfson, *The Philosophy of the Church Fathers*, 2nd ed., Harvard, 1964, I, 177 ff., who simply assumes without argument that 'proceeding to re-write Paul's sketch of the pre-existent Christ in terms of Philonic philosophy, John substitutes the term Logos for Paul's wisdom or Holy Spirit' (pp. 177 f.).

[2] Stauffer, *N.T. Theology*, p. 42.

[3] R. Bultmann, *Theology of the N.T.*, London, 1955, II, 9.

[4] Brown, *Commentary*, p. lviii; cf. R. McL. Wilson, 'Philo and the Fourth Gospel', *ExpT*, LXV (1953–4), 47 ff. F. M. Braun (*Jean le théologien*, II, 298): 'If Philo had never existed, the Fourth Gospel would most probably not have been any different from what it is.' Cf. also A. H. Armstrong and R. A. Markus, *Christian Faith and Greek Philosophy*, London, 1960, pp. 19 f.

[5] H. Odeberg, 'Ueber das Johannesevangeliums', *ZST*, 1939, quoted by P. H. Menoud, *L'évangile de Jean d'après recherches récentes*, p. 46.

flesh) with 'the only Son' in i. 14, he discards the concept, never to use it again. That fact, by itself, should be sufficient to put us on guard against seeking in the Prologue a developed doctrine of the Logos which reflects the varied forms of Logos-speculation in his environment. If those scholars are right who emphasise the essential Jewishness of St John's Gospel and the Palestinian-Jewish character of the Johannine tradition, it appears unnecessary and unwise to look beyond Palestinian Judaism for the background of this concept which plays so severely limited a role in St John's presentation of the Gospel message.

While the Prologue can stand by itself[1] it is evident that St John is far more interested in Jesus Christ, the Son of God, than he is in the Logos, and that he intended the Prologue to be interpreted in the light of the rest of the Gospel. Or, to put it more specifically, he intended the Logos of the Prologue to be interpreted in the light of Jesus the Christ, the Son of God, whose earthly life is the theme of the Gospel. The subject of the Gospel is Jesus Christ, not the Logos. Therefore, although we have insisted that the Palestinian-Jewish background of Johannine thought applies to the Logos-concept just as much as to the rest of the Gospel, the question of the meaning of the concept for St John is ultimately of only secondary importance and it may be asserted that in reality St John has no doctrine of the Logos.[2]

It is notoriously difficult, if not impossible, to decide at what exact point in the Prologue St John begins to think of the *incarnate* Logos, Jesus Christ, that is, at what point he passes from the pre-existent Logos to the historical Jesus. Serafin de Ausejo[3] holds that throughout the Prologue Logos means 'the Word-become-flesh', and that the whole hymn refers to Jesus

---

[1] An impressive array of scholars has argued that behind the Prologue lies a hymn either composed in Johannine circles or appropriated by them, interpolated to form a prologue for the Gospel. R. E. Brown, *Gospel according to St John*, pp. 18 f., lists the analyses made by eight scholars, and himself adds his own tentative reconstruction. That a hymn has formed the basis for the Prologue we do not doubt; what we are concerned with here is the Prologue as it stands in the context of the Gospel.

[2] W. F. Lofthouse, *The Father and the Son: A Study in Johannine Thought*, London, 1934, p. 64.

[3] 'Es un himno a Cristo el prologo de San Juan', *Estudios Biblicos*, xv (1956), 223-77, 381-427. Cf. R. E. Brown, *St John*, p. 25.

Christ. This view is not without its difficulties, yet in view of St John's emphasis on Jesus as Son of God, it must be agreed that from the beginning St John has Jesus Christ in mind. 'The Prologue, which can be read as Hellenistic philosophy, and as rabbinic mysticism, can also be read as history... The Logos exists, but is unknown and incomprehensible apart from the historical figure of Jesus.'[1] The Johannine perspective, in which the Logos-concept is far less important than the Son-concept, was not understood by some early Christian writers or by the gnostics, who magnified the Logos-concept to make it the master-concept of their religious thinking. Some filled the concept with the content of current Greek philosophy (Stoicism and Middle-Platonism); others filled it with content from the syncretistic system of Philo; while others interpreted it in the terms of the Jewish theology of the Word and Wisdom. Having thus formulated a doctrine of the Logos, they proceeded, each according to his own background, to interpret the rest of the Gospel in the light of his peculiar interpretation of the Prologue. Thus, very frequently christological views were built on a basic misunderstanding of St John's own intention.

The Prologue provides a summary of the Gospel, or perhaps rather an overture in which the stage is set and the atmosphere created for the drama of the Gospel, and the main themes of the Gospel are announced. The Logos is declared to be eternally pre-existent 'with' or 'in relation to' God (πρὸς τὸν θεόν, i. 1b) and himself 'God' (θεὸς ἦν ὁ λόγος, i. 1c; μονογενὴς θεός, i. 18).[2] He was and is the mediator of all of God's activity *ad extra*. A strong case can be made in support of the view that John i. 3a, πάντα δι᾿ αὐτοῦ ἐγένετο, has a wider field of reference than the traditional specific reference to creation. It refers to all God's activity *ad extra*, in creation, revelation and salvation, and is an announcement of the general theme of the mediatorship of the Logos-Son, which is to be specified later in the Prologue as mediatorship:

(a) *In creation* (i. 10).

(b) *In revelation*: the Logos is 'the light', 'the true light' (i. 4, 5, 9), 'full of grace and truth' (i. 14); thus 'grace and truth' have come

---

[1] C. K. Barrett, *The Gospel according to St John*, p. 129.

[2] The discovery of the reading μονογενὴς θεός in the Bodmer papyri, 𝔓66 and 𝔓75, has made the originality of this difficult reading almost certain.

'through him' (δι' αὐτοῦ); he, 'the only God, who is in the bosom of the Father has made him known' (i. 18).

(c) *In salvation*: to all who received him and believed in his name 'he gave power to become the children of God' (i. 12–13), and from his fullness believers receive 'grace upon grace' (i. 16).[1]

Thus the Prologue declares the threefold mediatorial activity of the Logos. Mediatorship in creation is not mentioned within the rest of the Gospel, which is concerned with the revelation of God and the redemption of men through Jesus Christ, God's only Son, through his life and words, his death and resurrection.

Further, the Prologue announces clearly the two stark paradoxes of the Christian faith: (i) the trinitarian paradox of the relationship between the Son and the Father, distinct yet one in the unity of the Godhead, the paradox of distinction-within-unity; and (ii) the paradox of the humanity and divinity of Jesus Christ, the Word-made-flesh. Both of these paradoxes, announced in the Prologue, become more explicit in the body of the Gospel itself.[2]

B. THE FATHER–SON RELATIONSHIP

The Gospel of St John is pre-eminently the Gospel of 'the Father and the Son'.[3] To say that is not to deny that the Fatherhood of God and the divine sonship of Jesus occupy an important place in the Epistles and Synoptic Gospels. For example, the famous Q-saying in Matt. xi. 27 (= Luke x. 22) and Jesus' use of the word *Abba* in address to God[4] show that 'awareness

---

[1] I have discussed John i.3 and its relation to the prologue in detail in 'Cosmology and the Prologue of the Fourth Gospel', *VC*, xII (1958), 147–53. My argument has been taken up and developed by Paul Lamarche, 'Le prologue de Jean', *RSR*, LII (1964), 497 ff., who strengthens my argument with additional evidence from LXX and *The Gospel of Truth*, 37.22–4.

[2] Objection may be made against the use of the word 'paradox', a word which has recently become suspect in systematic theology. The New Testament word μυστήριον (mystery) may be preferable, but any attempt to state the 'mystery' of the person of Christ, it seems to me, requires the use of 'paradoxical' language, and therefore the word 'paradox' is hard to avoid.

[3] This is the title of W. F. Lofthouse's excellent but seldom noticed study of Johannine theology; cf. p. 13, n. 2 above.

[4] Cf. T. W. Manson, *The Teaching of Jesus*, 2nd edn. Cambridge, 1935, pp. 330 f.; J. Jeremias, *The Central Message of the New Testament*, London, 1965, pp. 9 ff.

of Christ's divine sonship exists in the deepest stratum of the synoptic tradition as well as in John'.[1] Nevertheless, the divine sonship of Jesus, or rather the divine Father–Son relationship, is emphasised more strongly by St John than any other New Testament writer. For him the sonship of Jesus is 'unique' (μονογενής);[2] he asserts unequivocally that 'the Logos was God' (i. 1c), that 'the Logos became flesh' (i. 14), and that this enfleshed Logos is Jesus Christ (i. 16, 17) who is 'the only Son of the Father' (i. 14, 18; iii. 16, 18; cf. I John iv. 9). Later in the Gospel Jesus does not deny or refute the charge that by claiming to be the Son of God he is making himself God (ποιεῖς σεαυτὸν θεόν, x. 33). Throughout the Gospel Jesus alone is called 'the Son' (ὁ υἱός); those who welcome him and believe in his name become 'children' (τὰ τέκνα) of God (i. 12). He claims that he and the Father are 'one' (x. 30), that he is in the Father and the Father in him (x. 38; xiv. 10), that he who has seen him has seen the Father (xiv. 9). The climax of the Gospel is reached when, after the resurrection, for the first time one of his disciples explicitly acknowledges the divinity of Jesus with Thomas' confession: 'My Lord and my God' (xx. 28).[3]

The pre-existence of the Logos with God 'in the beginning' is emphatically stated in the opening words of the Gospel (i. 1–2). The pre-existence of Jesus Christ, the Son of God, is explicitly asserted in the Gospel itself (i. 15, 30; viii. 58; xvii. 5, 24); it is also implicit in the many references to his 'having come' (v. 43; vi. 14; vii. 28; ix. 39; x. 10; xi. 27; xii. 46;

[1] *Jerusalem Bible* comment on Matt. XI. 27.

[2] Cf. D. Moody, ' "God's Only Son": the Translation of John iii. 16 in the R.S.V.', *JBL*, LXXII (1953), 213 ff.; R. E. Brown, *St John*, pp. 13 f.; C. H. Turner, 'ὁ υἱός μου ὁ ἀγαπητός', *JTS*, XXVII (1926), 113 ff.

[3] It is interesting to note the sequence of 'confessions' concerning Jesus in the Gospel: 'Lamb of God' (i. 29, 36), 'Messiah' (i. 41), 'the Son of God, the King of Israel' (i. 49) where 'Son of God' is intended to be understood in kingly messianic terms, 'a teacher sent from God' (iii. 2), 'a' or 'the prophet' (iv. 19—the prophet awaited by the Samaritans?), 'the Holy One of God' (vi. 69), 'the prophet' (vii. 40—like Moses?), 'the Son of Man' (ix. 38), 'King of the Jews' (xix. 19), 'my Lord and my God' (xx. 28).

It is also interesting to compare Peter's confession in the four Gospels: Mark viii. 30: You are *the Christ*; Luke ix. 21: *The Christ of God*; Matt. xvi. 16: *The Christ, the Son of the living God*; John vi. 69: You are *the Holy One of God*. Is it possible that St John has preserved the authentic words of Peter's confession, of which the Synoptists give a more developed form?

xv. 22; xviii. 37), 'being from God' (vi. 46; vii. 29; ix. 33; xvi. 27, 28; xvii. 8), 'having been sent' (iii. 17, 34; iv. 34; v. 23, 24, 30, 36, 37; vi. 29, 38, 39, 40, 44, 57; vii. 16, 18, 29; viii. 16, 18, 26, 29, 42; ix. 4; x. 36; xi. 42; xii. 44, 45, 49; xiii. 20; xiv. 24; xv. 21; xvi. 5; xvii. 3, 8, 18, 21, 23, 25; xx. 21).

C. K. Barrett speaks of the sonship of Jesus having both an ontological and a moral sense for St John.[1] It is questionable whether St John gave any thought to the ontological nature of the sonship, although certainly for readers with minds nourished on Hellenistic philosophy his statements concerning Christ's sonship would raise questions of ontology. For minds nourished on Hebraic thought the moral nature of Jesus' sonship would be of first importance. For Hebrew minds a true son is one who reproduces the thought and action of his father.[2] This idea certainly receives strong emphasis in St John's teaching on the Father–Son relationship. Jesus says, 'The Son can do nothing of his own accord, but only what he sees the Father doing; for whatsoever he does, that the Son does likewise. For the Father loves the Son and shows him all that he himself is doing' (v. 19 f.). Jesus claims to reproduce not only the Father's thought and action, but also his very nature: 'If you knew me, you would know my Father also' (viii. 19); 'He who has seen me has seen the Father' (xiv. 9). Thus St John seems to be feeling after something more than moral likeness; 'John brings out more clearly than the Synoptics the meaning of sonship; both moral likeness and essential identity are included.'[3]

While he asserts the 'essential' identity[4] of the Son with the Father, at no time does St John lose sight of the distinction between them. The Son has been *sent* by the Father; he obeys his Father's commandments (xv. 10); he can do nothing of his own accord (v. 19–20); the words which he speaks are not his own but his Father's (xiv. 10, 24; xvii. 8); the deeds which he

---

[1] *The Gospel according to St John*, p. 60.
[2] Cf. E. Hoskyns, *The Fourth Gospel*, London, 1956, on John v. 19–20.
[3] C. K. Barrett, *The Gospel according to St John*, p. 60.
[4] The use of such terminology from a later stage of christological development must not be allowed to carry all the implications of its later meaning. Difficult though it may be to avoid speaking in terms like 'essence', 'essential', 'ontology', etc., we must not transform St John into a fourth-century Father.

does are the Father's (xiv. 10). Again and again St John emphasises the Son's total dependence on the Father;[1] he makes Jesus say, 'My Father is greater than I' (xiv. 28). Thus, for him, the 'essential' identity is never allowed to obliterate the distinction between the Father and the Son. 'John's thought is paradoxical, as perhaps all christological thought must be.'[2] The focal point of his Gospel is the Father–Son relationship, eternal and pre-existent, yet manifested to the eyes of faith in the earthly existence of the Son in the person of Jesus Christ, a relationship which he can only describe in terms of 'unity' or 'oneness' (x. 30), yet which allows distinctions within it, so that Father and Son are never identified. This is the first Johannine paradox—distinction-within-unity—expressed mid-way through the Gospel in the terse but staggering claim, 'I and the Father are one' (x. 30), which was to play a vital role in the trinitarian controversies from the beginning of the third century onwards.[3] Thus more explicitly and more emphatically than the other New Testament writers does St John declare the divinity of Jesus Christ as eternal Son of God and at the same time the distinction between the Son and the Father.

C. THE DIVINITY AND THE HUMANITY OF CHRIST

Despite its emphasis on the divinity of the Son of God, St John's Gospel is 'a history',[4] that is, it narrates the existence in history of Jesus Christ, God's Word who has become flesh, the God who has become a man. With all the emphasis on 'the glory' of the Son of God, the Son is 'a real man...(John) always sees him as having a human psychology (xi. 33; xii. 27; xiii. 27). The Logos-concept has not been able to obliterate the true

---

[1] Cf. J. E. Davey, *The Jesus of St John*, London, 1958, pp. 90–151. 'There is no more remarkable element in the Fourth Gospel than the consistent and universal presentation of Christ, in his life and work and words and in all aspects of his activities, *as dependent upon the Father at every point*' (p. 90, italics mine).

[2] Barrett, *The Gospel according to St John*, p. 77.

[3] Cf. my article, 'The Exegesis of John x. 30 in the Early Trinitarian Controversies', *NTS*, III (1956–7), 334–49.

[4] R. H. Lightfoot calls this Gospel 'a history of the Son of God: in (it) he who speaks and acts on earth is still always at his Father's side' (*History and Interpretation in the Gospels*, London, 1935, p. 224).

picture of Christ's humanity. The reality of his life stands too clearly in view.'[1] The earliest christological heresy of which we have any evidence was docetism,[2] which so emphasised the divinity of Jesus that it reduced his humanity to mere appearance or fantasy.[3] That St John has such a docetic christology in mind both in the Gospel and First Letter is clear: 'The Logos became flesh and dwelt among us' (i. 14), subject to the same passions and limitations as men. For all his emphasis on the divinity of Christ, Christ for him is *a man* (i. 30; iv. 29; viii. 40; ix. 11, 16; x. 33); belief that he *is* a man 'come in the flesh' is as essential to Christian faith (I John iv. 2–3) as the belief that he is 'the Christ' (I John ii. 22–3). Writing of the Letter to the Hebrews, M. Barth says, 'No other book of the New Testament (except the Fourth Gospel) puts the real deity and true humanity of Jesus Christ so clearly side by side.'[4] He who as Logos-Son clearly belongs to the sphere of the divine ('What God was, the Word was', John i. 1c NEB), as Jesus of Nazareth belongs also and equally to the sphere of the human. This conjunction of divine and human, Logos and flesh, God and a man, is nowhere defined or analysed by St John; it is simply part of his witness that this Jesus is the God-man through faith in whom men may have eternal life. The analysis and explication of this conjunction was attempted by the church: the second Johannine paradox which became the focus of controversy up to the Council of Chalcedon (A.D. 451) and beyond.

[1] Grillmeier, p. 34. Cf. E. K. Lee, *The Religious Thought of St John*, London, 1950, p. 135: 'This is the cornerstone upon which the whole structure of Johannine thought depends. The visible historical Jesus is the place in history where the glory of God was manifested.'

[2] 'It is not by accident that Docetism is the primal heresy of ancient Christianity, the only one which we can distinctly see to be attacked by the New Testament' (O. Cullmann, *Salvation in History*, London, 1967, p. 91).

[3] Cf. the quaint words of Jerome: 'While the Apostles yet remained upon the earth, while the blood of Jesus was almost smoking upon the soil of Judaea, some asserted that the body of the Lord was a phantom' (quoted by E. K. Lee, p. 135).

[4] 'The Old Testament in Hebrews', in *Current Issues in N.T. Interpretation* (ed. W. Klassen and G. F. Snyder), p. 58.

D. THE MEDIATOR

If the master-concept of the Fourth Gospel is the Father–Son relationship, its recurring theme is that as Son of God Jesus Christ is the one and only mediator between God and man, a theme which St John develops, as we have already seen, along three distinct yet closely integrated lines.[1]

(i) He places God's activity in Christ in its widest possible setting; as Logos, Christ is mediator of God's activity in creation. This idea, of course, is not original or unique to St John. St Paul describes Christ as 'the first-born of all creation, for in him all things were created...all things were created through him (δι' αὐτοῦ) and for him. He is before all things and in him all things hold together' (Col. i. 15–17). The author of Hebrews says that God 'has spoken to us by a Son...through whom also he created the world (Heb. i. 2). The activity of creation does not belong to the Logos-Son *simpliciter*; it is the activity of God 'through him' (δι' αὐτοῦ, John i. 3). He is the mediator, not some intermediary who performs a function which God, being sublime above all matter, cannot perform himself. The emphasis on mediatorship, as opposed to any notion of a demiurge or intermediary, differentiates St John's Logos-concept from that of Philo or of Greek philosophy. Yet St John appears to be much less interested in cosmology than St Paul is.[2] Apart from one, or possibly two references to creation in the Prologue (i. 10 and possibly i. 3, see above), there is no reference to mediatorship in creation in the Gospel itself. 'John is not interested in cosmology. He is not thinking of creation but of redemption.'[3]

---

[1] There is no Greek word in St John's Gospel which can be translated 'mediator', yet the idea of mediation is present throughout the Gospel. Cf. H. Clavier, 'Mediation in the Fourth Gospel', *Bull. SNTS*, no. 1, Cambridge, 1950, pp. 11–25.

[2] Is Paul's interest in cosmology due to the fact that he had to combat speculations about 'principalities and powers, etc.', speculations which make no appearance in St John's Gospel?

[3] Lofthouse, *The Father and the Son*, p. 47. He goes on to say: 'Possibly some of his friends and expected readers had been attracted to Philo's ingenious attempt at reconciling the best Greek philosophy of the time with the Pentateuch. "Well," he seems to say, "if you want to relate the Logos to your faith, you may. But when you use the term, observe what it is that you mean by it. You may find it in the first chapter of Genesis, where in the beginning, God utters the creating word and the world is made. But it is

(ii) For St John Jesus Christ is the sole mediator of God's activity in self-revelation (i. 17, 18; viii. 19, 38; xiv. 7, 9; xvii. 25). Here again the idea is not unique or original to St John; it is implicit throughout the New Testament, and particularly explicit in Hebrews i. 1–2 and in the Q-saying: 'No one knows the Father except the Son and any one to whom the Son chooses to reveal him' (Matt. xi. 27; Luke x. 22).[1] For St John Jesus is 'the light of the world' (viii. 12), 'the way, the truth and the life' (xiv. 6); 'He who has seen' Jesus 'has seen the Father' (xiv. 9). The idea of Jesus as the revelation of the Father, or the one through whom the Father reveals himself, is present throughout the Gospel—'the glory' of the Father is to be seen in all that the Son does and says.

(iii) Above all, Jesus Christ is the mediator of God's activity in saving men and adopting them into his family (i. 12). John the Baptist acclaims him as 'the Lamb of God that takes away the sins of the world' (i. 29); the Samaritans hail him as 'the Saviour of the world' (iv. 47). He is 'the only Son' whom the Father, in his love, has given that men 'should not perish but have eternal life' (iii. 16), that 'the world might be saved through him' (δι' αὐτοῦ, iii. 17). The Father's self-revelation through the Son has as its end that men should receive eternal life, or life in its fullest sense (vi. 40; x. 10, 28; xvii. 3; xx. 31); salvation comes through faith in the Son of God (i. 12; iii. 16 f.; ix. 35 ff.; xvii. 38; xx. 31). This theme is even more explicit in the First Letter: 'the blood of Jesus Christ his Son cleanses us from all sin' (i. 7 ff.); 'we have an advocate with the Father, Jesus Christ the righteous; and he is the expiation (ἱλασμός)

more than that. It is the means of life, the illumination of men. And only in these days have we come to know it. It is no idea, or force. It appeared as a human being. By it we are empowered to become children of God; neither Philo nor the Stoics ever told you that. We see it, with all the glory of heaven like a Shekinah around it, in Jesus, the *Son* of God. And after this, let us have no more about the Logos; let us contemplate the glory of the Son."'

[1] Cf. the interesting suggestion by Jeremias (*The Central Message of the N.T.*, pp. 23–5) supported by R. E. Brown ('How much did Jesus Know?', *CBQ*, xxix (1967), 32) that in this Q-saying Jesus 'is drawing on a maxim that a father and son know each other intimately, and a son is the best one to reveal the innermost thoughts of the Father' (Brown). However, in this saying Jesus claims to reveal not merely the innermost thoughts of the Father, but the Father himself.

for our sins, and not for ours only but also for the sins of the whole world' (ii. 1–2); 'God sent his Son into the world, so that we might live through him' (iv. 9–10). Once again the idea is by no means unique or original to St John; it is present throughout the New Testament and indeed it is the very centre of its message.

For St John, then, it is the one God who creates, reveals and saves, the Father of Jesus Christ, his only Son, his Word-become-flesh. It is through (διά) the Son that the Father accomplishes all things (πάντα δι' αὐτοῦ ἐγένετο, i. 3). St John asserts the mediatorship of the Son in creation in order to provide the cosmological setting for the self-revelation of the Father and the salvation of mankind.[1] Like St Paul, St John focuses his attention on the redemption which God has wrought through Jesus Christ, and like St Paul also he argues back from the mediatorial work in redemption (the re-creation of man and the cosmos) to the mediatorial work in the original creation.[2] The one who in these last days has been the mediator of the Father's self-revelation for the redemption of the world is the one who was in the beginning with God and mediator in the creation of all things. He who re-creates the created order is none other than he who created it in the beginning.

This emphasis on the three-fold mediatorship of the Son of God is necessary here because it plays an important part in the interpretation of St John's Gospel by the early church. The problem which St John's Gospel set for the church in the succeeding centuries was the complex problem of formulating a doctrine of God and of the person of Christ which would keep the paradoxical balance between the essential unity of the Son with the Father and the distinction between them, and the paradoxical balance between the divinity and the humanity of Christ, while at the same time keeping in proper perspective the threefold nature of the mediatorial role of the Son. To a very large extent this complexity may be reduced to the question of keeping the Logos-concept in the Johannine perspective.

[1] Cf. p. 20, n. 3 above; also A. E. J. Rawlinson, *The N.T. Doctrine of the Christ*, London, 1929, pp. 209 ff.

[2] Cf. S. Hanson, *The Unity of the Church in the N.T.*, Uppsala, 1946, pp. 109 ff., for a discussion of the relationship between cosmology and soteriology in Paul.

CHAPTER 2

THE DEVELOPMENT OF CHRISTOLOGY IN THE SECOND CENTURY

For over thirty years there has been a continuing debate over the question of the church's attitude towards St John's Gospel and its use of it during the second century, a question which is of considerable importance for understanding the development of Christian doctrine during this period. The first major contribution was made by W. von Loewenich in 1932.[1] In 1941 R. Bultmann's commentary was published,[2] in which he proposed the view that the basis of the Gospel was a gnostic writing which had been redacted in the interests of orthodoxy. In 1943 J. N. Sanders,[3] from an examination of the writings of the second century, reached mainly negative conclusions concerning the church's use of the Gospel in the first half of the second century. Because of its popularity in gnostic circles and the lack of clear quotations from the Gospel in surviving ecclesiastical writings written prior to A.D. 180, Sanders concluded that if the church knew of the existence of the Gospel, it treated it with suspicion; he further argued that the most likely place of the Gospel's origin was Alexandria.[4] C. K. Barrett, in 1955,

[1] *Das Johannesverständnis im zweiten Jahrhunderte* (*ZNTW*, Beiheft 13), Giessen, 1932. For a brief summary of the discussion before von Loewenich, cf. H. Chadwick, *Early Christian Thought and the Classical Tradition*, Oxford, 1966, pp. 124 f.

[2] *Das Evangelium des Johannes*, Göttingen, 1941.

[3] *The Fourth Gospel in the Early Church*, Cambridge, 1943.

[4] Sanders later modified his view of the place of the Gospel's origin: 'Syria may be a more likely place. His Gospel soon travelled to Ephesus' (*The Foundations of the Christian Faith*, London, 1951, p. 162). The possibility of a close connection between the Gospel (or the tradition it records) and Syria (Antioch) is supported by T. W. Manson, 'The Life of Jesus: A Survey of the Available Material. (5) The Fourth Gospel', *BJRL*, xxx (1946–7) (= *Studies in the Gospels and Epistles*, Manchester, 1962, ch. 6). Manson urges that more serious consideration should be given to Sanday's suggestion (*The Criticism of the Fourth Gospel*, London, 1905, p. 199) that there was 'an anticipatory stage of Johannine teaching, localised somewhere in Syria, before the Apostle reached his final home in Ephesus'. C. F.

simply reaffirmed Sanders' negative position: 'To trace the influence of the Fourth Gospel upon Christian theology would be more than the task of a lifetime; to trace its influence upon the thought of the first half of the second century is easy, for it had none.'[1]

Recently F. M. Braun[2] has made an exhaustive study of the question, decisively criticising Sanders' negative conclusions and demonstrating by an examination of a far wider range of evidence than his predecessors could take into account that St John's Gospel was not only used but also held in high esteem in the church in Egypt, Asia Minor, Syria and Rome early in the second century. Braun has investigated not only the second-century writings, both orthodox and heterodox, the recently discovered papyrus manuscripts and the Nag-Hammadi literature, but also the frescoes of the Roman catacombs which give ample proof of the popularity of Johannine symbolism in second-century Roman Christian art. Yet for all the weight of evidence which Braun adduces, the fact that in no extant 'orthodox' writing from before A.D. 170 is there any explicit quotation from the Gospel and First Letter of St John still remains a problem. Did early second-century writers know the Johannine writings or were they acquainted only with a Johannine type of theology? Braun's work makes it clear that Johannine motifs played an important role in the piety and devotion of the Church; this makes it difficult to suppose that the writings in which these motifs occur were not known and highly respected. Why, then, did ecclesiastical writers not quote

Burney (*The Aramaic Origin of the Fourth Gospel*, Oxford, 1922, pp. 129 ff.) also argues that the Gospel was written near Antioch. P. N. Harrison (*Polycarp's Two Letters to the Philippians*, Cambridge, 1936, pp. 263 f.) and H. Schlier (*Religions-geschichtliche Untersuchungen zu dem Ignatiusbriefen* (*ZNTW*, Beiheft 8), Giessen, 1929, p. 176, n. 1) set the place of writing somewhere near the Syrian border of Palestine. R. M. Grant ('The Odes of Solomon and the Church of Antioch', *JBL*, LXIII (1944), 377) and Virginia Corwin (*St Ignatius and Christianity in Antioch*, Yale, 1960, pp. 70 f.) agree that St John was influenced by the spiritual atmosphere of Antioch, while holding that the Gospel was probably written in Ephesus. On the other hand, R. E. Brown (*Commentary*, p. ciii) says that the arguments advanced in support of Antioch 'can be explained if some Johannine thought made its way to Syria'.

[1] *The Gospel according to St John*, London, 1955, p. 52.
[2] *Jean le théologien et son évangile dans l'église ancienne*, Paris, 1959, pp. 69–300.

from them, especially when quotation could have added considerable force to their arguments? Two pieces of evidence support the view developed by J. N. Sanders[1] that gnostic use of the Johannine writings made 'orthodox' writers hesitate to use them openly. Early gnostic use of them has been confirmed by the discovery of *The Gospel of Truth*[2] and the fragment of an unknown gospel (Papyrus Egerton 2).[3] It is known that the first commentary on the Gospel was written by the gnostic Heracleon, while Epiphanius records the existence of a group in Rome, whom he calls *Alogoi*, who rejected the Gospel because they believed it had been written by Cerinthus the gnostic.[4] It would not be unusual for theologians to be hesitant about writings which popular piety was prepared to use without hesitation.

Acceptance of the view that second-century writers hesitated to use St John's Gospel because gnostic use of it made them either suspicious of its orthodoxy or afraid that to use it might give the impression that they were allying themselves with gnosticism, does not mean that we have to go on to assert with Bultmann that the Fourth Gospel is of gnostic origin. Recent research into the origins of gnosticism, particularly since the discovery of *The Gospel of Truth* and the other Nag-Hammadi literature, has shown that Bultmann's view is untenable. Bultmann's main reason for asserting that the Gospel is an orthodox redaction of a gnostic original appears to be his assumption that the Iranian mystery of redemption with its 'pre-Christian Gnostic redeemer' had influenced the theology of St John. From a study of *The Gospel of Truth* Quispel is able to assert that 'there would appear to be good grounds for supposing that it was from Christianity that the conception of redemption and the figure of the Redeemer were taken over into Gnosticism. A pre-Christian redeemer and an Iranian mystery of redemption perhaps never existed.'[5]

In the writings of the second century we can see Christian

---

[1] *The F.G. in the Early Church.*

[2] Cf. G. Quispel, in *The Jung Codex* (ed. F. L. Cross), London, 1955, p. 49.

[3] Cf. C. H. Dodd, *New Testament Studies*, Manchester, 1953, pp. 13–25.

[4] *Panarion*, LI, 2 f.

[5] In *The Jung Codex*, pp. 77 ff. In a paper read at the Second International Conference on Patristic Studies, Oxford, 1955, Quispel said that *The Gospel of Truth* is 'the transposition of Johannine thought into a gnostic framework ...The Gospel of John is definitely not of gnostic origin.'

thinkers grappling with the questions raised by the paradoxes of Johannine theology. The recent work of writers like Daniélou[1] and Grillmeier[2] has demonstrated the kaleidoscopic variety of theological expression in second-century Christianity as Christians seized on a very diverse assortment of concepts to use in the explication of their faith and in their expression of it in worship. As a result theology was in a state of flux. By a process of trial and error concept after concept was introduced; many were discarded as inadequate or misleading, and a few retained as fitting and valuable. Always the adequacy of the concepts used was tested against the witness of scripture and the tradition of the church's faith and worship. St John's witness to Jesus Christ as the Son of God, God's eternally pre-existent Word made flesh, posed for the church the problem of christology, the task of elucidating for herself and for those whom she confronted with the claims of the Gospel her faith in God through Jesus Christ. Gradually there developed within the church different traditions of theology and of interpretation of St John's Gospel, the beginnings of which we can see in the writings of the second century.

A. IGNATIUS OF ANTIOCH

Despite his categorical assertion that St John's Gospel had no influence on Christian thought in the first half of the second century,[3] C. K. Barrett acknowledges that there are similarities between the Gospel and Ignatius' letters, and he accounts for them by pointing to the similar influence to which both writers were subject—controversy with Judaism and incipient docetism.[4] His list of similarities, however, is minimal as an examination of Braun's more comprehensive list shows.[5] Further, in his controversy with Judaism and his battle against incipient docetism, Ignatius presents a christology strikingly similar to St John's.

[1] *A History of Early Christian Doctrine*: vol. I (ETr.), *The Theology of Jewish Christianity*, London, 1964, and vol. II, *Message évangelique et culture hellénistique des IIe et IIIe siècles*, Paris, 1961.
[2] *Christ in Christian Tradition.*   [3] Cf. p. 24, n. 1 above.
[4] *The Gospel according to St John*, pp. 53 f.
[5] *Jean le théologien et son évangile dans l'église ancienne*, pp. 271 ff.

In Ignatius' letters the title *Logos* plays a very minor role. The term *Logos* appears only three times in the Ignatian corpus (*Rom.* ii. 1; *Magn.* viii. 2; *Smyrn. praef.*); in only one of these is it applied directly to Christ, in the much-debated passage, *Magn.* viii. 2.[1]

The context in *Magnesians* emphasises the oneness of Jesus with the Father as a pattern of the oneness which members of the Church must have with their bishop and presbyters. Jesus 'did nothing without the Father[2]... because he was at one with him (ἡνωμένος ὤν)'. Ignatius emphasises this oneness in a series of phrases: 'you must have *one* prayer, *one* petition, *one* hope... Run off—all of you—to *one* temple, as it were, to *one* altar, to *one* Jesus Christ, who came forth from *one* Father, while still remaining *one* with him, and returned to him (ἐπὶ ἕνα Ἰησοῦν Χριστὸν τὸν ἀφ' ἑνὸς πατρὸς προελθόντα καὶ εἰς ἕνα ὄντα καὶ χωρήσαντα).[3] Then follows a warning against 'wrong views and outmoded tales' by which Ignatius appears to mean 'apocryphal Jewish legends',[4] and this leads him to warn his readers against falling back into Judaism by reminding them of God's self-revelation in Christ:

The divine prophets... were inspired by his grace to convince unbelievers that God is one, and that he has revealed himself in his

[1] In *Smyrn. praef.* Ignatius says ἐν ἀμώμῳ πνεύματι καὶ λόγῳ θεοῦ πλεῖστα χαίρειν. H. A. Wolfson (*The Philosophy of the Church Fathers*, 2nd ed. 1964, pp. 184 f.), who argues that Ignatius identifies Holy Spirit and Logos, translates, 'in an unblamable Spirit and the Logos of God', although he admits that it is not clear whether 'Spirit' and 'Logos' are 'to be taken as two alternative expressions of the same thing or as two distinct expressions of two distinct things'. C. C. Richardson (*Early Christian Fathers* (LCC, vol. i), p. 112) translates, 'in all sincerity and in God's Word', where the capitalisation of 'Word' implies a reference to Christ as the λόγος θεοῦ. J. B. Lightfoot (*The Apostolic Fathers*, pt. ii, vol. ii, 2nd ed. 1899, p. 567) translates 'in a blameless spirit and in the word of God', where the lack of capitalisation for both 'spirit' and 'word' implies that he sees no reference either to the third or to the second person of the Trinity. In *Rom.* ii. 1 Ignatius sees himself, in his approaching role as a martyr, as a 'word of God' (ἐγὼ λόγος θεοῦ).

[2] A clear reminiscence of John v. 19, 30; viii. 28.

[3] This use of the oneness of the Son with the Father as a pattern for the oneness of Christians with one another is similar to the argument of John xvii. 21 ff. Cf. my article '"That they all may be one" (John xvii. 21)—and the Unity of the Church', *ExpT*, LXX (1959), 149–50.

[4] C. C. Richardson, *Early Christian Fathers*, p. 96, n. 46.

Son Jesus Christ, who is his Word issuing from the silence (ὅς ἐστιν αὐτοῦ λόγος ἀπὸ σιγῆς προελθών) and who won the approval of him who sent him...Through this mystery we got our faith... (*Magn.* viii. 1–ix. 2).

The use of the term *Sige* in connection with *Logos* has raised the question of the possible contact of Ignatius with Valentinian gnosticism in which *Sige* (also called *Ennoia* and *Charis*) is the female counterpart of God, the Perfect Aeon (also called *Bythos*). From *Bythos* and *Sige* were born *Nous* and *Aletheia*, and from the latter pair *Logos* and *Zoe* emanated.[1] Sanders says that the use of *Logos* in *Magn.* viii. 2 is much closer to this form of gnosticism than it is to St John's Gospel.[2] On the other hand, Virginia Corwin acknowledges a close similarity between the theology of the two writers and emphasises that 'the connection of *Sige* and *Logos* does not establish the priority of a pre-Valentinian gnosis'.[3] She shows that a connection of *Logos* and *Sige* occurs in *The Gospel of Truth*, the early Valentinian meditation on the Gospel (written some thirty years or more after Ignatius' letters),[4] without any hint of the later development of syzygies in the Valentinian Ogdoad. In *The Gospel of Truth* 37.4–21 the Logos, 'the first (of God's words) to emerge, revealed them (i.e. God's words) and a mind which speaks the Word which is characterised by a silent grace'. In this primitive Valentinian treatise there is no suggestion that the Logos

[1] Cf. R. McL. Wilson, *The Gnostic Problem*, London, 1958, p. 128; J. Doresse, *The Secret Books of the Egyptian Gnostics*, London, 1960, p. 27.

[2] He says that *Logos* is used 'in a way which can hardly be considered consistent with the assumption that Ignatius' theology is derived from that of the Gospel' (*The Fourth Gospel in the Early Church*, p. 12). Similarly, C. C. Richardson, *Early Christian Fathers*, p. 78.

[3] *St Ignatius and Christianity in Antioch*, p. 183.

[4] The view that *The Gospel of Truth* is a *primitive* Valentinian document, held by W. C. van Unnik (in F. J. Cross (ed.), *The Jung Codex*), K. Grobel (*The Gospel of Truth*), R. M. Grant (*Gnosticism and Early Christianity*, pp. 128 ff.) and tentatively accepted by R. McL. Wilson (*The Gnostic Problem*, pp. 161 ff.), has been challenged by R. A. Markus (review of Wilson, *The Gnostic Problem*, in *NTS* VI (1959–60), 99 f.) and Hans Jonas (in *SP* VI, 96 ff.), who argues that *The Gospel of Truth* in fact presupposes the developed Valentinian system. On the other hand, H. M. Schenke (*Die Herkunft des sogennanten Evangelium Veritatis*, Berlin, 1958) denies that *The Gospel of Truth* is Valentinian. For a full discussion see R. McL. Wilson, *Gnosis and the New Testament*, Oxford, 1968, pp. 89 ff.

issues from Silence—the Logos is characterised by *silent grace*—the Silence and Grace (*Sige* and *Charis*) which in later Valentinianism were other names for *Ennoia*, God's feminine counterpart. In both this passage and *Magnesians* the context is concerned with God's self-revelation and both emphasise the pleasure which the Father finds in the Logos through whom he reveals himself.[1]

The connection of *Sige* and *Logos* also occurs in a considerable number of the new gnostic documents from Nag-Hammadi,[2] but all of these appear to belong to a much later and more highly developed stage of gnostic speculation. No extant gnostic literature is early enough to give any indication of a possible gnostic background for Ignatius' use of *Sige* in connection with *Logos*.[3]

Miss Corwin emphasises correctly that for Ignatius *Logos* means 'the Spoken Word, not indwelling Reason'. 'Jesus Christ as the Logos is a meaningful declaration of what in the Father is otherwise unfathomable.'[4] The Silence from which the Logos issues is the incomprehensibility, the hiddenness of God, which God breaks at the incarnation by speaking his Word in

[1] The parallels between *Magn.* viii. 2 and *The Gospel of Truth*, 37.4–21 raise the question whether the latter may not be a 'gnosticised' version of the idea expressed in the former.

[2] Cf. Doresse, *The Secret Books of the Egyptian Gnostics*, index, under 'Silence'.

[3] Doresse (p. 17) draws attention to the occurrence of the two terms in a quotation in Hippolytus, *Refutation of all Heresies*, VI, xiii, said to be from Simon Magus' *The Great Revelation*. If this writing was from the hand of Simon, it is pre-Ignatian, but the highly developed dualism in the quotations makes it likely that it was a pseudonymous work from a considerably later period. L. W. Barnard (*Studies in the Apostolic Fathers and their Background*, Oxford, 1966, p. 27) draws attention to the fact that the late fifth-century comic poet Antiphanes used the concept of *Sige* in his cosmological speculations and that the term appears in the Magical Papyri 'where Silence is a symbol of the living, incorruptible God'. Barnard suggests that Ignatius simply 'took over *the terminology* of contemporary speculation', but 'gave it a new content by his grasp of the reality of the Incarnation and the centrality of the Work of Christ accomplished on the Cross' (*ibid.*).

[4] *St Ignatius*, p. 126. For the meaning of λόγος as 'spoken word', cf. Lightfoot's note on the distinction between λόγος, φωνή and ψόφος (*op. cit.* pp. 198–9): λόγος = 'the utterance of a rational being'; φωνή = 'the cry of an animate creature, whether articulate or not'; ψόφος = 'a mere confused indistinguishable sound'.

Jesus Christ. But she goes beyond the evidence when she asserts that for Ignatius 'Silence is not an attribute of God; it is God himself'.[1] 'It may be said that for Ignatius "Silence" seems to mean roughly what in more philosophical circles would be expressed by the metaphysical term οὐσία. He never uses οὐσία and it would clearly be foreign to his thought, for his terms come from myth not metaphysics. But Silence is its equivalent.'[2]

It is unwarranted to give such a technical meaning to a word which occurs in this context only once. That it does not have a technical meaning is supported by the fact that elsewhere in a similar context of God's revelation of 'mysteries' (μυστήρια) (*Eph.* xix. 1 f.) Ignatius uses the almost synonymous term ἡσυχία: 'Now, Mary's virginity and her giving birth escaped the notice of the prince of this world, as did the Lord's death— these three secrets (μυστήρια) crying to be told, but wrought in God's silence (ἐν ἡσυχίᾳ θεοῦ).' Both here and in *Magn.* vii. 2 Ignatius is speaking of the secrets which God reveals when he breaks his silence in speaking his Word in Jesus Christ. 'God was revealing himself as a man' (lit. 'humanly', ἀνθρωπίνως) (*Eph.* xix. 3).

Further, the declaration that God *is* Silence creates a difficulty which the context of *Magn.* viii. 2 itself obviates. Miss Corwin says, 'If there is one thing that can be said of both (i.e. Judaism and Christianity) it is that the will of the Father has always been accessible to men as it was revealed to the Jews. The very idea that the Father could be considered to be Silence is astonishing.'[3] She claims to find in both John and Ignatius the idea that until the incarnation God was silent, hidden and unknown, i.e. that there was no revelation of God in the Old Testament. Earlier she says that in his anti-docetic concern to emphasise 'the inescapable reality of the fact' of the incarnation, Ignatius believes that Christ fulfilled the prophecies of the Old Testament.[4] This thought is present in the context of

---

[1] Corwin, *St Ignatius*, p. 123.

[2] *Idem.* Later (pp. 175 ff., 199 ff.) she makes it clear that by 'myth' she means not 'the gnostic redeemer-myth', but rather 'mythological' material much nearer to Jewish thought (p. 183). Miss Corwin's view that God *is* Silence is repeated by L. W. Barnard, *Studies in the Apostolic Fathers*, p. 26.

[3] *Ibid.* p. 144.   [4] *Ibid.* p. 114.

Magn. viii. 2 where he says 'the divine prophets...were inspired by (God's) grace to convince unbelievers that God is one...'. The same point is made at greater length in *Philad.* v. i–ix. 2, of which Richardson says, 'This is an answer to the criticism of the judaisers that Ignatius was disparaging the Old Testament.'[1] It is true that in *Magnesians* 'the Word issuing from the Silence' refers specifically to the incarnation, but this does not imply that God broke his silence *only* at the incarnation and that there was no revelation prior to the incarnation. The prophets 'were inspired by God's grace' (*Magn.* viii. 2); 'they anticipated the Gospel in their preaching and hoped for and awaited him' (*Philad.* v. 2).

For Ignatius the Logos is God's Word of self-revelation, the *d^ebhar Yahweh*, as it is for St John; but like St John, Ignatius has his attention so fixed on the incarnation—'the gospel is the crowning achievement forever' (*Philad.* ix. 2)—that his thought always passes beyond the Logos to the Son, and he transfers to the Son, incarnate in Jesus Christ, the pre-existent activity ascribed to the Logos. His christology is a Son-christology, not a Logos-christology.

The Hebraic background of Ignatius' thought is evident too from his strong monotheistic emphasis. He bases his argument for the unity of the Church and for the unity of Christians with their bishops and presbyters on the oneness of God, the oneness of the Father with the Son.[2] So strong is his monotheism that at times he appears to be in danger of falling into a modalism which loses sight of the distinction between the Father and the Son, a danger which was to beset Antiochene theology for centuries to come. Ignatius frequently calls Christ 'God' or 'our God' (*Eph. praef.* xv. 3; xviii. 2; *Trall.* vii. 1; *Rom. praef.* (twice); iii. 3; *Smyrn.* i. 1; *Poly.* viii. 3); he speaks of 'the blood of God' (*Eph.* i. 1) and 'the passion of my God' (*Rom.* vi. 3). This emphasis on the full divinity of the Son and his 'oneness with the Father' (ἕνωσιν...Ἰησοῦ καὶ πατρός, *Magn.* i. 2) is balanced by an equal emphasis on the distinction between Father and Son. He frequently combines 'God the Father' and 'the Lord Jesus Christ' as co-ordinate phrases; his favourite designation for God is 'the Father of Jesus Christ', and for Christ, 'Son'. Christ 'comes forth from the one Father'

---

[1] *Early Christian Fathers*, p. 109, n. 93.   [2] Cf. above, pp. 27 ff.

(*Magn.* vii. 2); he has been 'sent' by the Father (*Magn.* viii. 2); his Father raised him (*Trall.* ix. 2); he returns to the Father (*Rom.* iii. 3); he defers to the Father (*Magn.* xiii. 2). He maintains his belief in 'the unequivocal unity'[1] between Father and Son while maintaining equally the distinction between them. Both the unity and the distinction are eternal: the Son was 'with the Father from eternity and appeared at the end' (*Magn.* vi. 1), and he is 'above time, the Timeless, the One who became visible for our sakes, who was beyond touch and passion, yet who for our sakes became subject to suffering, and endured everything for us' (*Poly.* iii. 2). This double emphasis rules out both modalism and adoptionism.

The focal point in Ignatius' theology is the incarnation. He nowhere speculates on the nature of the relation between Father and Son; he simply states their unity and recognises the distinction within that unity without attempting in any way to soften or resolve the paradox. The fullness and actuality of the divinity of Christ is essential to his faith in the incarnation. But this faith also demands the fullness of the humanity; real incarnation means that Christ is 'God in a man' (ἐν ἀνθρώπῳ θεός *Eph.* vii. 2). 'He was in fullness and actuality God entered into human life on the scene of history.'[2] Ignatius' letters reveal a lively and extensive interest in Christ's historical life.[3] His horror of docetism which would make the sufferings of Christ a phantasy and a sham leads him to pile up phrases with the adverb ἀληθῶς ('actually', 'really', 'genuinely'). Two passages are sufficient to demonstrate his emphasis on the real humanity of Christ:

Be deaf, then, to any talk that ignores Jesus Christ, of David's lineage, of Mary; who was really (ἀληθῶς) born, ate, and drank; was really (ἀληθῶς) persecuted...was really (ἀληθῶς) crucified and died...He was really (ἀληθῶς) raised from the dead, for his Father raised him, just as his Father will raise us, who believe on him, through Christ, apart from whom we have no genuine life (*Trall.* ix. 1–2).

Regarding our Lord, you are absolutely convinced that on the human side (κατὰ σάρκα) he was actually (ἀληθῶς) sprung from David's line, Son of God according to God's will and power, actually

---

[1] Corwin, *St Ignatius*, p. 137. [2] *Ibid.* p. 91.
[3] Cf. Miss Corwin's list, *op. cit.* pp. 94 f.

(ἀληθῶς) born of a virgin...actually (ἀληθῶς) crucified for us in the flesh under Pontius Pilate and Herod the Tetrarch...It was for our sakes that he suffered all this, to save us. And he genuinely (ἀληθῶς) suffered, as even he genuinely (ἀληθῶς) raised himself. It is not as some unbelievers say, that his Passion was a sham (*Smyrn.* i. 2–ii. 1).

For Ignatius the reality of revelation, salvation, and of his own existence as a Christian depends on the reality of the manhood of Christ. Christ is God revealing himself 'as a man' or 'in a human way' (ἀνθρωπίνως, *Eph.* xix. 3). 'It was for our sakes that he suffered all this, *to save us*' (*Smyrn.* ii. 1). 'If what our Lord did is a sham, so is my being in chains' (*Smyrn.* iv. 2). 'His total theology...springs from the paradox that Christ is *both* God and Man.'[1] He does not speculate on the manner of the incarnation; without seeking to resolve the paradox, he states it unequivocally in his conjunction of the titles 'Son of God' and 'Son of Man' (*Eph.* xx. 2) and in the more elaborate antithetic formula:

> There is only one Physician—
> of flesh   yet spiritual
> born   yet unbegotten
> God in a man
>
> Genuine life in death
> sprung from Mary   as well as from God
> first subject to suffering   then beyond suffering
> —Jesus Christ our Lord.   (*Eph.* vii. 2)

The paradox of the incarnation, of the God–Man, stands out stark and unrelieved.

In summarising we may say that for Ignatius, as for John, the Logos-concept, interpreted in the light of the Hebraic concept of the revealing Word of Yahweh, is strictly subordinated to the Son-concept, while Ignatius preserves the two Johannine paradoxes without in any way trying to analyse either the Father–Son relationship or the relationship of God and man in Jesus Christ. In these two crucial aspects of Christian faith he makes little advance on the witness of St John.

[1] Corwin, *op. cit.* p. 92.

B. THE ODES OF SOLOMON

The affinities between Ignatius of Antioch, the Odes of Solomon, and St John's Gospel have been noted by a number of scholars.[1] There is general agreement that they come from the same spiritual environment and, if some connection between the Johannine tradition and Antioch is accepted, from the same geographical area as well.[2]

The key christological concept in the Odes is the Logos-concept. The Logos is mediator of creation (xvi), of God's self-revelation (vii. 7, 12; viii. 8; xii. 10; xli. 13 f.), of salvation (xli. 11, 15; xxxi. 14). The Logos became incarnate, although the Odes do not assert the reality and fullness of the humanity of Christ as unequivocally as Ignatius had done. For example, Ode vii. 4, 6 says, 'He became like me that I might receive him. In similitude was he reckoned like me that I might put him on ... Like my nature he became, that I might learn him, and like my form, that I might not turn back from him.'

C. MELITO OF SARDIS (c. A.D. 160)

The discovery of Melito's *Homily on the Passion*, first in a papyrus codex in the Chester Beatty collection[3] and more recently in the Bodmer collection of papyri,[4] has provided additional important evidence for the Asia Minor tradition of christology in the second century.[5]

---

[1] E.g. F. M. Braun, *Jean le théologien dans l'église ancienne*, pp. 224 ff.; J. Dupont-Somner, 'Le problème des influences étrangères sur la secte juive à Qumran', *RHPR*, xxxv (1955), 75–94; V. Corwin, *St Ignatius*, 71 ff.; cf. R. M. Grant, 'The Odes of Solomon and the Church of Antioch', pp. 363–77.

[2] In any case Christianity in Asia Minor seems to have retained close links with Antioch. F. Loofs (*Leitfaden zum Studium der Dogmengeschichte*, §§18 and 21; *Paulus von Samosata*, p. 208; *Theophilus von Antiochien*, p. 248) includes Antiochene Christianity in what he calls the *kleinasiatische Tradition*.

[3] Edited by Campbell Bonner, *SD*, xiii (1940).

[4] Edited by M. Testuz, *Méliton de Sardes, Homélie sur la Pâque*, Geneva, 1960.

[5] The attribution of this homily to Melito has been contested by P. Nautin, *Le dossier d'Hippolyte et de Méliton dans les florilèges dogmatiques et chez les historiens modernes*, Paris, 1953, pp. 43–56. His argument has proved unconvincing; cf. J. Liébaert, *L'incarnation*: 1. *Dès origines au Concile de*

Like Ignatius and John, Melito rarely attributes the title *Logos* to Christ,[1] whom he usually designates by the titles *Lord* and *Christ*. The word *Logos* is used especially in opposition to *nomos*, Law,[2] a probable reminiscence of John i. 17; once *Logos* is used with reference to the function of Christ as mediator of revelation.[3] The whole homily has a soteriological, *heilsgeschichtlich* framework;[4] for Melito, as for Ignatius, the real divinity and the incarnation in real humanity are essential for the salvation of mankind. In one fragment, Christ's eternal pre-existence as the Logos is clearly stated: 'his Christ, who is Word of God before the ages' (τοῦ Χριστοῦ αὐτοῦ, ὄντος θεοῦ λόγου πρὸ αἰώνων).[5] Some scholars[6] find in the homily hints of modalism, as in the following passage, in which the distinction between Father and Son is obscured:

[Christ] is all things: in that he judges, Law; in that he teaches, Word; in that he saves, Grace; in that he begets, Father; in that he is begotten, Son; in that he suffers, a (sacrificial) sheep; in that he is buried, man; in that he arises, God.[7]

None the less, Melito does emphasise elsewhere the distinction between the Father and the Son.[8] We have to recognise, of course, that *The Homily on the Passion* and the collection of fragments form only a small part of the total corpus of Melito's writings; it would be unjust to form a rigid view of his theology on the basis of one brief sermon and a few quotations. However, we can see in his language here clear indications of the modalism which was to be a mark of later Antiochene (Asia Minor) theology.

Melito is emphatic that Jesus Christ is the God–Man. Eusebius of Caesarea speaks of him as one who, with Irenaeus and others, 'announced Christ as God' (*Hist. Ecc.* v, 28, 5).

Chalcédoine, Paris, 1966; F. L. Cross, *The Early Christian Fathers*, London, 1960, p. 104; A. Grillmeier, *Christ in Christian Tradition*, p. 111, n. 2.

[1] Cf. Bonner, *The Homily on the Passion of Melito of Sardis*, p. 28.
[2] *Ibid.* p. 1, line 10; p. 2, line 9.
[3] *Ibid.* p. 2, line 18: 'in that he teaches, Logos'.
[4] Cf. Grillmeier, *Christ in Christian Tradition*, pp. 111 f.
[5] Otto, *Corpus Apologetarum*, IX, fr. II.
[6] E.g. Liébaert, *L'incarnation*, I, 63; Bonner, *Homily on the Passion*, pp. 27 f.
[7] Bonner, *op. cit.* p. 2, lines 17–21.
[8] Liébaert (*L'incarnation*, I, 64) refers to fr. II, XIII and xv in the edition of M. Testuz.

For him 'the divine-human being of Jesus Christ is the guarantee of our salvation and of man's return to his original home with God'.[1] Christ is 'by nature God and man' (φύσει θεὸς ὢν καὶ ἄνθρωπος, Bonner, p. 2, line 16).[2] Anastasius Sinaita records that Melito wrote a treatise against Marcion, περὶ σαρκώσεως Χριστοῦ (PG, 89 col. 229). If a fragment preserved by Anastasius is genuine,[3] then Melito speaks of Christ as 'being at the same time God and perfect man' (θεὸς γὰρ ὢν ὁμοῦ τε καὶ ἄνθρωπος τέλειος), and refers to 'his two οὐσίαι'. Whether or not Melito used this more sophisticated christological terminology, it is clear from his *Homily* that like Ignatius he strove to maintain a christology in which both humanity and divinity received equal emphasis.

D. JUSTIN MARTYR

Of the group of second-century writers usually called 'Apologists', two may be selected as representative—Justin Martyr and Theophilus of Antioch—although each 'Apologist' makes his own contribution in the development of doctrine. Justin is of particular importance, however, because of the successors in his tradition, Clement of Alexandria and Origen, while Theophilus is the precursor of Irenaeus, and finds lineal descendants in the later Antiochene tradition.

In Justin Martyr we meet a Samaritan, born of pagan parents at Flavia Neapolis (ancient Shechem),[4] who came to Christian faith after wandering in turn through the philosophical schools of Stoicism, Aristotelianism and Pythagoreanism,[5] finally settling as a Christian in Rome where his life ended in martyrdom probably in A.D. 165.[6] He was one of the first Christian writers—the first at least from whom we have sufficient literary

---

[1] Grillmeier, *Christ in Christian Tradition*, p. 111.

[2] ' "Nature" (φύσις) still, of course, has no philosophical sense; it simply means "real", "true", like the ἀληθῶς in Ignatius of Antioch' (Grillmeier, *op. cit.* p. 114).

[3] PG, 89, col. 299; Otto, fr. VI. Its genuineness is challenged by Nautin (*Le dossier d'Hippolyte et de Méliton*, p. 84), Grillmeier (*Christ in Christian Tradition*, p. 114) and Liébaert (*L'incarnation*, I, 65).

[4] *Apol*, I, 1.   [5] *Dial. c. Tryph.* 2–8.

[6] For an outline of what is known of Justin's life, cf. L. W. Barnard, *Justin Martyr: His Life and Thought*, Cambridge, 1967, ch. I.

remains to enable us to make any accurate assessment—to raise the question of the relationship between the faith of the Church and the philosophy of the Greeks.[1] Having come to Christianity by way of the philosophical schools he continues to have a profound respect for philosophy which he acknowledges contains many things which 'were rightly said',[2] even though 'our doctrines are...indeed more lofty than all human philosophy'.[3] Yet 'he continues to speak the language of his pre-Christian philosophy after his conversion';[4] he is 'the classical instance of the semantic conflict arising from a Christian conversion',[5] a conflict which makes him speak 'a double language'.[6]

Ragnar Holte[7] has argued that the key to the theological content of Justin's *Apologies* is to be found at the end of the second apology where, in spite of his recognition of the partial agreement between the philosophies and Christianity, he 'abandons all philosophical systems and confesses his wish to be considered solely as a Christian';[8] here he has passed beyond apologetic argument to the level of personal confession of faith, recognising the inadequacies of philosophical language to explicate the depths of his personal faith. None the less, throughout his apologies his method of apologetic argument assumes that faith can be given logical and rational expression, and that 'an intelligent man will be able to comprehend' why Christ 'was born of a virgin as a man...and was crucified and died, and rose again and ascended into heaven'.[9] His appeal, both in the *Apologies* and in the *Dialogue with Trypho*, is primarily an appeal to the intelligence. Further, as Holte points out,[10] Justin's theological significance lies in his attempt to amalgamate a 'theological traditionalism' (unreserved attachment to the Christian doctrinal tradition) with 'philosophical eclecticism' (the attempt to appropriate the occasional truths found by the philosophers), but Holte fails to see that the expression

---

[1] Cf. R. Holte, 'Logos Spermatikos: Christianity and Ancient Philosophy in St Justin's Apologies', *ST*, xii (1958), 109.

[2] *Apol.* ii, 13.   [3] *Ibid.* 15.

[4] S. Laeuchli, *The Language of Faith*, New York, 1962, p. 180.

[5] *Ibid.* p. 178.

[6] *Ibid.* p. 183. Cf. Barnard, *Justin Martyr*, pp. 77 ff.

[7] 'Logos Spermatikos', pp. 110 ff.

[8] *Ibid.* p. 111.   [9] *Apol.* i, 46.

[10] 'Logos Spermatikos', p. 112.

of Christian faith in the language of the philosophers and the appropriation of philosophical 'truths' involve Justin ultimately in a form of schizophrenia[1] in which philosophy tends to dominate and transform the biblical elements in his faith received through tradition.

Justin's God is the God of the philosophers and the problem he seeks to solve is the philosophical problem of transcendence. God is ineffable and nameless[2] beyond all comprehension; he dwells in the super-celestial regions,[3] and cannot be thought to have direct contact with the world.[4] Between this transcendent God and the created world there is a gulf; to bridge it an intermediary is necessary. Justin finds in the Logos-concept this necessary bridge, the intermediary through whom God creates the world and communicates with it. 'The Logos is therefore the guide to God and the instructor of man. Originally he dwelt as a power in God, and shortly before the creation of the world he emanated and proceeded from him and he himself created the world.'[5] But the Logos-concept not only provides the bridge between God and the world; it also provides the bridge between pagan philosophy and Christianity. Whatever truth the philosophers apprehended, they did so through the Logos. Justin makes use of the concept of the *Logos Spermatikos*, 'the Logos of whom every race of men were partakers'.[6] Because of the immanence of the Logos in the world as Reason, those who have lived 'reasonably' (μετὰ λόγον), both Greeks like Heraclitus and Socrates, and barbarians like Abraham and Elijah, were Christians before Christ.[7]

---

[1] Laeuchli, *The Language of Faith*, p. 184. An opposite point of view is expressed by H. Chadwick (*Early Christian Thought and the Classical Tradition*, pp. 9 ff.) who asserts that Justin is primarily a 'biblical theologian': 'What is central in his thought is the way in which the biblical doctrine of God and his relation to the world provides him with a criterion of judgement, in the light of which he evaluates the great names in the history of Greek philosophy. Justin does not merely use Greek philosophy. He passes judgement upon it' (p. 20).

[2] *Apol.* I, 10; II, 6; cf. Pseudo-Justin, *Cohortatio ad Graecos*, 21.

[3] *Dial. c. Tryph.* 60.   [4] *Ibid.* 127.

[5] J. Quasten, *Patrology*, Utrecht and Brussels, 1951, I, 208.

[6] *Apol.* I, 46.

[7] *Idem.* There has been considerable discussion concerning the source of Justin's idea of the λόγος σπερματικός. For a long time it was assumed that Justin took the idea from Stoicism (P. Pfättisch, *Der Einfluss Platos auf die*

Yet, despite this speculation about the function of the Logos in teaching men of all races before the incarnation, Justin frequently equates the Logos with the Son of God and Jesus Christ. The Logos 'has taken shape, and become man, and was called Jesus Christ' (μορφωθέντος καὶ ἀνθρώπου γενομένου καὶ 'Ιησοῦ Χριστοῦ κληθέντος).[1] Christians 'hold him in the second place' (ἐν δευτέρᾳ χώρᾳ) after 'the true God himself'.[2] Justin is aware that the incarnation is a scandal to the Greeks, and he does not seek to minimise it: 'They proclaim our madness to consist in this, that we give to a crucified man a place second to the unchangeable and eternally existing God, the creator of all' (δευτέραν χώραν μετὰ τὸν ἄτρεπτον ‖καὶ ἀεὶ ὄντα θεόν).[3] Yet this Logos, 'who is called God, is distinct from him who made all things, numerically, I mean, but not in will' (ἕτερός ἐστι τοῦ πάντα ποιήσαντος θεοῦ, ἀριθμῷ λέγω, ἀλλ' οὐ γνώμη).[4]

The lack of indisputable quotation from St John's Gospel in Justin's writings, especially in view of the fact that there are verbal reminiscences at numerous points[5] and that quotation from the Gospel could often have added weight to his arguments, poses an interesting problem to which only hypothetical solutions can be given. Sanders concludes his discussion of the question: 'Justin's writings illustrate rather the first tentative use which was made of the Fourth Gospel by an orthodox writer, and this tentativeness makes it difficult to believe that Justin regarded the Fourth Gospel as Scripture, or as the work of an Apostle.'[6] While St John's idea of the pre-existent Logos

Theologie Justins des Märtyrers, Paderborn, 1910; V. A. Spence Little, *The Christology of the Apologists*, London, 1934, pp. 131 ff.). More recently C. Andresen ('Justin und der mittlere Platonismus', *ZNTW*, XLIV (1952–3), 157–95) has shown that Justin's concept has more affinities with Middle-Platonism. Andresen has been criticised by Ragnar Holte ('Logos Spermatikos', pp. 115 ff.) who argues that Justin has derived the concept from Philo, but is supported by J. Daniélou (*Message évangelique*, pp. 317 ff.) and L. W. Barnard (*Justin Martyr*, pp. 96 ff.).

[1] *Apol.* I, 5.
[2] *Ibid.* 13. Cf. Justin's 'confession of faith' (*Apol.* II, 13): 'For next to God, we worship and love the Logos...'; also, *Apol.* I, 6, 13, 61.
[3] *Idem.*   [4] *Dial. c. Tryph.* 56.
[5] Cf. J. N. Sanders, *The Fourth Gospel in the Early Church*, pp. 27 ff.
[6] *Ibid.* p. 31. Cf. Barnard, *Justin Martyr*, p. 60, and H. Chadwick, *Early Christian Thought*, p. 4 and pp. 124 f.: 'In Justin we find a theologian on

and of his becoming incarnate in Jesus Christ would have been congenial to Justin's thought, St John's emphasis on the unity of the Son with the Father would have been difficult for him to reconcile with his view of the Logos as 'in the second place' and 'numerically' distinct from the God who created all things.

While Justin lived and wrote and died in Rome, his theology appears to have had little influence on the development of Western theology; the tradition which he established, a tradition of interpreting the Christian faith as a philosophy,[1] finds its natural home and growth in the philosophical theology of Alexandria. The theological tradition which is to find its natural home in the west is that hammered out by Irenaeus in his polemic against the gnostics, a tradition in which philosophical speculation plays a decreasingly important role.

E. THEOPHILUS OF ANTIOCH

Theophilus is the first Christian writer to attribute the fourth gospel to 'John', the first to quote explicitly from the Gospel and the first to use the technical term τριάς (= trinitas, trinity) for the union of three persons in the godhead; his trinity, however, is not that of Father, Son and Holy Spirit, but 'of God, and his Word, and his Wisdom'.[2] G. Bardy points out that Theophilus habitually identifies Wisdom with the Spirit,[3] as also does Irenaeus on a number of occasions.[4]

The scope of his three books ad Autolycum is limited by the specific criticisms against which he seeks to defend the Christian faith, and in particular the criticism of the Christian doctrine of creatio ex nihilo. He seeks to demonstrate the superiority of the latter over the Platonic doctrine that the universe was fashioned out of pre-existing matter, on the basis of the Genesis creation stories and the Prologue of St John's Gospel. He asserts that

whom no real Johannine influence is discernible...So we have the strange paradox that the man chiefly responsible for making the Logos idea at home in Christian theology was little influenced by St John. It is not even certain that he had read Philo' (p. 4).

[1] Cf. Dial. c. Tryph. 8: 'I found this philosophy alone to be safe and profitable.'

[2] ad Autolycum, II, 15.

[3] Trois Livres à Autolycus (SC, xx), Paris, 1948, p. 43.

[4] adv. Haer. II, 30, 9; III, 24, 2; IV, 7, 4; IV, 20, 1, 3; Demonstratio, 5.

the prophets taught us with one accord that God made all things out of nothing, for nothing was co-eternal with God...God, then, having his own Word immanent (ἐνδιάθετος) within his own bowels begot him, emitting him along with his own Wisdom before the universe (πρὸ τῶν ὅλων). He had this Word as a helper (ὑπουργόν) in the things that were created by him, and through him he made all things (II. 10).

This is the first known use in a Christian writing of the Stoic term ἐνδιάθετος. Later Theophilus uses the correlative Stoic term προφορικός: 'When God wished to make all that he had determined on, he begot this Word uttered (προφορικός), the first-born of all creation,[1] without emptying himself of the Word, but having begotten the Word and always conversing with his Word' (II. 22). Although he makes use of Stoic terminology, Theophilus appears to be unconscious of doing so. Bardy[2] quotes with approval the comment of A. Puech that

Theophilus makes no allusion to their Stoic origin. Is it because this opponent of philosophy does not wish to admit that he owes the least thing to them? It is possible; but I believe that he would have been very surprised, if he had been reproached for thus borrowing from Hellenism in the same way as Hellenism, according to him, had borrowed from Judaism...Theophilus found these words convenient and adopted them...he thought he was doing nothing extraordinary.[3]

Theophilus' use of the 'twofold stage theory of the Logos' is probably no more than a convenient way of stating the belief that God creates through the mediation of the Logos, through the Word which he speaks in creation (Genesis i). None the less it was to play an important part in later Antiochene theology. The idea that 'at first God was alone and his Word was in him' (ad Autol. II. 22) is crucial in the theology of Marcellus of Ancyra during the fourth century, who asserted that in the beginning 'there was nothing but God' (οὐδὲν ἕτερον ἦν πλὴν

---

[1] Colossians i. 15. [2] Trois Livres, p. 41.

[3] J. Daniélou (Message évangélique, p. 325) points out that the opposition of ἐνδιάθετος and προφορικός is found in Philo, and 'it is never applied by him or by any other pre-Christian writer to the divine Logos. It seems then that it comes from a common philosophical language. It does not imply any reference to Stoicism. It is the Christian writers who use it to express their theology of the Logos.' Cf. also H. A. Wolfson, The Philosophy of the Church Fathers, pp. 192 ff.

θεοῦ),[1] the Monad,[2] and 'the Logos was in God' (ἐν τῷ θεῷ τοῦ λόγου).[3]

Theophilus does not mention 'Jesus Christ' and he does not discuss the incarnation or the atonement. S. Laeuchli points out that in *ad Autolycum* we see 'the first grave problem of Christian apologetic language', and suggests that a pagan reading it could just as well 'be converted to Diaspora Judaism'.[4]

F. IRENAEUS OF LYONS

A native of Asia, Irenaeus became Bishop of Lyons in Gaul; thus he provides a link, a bridge between the theology of Asia Minor and the Western Church. If the Western Church treated St John's Gospel with suspicion because of its popularity with the gnostics, then it was probably due to Irenaeus' masterly use of it in the task of refuting gnosticism that this suspicion was dispelled and the gospel accepted. In opposition to gnosticism with its abhorrence of the physical and material world and its dissolution of history into romance and mythology,[5] Irenaeus sets forth a theology of salvation-history with its primary emphasis on God's saving work in Jesus Christ. The fact that he was first and foremost a biblical theologian—'the first intentionally biblical theologian of the Christian Church'[6]—is now generally recognised.[7] Grillmeier quotes with approval Cullmann's statement:

[1] Marcellus, fr. 60; cf. fr. 63, 103, 104, 121. References are given according to the numbering in the collection of fragments in Klostermann's edition of Eusebius, *contra Marcellum* and *de Ecclesiastica Theologia* (*GCS*, vol. IV).

[2] Fr. 68, 69.   [3] Fr. 103.

[4] *The Language of Faith*, New York, 1962, p. 165.

[5] Cf. Laeuchli, *op. cit.* pp. 69 ff., 74 ff.; R. L. P. Milburn, *Early Christian Interpretations of History*, London, 1954, p. 26: 'The cultured gnostics recoiled in horror from the scandal of a true incarnation and strove to convert historic fact into edifying and ingenious romance.'

[6] G. T. Armstrong, *Die Genesis in der Alte Kirche*, Tübingen, 1962, quoted by Grillmeier, *Christ in Christian Tradition*, p. 118.

[7] Cf. A. Benoit, *Saint Irénée. Introduction à l'étude de sa théologie*, Paris, 1960; A. Houssiau, *La christologie de saint Irénée*, Louvain, 1955; J. Lawson, *The Biblical Theology of St Irenaeus*, London, 1948; G. Wingren, *Man and the Incarnation*, Edinburgh and London, 1959; S. Laeuchli, *The Language of Faith*, pp. 191 ff.

Down to the theologians of the 'redemptive history' school in the nineteenth century...there has scarcely been another theologian who has recognised so clearly as did Irenaeus that the Christian proclamation stands or falls with the redemptive history, that this historical work of Jesus Christ as Redeemer forms the mid-point of a line which leads from the Old Testament to the return of Christ.[1]

Irenaeus emphasises the threefold mediatorial work of the Son of God, but cosmology, the mediation in the work of creation, is strictly subordinated to the mediation in revelation and redemption. He says that John,

desiring...to establish the rule of truth in the Church, that there is one almighty God, who made all things by his Word, both visible and invisible, showing at the same time that by the Word, through whom God made the creation, he also bestowed salvation on the men who are included in the creation, thus commenced his teaching in the Gospel: 'In the beginning was the Word, etc...' (John i. 1–5).[2]

When he does speak of creation it is usually in order to assert that it is the work of the one God who 'created all things, since he is the only God, the only Lord, the only creator, the only Father (*solus deus, solus dominus, solus conditor, solus pater*), alone containing all things, and himself ordering all things into existence';[3] thus he denies the gnostic distinction between God and the Logos or Son.

Irenaeus, however, is far more interested in the gnostic denial of salvation through Christ; against their docetism he emphasises the reality of salvation through Jesus Christ, the Word made flesh, the God–man, and the authenticity of God's self-revelation through his Son. If Christ is not true God and true man, there is no real salvation and no authentic revelation. When God created man he made him in his image and likeness, and willed that he should remain in the state wherein he was

---

[1] Grillmeier, *Christ in Christian Tradition*, p. 115, quoting O. Cullmann, *Christ and Time*, 2nd ed. London, 1962, pp. 56–7. L. G. Patterson (*God and History in Early Christian Thought*, London, 1967, pp. 40–2) speaks of 'Irenaeus' lack of interest in *historia*', but underestimates the importance of *historia* in Irenaeus' central doctrine of *recapitulatio*, and the fundamental importance of history in Irenaeus' only extant non-polemical work, *The Demonstration of the Apostolic Preaching*. Cf. A. Luneau, *L'histoire de salut chez les Pères de l'Église*, Paris, 1964, pp. 93 ff.

[2] *adv. Haer.* III, 11, 1 (Harvey, I, 251).

[3] *Ibid.* II, 1, 1 (Harvey, I, 251); *Demonstratio*, 6.

created; through the sin of Adam, however, the image of God has been lost.[1] The incarnation takes place in order that 'what we had lost in Adam...we might receive again in Christ Jesus'.[2] Emphasising the necessity of a real, and not a merely apparent, incarnation for our salvation to be real and effective, Irenaeus says that

thus the Word of God was made man (*verbum dei homo factus est*), as also Moses says: 'God, true are his works' (Deut. xxxii. 4). But if, not having been made flesh, he appeared as if flesh, his work was not a true one. But what he appeared (to be), that he also was. God recapitulated in himself the ancient formation of man, that he might kill sin, deprive death of its power, and give life to man; and therefore his works are true.[3]

Man is made living and perfect, 'receiving the perfect Father', because 'the Word of the Father and the Spirit of God' have, in the incarnation, become 'united with the ancient substance of Adam's formation...in order that, as in the natural (Adam) we all were dead, so in the spiritual we may all be made alive'.[4] Through Jesus Christ, the Son of God, who 'passed through every stage of life, restoring to all communion with God',[5] sin is destroyed, death's power is broken, the image of God is renewed in man, and man is restored to that fellowship with God for which he was created.[6]

Closely interwoven with Irenaeus' doctrine of the mediatorship of the Son in the work of redemption is his doctrine of God's self-revelation through the Son. In Jesus Christ, the

---

[1] On the importance of Gen. i. 26 in Irenaeus' theology see L. M. Froidevaux, *Irénée de Lyon: Démonstration de la prédication apostolique* (*SC*, LXII), ch. 22, n. 8; ch. 55, n. 3; 'One can hardly exaggerate its importance in St Irenaeus' thought; he puts the image and likeness of the Father, not only at the beginnings of the first creation, but at the centre of the work of redemption' (ch. 55, n. 3). Cf. also G. Wingren, *Man and the Incarnation*, pp. 14 ff., 90 ff.; R. McL. Wilson, 'The Early Exegesis of Gen. i. 26', *SP*, I, 420–32. It is strange that Houssiau (*Saint Irénée*) makes no mention of this concept in his otherwise very satisfactory study of Irenaeus' Christology.

[2] *adv. Haer.* III, 18, 1 (Harvey, II, 95); cf. *Demonstratio*, 32.

[3] *Ibid.* III, 18, 7 (Harvey, II, 102); cf. *Demonstratio*, 30, 53, 71.

[4] *Ibid.* V, 1, 1 (Harvey, II, 317).

[5] *Ibid.* III, 18, 7 (Harvey, II, 101); cf. *Demonstratio*, 31: 'So he united man with God and brought about a communion of God and man' (translation J. P. Smith, *ACW*, XVI).

[6] Cf. *Demonstratio*, 97.

incarnate Word, and nowhere else do we see God and receive life.[1] 'That revelation which comes through the Word gives life to those who see God.'[2] In a long section by exegesis of Matt. xi. 27 he sets forth his doctrine of revelation through the Word, connecting the revelation in the historical Jesus with the revelation through the Word which came to the patriarchs and prophets of the old dispensation. 'Through the Word himself who had been made visible and tangible,[3] the Father was shown forth, although all did not equally believe in him; but all saw the Father in the Son; for the Father is the invisible of the Son, but the Son is the visible of the Father.'[4] If the revelation through the Son or Word is to be really revelation, the Word must become flesh, the Son must become a man. 'For in no other way could we have learned the things of God unless our Master, existing as the Word, had become a man (*homo factus fuisset*). For no other being had the power of revealing to us the things of the Father, except his own proper Word.'[5]

If the authenticity of God's self-revelation demands the reality of Christ's manhood, it equally demands the reality of his divinity. The gnostics err in seeking to separate Mind (*Nous*) and Word (*Logos*) as aeons which have emanated from him. Against them Irenaeus asserts that 'He who is over all... he is all Mind and all Word (*totus Nous et totus Logos*)'.[6] Unlike the word of a man the Word of God is not an emanation or an utterance; he asks, 'In what respect will the Word of God— yea, rather God himself, since he is the Word—differ from the word of a man?'.[7] Houssiau[8] points out that Irenaeus' criticism of the concept λόγος προφορικός has no bearing on the philosophical distinction between λόγος ἐνδιάθετος and λόγος προφορικός, for this distinction was not used by his adversaries. 'He is content to demonstrate that if the Logos is emitted, he

---

[1] *adv. Haer.* IV, 20, 5 (Harvey, II, 216).
[2] *Ibid.* IV, 20, 7 (Harvey, II, 219).   [3] Cf. I John i. 1–3.
[4] *adv. Haer.* IV, 6, 6 (Harvey, II, 160–1).
[5] *Ibid.* V, 1, 1 (Harvey, II, 314). Concerning this passage E. Brunner (*The Mediator*, London, 1946, p. 260) says, 'Note how very clearly Irenaeus sees what it means to be the Logos: "What God has to say to us".' Brunner gives a catena of quotations (*idem*, n. 2) in which Irenaeus emphasises the Mediatorship of the Son in revelation.
[6] *Ibid.* II, 13, 8 (Harvey, I, 285).
[7] *Idem.*   [8] *Saint Irénée*, pp. 165 ff.

cannot be interior but only uttered (προφορικός); it follows that he is like the human word (προφορά). *A fortiori*, Irenaeus does not allude in any way to the apologetic theory of the double state of the Logos.'[1] God is ὅλος Νοῦς, ὅλος Λόγος. The Word is God himself speaking for the creation of all things, the redemption of man and the revelation of himself. F. Loofs frequently refers to the 'identity of revelation' (*Offenbarungsidentität*) of God and his Word, of Father and Son in Irenaeus.[2]

It has already been pointed out that Irenaeus is anxious to preserve the unity of God. In the *Demonstratio*, 6 he says that the first and foremost article of our faith is 'God, the Father, uncreated, beyond grasp, invisible, one God the maker of all'.[3] But in the 'economy', which, for Irenaeus, always refers to redemptive history and not, as with later Fathers, to the internal arrangement of the Godhead, there is revealed the distinction between Father and Son (and Holy Spirit).

Therefore the Father is Lord, and the Son is Lord, and the Father is God and the Son is God. Thus God is shown to be one according to the essence of his being and power; but at the same time, as the administrator of the economy of our redemption, he is both Father and Son; since the Father of all is invisible and inaccessible to creatures, it is through the Son that those who are to approach God must have access to the Father.[4]

In his discussion of the rule of faith and the three articles of faith he clearly sets forth the unity of God and the distinction between Father, Son and Holy Spirit.[5] Although he sets the distinctions within the framework of salvation-history, he avoids modalism by his insistence on the eternity of the Son. Further, his emphasis on the mediatorship of the Son in creation, redemption and revelation prevents him from obscuring the distinction between Father and Son.

In opposition to the emanationism of the gnostics, which implies the posteriority of the Logos to God, Irenaeus repeatedly

---

[1] *Ibid.* p. 166; cf. J. P. Smith, *Proof of the Apostolic Preaching* (*ACW*, XVI), pp. 181 ff. Wolfson confirms this view by ascribing to Irenaeus a 'single stage theory of the Logos' (*Philosophy of the Church Fathers*, pp. 198 ff.).

[2] *Leitfaden*, §15, 4; 22, 2a; *Theophilus von Antiochien*, p. 335; cf. H. E. W. Turner, *The Patristic Doctrine of Redemption*, London, 1952, pp. 36 ff.

[3] Cf. *adv. Haer.* II, 1, 1 (Harvey, I, 251) (quoted p. 43, n. 3 above).

[4] *Demonstratio*, 47.   [5] *Ibid.*, 3, 6.

insists on the eternity of the Son with the Father.[1] In *adversus Haereses* (II, 13, 8) he speaks of 'the Word eternal in God' (*in deo aeternum verbum*). But Irenaeus, reacting against the highly speculative systems of the gnostics, refuses to speculate on the manner of the Son's generation: 'No one understands that production, or generation, or calling, or revelation, or by whatever name one may describe his generation, which is in fact altogether indescribable.'[2] It is sufficient to know that the Son is co-eternal with the Father, that 'in the beginning was the Word and the Word was with God, and the Word was God' (John i. 1), that Father and Son (and Holy Spirit) are one God.

Thus, without speculation, Irenaeus preserves the Johannine emphasis on the identity of the Word with God, of the Son with the Father and, at the same time, on the distinction between them. The one God reveals himself as Father through the Son.[3] The regulative concept in his theology, as in the Johannine, is that of sonship,[4] and because of his concentration on the historical manifestation in the incarnation, his theology is soteriological and christocentric throughout.

Further, it has already been shown that a real incarnation is the very centre of Irenaeus' thought. Revelation and redemption demand a real incarnation. The Word becomes flesh or, as Irenaeus prefers to put it, God becomes man (*homo factus est*).[5] Christ is 'man, the formation of God...he took up man into himself, the invisible becoming visible, the incomprehensible becoming comprehensible, the impassible becoming passible, and the Word being made man'.[6] Irenaeus' christology is a God–man christology in which the fullness of divinity and full-

---

[1] *adv. Haer.* II, 25, 3; II, 30, 9; III, 18, 1; IV, 6, 2; IV, 14, 1; IV, 20, 7; *Demonstratio*, 30; 'Son of God, pre-existent with the Father, born before all the building of the world'; *Demonstratio*, 43, 52.

[2] *adv. Haer.* II, 28, 6 (Harvey, I, 355): *prolationem istam, sive generationem, sive nuncupationem, sive adapertionem, aut quolibet quis nomine vocaverit generationem ejus inenarrabilem existentem, nemo novit.*

[3] Cf. E. Brunner (*The Mediator*, p. 260): 'The redemption through the Son is the redemption through the Word of revelation.'

[4] Houssiau points out (*Saint Irénée*, p. 30) that the title 'Son' is used almost 500 times in *adv. Haer.*

[5] *adv. Haer.* V, 1, 1; III, 22, 1; III, 18, 17; for further references cf. Houssiau, *Saint Irénée*, pp. 186 ff.

[6] *Ibid.* III, 16, 6.

ness of humanity are equally emphasised as both necessary for the reality and efficacy of revelation and redemption.

It remains to ask briefly what is the content of Irenaeus' Logos-concept. For him the Logos is no second or inferior God, but God himself in his self-communication, in creation, revelation and redemption. In no sense is the Logos an emanation of God; he is the biblical 'Word of the Lord'. His rejection of the two-stage theory of the Logos involves also a rejection of the equation of the Logos with Wisdom, which he equates rather with the Holy Spirit.[1] Metaphysical speculation about the nature of the Logos and the relationship between God and the Logos is absent from his thought.[2]

The theology of Asia Minor and Syria comes to self-consciousness in the biblical theology of Irenaeus. He has made the Johannine theology his own, developing the Johannine witness to the Son of God as mediator of God's activity in creation, revelation and redemption. On this basis he holds firmly to the two Johannine paradoxes without seeking in any way to dissolve or soften them. The concept of the Word of the Lord is useful to him, but for him, as for John, the regulative concept is that of sonship, or perhaps, rather, the concept of the Father–Son relationship. With Irenaeus, the Asian[3] who became a bishop in the Western Church, the Antiochene or Asia Minor theology with its strong Johannine flavour becomes a dominant theological influence in the west.

---

[1] *Demonstratio*, 5: 'The Word is fitly and properly called the Son, but the Spirit the Wisdom of God.' Cf. also *Demonstratio*, 10; *adv. Haer.* III, 38, 2; IV, 20, 3; IV, 34, 1; IV, 34, 3; *et al.*; J. P. Smith, *ACW*, XVI, 26 f., 42, 140. Froidevaux (*SC*, LXII, 36, n. 8) says, 'This identification of the Son with the Logos and of the Spirit with Wisdom is constant with Irenaeus.' Cf. also M. Simonetti, *Studi sull'Arianesimo*, Rome, 1965, p. 14.

[2] Cf. Grillmeier, *Christ in Christian Tradition*, p. 122.

[3] Harvey makes out a strong case for the view that Irenaeus was in fact a Syrian by birth who moved to Smyrna at an early age; cf. introd. to his edition of *adv. Haer.* I, cliii ff.

CHAPTER 3

CHRISTOLOGY IN THE THIRD CENTURY

If, during the second century, the church appeared not to be fully conscious of the theological task facing her, at the same time she was laying a foundation for the more specifically doctrinal development that lay ahead of her. The task of apologists like Theophilus and Justin, Athenagoras and Aristides and the rest, was to enter into dialogue with pagan detractors of the faith, a philosophical rather than a strictly theological exercise. The task of pastors like Ignatius, Irenaeus, and to a lesser extent Melito, was to proclaim the gospel to the faithful and to protect them from gnostic perversions of the faith. By the end of the century St John's Gospel had established its position within the church; it gave to the church a terminology which had points of contact with pagan thought and at the same time placed in her hand a weapon with which to defeat the syncretising forces of gnosticism.

This double stimulus—the necessity to defend her gospel on two points, against pagan attack from without and gnostic subversion from within—continued during the third century. In the west, Hippolytus and Tertullian continued the battle against gnosticism so ably begun by Irenaeus, using the same weapons of scripture and appeal to the traditional faith of the church,[1] based on scripture and handed down from apostolic times, enshrined in catechetical instruction and most succinctly expressed in the early baptismal creeds.[2] At the same time Tertullian continued the apologetic task in treatises like his *Apology* and *de Testimonio Animae*. In Alexandria, on the other

---

[1] Cf. D. van den Eynde, *Les normes de l'enseignement chrétien dans la littérature patristique des trois premiers siècles*, Gembloux, 1933; H. E. W. Turner, *The Pattern of Christian Truth*, London, 1954; E. Fleeseman-van Leer, *Tradition and Scripture in the Early Church*, Leiden, 1953; R. P. C. Hanson, *Tradition in the Early Church*, London, 1962; M. F. Wiles, *The Making of Christian Doctrine*, Cambridge, 1967.

[2] Cf. especially J. N. D. Kelly, *Early Christian Creeds*, London, 1940.

49

hand, the two tasks were faced as if they were one. Clement and Origen followed in the tradition of apologists like Justin, seeking to prove that Christianity is the true philosophy. Unlike the western opponents of gnosticism, however, they did not make a frontal attack on gnosticism; instead, they sought to portray Christianity as the true gnosis. Against pagan philosophy and gnostic theosophy they set out a single apologetic aimed at demonstrating that Christianity fulfils the highest hopes and yearnings of both.

This difference in attitude towards gnosticism is due largely to a difference in environment. Western theologians lived in an atmosphere that was practical rather than speculative, more interested in law and action than in philosophy; the only philosophy which had any lasting influence on the life and culture of the west was Stoicism with its strongly ethical and practical emphasis.[1] Alexandria, on the other hand, was a centre of cosmopolitan culture, where any and every philosophy and religion could gain a hearing and gather a following.[2] Valentinus and Basilides, founders of the two leading gnostic systems, were Alexandrians, while as early as the first century a brilliant attempt had been made by Philo Judaeus to reconcile or harmonise Judaism with current philosophy. In the first half of the third century Neo-Platonism was to be developed there at the very time when Clement and Origen were trying to achieve a reconciliation of the church's faith with Middle-Platonism and Alexandrian Judaism.[3]

As well as the continuing double stimulus provided by pagan attacks and gnostic subversion, another stimulus appears in the third century. Irenaeus had established the church's faith that it is the *one* God who is active both in the Old Covenant and the New, in opposition to the gnostic distinction between the creator and the Father of Jesus Christ, and the faith that Jesus

[1] Cf. e.g. Marcus Aurelius.

[2] Cf. E. R. Hardy, *Christian Egypt*, New York, 1952.

[3] If Alexandria finds no place in second-century history of dogma apart from the gnostic systems which flourished there, it is on Asia Minor and Syria that the curtain of silence falls in the third century, to be broken only in the brief controversy that led to the condemnation of Paul of Samosata in A.D. 269. Thus while Syria and the Western church are dominant in theological development in the second century, in the third it is Alexandria and the West which occupy the centre of the stage.

Christ is really man, over against the docetic christology of gnosticism. In the third century the church had to face the problem, from the beginning inherent in her worship and message, of defining more clearly the divinity of Christ and his place in the godhead. This challenge was raised in an acute form by the two varieties of Monarchianism which had only one thing in common, their desire to preserve the monotheism of the Bible, the church's faith in *one* God.

The challenge came first in the form of modalistic monarchianism, which preserved the unity of God and the divinity of Christ by denying any distinction between the Father and the Son and making the three dispensations of *Heilsgeschichte* no more than successive manifestations or aspects of the one God. Faced with this challenge, Hippolytus and Tertullian in the West were forced to define more closely the concept of distinctions within the unity of God. Later the challenge took the form of dynamic monarchianism which sought to preserve the unity of God and the distinction between the Father and the Son by denying the Son's divinity, asserting that he was a man raised to the status of divinity by adoption as Son of God. This form of monarchianism, 'a humanitarian doctrine which is neither Ebionite nor Theodotian, but may perhaps be that of Artemas',[1] brought forth Novatian's reply in his *de Trinitate*. In Antioch, a similar doctrine propagated by Paul of Samosata provoked the attacks of Origenist bishops who brought about his condemnation. In facing up to the challenges of monarchianism, the Western church anticipated by a century the trinitarian formulation of the Council of Nicaea (A.D. 325).

In Alexandria, on the other hand, the challenge of monarchianism was not strongly felt until the time of Dionysius (*c.* A.D. 260). Origen makes passing reference to those who deny the distinction between the Father and the Son;[2] the dominant influence of his theology, in which the μοναρχία of the Father was preserved by the subordination of the Son and the Holy Spirit within the hierarchy of the godhead, prevented monarchianism

---

[1] E. Evans, *Tertullian's Treatise against Praxeas*, London, 1948.

[2] *Comm. in Joh.* x, 37 (*GCS*, IV, 212, 13). In the *Dialogue with Heraclides*, discovered during the War and published in 1949, Origen combats a doctrine which bears many of the characteristics of modalistic monarchianism; cf. J. Scherer, *Entretien d'Origène avec Héraclide* (*SC*, LXVII), Paris, 1960, pp. 25 ff.

from being as strong a challenge in Alexandria as it was in the West. In A.D. 260, thirty years after Origen's departure from Alexandria for Caesarea, Dionysius attacked Sabellianism which had become rife in the Pentapolis, and was himself attacked for extreme subordinationism. Within the same decade the monarchianism and adoptionism of Paul of Samosata was condemned in Antioch by Origenist bishops.

The central theological task of the third century then was that of giving clearer definition to the Johannine paradox of the Son's unity with and distinction from the Father. The modalistic monarchians relied to a large extent on a small selection of scriptural texts (e.g. Deut. vi. 4; John x. 30; xiv. 9, 10) which, taken in isolation, seemed to support their view. It is largely by exegesis of St John's Gospel that their views are refuted. Hippolytus against Noetus, Tertullian against Praxeas, Novatian against the unnamed proponent of a humanistic christology (*psilanthropism*)—all three delivered their most telling blows by exegesis of St John. Clement and Origen, too, find in the Fourth Gospel support for their view of distinctions within the godhead.

As in the second century, so also in the third the strictly christological question of the relationship of the divine and human in Christ does not occupy the centre of the stage. None the less discussion of the relationship of the Father and the Son always involves some discussion of the christological question.

A. THE WESTERN CHURCH

(*i*) *Hippolytus*[1]

The monarchianism which provokes Hippolytus to write the *contra Noetum*, of which a substantial fragment is preserved,[2]

[1] The question of the identity of Hippolytus and the authenticity of the writings ascribed to him has been opened afresh by P. Nautin in three important studies: *Hippolyte et Josipe*, Paris, 1947; *Hippolyte: Contre les hérésies, Fragment*, Paris, 1949; *Le dossier d'Hippolyte et de Méliton dans les florilèges dogmatiques et chez les historiens modernes (Patristica,* i), Paris, 1953. It is unnecessary for the present purpose to enter the debate on these questions; the only treatise which concerns us is *contra Noetum* which Nautin ascribes to Hippolytus.

[2] Edited and translated into French in Nautin, *Hippolyte: Contre les hérésies*, pp. 234 ff.

originated in Asia Minor, either with Noetus of Smyrna or Epigonus, one of his disciples,[1] and appears to have gained a measure of popularity in Rome during the episcopates of Victor (193–202), Zephyrinus (202–19), and Calixtus (219–23).[2] The surviving fragment of Hippolytus' treatise gives a clear indication of the doctrine and exegesis both of Noetus and of Hippolytus.

Noetus' theology was a monarchianism of a naïvely modalistic kind which simply identified Christ with the Father: 'Christ was the Father himself, and the Father himself was born and suffered and died' (τὸν χριστὸν αὐτὸν εἶναι τὸν πατέρα, καὶ αὐτὸν τὸν πατέρα γεγεννῆσθαι καὶ πεπονθέναι καὶ ἀποτεθνηκέναι).[3]

Noetus preserved the monarchy of God by denying any distinction between the Father and the Son and by affirming their complete identity. It is possible to see in Noetian monotheism evidence of a strong reaction against the Logos doctrine which, as propounded by apologists like Justin and Theophilus, appeared to lead towards ditheism,[4] but whether the basis of this monotheism is biblical or philosophical is perhaps an open question. Hippolytus has no doubt at all that it is philosophical and traces its origin, not to the Old Testament, but to the philosophy of Heraclitus.[5] Further, he accuses the Noetians of 'using only one group of passages' of Scripture (μονοκώλως χρώμενοι),[6] selecting isolated texts—Exod. iii. 6; xx. 3; Isa. xliv. 6; Baruch iii. 36–8; Isa. xlv. 14–15—which teach the oneness of God, and ignoring those in which scripture teaches that there is a distinction between Father and Logos (Son). In his refutation of the Noetians' one-sided use of scripture Hippolytus frequently makes use of texts from St John's Gospel. They did not, however, ignore St John's Gospel entirely, for

---

[1] Hippolytus, *Philosophoumena*, IX, 2 ff.

[2] The best brief discussion of the monarchian controversy is to be found in E. Evans, *Tertullian's Treatise against Praxeas*, pp. 9–18. Cf. also J. N. D. Kelly, *Early Christian Doctrines*, 4th edn. London, 1968, pp. 115 ff.

[3] *c. Noet.* 1. Cf. *ibid.* 2: 'Christ who is himself God suffered, and consequently the Father suffered, for he himself was the Father...Christ was God.'

[4] Cf. Kelly, *Early Christian Doctrines*, pp. 109 f. In *Philos.* IX, 7, Hippolytus says that Callistus reproached his opponents: 'You are ditheists.'

[5] *Philosophoumena*, IX, 3–5.

[6] *c. Noet.* 3. Nautin (*Hippolyte*, p. 238) translates: 'Ils s'en servent à leur tour d'une manière unilatérale.'

they themselves quoted the crucial texts, John x. 30 and xiv. 9, to support their views.[1]

In opposition to their appeal to Isa. xlv. 15, 'God is in thee, and there is no God beside thee' as proving the oneness of God and the identity of the Father and the Son, Hippolytus appeals to John xiv. 10, 'I am in the Father and the Father in me.' 'God is in thee' refers to 'the mystery of the economy (μυστήριον οἰκονομίας) because when the Word had become flesh and became man (σεσαρκωμένου...καὶ ἐνανθρωπήσαντος) the Father was in the Son and the Son in the Father while the Son was living among men'.[2] Jesus himself bears witness to this when he speaks of the Son of Man who came down from heaven and is in heaven (John iii. 13).[3]

The Noetian appeal to John x. 30, 'I and the Father are one', is of particular interest because of the important role exegesis of this text was to play right through the trinitarian controversies.[4] Hippolytus points out that Jesus 'did not say, "I and the Father *am* (εἰμι) one" but "are (ἐσμεν) one". For "we are" does not refer to one person, but to two; it points to two persons, but a single power.'[5] That is to say, this text which *par excellence* points to the unity of Father and Son itself points also to the distinction between them. Hippolytus proceeds to argue that John x. 30 must be interpreted in the light of John xvii. 22, 23:[6] '...that they may be one even as we are one, I in them and thou in me, that they may become perfectly one so that the world may know that thou hast sent me'. Hippolytus

---

[1] They appear to have accepted St John's Gospel as canonical, but side-stepped the Prologue by interpreting it allegorically: 'But, someone will say to me, you introduce a strange thing to me when you call the Son "Logos"; for John indeed speaks about the Logos, but he gives it a different meaning by allegorising' (ἀλλ' ἄλλως ἀλληγορεῖ) (*c. Noet.* 15).

[2] *c. Noet.* 4. We shall return to Hippolytus' view of 'the mystery of the economy'.

[3] *Idem.*

[4] Cf. my article, 'The Exegesis of John x. 30 in the Early Trinitarian Controversies', *NTS*, iii (1956–7), pp. 324–49.

[5] *c. Noet.* 7.

[6] The question of the interpretation of John x. 30 and xvii. 22, 23 in relation to each other is a crucial exegetical point in the Arian and Marcellan controveries. Hippolytus takes the same line as the Arians and Eusebius of Caesarea. Athanasius, on the other hand, insists that John xvii. 22 f. must be interpreted in the light of John x. 30. See below, pp. 227–32.

argues that Jesus does not mean that we are all to be 'a single body physically' (ἓν σῶμα...κατὰ τὴν οὐσίαν) but 'one by power and harmony of attitude' (τῇ δυνάμει καὶ τῇ διαθέσει τῆς ὁμοφρονίας ἕν). 'In the same way the Son who was sent and was not known by those who are in the world, confessed that he was in the Father by power and disposition, for the Son is the mind of the Father.'[1]

Having refuted the Noetians' interpretation of their favourite texts, by which they support their philosophically derived doctrine, Hippolytus goes on to set out his own views which he claims are based on scripture and nothing else. 'There is, brethren, a single God, whom we know from the holy scriptures and from no other source.'[2] Taking account of the witness of scripture as a whole we are 'compelled to acknowledge God the Father Almighty, and Jesus Christ the Son of God, who, being God, became man, to whom also the Father made all things subject, himself excepted, and the Holy Spirit, and these are really three' (ταῦτ' εἶναι ὄντως τρία). God is one in power. 'His power is one' (μία δύναμις τούτου); 'as far as power is concerned God is one' (ὅσον κατὰ τὴν δύναμιν εἷς ἐστιν θεός), 'but as far as the economy is concerned the manifestation is threefold' (ὅσον δὲ κατὰ τὴν οἰκονομίαν τριχῆς ἡ ἐπίδειξις).[3]

The doctrine which Hippolytus sets forth is a form of economic trinitarianism, although as R. A. Markus points out[4] it is necessary to be cautious in applying this label to Hippolytus. Markus has shown that for Hippolytus 'economy' (οἰκονομία) means the incarnation. Of the passage quoted above he says,

the 'manifestation' in the course of the 'economy' spoken of would seem to suggest the historical manifestation of the Trinity in Creation, Incarnation, and the work of the Holy Spirit. This threefold manifestation is in fact the plan on which the 'demonstration of the truth'

---

[1] c. Noet. 7. In this and a number of other passages Hippolytus uses παῖς instead of υἱός, continuing a primitive Christian tradition (Acts iii. 13, 26; iv. 25, 27, 30; Didache, ix. 2 f.; x. 2 f.; Ps.-Barnabas, v. 1; ix. 2) probably derived ultimately from the Deutero-Isaianic Servant Songs. Cullmann claims that here we have a very primitive Christology or Paidology: Peter Disciple, Apostle, Martyr, London, 1st ed. 1952, pp. 66 ff.; Christology of the New Testament, London, 1959, pp. 73 ff.

[2] c. Noet. 9.　　　　　　　　　[3] Ibid. 8.

[4] 'Trinitarian Theology and the Economy', JTS, N.S. IX (1958), 89 ff., especially pp. 98–102.

which follows immediately is constructed. Summarising this 'three-fold demonstration' Hippolytus says: 'This is the economy delivered to us by the blessed John who bears witness to it in his gospel'; and, 'I shall certainly not speak of two gods but of one, and of two persons by the economy, and of the Holy Spirit in the third place. For though the Father is one, the persons are two, as there is also the Son; and there is the Holy Spirit for a third. The Father commands, the Word fulfils, the Son—through whom we believe in the Father—is shown forth. The economy is thus harmoniously reconciled with the one God.' (*c. Noet.* 14.)[1]

Being concerned with the problem of reconciling the unity of the godhead with the manifestation of the Son in the incarnation, Hippolytus appears, however, to be reluctant to call the second Person of the trinity 'Son' before the incarnation, so that frequently he seems to suggest that the Word became Son at the incarnation. Thus he foreshadows the economic trinitariansim of Marcellus of Ancyra. In the beginning 'God was alone, having nothing contemporaneous with himself' (θεὸς μόνος ὑπάρχων καὶ μηδὲν ἔχων ἑαυτοῦ σύγχρονον). Yet this unity was by no means undifferentiated, for 'although he was alone, he was multiple (αὐτὸς δὲ μόνος ὢν πολὺς ἦν), being neither without Logos (ἄλογος), nor without wisdom, nor without power, nor without counsel'.[2] 'When he willed and as he willed, he begot his Logos (ἐγέννα τὸν λόγον αὐτοῦ) through whom he made all things.' But this begetting of the Logos is not the origination of the Logos; rather it is the beginning of his separate subsistence. God always has the Logos in himself (ἐν ἑαυτῷ)—God is never ἄλογος[3]—but the Logos comes into separate existence for the creation of the world; 'conceiving the world in mind, and willing and uttering the word, he made it' (κόσμον ἐννοηθεὶς θελήσας τε καὶ φθεγξάμενος ἐποίησεν).[4] Thus 'there appeared another (ἕτερος) beside himself. But when I say *another*, I do not mean that there are two gods, but that it is only as light from light, or as water from a fountain, or as a ray from the sun.'[5] When St John says that 'the Logos was with God, and the Logos was God' (i. 1), he is not speaking of

---

[1] *Ibid.* p. 101.   [2] *c. Noet.* 10.

[3] *Idem.* In the fragment of the *Refutatio* edited by P. Nautin (*Hippolyte et Josipe*, p. 111) which he ascribes to Josippus, we have the technical adjective ἐνδιάθετον qualifying not λόγον but λογισμόν.

[4] *c. Noet.* 10.   [5] *Ibid.* 11.

two gods, but of one, and of two persons by the economy, and of the Holy Spirit in the third place.[1]

Thus Hippolytus endeavours to take seriously the implications of St John's witness to the distinctions within the unity of the one God, but St John's use of the two titles *Logos* and *Son* creates a problem for him. St John uses *Logos* as a title for the pre-existent, never as a title of the incarnate, yet in the body of the Gospel the Son claims to have pre-existed. These last passages Hippolytus overlooks. For him the Logos is called Son only proleptically. He was called Son of God and Son of Man only because he was to become such at the incarnation. When the Logos became flesh, he became 'Son of God and the perfect man'.[2] The Son of God is Logos *plus* flesh. This Hippolytus makes clear in anticipating the objection that St John used *Logos* only in a figurative way:

What then is this Son of his own whom God has sent in the flesh, if it is not the Logos, whom he called *Son* because he was going to become man...For neither was the Logos, unincarnate and in himself, true Son (τέλειος υἱός) although true Only (τέλειος μονογενής), nor could the flesh exist in itself apart from the Logos, for it is in the Logos that it has its subsistence. Thus he was manifested true Son of God.[3]

Hippolytus' emphasis on the economy of the incarnation leads him into a form of economic trinitarianism which involves a type of modalism. Over against the *successive* modalism of Noetus he propounds an *expansionistic* modalism. The one God expands into a trinity in the course of *Heilsgeschichte*. This attempt to solve the trinitarian paradox was to be repeated and developed in the 'Sabellianism' of which Marcellus of Ancyra was accused during the Arian controversy.[4]

At the same time as he tries to emphasise the distinctions within the unity of the godhead, Hippolytus emphasises the reality of the manhood which the Logos assumed at the incarnation. His christology, however, is a confusion of the *Logos–Sarx* schema and the *Word–Man* schema. He explicitly asserts that the flesh has its subsistence in the Logos, i.e. that

---

[1] *Ibid.* 14. For a fuller quotation of *c. Noet.* 14 see the quotation from R. A. Markus (p. 56, n. 1 above).
[2] *Ibid.* 5.   [3] *Ibid.* 15.
[4] Cf. R. A. Markus, 'Trinitarian Theology', and below, pp. 246 ff.

the Logos is the centre of consciousness in the historical Jesus;[1] yet he continually emphasises that the Logos, or God, has become man. Jesus Christ is 'the God who has become man for our sakes' (ὁ θεὸς ὁ ἄνθρωπος δι' ἡμᾶς γεγονώς).[2] The whole of c. Noetum 18 emphasises the reality of the humanity assumed at the incarnation. The problem of the closer definition of the divine–human relationship in Christ had not yet arisen; Hippolytus seeks to do justice to it as best he can.

Judged by later formulations of the doctrine of the trinity and of the person of Christ, that of Hippolytus may appear open to objection. Judged in its historical setting it marks an important step forward in the church's attempt to understand her faith in God as Father, Son and Holy Spirit, and in Jesus Christ as the Son of God made man for us men and our salvation. Hippolytus repeatedly confesses the church's faith and ends his refutation of Noetus with a doxology in which this confession is clearly stated. Jesus Christ is 'God made man for our sake, to whom the Father has subjected all things. To him be the glory and the power with the Father and the Holy Spirit in the holy church, both now and always and to the ages of ages. Amen.'[3]

(ii) Tertullian

When we pass from Hippolytus to Tertullian, we pass from the naïve stage of controversy with the modalistic monarchians to a more sophisticated stage.[4] Hippolytus makes the oneness of the godhead reside in 'power' (μία δύναμις)[5] while the trinity is 'a threefold manifestation' (τριχῆς ἡ ἐπίδειξις)[6] in which the one God manifests himself in three persons (πρόσωπα), Father, Son and Holy Spirit.[7] Tertullian, on the other hand, makes the oneness reside not in something that God has—'power' (potestas)—but in what God is—'substance' (substantia).[8] Tertullian develops more fully the implications

---

[1] Cf. p. 57 n. 3 above. [2] c. Noet. 18 fin.; cf. also ibid. 4; 8. [3] Ibid. 18.
[4] E. Evans (Tertullian's Treatise against Praxeas, pp. 23 f.) assumes that Hippolytus is dependent on Tertullian. Because of the more sophisticated nature of Tertullian's argument it appears more likely that if there is dependence, Tertullian is dependent on Hippolytus.
[5] c. Noet. 8. [6] Idem 8. [7] Idem; cf. ibid. 14.
[8] Cf. Evans (Tertullian's Treatise against Praxeas, pp. 39–46) for a discussion of the meaning of substantia in adv. Prax., and the criticism of Evans' view by G. C. Stead in 'Divine Substance in Tertullian', JTS, N.S. xiv (1963), 46 ff.

of the Johannine witness to the distinctness of Father and Son within the unity of the godhead than does Hippolytus.[1] Furthermore, the christology of Hippolytus is far less consistent than that of Tertullian. The former confuses the *Logos–Sarx* schema of the apologetic tradition (and later Alexandrian tradition) with the *Word–Man* schema which belongs distinctively to the Syrian–Asia Minor tradition. Tertullian, on the other hand, passes beyond these two schemata to a third, the *God–Man* schema which alone safeguards the fullness of the divinity and the fullness of the humanity in Christ. B. B. Warfield leaves the question of dependence open, merely asserting the probability that 'the two treatises embody a point of view already traditional in the church'.[2]

Tertullian had a double reason for hostility towards Praxeas. Praxeas was not only a patripassian; he had also been responsible for a sudden change in policy on the part of the Roman bishop with regard to Montanism, of which sect Tertullian was by the time he wrote the treatise an acknowledged adherent. 'At Rome Praxeas managed two pieces of the devil's business: he drove out prophecy and introduced heresy: he put the Paraclete to flight and crucified the Father.'[3]

He commences his refutation of Praxeas by a threefold statement:

(*a*) a terse statement of Praxeas' teaching: 'A Father who was born, a Father who suffered, God himself the Lord Almighty, is preached as Jesus Christ.'[4]

(*b*) a statement of the rule of faith which he claims 'has come down from the beginning of the gospel'[5] and which he claims is true because it is more primitive than the doctrine of Praxeas.[6] He states the rule of faith thus:

We however as always...believe (as they do) in one only God, yet subject to this dispensation (which is our word for 'economy') that the one only God has a Son, his Word who has proceeded from

---

[1] Compare *c. Noet.* 7 with *adv. Prax.* 22.

[2] 'Tertullian and the Doctrine of the Trinity', in *Studies in Tertullian and Augustine*, New York, 1930, p. 17.

[3] *adv. Prax.* 1 (Evans, p. 89, 31 f.).   [4] *Ibid.* 2 (90, 12 f.).

[5] *Idem* (90, 26); cf. *de Praescriptione Hereticorum*, 13; 'This rule taught by Christ'.

[6] *id esse verum quodcunque primum, id esse adulterum quodcunque posterius* (*idem* (90, 30 f.)); cf. *de Praescr.* 29 ff.

himself, by whom all things were made and without whom nothing was made (John i. 3); that this Son was sent by the Father into the virgin and was born of her both man and God, Son of man and Son of God, and was named Jesus Christ: that he suffered, died...[1]

(*c*) a statement of the trinitarian doctrine which Tertullian opposes to the monarchianism of Praxeas:

It (*sc.* the heresy) thinks it impossible to believe in one God unless it says that both Father and Son and Holy Spirit are one and the same (*ipsum eundemque*): as though the one (God) were not all (these things) in this way also, that they are all of the one (*ex uno omnia*), namely by unity of substance (*per substantiae unitatem*), while none the less is guarded the mystery of that economy (οἰκονομίας, *sacramentum*) which disposes the unity into trinity, setting forth Father and Son and Spirit as three, three however not in quality but in sequence, not in substance but in aspect, not in power but in (its) manifestation (*non statu sed gradu, nec substantia sed forma, nec potestate sed specie*), yet of one substance and one quality and one power, seeing it is one God from whom these sequences and aspects and manifestations are reckoned out in the name of the Father and the Son and the Holy Spirit. How they admit of plurality without division (*numerum sine divisione*) the discussion will show as it proceeds.[2]

Having thus set out the doctrine of Praxeas, the church's rule of faith, and his own statement of the implications of the rule of faith, Tertullian argues that Praxeas does not understand what 'monarchy' means. The idea does not preclude a sharing of the 'single and sole empire'[3] by two persons, a father and a son for example. The Son and the Spirit, 'occupying second and third place', are 'conjoint of the Father's substance' (*consortibus substantia patris*).[4] Tertullian claims that he 'derives the Son from no alien source but from the Father's substance...(and) the Spirit from nowhere else than from the Father through the Son'.[5]

Warfield has argued[6] that Tertullian's doctrine of the trinity is an attempt to expound the rule of faith in the light of the apologetic Logos-doctrine, but in doing so he stretches the latter so far that it tears apart in his hands. The monarchians'

---

[1] *Idem* (90, 13–21).
[2] *Idem* (90, 36–91, 8).
[3] *Ibid.* 3 (91, 24 f.).
[4] *Idem* (92, 6 f.).
[5] *Ibid.* 4 (92, 17 f.).
[6] *Studies in Tertullian and Augustine*, pp. 3–37.

identification of the Father and the Son and their aversion to the Logos-concept of the apologists make it necessary for Tertullian to meet them on their own ground and concentrate his attention on the concept of sonship, or rather on the Father–Son relationship. He commences with the Logos-concept but eventually is forced to leave it behind as inadequate, much as St John leaves it behind, in favour of the more personal and biblical concept of the Son of God.

At first Tertullian sets forth what may be called 'the evolution of the Logos'. Like Hippolytus he starts from the idea of God's solitariness before the creation of the world: 'before all things God was alone (*ante omnia deus erat solus*)...because there was nothing external to him'.[1] Yet God was not alone, for he had Reason (*ratio*) within him, the *ratio* which is his 'consciousness' (*sensus*).[2] This *ratio* is what the Greeks call λόγος, which also means 'speech' or 'discourse' (*sermo*), and it is *sermo* that Tertullian finds in his Latin version of John i. 1. He says that *ratio* is a better translation of λόγος, since Reason is prior to Speech, *ratio* is prior to *sermo*. Nevertheless, he says, it makes no difference. For

although God had not yet uttered his *sermo*, he always had it within himself along with and in his *ratio*, while he silently thought out and ordained within himself the things which he was shortly to say by the agency of *sermo*; for while thinking out and ordaining them in company of his *ratio*, he converted into *sermo* that *ratio* which he was discussing in *sermo*.[3]

Thus for him ὁ λόγος of John i. 1 includes both the idea of *Reason* (*ratio*) and that of *Speech* (*sermo*). Although he talks about them in terms of temporal succession, he makes it clear that he does not consider them to be two stages in the existence of the Logos. *Ratio*, in which *sermo* has its ground (*sermo ratione consistens*), is the substance of *sermo* (*substantia sua*).[4] The priority of *ratio* to *sermo*, then, is not temporal but logical. 'Before the establishment of the universe, God was not alone, seeing he had continually in himself *ratio*, and in *ratio sermo*, which he made another beside himself by activity within himself.'[5]

[1] *adv. Prax.* 5 (93, 13 ff.).   [2] *Idem* (93, 18).
[3] *Idem* (93, 25 ff.).   [4] *Idem* (93, 24 f.).
[5] *Idem* (94, 10 f.).

Scripture calls *ratio* by the name 'Wisdom' (*sophia*) which is 'established as a second person' (*secundam personam conditam*).[1] *Sermo*, which has within itself its own inseparable *ratio* and wisdom, receives 'its manifestation and equipment, namely sound and voice, when God says, "Let there be light." This is the complete nativity of *sermo* (*nativitas perfecta sermonis*), when it comes forth from God.'[2] *Sermo* was first 'established for thought under the name of Wisdom (Prov. viii. 22), then begotten for activity (Prov. viii. 27), thereafter causing him to be his Father by proceeding out of whom he became Son, the first-begotten as begotten before all things, the only-begotten as alone begotten out of God in a true sense'.[3] The monarchians are wrong in refusing to think of *sermo* as 'substantive in objectivity (*substantivum in re*), as being a substance which is himself, that (thus) he may be seen to be an object and a person (*res et persona*), and so may be capable, inasmuch as he is another beside God (*secundus a deo*), of causing there to be two, the Father and the Son, God and *sermo*'.[4] Tertullian rejects the idea that a word is a mere voice or sound made by the mouth—something empty and incorporeal, for nothing empty or incorporeal can come forth from God. The *sermo* of God is *substance*; 'what the substance of the *sermo* was, that I call a Person, and for it I claim the name of Son; and while I acknowledge him as Son, I maintain he is another beside the Father'.[5]

Up to this point Tertullian is trying to express the church's confession of faith in one God, Father, Son and Holy Spirit, in terms of a Logos-theology. The result is considerable confusion because he finds it impossible to reconcile the implications of the Logos-theology with the concept of sonship. The framework of his argument has been an attempt to narrate what Warfield calls 'a complete history of the Logos'.[6] in terms of a process

---

[1] *Ibid.* 6 (94, 17).   [2] *Idem* (94, 33 f.).

[3] *Idem* (94, 35–96, 5). On Tertullian's exegesis of Prov. viii. 22 ff. in *adv. Hermogenem* and *adv. Praxean* cf. M. Simonetti, 'Sull'interpretazione patristica di Prov. 8. 22', in *Studi sull'Arianesimo*, pp. 14 ff. Simonetti argues that Tertullian breaks with the apologetic two-stage theory of the Logos in favour of a three-stage theory—impersonal *ratio*, personal *sophia*, Logos (Son). It is possible, however, that the difference is better explained by the hypothesis which I develop later, that in *adv. Prax.* two separate arguments are confused: see below, pp. 63 f.   [4] *adv. Prax.* 7 (95, 24 ff.).

[5] *Idem* (96, 12 ff.).   [6] *Studies in Tertullian and Augustine*, p. 57.

which takes place temporally, or rather 'pre-temporally temporally'.[1] In the beginning God was alone, but not without *ratio*, for he is always *rationalis*; this *ratio* is what Scripture calls *Wisdom*, and is prior to the spoken word (*sermo*) which is begotten as Son when God speaks the creative word (Gen. i. 3). Tertullian, that is, makes use of the distinction between λόγος ἐνδιάθετος and λόγος προφορικός and the latter, the uttered word, he calls *Son*. The Son comes to substantive existence as a person distinct from God only at the moment of creation, and Tertullian draws the inevitable conclusion that God then also became Father. In *adversus Hermogenem* he draws this conclusion more explicitly, asserting that because God was always God, it does not necessarily follow that he was always Father, 'for he could not have been a Father before the Son...but there was a time when there was no Son' (*fuit tempus cum filius non fuit*).[2]

Within the framework of this 'complete history of the Logos' there appears a second argument, based on the rule of faith, which leads to a conclusion which bursts the framework. At the beginning Tertullian differentiates between the two meanings of λόγος, making *ratio* prior to *sermo* as its *substantia* and reserving the title Son (*filius*) for the uttered *sermo*. Towards the end of the argument, however, he says that the *substantia* of *sermo* is a *persona* and that this *persona* is called *filius*. Now the Son, originally the final stage of the evolution of the Logos, is equated with the first stage, with the *ratio* which is the substance of *sermo* and which is co-eternal with God who is always *rationalis*. Thus Tertullian carries back the distinction between God and the Logos into the very *substantia* of God. The Logos-theology has foundered on the rock of the rule of faith, and as the rest of *adv. Praxean* shows, on the rock of scripture, both of which acknowledge that there is one God, Father, Son and Holy Spirit. What began in Tertullian's argument as a distinction between God and the Logos (*ratio*) has now become a distinction between two persons who are one substance. From this point Tertullian leaves behind the Logos-concept and concentrates on the name Son. The Logos-theology was inadequate to combat Praxeas' doctrine. In the rest of the treatise he discusses the Father–Son relationship.

---

[1] Warfield, *op. cit.* p. 50.   [2] *adv. Hermog.* 3.

It was shown above that Tertullian's attempt to trace the history of the Logos led him to draw the conclusion (for which the Arians were later to be anathematised) that God was not always Father and that 'there was a time when there was no Son'. Now he discusses the Father–Son relation in terms of the Aristotelian doctrine of relations, that correlative beings, by virtue of their very nature, necessarily co-exist.[1] Praxeas' identification of Father and Son means that the Father—or the Son—is both terms in the Father–Son relation:

Those who become what they are by relationship with one another [says Tertullian] cannot by any means so become by relationship with themselves, as that a father should make himself his own son, or a son should cause himself to be his own father. The rules God has made he himself observes. A father must have a son so as to be a father, and a son must have a father so as to be a son.[2]

That is, the father–son relation implies two co-existing persons, father and son. Therefore the Father and the Son are two persons.

This same doctrine Tertullian applies to the relation between 'speaker and person spoken of and person spoken to'.[3] In scripture the Father speaks of the Son and to the Son, and the Son speaks of the Father and to the Father; thus 'the distinctness of the trinity is clearly expounded' (*distinctio trinitatis exponitur*), these scriptural passages 'establish each several person as being himself and no other'.[4] But the distinction between Father and Son thus testified does not mean that they are two gods, but 'two manifestations of one undivided substance' (*duas species unius et indivisae substantiae*).[5] Tertullian is always conscious of the dangers of ditheism—and of the fact that this was a common reproach levelled by the monarchians:

We are rendering an account...how the Father and the Son are two, and this not as a result of separation of substance, but as a result of ordinance,[6] while we declare the Son indivisible and

---

[1] Aristotle, *Categories*, vii; cf. R. Arnou, 'Arius et la doctrine des relations trinitaires', *Greg*, xiv (1938), 270 ff. This doctrine of relations is also appealed to by Dionysius of Alexandria, Arius and Athanasius.

[2] *adv. Prax.* 10 (98, 16 ff.).   [3] *Ibid.* 11 (100, 23).

[4] *Idem* (101, 13–18).   [5] *Ibid.* 13 (104, 21 f.).

[6] Evans translates *dispositio* by 'ordinance' (p. 193): ' "Ordinance" implies something more fundamental than "law", a fact inherent in the very nature of things.'

inseparable from the Father, another not in quality but in sequence, who, although he is called God when he is named by himself, yet does not for that reason make a duality of gods, but one God, by the very fact that he has to be called God as a result of his unity with the Father.[1]

The conflict between the rule of faith and the Logos-theology becomes apparent again when Tertullian tries to account for the relationship of the Son with the Father in the oneness of the godhead. His Logos-theology makes him say that 'the Father is the whole substance, but the Son is a derivation and part of the whole' (*pater tota substantia est, filius vero derivatio totius et portio*).[2] The Son, as God's *ratio* (λόγος), is a part of the substance of God. The rule of faith and scripture, however, speaks in terms not of a God–Logos relationship, but of a Father–Son relationship, and of two persons, Father and Son, who are both God. There can be no division or partition of the divine substance which is one; God is 'one substance in three who cohere' (*unam substantiam in tribus cohaerentibus*).[3] The 'minoration' implied by his use of *derivatio et portio* is balanced by the emphasis on *una substantia* which admits no *divisio* or *separatio*. The implications of scripture and the rule of faith are rending asunder the inadequate garments of the Logos-theology in which Tertullian had clothed his thought. *Logos* is inadequate as a description of him whom scripture and the rule of faith attest as Son of God.

Like Hippolytus, Tertullian criticises the monarchians for the way in which they misuse scripture, supporting their doctrine on a few isolated texts and ignoring the many which are contrary to their view. Doubtless with some exaggeration, he says that they rely on only one text from the Old Testament (Isa. xlv. 5) and two from the New (John x. 30; xiv. 9, 10). They ignore the rule that 'the smaller number ought to be understood in accordance with the greater'.[4] Their use of these Johannine texts calls forth from Tertullian what he calls

---

[1] *adv. Prax.* 19 (112, 27 ff.).

[2] *Ibid.* 9 (97, 34 ff.). Evans translates *derivatio totius et portio* by 'outflow and assignment of the whole', but in his introduction (p. 44) he admits that 'in the third century *portio* was regularly used for *pars*, and in fact in the present passage Tertullian admits a certain minoration of the Son (not only in the incarnation but) in his divine being'.

[3] *adv. Prax.* 12 (102, 18).   [4] *Ibid.* 20 (113, 6).

'a complete study of John's Gospel'.[1] It is by exegesis of John's Gospel that he demolishes his opponents' position and establishes the doctrine of distinctions within the unity of the godhead. As he works his way through the gospel, his exegesis finds its focal point in the Father–Son relationship; its regulative concept is *Son*, not *Logos*.

It is unnecessary to follow Tertullian's exegesis in detail. In order to establish the distinction-within-unity in the Father–Son relationship he comments on the following texts: John i. 1–3; i. 14; i. 18; i. 29, 36; i. 49, 50; ii. 16; iii. 16–18; iii. 35; iv. 25; iv. 34; v. 17; v. 18; v. 19–27; v. 36, 37; v. 43; vi. 29; vi. 32–44; vi. 69; vii. 15–16; vii. 26–9; vii. 32–3; viii. 16; viii. 18; viii. 19; viii. 26–7; viii. 28; viii. 38, 40; viii. 42; viii. 49, 54–5; viii. 56; ix. 4; ix. 35; ix. 36–7; x. 15–17; x. 24–5; x. 28–9; x. 30; x. 32; x. 34–8; xi. 27; xi. 41–2; xii. 27–8; xii. 30; xii. 44–9; xii. 50; xiii. 1, 3; xiii. 31; xiii. 32; xiv. 5–9; xiv. 10.[2] Having reached xiv. 9–10, a crucial text to which the monarchians appealed, Tertullian is content to compress the rest of the evidence from St John's Gospel into one short chapter (ch. 25), saying that the whole gospel is written in the same strain, demonstrating that Father and Son are 'distinguished as each being himself' (*in sua proprietate distinguuntur*). He takes advantage, however, of the Johannine references to the sending of the Holy Spirit in order to link the Spirit with the Father and the Son, and at the same time to distinguish him from them. In this connection he quotes and comments on John xiv. 16 and xvi. 14, declaring:

So the close series of the Father in the Son and the Son in the Paraclete makes three who cohere (*tres cohaerentes*), the one attached to the other. And these three are one thing, not one person, in the sense in which it is said 'I and the Father are one' in respect of unity of substance, not of singularity of number.[3]

Out of the abundance of his exegesis of Johannine texts it is sufficient to choose the two texts to which he gives most attention, two which the monarchians themselves claimed in support of their identification of Father and Son:

(*a*) John x. 30: 'I and the Father are one.'
Hippolytus had emphasised the fact that the verb ἐσμεν is in

---

[1] *Ibid.* 26 (121, 34).   [2] *Ibid.* 21–4.   [3] *Ibid.* 25 (121, 9–13).

the plural, indicating the plurality of Father and Son. Tertullian goes into more detailed exegesis:

Here then they wish to make a stand, these fools, yea blind, who see
not, *first*, that 'I and the Father' is an indication of two; *secondly*, at
the end of the sentence, that 'we are' (ἐσμεν, *sumus*) is not from the
person of one, because it is spoken in the plural; and *then*, that he
says 'are one thing' (*unum*), not 'are one person' (*unus*)...When
he says that two, of the masculine gender, are one thing, in the
neuter—which is not concerned with singularity but with unity,
with similitude, with conjunction, with the love of the Father who
loves the Son, and with the obedience of the Son who obeys the
Father's will—when he says, 'One thing are I and the Father', he
shows that those whom he equates and conjoins are two.[1]

In a note on this passage Evans[2] remarks that 'the phraseology
here and a little later does not necessarily imply more than a
moral unity'. At this point Tertullian is content to emphasise
the unity in this way, as he continues to do in the exegesis of
John x. 32, 34–5, as a unity in action and will; but he has
made his point about unity of substance sufficiently strongly
elsewhere.

(*b*) John xiv. 9–10:

Jesus said to him, 'Have I been with you so long, and yet you do
not know me, Philip? He who has seen me has seen the Father; how
can you say, "Show us the Father"? Do you not believe that I am
in the Father and the Father in me? The words that I say to you
I do not speak on my own authority; but the Father who dwells in
me does his works.'

Tertullian asks,

As who does he say he ought to have been known by them?...
As the Father, or as the Son?...At every hour Jesus named the
Father, set forth the Father and honoured the Father, clearly
showing that he himself was distinct from the Father as the Son of
God. Now it is plain in what sense Jesus meant, 'He who sees me
sees the Father also.' This is said in the same sense as 'I and the
Father are one' (John x. 30), because 'I came forth and am come
from God' (John xvi. 28?), 'I am the way, the truth and the life'
(John xiv. 6), 'No one comes to me except the Father has drawn
him' (John vi. 44)..., 'As the Father gives life, so also the Son'
(John v. 21), and 'If you know me you know the Father' (John

[1] *Ibid.* 22 (117, 5–17).   [2] *Tertullian's Treatise against Praxeas*, p. 302.

xiv. 7). According to these texts he has revealed himself as the deputy of the Father (*vicarium patris*), by means of whom the Father was both seen in acts and heard in words, and known in the Son who was carrying out the Father's acts and words...If by John xiv. 9 he had wished the identity of the Father and the Son (*patrem eundem filium*) to be understood, he would not have added, 'Do you not believe that I am in the Father and the Father in me?' Rather he would have added, 'Do you not believe that I am the Father?...'

Tertullian goes on to emphasise that Jesus did not wish men to identify him with the Father, for 'he always professed to be the Son and to have come from the Father'; thus he makes plain 'the conjunction of the two persons so that the Son might be accepted as he who makes the Father present'. Further:

Jesus explained in what manner the Father was in the Son and the Son in the Father. 'The words that I speak are not mine' because they were the Father's, 'but the Father abiding in me does the works'...Therefore, the Father, abiding in the Son through works of power and words of doctrine, is seen through those things through which he abides and through him in whom he abides; from this it is clear that each person is himself and no other.

Earlier in the chapter he has emphasised that the Father, who is invisible, 'becomes visible in the Son, in consequence of acts of power, not in consequence of actual manifestation of his person' (*non ex personae repraesentatione*).[1]

(*c*) Tertullian's exegesis of one further Johannine text should be noted although it does not occur in his running commentary on the Gospel, but earlier, at the beginning of his argument about distinctions within the divine unity. This is the most 'subordinationist' text in St John's Gospel, John xiv. 28: 'My Father is greater than I', a text which, of course, supports strongly his emphasis on the distinction between Father and Son. Tertullian says:

The Son is not other than the Father by diversity, but by distribution, not by division but by distinction, because the Father is not identical with the Son, they even being numerically distinct from one another. For the Father is the whole substance, while the Son is the outflow and assignment of the whole, as he himself professes, 'Because my Father is greater than I', and by him, it has also been

---

[1] *adv. Prax.* 24 (119, 30 ff.).

sung in the psalm (viii. 6), he has also been made less, 'a little on this side of the angels'. So also the Father is other than the Son as being greater than the Son, as he who begets is other than he who is begotten, as he who sends is other than he who is sent, as he who makes is other than he through whom a thing is made.[1]

This text was to play a considerable role in succeeding controversies although, for some strange reason, the Arians made little appeal to it,[2] and Athanasius refers to it only three times and devotes one short sentence to its exegesis.[3] It is significant that Tertullian interprets the contrast between Father and Son simply in terms of the Johannine distinction between Sender and Sent, between Begetter and Begotten, between Maker and Agent or Mediator. With all his emphasis on the distinction between Father and Son, so necessary in combating the Sabellian identification of them, Tertullian avoids any subordinationism which would make the Son an inferior or second God.

Very largely by exegesis of St John's Gospel Tertullian has demonstrated the monarchian error and established within the Western theological tradition the Johannine paradox of distinction-within-unity in the Father–Son relationship. In the concluding section of his *adversus Praxean* he turns his attention to the second Johannine paradox of the incarnation of the Word, the paradox of the God–man.

It appears that some of the modalistic monarchians, seeking to escape the difficulties which followed from their identification of Father with Son, changed their ground, saying that 'the Son is the flesh, that is, the man, Jesus, while the Father is the Spirit, that is God, that is Christ'.[4] In reply to this manœuvre —'now they begin to divide them rather than call them one'[5] —Tertullian enquires into the meaning of John i. 14, 'The Word became flesh.' In answer to the question how the Word became flesh, he replied, 'Not by being transformed into flesh, but by clothing himself in flesh (*indutus carnem*).' If the incarnation is the transformation of the Word of God into flesh, Jesus will be one substance composed of two, flesh and spirit. 'In that case Jesus will not be God, for he has ceased to be the Word,

[1] *Ibid.* 9.
[2] Cf. G. Bardy, *Recherches sur saint Lucien d'Antioche et son école*, Paris, 1936, p. 209.
[3] *Or. c. Ar.* 1, 58 *fin.*   [4] *adv. Prax.* 27 (123, 25f.).   [5] *Idem.*

since it has become flesh; neither will his manhood be flesh, for it is not properly flesh, seeing it has been the Word.' But scripture sets Jesus forth as 'both God and man' (*et deum et hominem*). 'Certainly we find him set forth as in every respect Son of God and Son of man, since we find him as both God and man, without doubt according to each substance as it is distinct in what it itself is, because neither is the Word anything else but God, nor the flesh anything else but man.' Thus there is a double quality which is 'not confused but combined, Jesus in one person God and man' (*non confusum sed coniunctum, in una persona deum et hominem Iesum*).[1] For Tertullian the statement in John i. 14 means that God became man; Jesus Christ is the God–man, one person who is both God and man. Nowhere does he attempt to define how the two 'natures'[2] exist together in Christ; he is content, like St John, to state that they do and to rule out any notion which would confuse them or truncate either of them.

It has been necessary to deal with Tertullian's theology and exegesis of St John at length because of his importance in the history of the formulation of the doctrine of the trinity. He is the first author to attempt a systematic exposition of the trinitarian and christological implications of St John's Gospel. Although he starts from an examination of the Logos-concept he quickly passes beyond it to the Son-concept, concentrating his attention on the Father–Son relationship instead of the God–Logos relationship, and on Jesus as the *God–man* and not the *Logos–sarx*. His emphasis on Christ as Son rather than as Logos saves him from the difficulties which were to beset the Alexandrians and the Antiochenes because of their concentration on the Logos-concept, interpreted by the former in the light of Philonic and Middle-Platonist Logos speculation, and by the latter in the light of an impersonal or sub-personal Word-concept drawn from Hebraic thought. 'Briefly expressed, the contribution of Tertullian to Christian thought is the expansion of the idea of *Sonship*...The term "Logos" by itself was an abstraction: it was incapable of conveying the fullness of

[1] *Idem.* Tertullian is feeling after the position later laid down at Chalcedon.
[2] Neither Tertullian nor Novatian uses the term *natura*; instead they use *substantia* in christological contexts in the sense in which *natura* was to be used later.

Christian thought.'[1] Or as J. A. Dorner says, 'The age of
Logology was now succeeded, in consequence of his labours, by
the age of sonship.'[2]

Within his lengthy theological and exegetical arguments for
the distinction between Father and Son within the unity of
the godhead and for the reality of the incarnation, there lies
an emphasis on the mediatorial role of the Son in all things—
in creation, revelation and redemption. The *adversus Praxean*
gives little indication which aspect of the Son's mediatorial
work holds the pre-eminent place in his thought, yet the second
clause of his statement of the rule of faith emphasises the soteriological purpose of the incarnation, and underlying his
whole argument is the thought of the necessity of the reality of
Christ's sonship and of his humanity for the accomplishment of
God's redemptive purpose. Elsewhere, particularly in his
adversus Marcionem, the central place of soteriology is obvious.

(iii) Novatian

Novatian's treatise, *de Trinitate*, is to a large extent dependent
on Tertullian, although on several points he makes a distinct
advance on the position reached by his forerunner. Tertullian
has been concerned solely with modalistic monarchianism;
Novatian expounds his doctrine of the trinity by controversion
of the errors of gnosticism, docetism, modalistic monarchianism,
and especially with a humanitarian form of monarchianism
which preserved the 'monarchy' of God by denying the divinity
of the Son.

Like Tertullian his starting point is the rule of faith or, as
he prefers to call it, the rule of truth (*regula veritatis*), which
provides the framework for his treatise, which falls into three
main sections: God the Father (chs. 1–8), God the Son (chs. 9–
28), and God the Holy Spirit (ch. 29), with a short concluding
section on the Unity of God (chs. 30–1). It is with the section on
God the Son that we are concerned here. Of it E. Evans says,

In this section the influence of Tertullian is very apparent: the themes
and the scriptural quotations and many of the interpretations are

---

[1] R. L. Ottley, *The Doctrine of the Incarnation*, 7th edn. London, 1902, p. 262.
[2] *History of the Development of the Doctrine of the Person of Christ*, Edinburgh,
1878, I, ii, p. 79.

borrowed from him, but with the difference that what he uses to prove that the Son is a second divine Person beside the Father, Novatian (whose adversaries admit Christ's personal existence) finds equally apposite to prove his deity (which Tertullian's adversaries did not deny).[1]

A brief discussion of docetism, which he criticises on the grounds that if Christ's humanity were unreal we would have no salvation,[2] leads Novatian to affirm the full and complete humanity of Christ; on that point he and his main adversaries are agreed. But this assertion does not mean that he agrees with their view 'that he was solely and simply man...mere man and nothing more' (*hominem tantum et solum...hominem nudum et solitarium*). The heretics see only one part of Christ, his human frailty, and ignore the 'tokens of his majesty' (*maiestates*) which declare his divine power. If our faith is to be complete we must accept both the humanity and divinity of Christ.[3]

After brief exegesis of some Old Testament texts, Novatian sets forth the New Testament evidence for the divinity of Christ, using St John's Gospel as the framework for his argument and commencing with what he calls 'John's account of the nativity of Christ' (*Ioannes nativitatem Christi describens*),[4] John i. 14, which shows that Christ 'is man, seeing that he was made flesh, and God, seeing that he is Word of God', for the Gospel 'has associated both natures[5] in the single harmony of Christ's birth'.[6] The greater part of Novatian's refutation of the view that Christ is a mere man (chs. 14–16) consists of a series of arguments which begin, 'If Christ is only man, how ...?' (*si homo tantummodo Christus, quomodo...?*), followed by statements about Christ or claims made by him, most of which are drawn from St John's Gopsel. The texts quoted within this formula are: John i. 11; i. 3; Col. i. 16; John i. 14; iii. 31, 32; i. 15; v. 19; v. 26; vi. 51; vi. 46; vi. 62; viii. 14, 15; viii. 23; viii. 42; viii. 51, 58; x. 27; x. 30, 35, 36, 32; xi. 26; xvi. 14; xvii. 3, 5. Novatian concludes the argument by confronting his opponents with a choice: 'Either they must cut out of the

---

[1] *Tertullian's Treatise against Praxeas*, p. 27.   [2] *de Trin.* 10.
[3] *Ibid.* 11.   [4] *Ibid.* 13.
[5] Like Tertullian (cf. p. 70, n. 2) Novatian uses *substantia* in the sense that *natura* bore in later christological controversy. Here *substantia* is translated 'nature'.   [6] *de Trin.* 13.

scriptures all these passages, and rob Christ of his divinity, or, if they cannot do that, they must restore to him the divinity which is rightly his.'[1] Later he returns to the Fourth Gospel, finding further proofs of Christ's divinity in John ii. 19 and x. 18; then after a catena of passages on which he has already commented (John i. 1, 3; iii. 31, 32; vi. 38; i. 14) he concludes that the subject of these statements is 'this Christ, who is from us (i.e. a man like us), proved to be not man only, because Son of man, but also God, because Son of God'.[2]

After refuting the denial of Christ's divinity, Novatian turns to the modalists' denial of his distinction from the Father; in doing so he reproduces many of the arguments already used by Hippolytus and Tertullian. He sets forth the modalistic argument in almost syllogistic form:

> If God is one,
> and Christ is God,
> and the Father is God,
> then Christ and the Father are one
> and Christ must be called the Father.[3]

Like Tertullian he argues against this position on the basis of a series of Johannine texts (John vi. 38; xiv. 28; xx. 17; viii. 17, 18; xii. 28; xvii. 5; xi. 42; xvii. 3), and pays special attention to the two crucial Johannine texts, John x. 30; xiv. 9, 10. On John x. 30 he says:

'And' shows that the 'I' is distinct from 'the Father'; 'One' (*unum* not *unus*) expresses 'a harmony of fellowship not a unity of person' (*societatis concordiam non unitatem personae*); 'are' (*sumus*) points to the two who are distinct.

He explains what he means by 'harmony of fellowship' by the analogy of fellowship between two human persons:

For where between two persons there is a unity of thought, a unity of truth, a unity of faith, a unity and identity of religion, a unity in the fear of God, the two are one, for all their being two (*unum sunt, etiam si duo sint*).[4]

Although he does not refer to John xvii. 22, 23, it is clear that Novatian is interpreting John x. 30 in the light of Christ's prayer that his disciples 'may be one as we are one'; that is, for him the unity of Father and Son is a moral unity, not an essen-

---

[1] *Ibid.* 16.   [2] *Ibid.* 21.   [3] *Ibid.* 26.   [4] *Ibid.* 27.

tial or substantial unity. He does not affirm an *unitas substantiae* or the *una substantia* as Tertullian does, but speaks rather of a *substantiae communio*;[1] the Father and the Son are one *per concordiam et per amorem et per dilectionem*.[2]

Novatian fails to realise that the assertion of two distinct *personae* united only in a moral relationship of harmony and fellowship lays him open to the charge of ditheism. 'The fact is that Novatian was as deeply impressed as were his opponents by the fact of the divine "monarchia", and finds it difficult so to reconcile this with the separate personality of the Son as to maintain the eternity of his divine essence.'[3] Yet he does come near to the idea of eternal generation at the conclusion of his treatise when he asserts, 'The Son is eternally in the Father; otherwise the Father were not always Father.'[4] Yet, as Father, God is antecedent to the Son: the Father alone is without origin (*solus originem nesciens*),[5] while the Son has an origin in that he is begotten by the Father. This antecedence, however, must not be thought of in terms of time, 'for a date in time cannot be fixed for him who is before time'.[6] Thus like Tertullian he thinks of the generation of the Son by the Father 'pre-temporally temporally'.[7]

It is by appeal to St John's Gospel and by exegesis of it that Novatian maintains the divinity of Christ and his unity with the Father in a oneness which admits of distinctions, and at the same time his complete humanity. It had been Tertullian's task to maintain the distinction between Father and Son against those who asserted that it was the Father who became incarnate and suffered and died. To Novatian fell the task of showing that the distinction did not mean that the Father alone was God, and the Son a mere man (*homo nudus*). Thus in the first half of the third century each of the Johannine paradoxes was challenged, and both challenges were repulsed by exegesis of St John's Gospel. In Hippolytus, Tertullian and Novatian we see the struggle to grasp the full significance of these paradoxes and the inadequacy of a Logos-theology for their preservation;

---

[1] *Ibid.* 31. [2] *Ibid.* 27.
[3] W. Y. Fausset, *Novatian: de Trinitate Liber* (*CPT*), Cambridge, 1909, p. xlviii.
[4] *de Trin.* 31. Novatian appears to have in mind the doctrine of relations appealed to by Tertullian, cf. p. 64, n. 1 above.
[5] *Idem.* [6] *Idem.* [7] Cf. p. 63, n. 1, above.

only by passing beyond the Logos-concept to the Son-concept was it possible for them to accomplish their task. This they did so successfully that the great trinitarian controversies of the fourth century and the christological controversies of the late fourth and early fifth centuries appear to have had little impact on the Western church.

B. ALEXANDRIA

In the development of the interpretation of St John's Gospel during the second century and in the third-century writers of the Western church, little mention has been made of Philo Judaeus and of his possible influence on the development of Christian doctrine. This omission has not been due to oversight. Although Wolfson bases the main argument of his *The Philosophy of the Church Fathers* on the belief that Philo's influence is discernible even within the New Testament itself, there is, in fact, no definite evidence of unmistakable Philonic influence on any of the writers studied so far.[1] The main extra-biblical influences are Middle-Platonism and Stoicism, with their idea of the Logos as the Reason which pervades the Cosmos and in which rational (λογικός) man participates, and with their distinction between the immanent Logos (λόγος ἐνδιάθετος) and the uttered Logos (λόγος προφορικός). It is only when we come to the earliest Christian writings to emerge from Alexandria that we find clear evidence of Philonic influence on Christian thought.

The neglect of Philo, whose teaching provides some striking similarities with the Prologue of St John's Gospel,[2] before the time of Clement of Alexandria may be attributed to at least two possible causes: (*a*) Just as St John's Gospel was treated with some suspicion in some Christian circles because of gnostic use of it, so also the kinship between gnosticism and Philo's thought would have caused ecclesiastical writers to be hesitant to use the latter; (*b*) The bitterness between Christians and Jews in the early Christian centuries would make the former averse to putting themselves under a debt of obligation to a

[1] E.g., see H. Chadwick (*Early Christian Thought and the Classical Tradition*) on Justin Martyr: 'It is not certain that he had read Philo' (p. 4).
[2] Cf. C. H. Dodd, *Interpretation*, pp. 54 ff.

Jew.[1] It was in Alexandria, the home of Philo, that the first attempts were made by a Christian writer to use Philo's contribution to religious thought in the service of Christian theology.

(i) Clement of Alexandria

Important though he may be in the development of Christian thought, Clement contributes little to our understanding of the use of St John's Gospel in the explication of the Christian doctrine of God and of the person of Christ. Clement is a moralist rather than a speculative theologian, 'not a missionary bishop, like Irenaeus, but a converted philosopher who remained a professor and a scholar'.[2] He found himself in an environment in which all of the currents of the religious and cultural life of the hellenistic world flowed together—Philonic Judaism, the Mystery Religions, Gnosticism, Stoicism, Middle-Platonism—and he writes against a background of 'extraordinary spiritual, intellectual and moral ferment'.[3] All these currents, together with his newly found Christian faith, influence his thought, with the result that his ideas

are set forth without much order, in a complex and synthetic fashion which makes their analysis difficult; since it is impossible to speak about all of it at once, it is very necessary to draw distinctions, to make divisions and to select a scheme for exposition, but even then it is impossible not to be almost constantly troubled with the feeling that one is betraying or deforming the author...A certain unfaithfulness is perhaps inevitable.[4]

Clement himself admits that he has set forth his thoughts 'in a studied disorder' (ἐπίτηδες ἀναμίξ).[5] This 'studied disorder' of his thoughts, taken with the eclectic nature of his system,

---

[1] Cf. G. A. F. Knight (*A Biblical Approach to the Doctrine of the Trinity*, p. 2): 'In the great formative days of Christian theology the Catholic Church and the Synagogue were bitter enemies.'

[2] H. Crouzel, *Théologie de l'image de Dieu chez Origène*, Paris, 1956, p. 67.

[3] C. Mondésert, *Clément d'Alexandrie*, Paris, 1944, p. 41.

[4] *Ibid.* p. 81, n. 1.

[5] *Strom.* VI, 1, 2 (*GCS*, II, 423f.). Cf. E. Molland (*The Conception of the Gospel in the Alexandrian Theology*, Oslo, 1938, p. 9): 'The dilemma of Clement is that he shall divulge the truth and he shall not...He conceals in order to be understood only by the right readers and to be rightly understood only when diligently and attentively read.'

makes interpretation of his thought exceptionally difficult. The scheme of exposition to be followed here will begin by asking (*a*) what Clement was seeking to accomplish, and then (*b*) how this aim affected his understanding of the Christian message and his interpretation of St John's Gospel.

Clement's method of meeting the double challenge of gnosticism and of pagan philosophy differs from that of Irenaeus and Tertullian. 'Irenaeus had already denounced and opposed the pseudo-gnostics; but one only suppresses what one replaces. Clement goes much farther; he wishes to be, and in fact he is, a true gnostic, a Christian gnostic.'[1] Against the gnostic claim to a secret tradition of esoteric knowledge, Clement sets, not the church's rule of faith, but the true tradition of knowledge, the γνωστικὴ παράδοσις which he claims to have received from his own teachers.[2] He nowhere states what is the content of this tradition of knowledge, but it seems likely that in it Clement has confused three separate and different things:

first, his own private speculations, which are often of a gnostic cast, second, a tradition of doctrinal speculation inherited from eminent teachers before him, not least among whom were...Philo, and Pantaenus, a tradition which he attributed quite mistakenly to Barnabas, whom he imagined to have derived it through the Twelve from our Lord, third...διδασκαλία, the Church's interpretation of her tradition in teaching and preaching.[3]

Clement's appeal was primarily to educated, wealthy, cultured pagans in Alexandria to whom he offered 'a more excellent way' of *gnosis*, a superstructure of knowledge raised on the foundation of faith.[4] This attempt to create a spiritual and intellectual *élite* in the church inevitably laid him open to suspicion within the church, the majority of whose members were content with the 'more simple' faith traditional in the

---

[1] J. Tixeront, *Mélanges de patrologie et d'histoire des dogmes*, Paris, 1921, pp. 93 f.

[2] *Strom.* I, I, 15 (*GCS*, II, 11, 19).

[3] R. P. C. Hanson, *Origen's Doctrine of Tradition*, London, 1954, pp. 71 f.; cf. also *ibid*. p. 63: This true *gnosis* contained 'suspiciously Alexandrine speculations, and certainly a thoroughgoing licence for allegorisation is part of it'.

[4] Cf. Mondésert, *Clément d'Alexandrie*, ch. 1.

church, expressed in the tripartite rule of faith. The result was a tension between 'faith' and 'reason' which has continued in the church to the present day.[1] Clement's caustic ridiculing of the *simpliciores* shows that he is aware that his teaching is not representative of the faith of the Alexandrian church,[2] and we must be on guard against equating the theology of the Alexandrian 'school'—Clement, Origen, Pierius and, to a lesser extent, Dionysius—with the faith of the Alexandrian church. The latter was to find its literary expression at the end of the third century and the beginning of the fourth in the writings of Peter, Alexander and Athanasius.

For Clement, before his conversion, it had been a case of *intellectus quaerens fidem*; after his conversion it is a case of *fides quaerens intellectum*.[3] But, so great is his emphasis on *intellectus*, there is little wonder that his attempt to set knowledge above faith, *gnosis* above *pistis*, met with opposition.[4] His equation of Christianity with wisdom, with *gnosis*, raises the perplexing question whether the framework of his thought is biblical or philosophical. De Faye[5] answers that he is first and foremost a philosopher who has grafted on to his philosophy his faith as a Christian, while Mondésert[6] says that he is primarily a Christian whose philosophy has been re-oriented by his faith. Yet Mondésert admits that he does not develop his thought by exegesis of scripture, but uses scripture, interpreted allegoric-

---

[1] Cf. E. de Faye, *Clément d'Alexandrie: Étude sur les rapports du christianisme et de la philosophie grecque au II* siècle, Paris, 1898, chs. I and III; Mondésert, *Clément d'Alexandrie*, pp. 39 ff.; J. Lebreton, 'Le désaccord de la foi populaire et de la théologie savante dans l'église chrétienne du III* siècle', *RHE*, XIX (1923), 481–506; XX (1924), 5–37; H. E. W. Turner, *The Pattern of Christian Truth*, pp. 391–5; H. Chadwick, *Early Christian Thought*, pp. 33 f.

[2] *Strom.* VI, 11, 89 (*GCS*, II, 476, 14 ff.): 'It seems that most of those who are inscribed with the Name are like the companions of Ulysses; they approach the word as rustics, passing by, not the Sirens, but the rhythm and the melody; in their ignorance they have stopped their ears, since they know what will happen once they lend their ears to the studies of the Greeks; it will be impossible for them to retrace their steps.'

[3] Cf. Mondésert, *Clément d'Alexandrie*, p. 122.

[4] Cf. Molland (*The Conception of the Gospel in the Alexandrian Theology*, p. 42): 'Clement finds it necessary to expand at length the meaning of these words. In his interpretation of them he betrays how intellectualistic his conception of the Gospel is. He always clings to the idea that wisdom is the supreme element of the spiritual life, and that Christianity is wisdom.'

[5] *Clément d'Alexandrie.*   [6] *Clément d'Alexandrie*, p. 263.

ally, to support his eclectic philosophy of which the specifically Christian and biblical data form only one element: 'he makes use of scripture, rather than putting himself at its service'.[1]

Basically Clement's conception of God is that of Plato: God is 'the Monad',[2] 'the Absolute' (τὸ ὄν),[3] 'the Father of the universe',[4] 'the Ruler of all, a being difficult to grasp and apprehend, ever receding and withdrawing from him who pursues',[5] 'the remoter Cause, the Father of the universe, the most ancient and most beneficent of all existences'.[6] God is far removed from the world in utter transcendence so that any commerce between him and the world is impossible. He is unknown and unknowable; no names or predicates are applicable to him.[7] Yet he has not left mankind entirely without knowledge of himself, for in his goodness he has always made himself known through his Logos: 'we comprehend the Unknown (τὸ ἄγνωστον) by divine grace, and by the Logos that alone proceeds from him'.[8] Therefore Clement concentrates his attention on the Logos: he 'attempted to set up a theological system with the idea of the Logos as its beginning and basis. All his thinking and reasoning are dominated by this idea...He made it the highest principle for the religious explanation of the world.'[9] Like his conception of God, his conception of the Logos is philosophical rather than biblical, and his attention is concentrated not on Jesus Christ, the Logos made flesh, but on the pre-existent Logos whom he describes largely in terms derived from philosophy. Mondésert, who argues that the foundation and framework of Clement's thought is biblical, gives his case away when he admits that 'it can be shown that the Prologue of St John has certainly

[1] *Ibid.*   [2] *Protrept.* 9, 88 (*GCS*, I, 65, 31).
[3] *Strom.* v, 12, 82 (*GCS*, II, 380, 26).
[4] *Paed.* I, 5, 21 (*GCS*, I, 102, 19) *et frequenter.*
[5] *Strom.* II, 21, 5 (*GCS*, II, 115, 19 f.).
[6] *Ibid.* VII, 1, 2 (*GCS*, III, 4, 7 f.).
[7] *Ibid.* v, 12, 81 f. (*GCS*, II, 380, 14 ff.).
[8] *Ibid.* v, 12, 83 (*GCS*, II, 381, 7 f.).
[9] J. Quasten, *Patrology*, II, 21; cf. J. F. Bethune-Baker, *An Introduction to the Early History of Christian Doctrine*, London, 1903, p. 133; Molland, *The Conception of the Gospel in the Alexandrian Theology*, p. 11; R. L. Ottley, *The Doctrine of the Incarnation*, p. 202; F. Loofs, *Leitfaden*, §23, 2; H. R. Mackintosh, *The Person of Jesus Christ*, Edinburgh, 1912, p. 162; Mondésert, *Clément d'Alexandrie*, pp. 97 f.

oriented, given precision to and enriched his conception of the Logos, *wherever he had derived it from*'.[1]

A comparison of the index of Stahlin's edition of Clement's works[2] with Leisegang's index to Cohn and Wendland's edition of Philo's works, under the word λόγος, reveals how much Clement has borrowed from Philo. After pointing out that Philo's emphasis on the absolute transcendence of God forces him to introduce a host of intermediaries in order to connect God with the world, Crouzel[3] summarises Philo's Logos-doctrine thus:

From this there comes a whole proliferation of hypostases: Wisdom, the Bride of God, the Logos, his eldest Son, the Spirit, Angels, Divine Powers, etc. The Logos, the chief of these half-abstract, half-personal, intelligible beings, is derived from varied sources. It (he?) is the principle of unity and coherence of the world, being scattered in all beings as a seed—a Stoic conception. At the same time it preserves in the universe the distinctions and oppositions between contraries; that is the Logos, the Divider (τομεύς), inherited from Heraclitus. It is the intelligible world, the place of the Ideas, according to which the sensible world has been created: borrowed from Platonism. It is lastly the Hebraic Word of God, and it is through it that God reveals himself in the theophanies and communicates himself to souls. And, above all, it is the link, the intermediary, the mediator between God and the world, the way by which man knows God and approaches God.

All of these elements Clement takes over from Philo. It is true that he calls the Logos 'Son of God', 'Only' (μονογενής), 'Saviour'; it is true that he can apply to the Logos phrases from St John's Gospel:[4] God and the Logos 'are one',[5] 'the Son is in him, and the Father is in the Son',[6] 'at the same time that he is the Father, he is the Father of the Son'.[7] But the Johannine element in his concept of the Logos (Son) is slight compared with that derived from his philosophical heritage and from Philo.

It is in the *Excerpta ex Theodoto* that Clement discusses the relation between the Logos and Jesus Christ and links his

---

[1] *Op. cit.* p. 264 (my italics).   [2] *GCS*, IV.

[3] *Théologie de l'image de Dieu chez Origène*, pp. 52 f.

[4] Cf. Wolfson, *Philosophy of the Church Fathers*, pp. 204 f.

[5] *Paed.* I, 8 (*GCS*, I, 127, 5).   [6] *Ibid.* I, 7.   [7] *Strom.* V, I, I (*GCS*, I, 121, 26).

thought more closely with St John's Gospel. After criticising Valentinian gnostic exegesis of the Prologue of the Gospel, he sets out his own exegesis, drawing a distinction between 'the essential Logos' (ὁ ἐν ταὐτότητι λόγος) and 'the child of the essential Logos' (τέκνον τοῦ ἐν ταὐτότητι λόγου).[1] The essential Logos is 'God in God, who is also said to be "in the bosom of the Father" (John i. 18), continuous, undivided, one God'.[2] Like Tertullian[3] Clement makes 'bosom' (κόλπον) the object of ἐξηγήσατο in John i. 18—οὗτος τὸν κόλπον τοῦ πατρὸς ἐξηγήσατο: the Logos exists in the bosom of the Father which is his thought (ἔννοια) and it is his function to explain or reveal the bosom (thought) of the Father. That is, for Clement the essential Logos is the λόγος ἐνδιάθετος[4] and it is to this Logos that John i. 1 refers.

Having drawn a distinction between 'the essential Logos' and 'the child of the essential Logos' Clement goes on to describe what may be called 'the triple incarnation' of the Logos: (a) when the essential Logos became a Son, (b) when he acted through the prophets, and (c) at his advent on earth as Saviour:

'And the Logos became flesh' (John i. 14) not only by becoming man at his advent on earth, but also 'at the beginning' (John i. 1) the essential Logos became a son by circumscription and not in essence (κατὰ περιγραφὴν οὐ κατ' οὐσίαν). And again he became flesh when he acted through the prophets. And the Saviour is called a child of the essential Logos; therefore, 'in the beginning was the Logos, and the Logos was with God' (John i. 1), and 'that which came into existence in him was life' (John i. 4), and Life is the Lord. And when Paul says, 'Put on the new man created according to God' (Eph. iv. 24), it is as if he says, Believe on him who was 'created' by God, 'according to God', that is, the Logos in God (τὸν ἐν θεῷ λόγον). And 'created according to God' can refer to

---

[1] *Exc. ex Theod.* 8, 1 (*GCS*, III, 108, 20).

[2] *Idem* (*GCS*, III, 108, 20 f.). In *Paed.* I, 8, 62 Clement says of God and the Logos, ἓν γὰρ ἄμφω, ὁ θεός, ὅτι εἶπεν ἐν ἀρχῇ ὁ λόγος ἦν ἐν τῷ θεῷ, καὶ θεὸς ἦν ὁ λόγος. Similarly in *Protrept.* 11, 110 (*GCS*, I, 78, 14) Clement reads ἐν τῷ θεῷ instead of πρὸς τὸν θεόν, while in *Paed.* I, 2, 4 (*GCS*, I, 91, 24), he speaks of λόγος θεός, ὁ ἐν τῷ πατρί.

[3] *adv. Prax.* 21: 'He, the only one, has revealed the bosom of the Father, not the Father his own bosom.'

[4] On Clement as a representative of the 'twofold stage theory' of the Logos, cf. Wolfson, *Philosophy of the Church Fathers*, pp. 204 ff. Cf. also R. P. Casey, *Excerpta ex Theodoto* (*SD*), Cambridge, 1934, p. 28.

the end of advance that man will reach, as does...[1] he rejected the end for which he was created. And in other passages he speaks still more plainly and distinctly: 'Who is an image of the invisible God' (Col. i. 15); then he goes on, 'first-born of all creation' (*idem*). For he calls the Son[2] of the essential Logos 'an image of the invisible God', but 'first-born of all creation'. Having been begotten without passion, he became the creator and progenitor of all creation and substance, for by him the Father made all things. Wherefore it is also said that he 'received the form of a servant' (Phil. ii. 7), which refers not only to his flesh at his advent, but also to his substance, which he derived from its underlying reality, for substance is a slave, inasmuch as it is passive and subordinate to the active and dominating cause.[3]

In this important passage several points of Clement's confused thought become clearer:

(i) The essential Logos, 'the Logos in God', proceeds from God to become a Son. This procession does not involve a division of the essence of the godhead (οὐ κατ' οὐσίαν); it is a περιγραφή, a de-limitation,[4] a circumscription;[5] perhaps it may even be called a 'hypostatisation'. Sagnard comments that περιγραφή 'is very important, and designates what was later called "hypostasis" or "person", that is, that through which the Son is distinguished from the Father, although they have only a single and identical essence'.[6]

(ii) Clement weakens the distinction between 'inspiration' and 'incarnation' by applying John i. 14 to the activity of the Logos in the prophets. The incarnation of the Logos in Jesus Christ does not differ from his activity in the prophets in kind, but only in degree; the latter is also a becoming-flesh. Because of his confusing use of the phrase 'became flesh', it is difficult to know which of the three 'incarnations' he means: the original 'generation' by which the Logos became a Son, the

---

[1] Casey supposes there to be a lacuna in the text; Stählin (*GCS*), Bunsen, and Sagnard (*Excerpta ex Theodoto* (*SC*, 23)) emend the text variously; cf. Sagnard, *op. cit.* p. 94.

[2] Stählin (*GCS*, III, 113, 8) and Sagnard (*loc. cit.*) read τὸν «υἱὸν» λέγει τοῦ λόγου; Casey (*op. cit.* p. 54, 216) reads τὸν λόγον τοῦ λόγου.

[3] *Exc. ex Theod.* 19 (*GCS*, III, 112, 27 ff.).

[4] So Sagnard.   [5] So Casey.

[6] *Exc. ex Theod.* p. 93, n. 2. For an excellent discussion of περιγραφή cf. Daniélou, *Message évangélique*, pp. 341 ff.

inspiration of the prophets, or the becoming flesh in Jesus Christ.

(iii) This passage makes a clear distinction between the essential Logos, the Logos in God, and Jesus Christ who is a child or a son of the essential Logos.

(iv) Clement reads back into the pre-existent state of the Logos statements which are made about the Logos incarnate in Jesus Christ: for example, John i. 14, 'became flesh', and Phil. ii. 7, 'the form of a slave'. He applies the latter to the οὐσία of the Logos which, according to Sagnard,[1] is the equivalent of the later term ὑπόστασις or of Tertullian's *persona*. The *persona* of the Son in the incarnate state is 'the form of a slave', subordinate to or derived from 'the underlying reality' (τὸ ὑποκείμενον), the essence of the godhead. Thus Clement, following the Philonic method of interpreting scripture, is reading into the text presuppositions which have no connection with it.[2]

(v) The influence of Stoicism is evident in the contrast between 'the essential Logos' and 'the child of the essential Logos'; it is the same as the distinction between λόγος ἐνδιάθετος and λόγος προφορικός. In the *Stromateis*,[3] Clement denies that the Logos is the λόγος προφορικός but says it is the wisdom, kindness and power of God. While he does not describe Jesus Christ as λόγος προφορικός this designation is implied a little later: 'Since the soul became too enfeebled for the apprehension of realities, we needed a divine teacher. The Saviour is sent down—a teacher and leader in the acquisition of good—the secret and sacred token of the great Providence.'[4] The Logos is the Wisdom of the Father; the Saviour is the teacher who leads to goodness.

Throughout Clement's writings the emphasis is on the intellect, and the primary function of the Logos is to impart knowledge, to explain or reveal the bosom (thought) of the Father, but not the Father himself. Nowhere does Clement refer to John xiv. 9: 'He who has seen me has seen the Father.'

[1] *Exc. ex Theod.* p. 97, n. 2.
[2] Cf. my article, 'The Origins of Christian Exegesis', *JRH*, 1 (1961), 138–47.
[3] *Strom.* v, 1, 6 (*GCS*, II, 329, 21 ff.).
[4] *Ibid.* v, 1, 7 (*GCS*, II, 330, 16 ff.).

The intellectual emphasis in his concept of the Logos comes out plainly in a passage where he talks about the Logos as the image of God: 'The image of God is his Logos, the genuine Son of (his) mind, the divine Logos, the archetypal Light of Light; and the image of the Logos is the true man... assimilated to the divine Logos in the affections of the soul, and therefore rational.'[1] For Clement the purpose of the incarnation seems to be simply an accommodation on the part of the Logos to the weakness of those who cannot accept anything without sensible proof: 'The Son is said to be the Father's face (πρόσωπον τοῦ πατρός) revealing God's character to the five senses, by clothing himself with flesh.'[2] The incarnation serves to make the truth of God plain to those who cannot perceive it spiritually. 'The Logos, issuing forth, was the cause of creation; then he also generated himself, when "the Logos became flesh" (John i. 14), in order that he might be seen.'[3] In its context, that refers equally to the theophanies, to the inspiration of the prophets, and to the incarnation in Jesus Christ. 'The Logos ἄσαρκος and the Logos ἐν σαρκί involve the same amount of ideas about God. The quantity of truth is unvarying; all the truth of the New Testament was known to the Old. The only superiority of the New is its kindergarten method of teaching through the incarnation, so that even children might understand.'[4]

If the emphasis on the triple incarnation of the Logos diminishes the importance of the incarnation in Jesus Christ, Clement carries the process of diminution still farther by dehumanising the flesh of Christ. He can affirm that 'the Son himself came to earth... he put on manhood',[5] but the manhood is a mask: 'Having assumed the mask of manhood and received fleshly form, he began to act the drama of salvation for humanity.'[6] The flesh which the Logos assumes is human flesh stripped of what makes it specifically human, with the result that Clement's view is close to the docetism of the gnostics

---

[1] *Protrept.* x, 98 (*GCS*, I, 71, 24 ff.); cf. Crouzel, *Théologie de l'image de Dieu chez Origène*, p. 67.

[2] *Strom.* v, 6, 34 (*GCS*, II, 348, 9 f.).

[3] *Ibid.* v, 3, 16 (*GCS*, II, 336, 12 ff.).

[4] H. S. Nash, 'The Exegesis of the School of Antioch', *JBL*, XI (1892), pt. I, p. 32.

[5] *Quis dives?* XXXVII (*GCS*, III, 184, 5).

[6] *Protrept.* x, 110 (*GCS*, I, 78, 15 f.).

whom he opposes. 'The Logos, having assumed the flesh, which is by nature subject to passion, trained it to a habit of impassibility.'[1] He has 'a soul devoid of passion'.[2] The Saviour, that is, the historical Jesus, has no need of food and drink:

In the case of the Saviour, it were ludicrous (to suppose) that the body, as a body, demanded the necessary aids in order to endure. For he ate, not for the sake of the body, which was kept together by a holy energy, but in order that it might not enter into the minds of those who were with him to entertain a different opinion of him just as some afterwards supposed that he appeared in phantasmal shape. But he was completely impassible, inaccessible to any movement of feeling, either pleasure or pain.[3]

Thus the earthly life of Jesus is play-acting on the part of the Logos, who dons the mask of manhood to act out the drama of salvation. The flesh which he assumes is not manhood like ours; he has assumed flesh, but in assuming it robs it of all that makes it specifically human. The Logos is a 'holy energy', less than God, while the 'manhood' is mere flesh, *sarx*, entirely passive, without human needs and emotions and incapable of suffering.[4]

From Clement's Logos-doctrine, and especially from the passage quoted earlier from *Excerpta ex Theodoto*,[5] it is possible to deduce the way in which he used St John's Gospel. The predominant role played by the Logos in his thought has made him concentrate attention on the Prologue of the Gospel, interpreting the Logos-concept which he finds there in the light of his eclectic philosophy, filling it with a non-biblical content and almost completely ignoring the earthly life of the Logos incarnate. Because of his Platonism, he treats all earthly realities as but shadows of eternal truth; hence the diminished importance of the incarnate life. He reads back into the pre-existence of the Logos what St John asserts of the incarnate life, making even the assertion that 'the Logos became flesh' (John i. 14) refer to the self-begetting of the Logos as Son of God, and to the activity of the Logos in the prophets. Concen-

---

[1] *Strom.* VII, 2, 7 (*GCS*, III, 7, 15 f.).
[2] *Paed.* I, 2, 4 (*GCS*, I, 91, 23).
[3] *Strom.* VI, 9, 71 (*GCS*, II, 467, 9 f.).
[4] Cf. my article, 'The Impassibility of God', *SJT*, VIII (1955), 353–64.
[5] Cf. p. 82, n. 3 above.

tration on the God–Logos relationship throws the Father–Son relationship, the central theme of St John, completely into the background. In Clement's hands, the intention of the evangelist, that the Prologue should be read in the light of the incarnate life narrated in the rest of the Gospel, is inverted—proof of Clement's failure to understand the real message of St John.

(ii) Origen

From his own time up to the present day Origen has been an enigmatic figure and the subject of debate.[1] The central point at issue today is whether he was primarily an exegete, a philosopher, a theologian or a mystic. E. de Faye argued that 'the material of the gospels was not one of the sources of his thought',[2] and that his professed loyalty to the scriptures and the *regula fidei* was a 'mere façade composed in order to hide the fact that Origen is composing his theological system from elements in contemporary philosophy and not from any genuine tradition of Christian thought'.[3] G. Bardy treats Origen as primarily an exegete and theologian, but sees a tension between Origen the philosopher and Origen the believer, suggesting that there is an inner conflict within his personality,[4] similar to the schizophrenia which Laeuchli sees in Justin Martyr.[5] W. Völker[6] claims that Origen is primarily a master of the spiritual life, while A. Lieske[7] has argued that his teaching about the spiritual life is derived from his Logos-doctrine. H. Koch,[8] building on the foundation of de Faye's view, has argued that the foundation and framework of Origen's thought is Neo-Platonic. Daniélou holds that in fact Origen is all these

---

[1] Cf. J. Daniélou, *Origen* (Eng. Tr.), London, 1955, pp. vii ff.

[2] *Origène: sa vie, son œuvre, sa pensée*, Paris, 1923–8, iii, 160.

[3] R. P. C. Hanson, *Origen's Doctrine of Tradition*, p. 185, summarising de Faye's position.

[4] 'Origène', *DTC*, xi, col. 1527.

[5] See Ch. 2, p. 38, n. 1 above.

[6] *Das Vollkommenheitsideal des Origenes*, Tübingen, 1931; cf. H. Crouzel, 'L'anthropologie d'Origène dans la perspective du combat spirituel', *RAM* xxxi (1955), 365.

[7] *Die Theologie der Logosmystik bei Origenes*, Münster, 1938; a similar view is held by Grillmeier, *Christ in Christian Tradition*, pp. 163 ff.

[8] *Pronoia und Paideusis: Studien über Origenes und sein Verhältnis zum Platonismus*, Berlin and Leipzig, 1932.

things at once and that all scholars who have studied him up to
the present have made the mistake of trying 'to reduce his
personality to one or other of its aspects; whereas the characteristic thing about Origen was that he combined several different kinds of activity and thus, more than any other Christian
thinker before St Thomas, came to see the world as a single
whole'.[1] Since those words were written in 1948 the debate
has continued.[2] H. de Lubac[3] has emphasised the biblical
foundation of Origen's thought, while H. Jonas[4] has portrayed
him as a gnostic somewhere between Valentinus and Plotinus.
H. Crouzel follows Bardy's view that there is a conflict within
the mind of Origen, a conflict of which Origen himself is
seldom conscious: 'The themes we are studying, like the whole
of his thought, have, with Origen, a double source, hellenistic
and scriptural. He supports them on scripture, but he speculates on them with the help of the materials with which Greek
philosophy abundantly supplied him.'[5] Crouzel suggests that
there is in fact in Origen's thought an unresolved contradiction
between his Platonist and his Christian view of the world.[6]
A similar point of view is taken by R. P. C. Hanson in his
exhaustive study of Origen's interpretation of scripture,
Allegory and Event:[7]

Origen began as a philosopher and never ceased to be a philosopher,
though as a Christian priest he saw the necessity and usefulness of
applying his philosophy to the personal problems of ordinary men
and women...Origen in his Homilies sincerely and carefully expounds scripture for the ordinary man and woman in the pew, but
we must not expect to find the full, the whole Origen there.[8]

The study of Origen's approach to and interpretation of St
John's Gospel leads to a conclusion similar to that reached by
Bardy, Crouzel and Hanson, namely that Origen's thought has

---

[1] *Origen*, pp. viii f.

[2] Cf. Daniélou's Appendix to the Eng. Tr. of *Origène*, p. 339.

[3] *Histoire et l'Esprit*, Paris, 1950.

[4] 'Die Origenistische Spekulation und die Mystik', *TZ*, 5 (1949), pp. 24 ff.

[5] *Théologie de l'image de Dieu*, p. 33.

[6] *Ibid.* p. 221. In a private letter of 5 April 1956 Father Crouzel writes:
'Origène n'a pas toujours conscience des différences de mentalité entre les
Grecs et l'Écriture, et il passera de l'une à l'autre sans s'apercevoir de leur
incompatibilité.'

[7] London, 1959.   [8] *Op. cit.* p. 186.

a double origin, scriptural and hellenistic, and that it is the hellenistic philosophical element which is dominant. At the same time he appears to be aware of the tension and strives to pass beyond the hellenistic cosmological mould in which he expresses his thought and which he appears to recognise as inadequate, but never wholly succeeds in doing so.

The situation in which Origen found himself as a Christian teacher in the catechetical school at Alexandria,[1] who was seeking to commend the faith to educated Alexandrians, led him quite naturally to emphasise those points at which Christian faith and hellenistic thought approached each other most closely.[2] In preparation for this teaching task he undertook a course of education in secular and philosophical studies,[3] and when he became head of the school he reorganised it, transforming it into 'a kind of university, or, if you wish, a faculty of theology, for the use of cultivated laymen',[4] and extending its curriculum to include subjects taught in pagan schools, such as philosophy and mathematics.[5]

His apparent starting point was the church's *rule of faith*, which he acknowledged to be derived from the Old and New Testaments.[6] Many of the concepts, however, which he mixes into the foundations of his teaching are drawn from extra-biblical sources, and he manages to find biblical support for them only by the use of allegorical interpretation. This is apparent in his doctrine of the threefold sense of scripture which he derived from Philo[7] and which appears to have its ultimate origin in the Platonic doctrine that earthly things are only symbols or shadows of heavenly realities. Origen finds support for this doctrine of scripture in one biblical text only, Prov. xxii. 20 f.: 'Portray them threefold in counsel and knowledge, that thou mayest answer words of truth to those

---

[1] Cf. G. Bardy, 'Pour l'histoire de l'école d'Alexandrie', *Vivre et Penser (RB)*, 2nd series (1942), pp. 86 ff.

[2] See Crouzel, *Théologie de l'image de Dieu*, preliminary chapter on 'The Themes Studied and their History', in which he outlines the Hellenistic, Jewish and Christian traditions on the idea of the Image of God.

[3] Eusebius, *H.E.* vi, 18, 3–4; cf. Daniélou, *Origen*, p. 73.

[4] Bardy, 'Pour l'histoire de l'école d'Alexandrie', p. 93.

[5] Eusebius, *H.E.* vi, 18, 3.

[6] Cf. Hanson, *Origen's Doctrine of Tradition*, p. 182.

[7] Cf. Daniélou, *Origen*, pt. ii, ch. iii, 2: 'Origen and Philo'.

who question thee'—a text which does not refer to scripture, and which in Hebrew has no word corresponding to the τρισσῶς of the LXX. From it Origen concludes: 'One must, therefore, portray the meaning of the sacred writings in a threefold way upon one's soul...for just as man consists of body, soul and spirit, so in the same way does the scripture which has been prepared by God to be given for man's salvation.'[1] Thus Origen finds support for his method of interpreting scripture only by interpreting one isolated verse according to that method.[2] His system of allegory, which owes much to Philo, is used 'to make scripture supply all his demands in the realm of metaphysics, and indeed of physics too'.[3]

Daniélou claims that the data out of which Origen's system was built were provided 'by revelation and, considered in the light of a certain set of problems, those of Middle-Platonism',[4] but a study of Daniélou's chapters on Origen's philosophical background and cosmology shows what a vast quantity of data Middle-Platonism provided. The central problem for religious and philosophical thought, which found expression in the Middle-Platonism of Maximus of Tyre, Numenius, Kronnius, Atticus, Taurus and Albinus, was the question of providence, the question of the possibility of relations between God and the created order, between the One and the Many.[5] This is also the problem for Origen, but parallel with it is another problem which arose from his conflict with gnosticism, the question of the freedom of the will which gnosticism denied. These two questions, divine providence and human freedom, are the key questions in Origen's system.

Origen's universe is not primarily the physical cosmos but the cosmos of spiritual beings created and providentially

---

[1] de Princ. IV, 2, 4 (GCS, V, 312, 1–313, 4).

[2] S. Laeuchli ('The Polarity of the Gospels in the Exegesis of Origen', CH, XXI (1952), 215 ff.) argues that Origen was forced into allegorical interpretation because of the impossibility of harmonising the gospels; if two or more gospels present divergent accounts of the ministry of Jesus, then the truth cannot lie in historicality, it must be on a higher plane.

[3] Hanson, Origen's Doctrine of Tradition, p. 185.

[4] Origen, p. 203.

[5] Cf. Daniélou, ibid. p. 205; E. von Ivanka, Hellenisches und christliches im frühbyzantinischen Geistesleben, Vienna, 1948, ch. I: 'Das Hellenische Grundmotiv'.

governed by God. But this immediately raises the problem of explaining the diversity of condition of spiritual beings, the difference, for example, between angels and men, and of reconciling this diversity with the idea of the goodness and providence of the Creator. The gnostics solved this problem by denying the goodness of the Creator, while Origen solves it by postulating that the inequalities are the result of the exercise of freedom of the will with which the good Creator endowed all spiritual beings. The introduction of the concept of freedom, however, solves the problem for Origen only by the further introduction of the Platonist idea of the eternal pre-existence of spiritual beings,[1] all originally equal to each other, for he recognised that all souls are not equal when they come into the world. Then, in order to bridge the gulf between their pre-existent equality and the inequality of their present condition, Origen introduces the Old Testament idea of the Fall, in which all spiritual beings (except the Logos and the Holy Spirit) participate. To fit the Fall into his system, however, Origen has to make it a pre-mundane fall. The creation of the physical world is a consequence of the Fall. God creates the world to provide a school of punishment and correction for those souls which have fallen farther than the angels but not as far as the demons. The clearest statement of this doctrine is to be found in *de Principiis* (I, 8, 1):

God did not begin to create minds...Before the ages minds were all pure, both demons and souls and angels, offering service to God and keeping his commandments. But the devil, who was one of them, since he possessed free-will, desired to resist God, and God drove him away. With him revolted all the other powers. Some sinned deeply and became demons, others less and became angels, others still less and became archangels; and thus each in turn received the reward for his individual sin. But there remained some souls who had not sinned so greatly as to become demons, nor on the other hand so very lightly as to become angels. God therefore made the present world and bound the souls to the body as a punishment. For God is 'no respecter of persons' that among all these beings who are of one nature (for all immortal beings are rational) he should make some demons, some souls, some angels; rather is it clear that God made one a demon, one a soul, and one an angel as a means to punishing each in proportion to its sin. For if this were

---

[1] *de Princ.* I, 8, 4 (*GCS*, v, 101, 28 f.); III, 3, 5 (*GCS*, v, 261, 10 f.).

not so, and souls had no pre-existence, why do we find some new-born babes to be blind when they have committed no sin, while others are born with no defect at all?

This is the cosmology which determines Origen's doctrine of the Logos and of the relation of the Logos to God.

Origen's doctrine of God, like his cosmology, is a fusion of Middle-Platonist and scriptural elements. De Faye argues that Origen reinforces his idea of monotheism by appeal to the Old Testament, but insists that the Old Testament 'has contributed nothing to the formation of his idea of God';[1] indeed he argues that Origen's idea of God is more abstract than Plato's.[2] He points out that Origen emphasises the absolute spirituality of God as pure intelligence, invisible and incorporeal. God is not only the μονάς, the One, but also the ἑνάς,[3] the absolutely Singular, the One and Simple.[4] He is absolutely transcendent and incomprehensible; he is Mind (Νοῦς),[5] and Being (Οὐσία),[6] but he is also 'beyond Mind and Being' (ἐπέκεινα νοῦ καὶ οὐσίας).[7] All this is Platonic and Philonic, and such a God has little in common with the God of the bible. De Faye points out, however, that Origen's God is also 'le Vivant par excellence';[8] he is 'God of the living'; and 'life in the full sense of the word ...belongs only to God'.[9] He is absolutely good (αὐτοαγαθός).[10] Above all God is the Father of the Son and our Father. These latter are certainly biblical contributions to Origen's doctrine of God, inconsistent or irreconcilable though they may be with the elements derived from Platonism.

The doctrine of the Logos is, for Origen, made necessary by the Platonist elements in his doctrine of God.[11] Just as Philo had found it necessary to introduce the Logos as an intermediary

---

[1] *Esquisse de la pensée d'Origène*, Paris, 1925, p. 52.   [2] *Ibid.* p. 47.
[3] *de Princ.* I, 1, 6 (*GCS*, V, 21, 13).
[4] *in Joh.* I, 22 (*GCS*, IV, 24, 23): εἷς καὶ ἁπλοῦς.
[5] *de Princ.* I, 1, 6 (*GCS*, V, 21, 13).
[6] *Idem* (*GCS*, V, 21, 7).   [7] *c. Cels.* VII, 38 (*GCS*, II, 188, 11).
[8] *Esquisse de la pensée d'Origène*, p. 49.
[9] *in Joh.* II, 11 (*GCS*, IV, 73, 26 ff. and 74, 30 ff.).
[10] By implication from the denial that the Son is αὐτοαγαθός; the Father is ἀπαραλλάκτως ἀγαθός: *de Princ.* I, 2, 13 (*GCS*, V, 47, 2 ff.).
[11] Cf. Daniélou (*Origen*, p. 252): Origen 'regards the relationship between the Logos and the Father as parallel to the relationship between the creatures of the spiritual world and the Logos. It is one of the factors in his system where the influence of Middle-Platonism is most clearly discernible.'

between the absolutely transcendent God and the created order, just as the Middle- and Neo-Platonists were obliged to postulate an intermediary between the One and the Many, so Origen ascribes to the Logos an intermediate position, function, status and power between God and created spiritual beings. The Logos is 'the mediator, midway between all creatures and God' (*harum omnium creaturarum et dei medium...mediatorem*);[1] he is 'between the nature of the Uncreated and the nature of all created beings' (μεταξὺ ὄντος ἀγενήτου καὶ τῆς τῶν γενητῶν πάντων φύσεως).[2] The Logos is inferior to God (the Father) but superior to the created spiritual beings.

Origen appears to be uncertain on the question of the relative distance between God and the Logos on the one hand, and between the Logos and spiritual beings on the other. In his *Commentary on St John* he says that

If the Saviour and the Spirit transcend all creatures not in degree only but in kind, they are in turn transcended by the Father as much as, or even more than, they themselves transcend all other creatures, even the highest.[3]

In the *Commentary on St Matthew*, however, he puts forward the opposite point of view:

The analogy between God's goodness and the goodness of the Saviour, who is the image of that goodness, is closer than the analogy between the Saviour and a good man.[4]

Perhaps the contradiction is to be explained as a modification of his view between the writing of the first (*c*. A.D. 235) and the writing of the second (*c*. A.D. 244).[5] The modification, however, does not affect his general position that the Logos is inferior to God, a middle being between God and spiritual beings.

Although he emphasises that the Logos is inferior to God, Origen always sets him within the divine sphere. He 'does not become Son in an external way, through the adoption of the Spirit, but is Son by nature' (*sed natura filius est*).[6] The title

---

[1] *de Princ.* II, 6, 1 (*GCS*, V, 139, 15).
[2] *c. Cels.* III, 34 (*GCS*, I, 231, 7 f.).
[3] *in Joh.* XIII, 25 (*GCS*, IV, 249, 18 ff.).
[4] *in Matt.* XV, 10 (*GCS*, X, 375, 31 f.).
[5] Cf. Quasten, *Patrology*, II, pp. 48 f.
[6] *de Princ.* I, 2, 4 (*GCS*, V, 33, 2).

Monogenes differentiates the Logos from created beings, for 'the *Monogenes* alone is Son by nature' (μόνου τοῦ μονογενοῦς φύσει υἱοῦ).[1] This Logos, who is Son 'by nature' and not 'by adoption', is eternally generated by the Father:

If we consider the Saviour, we will see that it cannot be said that the Father begat the Son, then allowed him to live as a being separated from him; on the contrary, he continually gives existence to him... The Saviour is always being begotten by the Father (ἀλλ' ἀεὶ γεννᾷ αὐτόν...ἀεὶ γεννᾶται ὁ σωτὴρ ὑπὸ τοῦ πατρός).[2]

In *de Principiis* he frequently asserts that 'God was always Father of his only-begotten (*unigeniti*) Son'[3] and denies that there ever was a time when the Son did not exist (οὐκ ἔστιν ὅτε οὐκ ἦν).[4] The Logos (Son) continually receives his divinity and his existence from God (the Father). 'The idea of a continual generation completes that of the generation *ab aeterno* and with it gives something which comes a little closer to the real idea of eternity: not a time without commencement or end, but the concentration of all in a single instant.'[5]

While asserting the divinity of the Logos, however, Origen does not acknowledge him to be God in the proper sense of the word; he is *God* but not *the* God. Discussing John i. 1 c, θεὸς ἦν ὁ λόγος, Origen draws a distinction between θεός and ὁ θεός, between God-without-the-article and God-with-the-article:

God is God in an absolute sense (αὐτόθεος), as the Lord said in his prayer to the Father, 'that they may know thee, the only true God' (John xvii. 3: τὸν μόνον ἀληθινὸν θεόν), and that all that is outside of him who is God in an absolute sense, being made God by participation (μετοχῇ) in his divinity, cannot be called God-with-the-article but God-without-the-article (οὐκ ὁ θεὸς ἀλλὰ θεός). This name belongs fully to the 'First-born of all creation' (Col. i. 15). First on account of the fact of being next to God, attracting to himself the divinity and being superior to other gods of whom God is the God, as it is written, 'The God of gods, the Lord, has spoken

[1] *in Joh.* II, 10 (*GCS*, IV, 65, 22); cf. Crouzel, *Théologie de l'image de Dieu*, p. 108.
[2] *Hom. Jer.* IX, 4 (*GCS*, III, 70, 14 ff. and 24 f.).
[3] E.g. I, 2, 2 (*GCS*, V, 29, 12).
[4] *de Princ.* IV, 4, 1 (*GCS*, V, 349, 17), a fragment preserved in Greek by Athanasius, *de Decr.* 27.
[5] Crouzel, *Théologie de l'image de Dieu*, pp. 88 f.

and called the earth' (Ps. xlix. 1), he [sc. the First-born] enabled them to become gods, and drew from God abundantly the means by which they may be made divine and communicated it to them according to his own goodness. God (ὁ θεός) is the true God, then; the others are gods formed according to him as images of the proto-type. But again, of the many images, the archetypal image is he who is with God, the Logos, who was in the beginning because he was God (θεός) always dwelling with God, and who would not continue to be God, unless he existed in the perpetual contemplation of the depths of the Father.[1]

Crouzel has pointed out that with Origen μετοχή means 'communication' rather than 'participation', for the latter implies divisibility, which is impossible for the indivisible God. What Origen means by the word in this context is that 'the Father and the Son possess a common nature, of which the Father is the origin and which he communicates to the Son'.[2] Yet Origen also uses the term μετοχή of the relation of the creatures to the divinity. According to Crouzel's interpretation the μετοχή of the Logos in God's being and that of the creatures in the divinity differ in three ways: (a) that of the Son is total, that of the creatures is partial; (b) the former is substantial (and therefore unchangeable), the latter is accidental (able to grow or shrink); (c) the Logos (Son) is the intermediary between the creatures and the Father.[3] Origen does not ask[4] how if the godhead is indivisible, the Father can communicate it *partially* to the creatures and *wholly* to the Logos. The in-divisibility of the divinity would demand total communication or none at all.

The solution to this difficulty would appear to lie in Origen's Logos-doctrine which, at this point, is closely linked with his doctrine of the Image of God which plays an important part in his interpretation of John i. 1c above, where we meet the distinction which Crouzel has made the subject of his exhaus-tive study: the Logos is *the Image of God*, while all the rest of the spiritual beings are made *according to the Image*. The crea-tures are images of the Image of God. As Crouzel points out, the influence of the Platonic doctrine of Ideas is strong here,

[1] *in Joh.* II, 2 (*GCS*, IV, 54, 30 ff.).
[2] Crouzel, *Théologie de l'image de Dieu*, p. 110. [3] *Idem*.
[4] Crouzel seems not to notice this point.

and it is the source from which Origen derives his idea of the divinisation of spiritual beings. The Logos, as Image, stands in an intermediate position between God and the creatures, not only in his incarnate state, but also in his very divinity. 'In order to make the connection between God and the world, in order to accustom men to the revelation of God, he [*sc.* the Logos] will be often represented as a diminished copy of the whole divine reality',[1] inferior to him whose Image he is. One of Origen's favourite texts in this connection is John xiv. 28, which he always quotes in an expanded form, 'The Father *who sent me* is greater than I'—an expansion which gives even greater subordinationist emphasis to the most explicitly subordinationist text in the whole New Testament.[2]

The Logos, then, in Origen's system, fulfils the function of an intermediary. While he recognises the Logos' mediatorial function in creation, his main emphasis is on the pedagogic role of the Logos. The world is a place created for the punishment and correction of fallen souls, and it is the Logos' task, before as well as after the incarnation, to educate souls so that they may return to their pre-fallen state and become divine. The task of the Logos is to reveal to men the *gnosis* of God so that, knowing God, they may again become divine.

Within the framework of this cosmology, both the idea of subordination of the Logos to God and that of the eternal generation of the Logos from God are necessary doctrines. The former is necessitated by his view of the absolute transcendence of God, and the latter by his belief in the eternal pre-existence of spiritual beings. Perhaps Origen's greatest contribution to trinitarian theology is his doctrine of eternal generation, yet its primary source for him is his Middle-Platonist cosmology. Here, however, a necessary implication of his cosmology coincides closely with a necessary implication of the worship and

---

[1] Crouzel, *Théologie de l'image de Dieu*, pp. 112 f.

[2] The addition of ὁ πέμψας με is found in all citations of John xiv. 28 in Origen's works; e.g. *de Princ.* IV, 4, 8 (*GCS*, V, 360, 1 f.); *in Joh.* XIII, 37 (*GCS*, IV, 262, 8); XIII, 25 (*GCS*, IV, 249, 14); XXXII, 29 (*GCS*, IV, 475, 18); *c. Cels.* VIII, 14 (*GCS*, I, 232, 6); VIII, 15 (*GCS*, I, 233, 9). Hautsch (*Die Evangelienzitate des Origenes*, *TU*, XXXIV, 152 f.) notes a similar addition in quotations of John xiv. 9, but not the more frequent addition in John xiv. 28. Eusebius of Caesarea also quotes the expanded form of John xiv. 28 in his *Letter to Euphration of Balanea* (Opitz, *Urkunde*, 3, 5, 1–3).

reverence which Christians from the beginning had found themselves compelled to offer to Jesus Christ.

If this interpretation of Origen's system is correct, then it must be concluded that the content of his Logos-doctrine is non-biblical in origin. The question remains, however, whether the Logos-concept is really regulative for his trinitarian and christological doctrine. J. F. Bethune-Baker,[1] C. W. Lowry,[2] and more recently M. F. Wiles[3] have argued that the Son-concept is regulative. Bethune-Baker, for example, concludes his discussion of Clement's Logos-doctrine thus:

> From this time forward the explanation of the Person of Christ and of his relation to the Godhead as a whole, which was furnished by the Logos-doctrine, tended more and more to recede into the background of theological thought. The main idea had no doubt in large measure passed into the common stock, but the name was less and less used and attention was concentrated rather on the group of ideas which the title Son suggests. The more philosophic conception gave way to the one which can best be brought to the test of conditions with which everyone is familiar. So the conception of Sonship occupies the chief place in the thought and exposition of an Origen no less than in a less speculative and more prosaic theologian like Tertullian.[4]

It is going too far to suggest, as Bethune-Baker does, that the speculative Logos-concept is superseded in the thought of Origen by the more specifically religious Son-concept, but it is clear that he was aware of the inadequacy of the former and tried to break through the bonds of the philosophical category in order to set the biblical concept of sonship, which is also the christological concept *par excellence* in the church's rule of faith, at the very centre of his thought. As with Tertullian and Novatian, so also with Origen there is a tension between the philosophical categories belonging to the Logos-concept and the biblical categories of the rule of faith. Because Origen's Logos-doctrine is more highly developed than theirs, the tension is greater in his thought.

Lowry points out that Origen makes it clear that the meaning of the title *Logos* applied to Christ is a matter for careful inter-

---

[1] *An Introduction to the Early History of Christian Doctrine*, p. 137.
[2] 'Origen as Trinitarian', *JTS*, xxxvii (1936), 225 ff.
[3] *The Spiritual Gospel*, Cambridge, 1960, pp. 93 ff. [4] *Ibid.*

pretation; that 'one of the canons of such interpretation is the concept of the Son', and that Origen criticises those who attach too much importance to the title and seek to explain it on the analogy of a man's spoken word.[1] Lowry quotes an important passage from the *Commentary on St John*, I, 23:[2]

For it is impossible for anyone to understand how a word which is spoken is a Son. And such an animated word, not being something separate from the Father, and therefore having no subsistence (τῷ μὴ ὑφεστάναι), is not a Son, or, if so, let them say that God the Logos is a separate being (κεχωρισμένον) and has an essence of his own (οὐσιωμένον). One must say, therefore, that, as in the case of each of the titles spoken of before, it is necessary to unroll the notion of the thing named from the naming and to adapt it, demonstrating how the Son of God is described by this title, so also one must act when he is called the Logos.

Thus Origen recognises explicitly that the title *Logos* must be interpreted in terms of sonship and not *vice versa*; he lays it down as 'a canon of interpretation', or what Wiles calls a 'methodological principle',[3] that sonship is the regulative concept.

Before examining the way in which Origen applies this canon in his interpretation of St John's Gospel, we must examine his understanding of the relation of the Logos to God and of the Son to the Father. He speaks of 'generation' not only as an eternal (pre-temporal) act but also as a continual or continuing process, but the question remains, 'What does he mean by generation?' Crouzel[4] points out that Origen refuses to consider the generation of the Son (Logos) on the analogy of human generation, which would suggest a division of the Father's substance.[5] He prefers to use the following analogies: (*a*) the uttering of a word expressing the thoughts of the mind,[6] an analogy which recalls the distinction between λόγος ἐνδιάθετος and λόγος προφορικός; (*b*) generation through contemplation, an idea reminiscent of Platonism;[7] (*c*) generation as of radiance

---

[1] 'Origen as Trinitarian', p. 226. [2] *GCS*, IV, 29, 27 ff.
[3] *The Spiritual Gospel*, p. 93.
[4] *Théologie de l'image de Dieu*, pp. 83 f.
[5] *de Princ.* I, 2, 4 (*GCS*, V, 32, 15 f.).
[6] *in Joh.* I, 38 (*GCS*, IV, 50, 4 ff.)—this is almost in direct contradiction to what he has said in *ibid.* I, 23 (n. 2 above).
[7] *in Joh.* II, 2 (see p. 94, n. 1 above); cf. Plato, *Phaedrus*, 249 C.

from light (*sicut splendor generatur ex luce*),[1] generation as of will proceeding from the mind (*velut quaedam voluntas eius ex mente procedens*).[2] All of these analogies are more fitting to the Logos-concept than to the Son-concept.

In the *Commentary on St John* Origen appears to follow the 'methodological principle' he has laid down, namely, that we must ask how the Son can be said to be the Logos and not *vice versa*. He says that we must first ask how the Son is all the other titles which St John applies to him so that 'we shall necessarily understand more about him, not only in his character as Logos, but in his other characters also'.[3] Therefore he discusses the titles given to Christ—Light, Resurrection, Way, Truth, Life, King, Teacher, Lord, Son, True Vine, Living Bread, Door, Good Shepherd—before he discusses the title *Logos*. An examination of his interpretation of these titles, however, makes it clear that Origen is unable to keep to the methodological principle he has laid down, a point which Wiles fails to notice.[4] Aware though he is of the inadequacy of the Logos-concept, and of the necessity to pass beyond it to the Son-concept, Origen is unable to transpose his interpretation of the gospel from the philosophical key into the more specifically biblical and religious key. It is necessary only to select representative examples.

(*a*) *Christ as Light* (John viii. 12): He is the Light of the intellectual world, that is, of the reasonable souls which are in the sensible world.[5] He is called the Light of men and the true Light of the world, because he brightens and irradiates the highest parts of men, or, in a word, of rational beings (τῶν λογικῶν).[6]

(*b*) *Christ as Truth* (John xiv. 6): The Only-begotten is Truth, because he embraces in himself according to the Father's will the Reason concerning all things (τὸν περὶ τῶν ὅλων...λόγον) and being the Truth communicates to each creature in proportion to its worthiness...It is from being the Truth that He is Saviour.[6]

(*c*) *Christ as Shepherd* (John x. 11): As he is a lover of men and

---

[1] *de Princ.* I, 2, 5 (*GCS*, V, 33, 1 f.).   [2] *Ibid.* I, 2, 6 (*GCS*, V, 35, 4).

[3] *in Joh.* I, 24 (*GCS*, IV, 30, 14 ff.).

[4] Cf. my review of M. F. Wiles, *The Spiritual Gospel*, in *NTS*, VII (1960), 95–7.

[5] *in Joh.* I, 25 (*GCS*, IV, 31, 1 f.).

[6] *Ibid.* I, 27 (*GCS*, IV, 33, 26 f.).

[7] *Ibid.* I, 27 (*GCS*, IV, 34, 19 f. and 27).

approves the impulse of human souls to what is better, even of those who do not hasten to Reason (ἐπὶ τὸν λόγον) but like sheep have a weakness and gentleness which is not enquired into but unreasonable (ἄλογον), so he is the Shepherd.[1]

These examples show how little Origen was able to follow his own methodological principle. These titles he discusses in the light of his Logos-concept. When he discusses the title *Son* he does so in only seven lines of text,[2] and then only in terms of his doctrine of eternal generation which, as we have seen, is a logical implication of his non-biblical doctrine of the eternal pre-existence of spiritual beings.

When, finally, he comes to ask how the Son of God is called *Logos* he says:

He is also called Logos, because he takes away from us everything irrational (πᾶν ἄλογον) and makes us truly rational (λογικούς),[3] so that we do all things, even to eating and drinking, to the glory of God, and discharge by the Logos (διὰ τὸν λόγον) to the glory of God both the commoner functions of life and those which belong to a more advanced stage...But the Son may also be the Logos because he reports the secret things of his Father who is Intellect (Νοῦς) in the same way as the Son is called Logos. For as with us the Word is a messenger of those things which the mind perceives, so the Logos of God, knowing the Father, since no created being can approach him without a guide, reveals the Father whom he knows.[4]

---

[1] *Ibid.* i, 27 (*GCS*, iv, 35, 7 ff.).

[2] *Ibid.* i, 29 (*GCS*, iv, 37, 6 ff.).

[3] Crouzel (*Théologie de l'image de Dieu*, p. 127) says that 'the meaning of these terms (*sc.* λογικόν and *rationabile*) is not primarily philosophical or natural, it is theological and supernatural; the better translation of λογικός would be "verbifié"'. Unfortunately English has no verb which corresponds to 'word' in the way in which 'verbifié' corresponds to 'verbe' in French. I am not convinced that Crouzel is right in undervaluing the philosophical element in Origen's use of the terms λόγος and λογικός, which always have strong overtones of 'rationality', however theological the context may be. In his article, 'L'anthropologie d'Origène' (*RAM*, xxxi (1955), 374 f.), after warning against the danger of translating λόγος and λογικός by 'reason' and 'rational', Crouzel says, 'Only a saint is a λογικόν; the demons and the damned have, through a free choice of their will, become ἄλογα like the animals without reason'. Is the distinction between λογικός and ἄλογος absolute, or are there in fact degrees of being λογικός between the saint and the demon? Origen's hierarchy of spiritual beings would suggest that there are.

[4] *in Joh.* i, 37 (*GCS*, iv, 47, 21 ff.); i, 38 (49, 2 ff.).

Ultimately Origen's doctrine of the godhead comes perilously close to tritheism. He is quite emphatic that the Logos (Son) and the Holy Spirit belong to the sphere of the divine, but so emphasises the distinction between the Father and the Son that he has difficulty in maintaining their unity as anything more than a unity of wills, i.e. a moral unity. In *contra Celsum* (VIII, 12) he answers the charge of ditheism, supporting his assertion that Christians do not worship 'another besides the supreme God' by appealing to John x. 30: 'I and my Father are one', John xvii. 21–2: 'As I and thou are one', John xiv. 10–11 and xvii. 21: 'The Father is in me and I in the Father'. He asserts, 'We worship but one God, the Father and the Son', but having affirmed their unity he proceeds to describe them as 'two distinct existences, but one in mental unity, in agreement, and in identity of will' (ὄντα δύο τῇ ὑποστάσει πράγματα, ἓν δὲ τῇ ὁμονοίᾳ καὶ τῇ συμφωνίᾳ καὶ τῇ ταὐτότητι τοῦ βουλήματος). Further in the *Commentary on St John* he appeals to John xvii. 3, ὁ μόνος ἀληθινὸς θεός, and to the distinction between ὁ θεός and θεός to support his view of the distinction between Father and Son. His commentary on John x. 30 is lost, but twice at least he expounds this crucial text:

(*a*) When discussing John iv. 34: 'My meat is to do the will of him that sent me' he argues that the will of God was in the will of the Son and the will of the Son became the same as the will of the Father, in order that there may no longer be two wills but one will. Wherefore, the unity of will was the reason for the Son's saying, 'I and the Father are one' (John x. 30).[1] Thus he interprets the ἕν of John x. 30 as a unity of will.

(*b*) Later, discussing John viii. 40, 'Now you seek to kill me', Origen draws a distinction which was to become a standard exegetical principle, between sayings which refer to the Son's manhood and those which refer to his divinity;[2] John x. 30, he says, belongs to the latter category.[3]

Placed together, these two expositions emphasise that the Son is divine (although inferior to ὁ μόνος ἀληθινὸς θεός) and that his unity with the Father is a moral unity of will. This comes out more clearly still in the Toura MS, *The Dialogue*

---

[1] *in Joh.* IV, 34 (*GCS* iv, 260, 31 ff.).
[2] See the excellent discussion of this 'two-nature' exegesis in M. F. Wiles, *The Spiritual Gospel*, ch. VII.   [3] *in Joh.* XIX, 2 (*GCS*, iv, 299, 14 ff.).

with Heraclides, where Origen develops the exegesis of John x. 30 more fully against what appears to be a representative of the Antiochene theological tradition which, a century later, was to be represented by Eustathius of Antioch and Marcellus of Ancyra, to show that the Father and the Son are two gods who become a unity.[1] In anticipation of monarchian objections, Origen goes on to give a lengthy explanation of the statement that there are two gods; 'we must...show in what sense they are two, and in what sense the two are one God.'[2] First he seeks to show how scripture teaches that 'several things which are two are one':[3] Adam and Eve are distinct, yet it is said of them, 'For they two shall be one flesh' (Gen. ii. 34); and the righteous man is distinct from Christ, yet it is said, 'For he that is joined to the Lord is one Spirit' (I Cor. vi. 17). From these two examples Origen then draws the conclusion:

So in relation to the God and Father of the universe, our Lord and Saviour is not one flesh, nor one spirit, but something higher than flesh and spirit, namely, one God. The appropriate word when human beings are joined to one another is flesh. The appropriate word when a righteous man is joined to Christ is spirit. The appropriate word when Christ is united to the Father is not flesh, nor spirit, but more honourable than these—God. That is why we understand in this sense, 'I and the Father are one' (John x. 30).[4]

Here Origen interprets the ἕν of John x. 30 as εἷς θεός: 'I and the Father are one God'. This assertion of the unity of Father and Son as 'one God', must, however, be understood in the light of Origen's whole doctrine of the divinity of the Son (Logos): the Son is θεός not ὁ θεός; he is inferior to 'the only true God'; he is distinct from the Father, even 'numerically distinct from the Father' (διαθέρειν τῷ ἀριθμῷ υἱὸν τοῦ πατρός, *in Joh.* x, 37).[5] He is God in a derivative sense, having

---

[1] *Dial.* 2, 26 (references according to Scherer's edition, *SC*, vol. 67). The series of questions Origen puts, all of which Heraclides answers in the affirmative without any qualification (except the last), indicates Origen's own method of argument: 'The Father is God?'...'The Son is distinct from the Father?'...'Though he is distinct from the Father, the Son is also God?'...'And the unity is that of two Gods?' (καὶ γίνονται ἓν δύο θεοί)...'We confess two Gods?' Heraclides replies to the last question, 'Yes. The power is one', which recalls Hippolytus, *c. Noetum;* see above.

[2] *Ibid.* 2, 30.   [3] *Ibid.* 2, 31 ff.   [4] *Ibid.* 3, 20–4, 1.

[5] Cf. Justin Martyr's ἀριθμῷ, p. 39 above.

his divinity by communication (μετοχή)[1] from 'the God and Father of the universe'. Origen knows that it is necessary to assert both the distinction and the unity, but his view of the unity is impaired by the ditheism implicit in his subordinationist view of the Son's divinity. As Chadwick remarks, 'For Origen the independence of the Son is theologically prior to his oneness with the Father. He begins by thinking of two Gods, and then tries to explain how they are one, never *vice versa*.'[2] The rightness of this judgement is supported by the same emphasis on the unity of Father and Son as a unity of wills as we found in *in Joh.* IV, 34.[3] Origen reverses the order of theological priority which we find in St John's Gospel. For St John the unity of Father and Son is theologically prior to the distinction between them; the creative, revealing and saving Word of God, who is with God in the beginning and is God, is, within the unity of the godhead, distinct from the Father.[4]

Origen, then, seeks to preserve the first Johannine paradox of distinction-within-unity in the godhead. He can, however, maintain the unity only by the doctrine of eternal generation and of the Father's 'communication' of his substance to the Son, and the distinction only by the doctrine of the Son's subordination and inferiority to the Father. Both of these doctrines are derived from his Logos-cosmology; the former from the Stoic doctrine of the Logos and the latter from the Platonic doctrine of the pre-existence of souls.

It is on this same Platonic doctrine of the pre-existence of souls that Origen's interpretation of the second paradox, the paradox of the incarnation, depends. 'A Greek could certainly think of no greater contradiction than that of "Logos" to "sarx", especially if the idea of suffering and dying was connected with it.'[5] In some places Origen seems to interpret the paradox in terms of the *God-Man* schema:

---

[1] Cf. J. Scherer, *Entretien d'Origène avec Héraclide* (*SC* 67), pp. 29 f.

[2] H. Chadwick, *Alexandrian Christianity* (*LCC*, III), p. 433.

[3] Cf. p. 100, n. 1 above.

[4] The above treatment of *The Dialogue with Heraclides* is largely drawn from my article, 'The Exegesis of John x. 30 in the Early Trinitarian Controversies', *NTS*, III (1956–7), 338 f.

[5] A. Grillmeier, *Christ in Christian Tradition*, p. 34; cf. also A. Grillmeier and H. Bacht, *Das Konzil von Chalkedon*, Würtzburg, 1951, I, 25.

First we must know this, that in Christ there is one nature, his deity, because he is the only-begotten of the Father, and another, the human nature, which in very recent times he took upon him to fulfil the divine purpose.[1]

He took upon him the whole man (ὅλον ἄνθρωπον).[2]

The whole man would not have been saved unless he had taken upon him the whole man (οὐκ ἂν δὲ ὅλος ἄνθρωπος ἐσώθη, εἰ μὴ ὅλον ἄνθρωπον ἀνειλήφει).[3]

Thus Origen clearly foreshadows the later formula, which was to become a christological axiom: 'What he did not assume, he did not redeem'. Nevertheless, when his christology is examined within his system it becomes clear that it is in fact a modification or refinement of the *Logos-sarx* christology. The key passage is *de Principiis*, II, 6, 3 ff.,[4] where, starting from 'the only-begotten Son of God', i.e. the pre-existent Logos whom he identifies with the Son, Origen argues that the pre-existent human soul of Jesus

clung to God from the beginning of the creation and ever after in an inseparable and indissoluble union, as being the soul of the Wisdom and Logos of God...This soul, then, acting as a medium between God and the flesh (for it was not possible for the nature of God to mingle with a body apart from some medium), there is born, as one said, the *God–Man* (*deus–homo*), the medium being that substance to whose nature it was not contrary to assume a body. Yet neither, on the other hand, was it contrary to nature for that soul, being as it was a rational substance (*substantia rationabilis*), to receive God, into whom, as we have said above, it had completely entered by entering into the Logos and Wisdom and Truth.[5]

From this passage it appears that Origen identifies the pre-existent human soul of Jesus with the 'soul' of the Logos. Elsewhere, however, he distinguishes between the two:

That he possessed a soul, the Saviour himself most clearly proves in the gospels when he says: 'No one taketh from me my soul, but

[1] *de Princ.* I, 2, 1 (*GCS*, v, 27, 21 ff.).
[2] *in Joh.* XIII, 21 (*GCS*, IV, 456, 9).
[3] *Dial. c. Herac.* 7, 5 ff. [4] *GCS*, v, 141, 25 ff.
[5] Cf. *c. Cels.* v, 39 (*GCS* ii, 43, 26 ff.): 'We say that this Logos dwelt in the soul of Jesus and was united with it in a closer union than that of any other soul, because he alone has been able perfectly to receive the highest participation in him who is the Logos, and the very Wisdom, and the very Righteousness himself' (Chadwick's translation).

I lay it down of myself. I have power to lay it down, and I have power to take it up again' (John x. 18). And again: 'My soul is sorrowful even unto death' (Matt. xxvi. 38); and also: 'Now is my soul troubled' (John xii. 27). For the soul that was 'troubled' and 'sorrowful' is certainly not the 'only-begotten' and the 'first-born of all creation' (Col. i. 15), nor God the Logos, who is superior to his soul, as the Son of God himself says: 'I have power to lay it down, and I have power to take it up' (John x. 18).[1]

The pre-existent soul of Jesus is united to the Logos, and as a result of this union or assimilation, the divine nature can be spoken of in terms of the human, and the human in terms of the divine.[2]

Thus Origen acknowledges that Christ has a rational soul, and it follows from this that the Logos assumed the whole man. The question arises, however, whether the pre-existent rational soul of Christ which is united to the Logos is wholly the same as the rational souls of men. To give an adequate answer would require a full discussion of Origen's anthropology, but it is sufficient for the present purpose to set it out briefly. The previous discussion of Origen's cosmology showed that he held that of the spiritual beings who fell through the exercise of their free will, some became angels and some demons and, in between, some became 'souls' which God imprisoned in the earthly body for punishment and correction so that they might have opportunity to ascend again to their original state. But there was *one* exception: 'all rational beings have fallen into sin except the soul which was destined to become incarnate with the Logos and which lived already the very life of the Logos'.[3] All souls were originally equal; their present inequalities are due to their having freely chosen to rebel against God. The pre-existent soul of Christ alone did not rebel because of its eternal union with the Logos. It is doubtful, then, whether the soul can be said to be wholly the same in nature as those of men.

Origen's christology, then, depends on his doctrine of the pre-existence of souls. If that doctrine is denied, his christology and his doctrine of the eternal generation of the Logos-Son collapse. The only way in which he can describe the union,

---

[1] *de Princ.* IV, 4, 4 (*GCS*, V, 353, 14 ff.).
[2] Cf. Crouzel, *Théologie de l'image de Dieu*, and 'L'anthropologie d'Origène'
[3] Crouzel, *art. cit.* p. 369.

assimilation, or fusion of the pre-existent soul of Jesus with the Logos is by the similes of iron in fire and of ointment and its odour: 'The soul, which, like a piece of iron in the fire, was forever placed in the Logos...forever in God, is God in all its acts and feelings and thoughts.'[1] The christology, which at first sight appears to be a *God-Man* christology, proves to be little more than a refinement of the *Logos-Sarx* christology, for ultimately the idea of the fusion of the soul with the Logos means that the Logos, subordinate and inferior to God, takes the place of the human soul in Christ.

Origen's doctrine represents the first attempt to work out a system of doctrine. Origen explicitly recognised the intention of St John that the fundamental concept for understanding the person of Christ, both in relation to the godhead and in relation to man, is the biblical concept of *Son*, not the philosophical concept of *Logos*, but his anxiety to commend the Christian message to educated pagans led him so to emphasise the Logos-concept that he was unable to break loose from the cosmology in which he clothed the Logos. His religious insight reached heights to which his theology could not attain. He recognised the need to pass beyond this Logos-theology to one in which the Father–Son relationship of the New Testament and the Church's rule of faith was central, but he himself could not take this step. The task he failed to accomplish he bequeathed to his successors—the task of transposing his insights into the God–Logos relationship from the philosophical key into a more strictly theological key. Despite their cosmological basis in his thought, the doctrines of eternal generation and of subordination are essential for the understanding of the person of Christ. The task to which the church had to set her mind was that of removing the inadequate garb of the Platonic cosmology of the Logos and reclothing the Christian message in a theology of the Father–Son relationship.

(iii) Alexandrian theology, A.D. 230–310

Origen's influence on Alexandrian theology did not end with his removal from the headship of the catechetical school and his departure for Caesarea. Bishop Demetrius who removed

---

[1] *de Princ.* II, 6, 6 (*GCS*, v, 145, 17 ff.).

Origen was succeeded first by Heraclas and then by Dionysius, both of them pupils of Origen; yet neither appears to have made any attempt to reinstate Origen as head of the school.[1] Little is known of the theology of the former, but sufficient fragments of Dionysius' writings have survived to enable us to see that he tried to preserve the essential teaching of his master,[2] and this appears to be true also of two later Alexandrian teachers, Theognostus and Pierius. By the end of the century, however, Origen's influence appears to have waned and the centre of Origenism had shifted to Caesarea where Pamphilus and Eusebius sought to keep alive the system and memory of the great Alexandrian.

It would be a mistake to assume that the theology of the Alexandrian school was representative of the theology of the Alexandrian church. Clement and Origen had both met opposition from the *simpliciores*, an opposition which was almost certainly a contributing factor to Demetrius' hostility to Origen. Dionysius also was to encounter similar opposition, and in the light of it to modify his terminology, if not his theology. As Origen's influence waned, a theology firmly rooted in scripture and the church's rule of faith asserted itself more strongly until at the end of the century it began to find literary expression.

(*a*) *Dionysius of Alexandria.* Athanasius records that Dionysius wrote to Ammonius, Bishop of Berenice, complaining that because of the popularity of Sabellianism in the Pentapolis 'the Son of God was scarcely any longer preached in the churches'.[3] In his zeal to oust Sabellianism, Dionysius restated Origen's subordinationism in an extreme form to emphasise the distinction between the Father and the Son, a re-statement to which the Arians were to appeal for support of their denial of the doctrine of eternal generation. Criticising the Sabellians, Dionysius wrote:

The Son of God is a thing made and originated (ποίημα καὶ γενητόν) not belonging to (the Father) by nature, but in essence (κατ' οὐσίαν) he is foreign to the Father just as the vine-dresser is foreign to the

---

[1] Cf. Bardy, 'Pour l'histoire de l'école d'Alexandrie'.

[2] Cf. Simonetti, *Studi sull'Arianesimo*, pp. 28 ff.

[3] *de Sent. Dion.* 5.

vine and the ship-builder to the ship. For inasmuch as he is a thing made, he did not exist before he came into existence (ὡς ποίημα, ὢν οὐκ ἦν πρὶν γένηται).[1]

The extreme subordinationism of such language aroused some within the Alexandrian see to appeal to Dionysius, Bishop of Rome, for his view of the orthodoxy of their bishop. C. L. Feltoe has deduced five errors into which his opponents alleged that he had fallen:[2]

(i) separating the Father and the Son.[3]
(ii) denying the eternity of the Son.[4]
(iii) naming the Father without the Son, and the Son without the Father.[5]
(iv) virtually rejecting the term ὁμοούσιος as descriptive of the Son.[6]
(v) speaking of the Son as a creature of the Father and using misleading illustrations of their relation.[7]

There can be little doubt that Dionysius' zeal to counteract Sabellian identification of Father and Son led him to assert an absolute distinction between them.

Dionysius of Rome replied by insisting that it is essential to preach the divine Monarchy:

If he came to be Son, once he was not; but he was always, if he is in the Father, as he says himself (John xiv. 10), and if the Christ be the Logos and Wisdom and Power...and these attributes be powers of God. If, then, the Son came into being, once these attributes were not; consequently, there was a time when God was without them, which is most absurd.[8]

He treats 'Sabellianism as a lesser evil than subordinationism',[9] over-emphasis on the unity of God as a lesser evil than over-emphasis on the distinction between Father and Son.

Whether it was his Roman namesake's letter which caused

---

[1] *apud* Athanasius, *de Sent. Dion.* 4.
[2] *The Letters and other Fragments of Dionysius of Alexandria (CPT)*, Cambridge, 1904, pp. 167 f.
[3] Athanasius, *de Sent. Dion.* 16.
[4] *Ibid.* 14.   [5] *Ibid.* 16.
[6] *Ibid.* 18.   [7] *Ibid.* 4.
[8] Athanasius, *de Decr.* 26 (Feltoe, *Dionysius of Alexandria*, p. 179, 11 ff.).
[9] E. Evans, *Tertullian's Treatise against Praxeas*, p. 29.

him to modify his language or not,[1] the Alexandrian's reply, *Elenchus et Apologia*, shows a remarkable change of emphasis. Whereas previously he had taken Origen's subordinationism to extremes, now he emphasises the eternity of the Father–Son relationship and their unity of essence, thus developing Origen's doctrine of eternal generation of the Logos in terms of the Father–Son relationship. Just as Tertullian had applied the Aristotelian doctrine of relations in order to prove that the Son is distinct from the Father,[2] so Dionysius uses it to prove that the Son is co-eternal with the Father in direct contradiction of his earlier statement, 'He did not exist before he was brought into existence'. He now says:

Never was there a time when God was not Father...Christ exists always, being Logos and Wisdom and Power. For it is not to be supposed that God, having at first no such issue, afterwards begat a Son, but that the Son has his being not of himself but from the Father...Since the Father is eternal, the Son is eternal, being Light from Light; for if there is a parent there is also a child. But if there were not a child, how and of whom can there be a parent? But there are both and they always exist.[3]

Dionysius' complete reversal of doctrine, however, is more apparent than real and indicates the difficulty which Origen's successors faced when they allowed the cosmological framework of their master's thought to be weakened. Within the latter's system the doctrines of subordination and eternal generation are complementary. Removed from the cosmological framework they become contradictory. At first, in opposition to the Sabellians, Dionysius lost sight of the eternal generation in his anxiety to emphasise the distinction between the Father and the Son. Then, when the implications of this are pointed out he grasps the doctrine of eternal generation again while endeavouring, as Origen did, to maintain the distinction as well.

[1] Evans suggests that the influence of Tertullian can be seen in the writings of Dion. Alex. There is nothing improbable in this, but it is possible that Dion. Rom. reminded Dion. Alex. of an essential fact which he had overlooked, namely the Church's faith in *One* God. Evans speaks of 'the unlikely heresy of tritheism' which Dion. Rom. attacks, yet tritheism was the logical result of the extreme subordinationism which Dion. Alex. opposed to Sabellianism.

[2] See above, pp. 64 f.

[3] Athanasius, *de Sent. Dion.* 15 (Feltoe, p. 186, 4–9; p. 187, 13–16).

In order to do this, however, he has to return to the concept of the Logos as an emanation of Mind:

For the Logos is an emanation of Mind (*Nous*), and, to borrow language applicable to men, the mind which finds expression by means of the tongue is derived from the heart through the mouth, becoming different from the word in the heart. For after sending forth the other, the latter remains as it was. But the other is sent forth and flies forth and is borne in every direction. And so each is in the other and each distinct from the other, and they are one and at the same time two (ἕν εἰσιν, ὄντες δύο). Likewise the Father and the Son were said to be one, and the One in the Other.[1]

While he is prepared to accept the co-eternity of the Son with the Father, Dionysius hesitates to go as far as the Western theologians and declare that Father and Son are two persons in one substance. He objected to the term (ὁμοούσιος) because it was unscriptural,[2] but claimed that the illustrations he had used suggest the idea contained in it. As parent and child are ὁμογενής, as seed, root and plant are ὁμοφυής, so Father and Son are ὁμοούσιος. The fact that he treats ὁμογενής and ὁμοφυής as 'near equivalents'[3] of ὁμοούσιος shows that he has not grasped the significance of ὁμοούσιος. For him the oneness of the godhead is not essential but generic.[4]

Within the theology of Dionysius of Alexandria and his correspondence with Dionysius of Rome we see in miniature the conflict between the doctrines of subordination and eternal generation which was to become the major doctrinal controversy of the fourth century.[5] Dionysius tries to think in terms of the Father–Son relationship rather than of the God–Logos relationship, but when he sees the danger of losing sight of the distinction between Father and Son he takes refuge in the Logos-doctrine; when he sees that the edifice of Origenism

---

[1] *de Sent. Dion.* 23 (Feltoe, p. 191, 1–8).

[2] *de Sent. Dion.* 18 (Feltoe, p. 188, 11 ff.).

[3] J. F. Bethune-Baker, *The Meaning of Homoousios in the Constantinopolitan Creed* (*TS*, VII, 1), Cambridge, 1901, p. 25.

[4] J. F. Bethune-Baker, *Introduction to the Early History of Christian Doctrine*, pp. 113 ff.

[5] Cf. Simonetti, *Studi sull' Arianesimo*, p. 25: 'nella questione dei duo Dionigi cominciassero a profilarsi con chiarezza questioni, problemi, prese de posizione, il cui contrasto si sarebbe rivelato con drammatica evidenza al tempo della crisi ariana'.

is developing cracks in its foundations, he endeavours to strengthen it with the mortar of the Logos-doctrine which had originally held it together. Dionysius' attitude to the paradox of distinction-within-unity makes no significant advance on Origen's position. He points the way, however, to the ascription to the Son of co-eternity with the Father on a foundation other than that of Origen's cosmology. If God is eternally Father, then the Father–Son relationship is eternal within the godhead, and the Son is co-eternal with the Father. It is this insight into the Father–Son relationship, to which St John is the pre-eminent biblical witness, that is taken up and developed by Alexander and Athanasius against the Arians' over-emphasis on the subordinationist side of Origen's system.

(b) *Theognostus and Pierius.* Little is known about the two teachers who succeeded Dionysius in the catechetical school at Alexandria, and few fragments of their writings have survived. Theognostus appears to have remained a firm adherent of Origenism with a strong emphasis on subordinationism. Photius records that 'in speaking of the Son he describes him as a creature (κτίσμα) who has charge of beings endowed with reason (λόγος)'.[1] Radford argues that this term must be read in the light of the terms ἀπαύγασμα and ἀπόρροια 'which Theognostus, like Origen and Dionysius before him, also used to describe the Son in order to illustrate the eternity of the relation of the Son to the Father...The light never existed without its radiance (ἀπαύγασμα). But an eternal κτίσμα is no "creature" in any sense of the word as it is commonly understood'.[2] However, Radford overlooks the fact that for Origen all spiritual beings are eternal κτίσματα.[3]

---

[1] Routh, *Reliquiae Sacrae*, III, 413.

[2] L. B. Radford, *Three Teachers of Alexandria: Theognostus, Pierius and Peter*, Cambridge, 1908, p. 18.

[3] Origen calls the Son a κτίσμα (*de Princ.* IV, 4, 1); cf. C. W. Lowry, 'Did Origen style the Son a Ktisma?', *JTS*, XXXIX (1938), 39–42. Simonetti (*Studi sull' Arianesimo*, p. 24) points out that in his interpretation of Prov. viii. 22 ff. Origen treats κτίζειν and κτίσμα as equivalents of γεννᾶν and γέννημα, and that he never uses Prov. viii. 22 (ἔκτισεν) in his attempt to describe the generation of the Son by the Father, 'while on the contrary he has made skilful use of the γεννᾷ which Prov. viii. 25 provided for him'.

Of Pierius, whom Jerome calls 'Origen Junior',[1] Photius says 'in regard to the Father and the Son his statements are orthodox, except that he asserts that there are two substances and two natures, using these terms. . .in the sense of hypostasis, not in the sense given by the adherents of Arius'.[2] Later he reports that there are hints in Pierius' writings that he accepted Origen's 'absurd idea' of the pre-existence of souls.[3] From our limited sources it appears then that both Theognostus and Pierius remained firmly in the Origenist tradition.

(c) *Peter.* 'The tide of Origenist thought and influence at Alexandria rose to its height with Pierius. The reaction came with Peter, catechist, bishop and martyr.'[4] In order to answer the question why the Origenist tradition should suddenly be broken we have to resort to hypothesis, for history does not provide us with clear data on which to base a firm judgment.[5] If, as Philip of Side, a notoriously unreliable historical source, records, Pierius was head of the school and lived until after the martyrdom of his pupil Pamphilus in the Diocletian persecution (A.D. 309–10), then he was not head of the school during the last years of the third century and the first decade of the fourth, for in A.D. 300 Peter became bishop after some years as head of the school. This gives the interesting situation that a former head of the school, a convinced Origenist, is still living at a time when a convinced anti-Origenist is in charge of the school and bishop of the diocese. These facts, if correct, lead to the conclusion that at last the opponents of the intellectualistic and speculative theology, which had been characteristic of the school, but not of the Alexandrian church as a whole, since the time of Origen, have gained control of the school. In Peter they found a man who could give literary expression to the faith of the church as expressed in her rule of faith and liturgy.

The reaction against Origenism represented by Peter takes the form of denial of two pillars on which Origen had supported the edifice of his system: (i) the allegorical interpretation of

[1] *de Viris Illustribus*, 76.
[2] Routh, *Reliquiae Sacrae*, III, 430.   [3] *Idem.*
[4] Radford, *Three Teachers of Alexandria*, p. 58.
[5] Cf. G. Bardy, 'Pour l'histoire de l'école d'Alexandrie', p. 109.

scripture, and (ii) the doctrine of the pre-existence of souls.[1] When the latter doctrine is denied the cosmological basis of Origen's doctrines of eternal generation and the incarnation is destroyed, while denial of the validity of allegorical interpretation removes the method by which he found scriptural support for the non-biblical elements in his system.

Three fragments of Peter's *de Divinitate* indicate that Peter taught the fullness both of the divinity and the humanity in Christ. ' "The Logos was made flesh" (John i. 14) and "was found in fashion as a man" (Phil. ii. 7), but was not left without his divinity.'[2] When this statement is taken with another preserved by Leontius of Byzantium, it is plain that Peter's christology differs from the *Logos–Sarx* christology of Origen and his successors: 'These things and the like, and all the signs which he showed and his miracles, prove that he is God made man (θεὸς εἶναι ἐνανθρωπήσαντα). Both things, therefore, are demonstrated, that he was God by nature, and that he became man by nature (θεὸς ἦν φύσει, καὶ γέγονεν ἄνθρωπος φύσει).'[3] That is, Peter's christology belongs to the *God–Man* type.

Peter's reaction against Origen's doctrine of the pre-existence of souls robbed the doctrine of eternal generation of its cosmological basis. The prospect of losing the deep religious insight contained in this latter doctrine placed Alexandrian theology in a dilemma, well summed up by H. Berkhof:

Theology stood once more face to face with the question whether the Son is eternal like the Father or begotten from him in time. Cosmological thought must accept the latter and return to the position of the Apologists, sharpened by the renunciation of Origenistic ditheism. That is what the Arians did. If anyone would maintain the doctrinal position of eternal generation, he could do so now only for soteriological reasons. With this the Logos-concept undergoes drastic alteration. The Logos is eternal for the reason that no incarnate demigod can lead fallen creation back to God. This

---

[1] Cf. Radford, *Three Teachers of Alexandria*, pp. 72 ff. Leontius of Byzantium (*contra Monophysitas*) quotes from Peter's *de Anima*: 'This (doctrine) comes from the philosophy of the Greeks; it is foreign to those who wish to live piously in Christ' (Routh, *Reliquiae Sacrae*, IV, 50).

[2] Preserved in the acts of the Council of Ephesus (A.D. 431); cf. Labbé, *Conciliorum omnium amplissima collectio*, IV, 1184; Routh, *op. cit.* IV, 56.

[3] *contra Nestorianos et Eutychianos*, 1; Routh, *op. cit.* IV, 48.

fundamental alteration of the Logos-doctrine is accomplished theologically by Alexander and ecclesiastically at Nicaea.[1] Peter's criticism of Origen's speculative theology and of the allegorical interpretation by which it was given scriptural support, together with the central position he gives to the incarnation, indicates that this process of altering the Logos-doctrine had already been commenced by the predecessor of Alexander.

C. ANTIOCH

The curtain of silence which covers Antiochene and Syrian Christianity during the third century is drawn aside momentarily for the drama of the deposition of Paul of Samosata from the see of Antioch in A.D. 269; even on this incident history has left us little information. It appears that the old Antioch–Asia Minor tradition continued in Antioch, retaining a strong emphasis on monotheism on the one hand, and on the real humanity of Christ on the other.

Paul of Samosata.[2] In the history of the deposition of Paul we see for the first time open conflict between the theological traditions of Antioch and Alexandria. The bishops responsible for Paul's condemnation were Syrians who had been educated in Caesarea at the feet of Origen. Bardy has argued that the limited data we possess shows that Paul's was a strictly monarchian theology which can be summed up in two articles: 'a unique God who possesses among his attributes Wisdom or Reason (σοφία or λόγος), and Jesus Christ, a man similar to others, to whom the divine Wisdom has been communicated in super-abundance'.[3] On the other hand, R. V. Sellers, following Loofs' view,[4] concludes that Paul's theology is neither

---

[1] *Die Theologie des Eusebius von Caesarea*, Amsterdam, 1939, p. 72.

[2] The fragments of Paul's writings are quoted according to the numbering of G. Bardy, *Paul de Samosate*, Louvain, 1923, and H. J. Lawlor, 'The Sayings of Paul of Samosata', *JTS*, XIX (1918), pp. 20 ff., 115 ff. They have also been collected by F. Loofs, *Paulos von Samosata*, and H. de Riedmatten, *Les actes du procès de Paul de Samosate*, Fribourg, 1952. The latter is the most definitive collection, but my access to it has been limited.

[3] *Paul de Samosate*, p. 380.

[4] Sellers, *Two Ancient Christologies*, London, 1940, p. 118; Loofs, *Paulus von Samosata*.

dynamic monarchianism nor psilanthropism, but a view closely akin to that which Marcellus opposed to Arianism. Even if this latter view is correct, Bardy is still right in his analysis of the two foci of Paul's theology as the Oneness of God and the humanity of Jesus Christ. Paul appears to have based his monotheism on Old Testament texts such as Deut. vi. 4: 'The Lord thy God is one Lord',[1] and to have argued from them that God is unipersonal:

God is a single person with the Word (πρόσωπον ἓν τὸν θεὸν ἅμα τῷ λόγῳ) just as a man and his word are one.[2] God with the Word and the Word with God, a single person of the Father with the Word and of the Word with the Father (ἓν πρόσωπον πατρὸς πρὸς τὸν λόγον καὶ τοῦ λόγου πρὸς τὸν πατέρα).[3]

Thus Paul denies any personal distinction between God and the Word, by making the relationship indicated by John i. 1 b, ὁ λόγος ἦν πρὸς τὸν θεόν, a reciprocal relationship.

For Paul λόγος and σοφία are equivalent terms. Both denote an attribute of God, a δύναμις, a power of God which, being always in God (ἐν τῷ θεῷ) comes into separate existence by utterance (κατὰ τὴν προφοράν).[4] According to the sixth-century treatise de Sectis, Paul used λόγος to signify 'an order or a command' proceeding from God.[5] This λόγος, separated from God by God's act in uttering it, is not, it appears, endowed with any separate *personal* existence, and what separate existence it has is temporary and spasmodic.

'The Word was not a man; he dwelt in a man (*verbum homo non erat*; *in homine habitavit*), in Abraham, in Moses, in David, in the prophets',[6] and finally in Christ 'as in a temple'. 'As in each of the prophets, so also is the dwelling of the divine Word in him. Consequently, there are in Christ two natures separated from each other and without anything in common with each other; Christ himself is one thing and the divine Word which dwells in him is another.'[7]

---

[1] Bardy, fr. xv; Lawlor, fr. ix.
[2] Bardy, fr. xvi (1); Lawlor, fr. x.
[3] Bardy, fr. xvi (3); Lawlor, fr. x.
[4] Bardy, fr. xvi (2); Lawlor, fr. x.
[5] PG, LXXXVI, 1213 D, quoted by Sellers, *Two Ancient Christologies*, p. 120.
[6] Bardy, fr. v.
[7] Bardy, fr. iv; Lawlor, fr. ii.

Paul denies that Jesus Christ is the Word:

The Word was greater than Christ, for Christ became great through Wisdom; let us not lower the dignity of Wisdom. For the Word is from above: Jesus Christ the man is from below. Mary has not given birth to the Word, for she did not exist before the ages. Mary has received the Word, and she is not older than the Word; but she has given birth to a man like us, although better in all things, since the grace which came upon him is from the Holy Spirit, from the promises, from the scriptures. Thus the anointed Son of David is not alien to Wisdom, and Wisdom does not dwell in this manner in any other; for it was in the prophets, more in Moses and many of the masters and still more in Christ as in a temple. For Jesus Christ is one thing, and the Word another.[1]

The union of the Word with Jesus is not an essential union (οὐσιωδῶς) but qualitative (κατὰ ποιήτητα),[2] and Christ is not 'righteous by nature' but 'by fellowship' (κατὰ κοινωνίαν).[3] He is 'a man honoured by God' because of his 'life full of virtue'.[4] Because God bestows on him in utmost fullness the gift of the Word or Wisdom, Paul can speak of Jesus as divine, 'God born of a virgin, God manifested at Nazareth', yet he qualifies this by saying that he has 'the beginning of his existence (τῆς ὑπάρξεως τὴν ἀρχήν) from below'; the Word was 'manifested in existence at Nazareth in order that, scripture says, he who is God above all, the Father, may be one'.[5]

Paul's emphasis is on God's self-communication through the Word. Whenever God speaks, the Word comes forth into separate existence, and pre-eminently in Jesus Christ. Paul's interest, in the surviving fragments at least, is not cosmological but revelational. The revelation, however, is not revelation of God, nor of his purpose of salvation; it is the revelation of an ethical example for men to follow:

Our Saviour has become holy and righteous, having conquered by struggle and toil the sin of our first father; having thus set up virtue again, he has been united to God, having one and the same will and energy as God, for the progress of man in goodness; and in order to preserve it inseparable, he obtained the name which is above every name which is given to him as a reward of love.[6]

---

[1] Bardy, fr. 11a; Lawlor, fr. 11.   [2] Bardy, fr. 1x; Lawlor, fr. 1v.
[3] Bardy, fr. xx (2).   [4] Bardy, fr. xx (1); Lawlor, fr. 1x (4).
[5] Bardy, fr. xvii; Lawlor, fr. 1x (4).
[6] Bardy, fr. xxvii; Lawlor, fr. xvi.

Bardy comments that Paul reduces salvation to an admirable example of perfection: 'By obeying the divine Wisdom which filled him, Jesus succeeded in conquering sin; there is no man who, in a certain measure, cannot aspire to the same victory, if he obeys the grace and imitates the conduct of the Christ of God.'[1]

Paul, then, reduces the Johannine paradox of distinction-within-unity by interpreting the unity of the Father and the Son as the unity of God with one of his powers or attributes. The distinction between the Father and the Son is the distinction between God and a man whom God fills with Wisdom. If Epiphanius is reliable, 'it is not impossible that in the Fourth Gospel (John i. 1 *b*) the Samosatene had read or had interpreted πρὸς τὸν θεόν as ἐν τῷ θεῷ ἦν ὁ λόγος in a way which would have favoured his monarchian doctrine and which would show that the Logos did not possess any separate hypostasis'.[2] So also Paul fails to understand the paradox of the incarnation; the Word did not *become* flesh; it came to dwell in flesh. The Word, as a divine power, is joined to a man. In no sense is there an incarnation of God in man. Paul takes the manhood of Jesus seriously, but the Word, being impersonal, is less than God.

If Alexandrian theology in the third century demonstrates the inadequacy of the Logos-concept as the basis for interpreting the witness of St John's Gospel to the Father–Son relationship in the godhead and to the fullness of the divinity and humanity in Jesus Christ, Antiochene theology as we see it represented in Paul of Samosata demonstrates the inadequacy of the Hebraic Word–Wisdom concept. Of the three ante-Nicene traditions, only Western theology understood St John's intention that the central concept for christology must be that of the Father–Son relationship; because of this clearer understanding of St John's intention and its stronger emphasis on the faith of the church as expressed in the *rule of faith*, the Western tradition appears to have been more representative of the faith of the majority of Christians everywhere. The anti-Origenist reaction of Peter of Alexandria prepared the way for a close alliance between Athanasius and Western theologians like Hilary of Poitiers during the Arian controversy.

[1] *Paul de Samosate*, p. 379.
[2] *Ibid.* p. 382; cf. Epiphanius, *Haer.* LXV, 4.

CHAPTER 4

THE TRADITIONS AT THE OUTBREAK OF THE ARIAN CONTROVERSY

In the period immediately before the outbreak of the Arian controversy, three theological traditions, each involving a different method of interpreting St John's Gospel, find illustrious representatives within the church. The 'Antiochene' tradition is represented by Eustathius of Antioch who was to be the first victim of the Arian reaction in A.D. 328–9; the 'Alexandrian' tradition is represented by Eusebius of Caesarea, an avowed admirer of Origen, who was to become a close ally of the Arians; the 'neo-Alexandrian' tradition, which, as it developed, came to resemble closely the 'Western' tradition, and in which the common faith of the church of Alexandria finds theological expression, was represented by Alexander and his young deacon, Athanasius, who carried on the anti-Origenist reaction of Peter the Martyr. By and large, the Arian controversy was to be an Eastern controversy, but it is significant that Athanasius, the 'neo-Alexandrian', was to find his strongest theological support from Hilary of Poitiers, heir to the 'Western' tradition of Tertullian and Novatian. In the initial stages of the controversy and immediately before its outbreak, Athanasius plays the role of a representative of the 'Western' tradition, although it may be impossible to demonstrate that he was at this time in any way familiar with the 'Western' theological tradition or the writings of its representatives.

The three traditions had existed side by side for more than a century. There had been a clash between the Antiochene and Alexandrian traditions in the affair of Paul of Samosata, and between the Alexandrian and Western traditions in the affair of the two Dionysii. The three traditions came into open and full-scale conflict in the Arian controversy, the Antiochene and the neo-Alexandrian being allied against Arianism and the supporters it found among the heirs of the old Alexandrian tradition of Origen. In setting the stage for the discussion of the Arian controversy and the part played in it by St John's Gospel, it is important that the situation in the first two decades of the fourth century should be outlined.

A. EUSTATHIUS OF ANTIOCH[1]

Eustathius of Antioch is chosen as the representative of the Antiochene tradition at this stage in preference to Marcellus of Ancyra, for the surviving fragments of the latter's works clearly come from his polemic against the Arians in the immediate post-Nicene period, whereas those of Eustathius' writings are not so clearly anti-Arian.

Eustathius' starting-point is the same as that from which Paul of Samosata had started, namely an insistence on the essential unity or oneness of God and on the complete manhood of Christ. His theology, however, avoids the crudities of Paul's naïve position. While he remains a true child of the Antiochene tradition, he makes significant advances and paves the way for the later development of this tradition in the latter half of the fourth and the early part of the fifth centuries.[2]

For Eustathius, God is the one God, the Almighty (παντο-κράτωρ),[3] the creator of all things,[4] who is perfect, infinite, incomprehensible (τέλειος, ἄπειρος, ἀπερινόητος),[5] above all things (ἐπὶ πάντων),[6] in everything (ἐν παντί),[7] and fills all things (τὰ πάντα πληρῶν).[8] Along with this monotheistic emphasis he equally strongly emphasises the completeness of the humanity of Jesus Christ.

Eustathius insists that *ipsa veritate totum hominem indutus est deus,*[9] and by his *totus homo* means that the manhood which God put on consists not only of a body but also of a soul which is homoousios with the souls of men and rational (λογική), having the power of choice[10]— a conception which is reflected in all he says concerning 'the Man of Christ'.[11]

---

[1] Cf. M. Spanneut, *Recherches sur les écrits d'Eustathe d'Antioche*, Lille, 1948. Unfortunately I have not been able to obtain a copy of this work.
[2] For this later development, cf. R. V. Sellers, *Two Ancient Christologies.*
[3] *de Engastrimytho,* 75, 19; 25, 18.   [4] *PG,* xviii, 691 c.
[5] *PG,* xviii, 685 B.   [6] *de Eng.* 75, 19.   [7] *PG,* xviii, 695 A.
[8] *Idem.*   [9] *PG,* xviii, 693, fr. 5.   [10] *Interpret. Ps. xv; PG,* xviii, 683 D.
[11] Sellers, *Two Ancient Christologies,* p. 185.

This emphasis on the oneness of God on the one hand and on the manhood of Christ on the other raises immediately the question of the relationship between God and the man Jesus. Unlike Paul of Samosata before him and Marcellus his contemporary, who thought that the pre-existent Word became Son of God at the incarnation,[1] i.e. that the impersonal Word became personal through its conjunction with the man Jesus, Eustathius has no hesitation in calling the pre-existent Word by the personal name Son. God is 'the most divine Father' and 'the most divine Begetter';[2] the Father and the only Son are a dyad within the one God (ἐκ δυάδος τὴν μίαν... θεότητα καὶ τὴν ἀληθῆ θεογονίαν).[3] The relation between the Father and the Son is a true theogony; Eustathius describes the Son as 'genuine Son of God by nature' (φύσει θεοῦ γνήσιος υἱός).[4] Sellers[5] points out that when speaking of the Son Eustathius uses, apparently synonymously, four other terms: λόγος, παῖς, σοφία and πνεῦμα. Everyone, he says, agrees that the only Son is called ὁ λόγος:[6] 'his Logos is God' (ὁ λόγος αὐτοῦ θεὸς ὤν)[7] 'the one who has been begotten from him' (ὁ γεννηθεὶς ἐξ αὐτοῦ),[8] 'God by nature' (τὴν φύσιν θεός).[9] He is 'the image of the divine substance' (imago divinae substantiae),[10] possesses the eternal Kingdom of the Father,[11] is the cause of all created things,[12] and mediator of God's activity in creating the heavens and the earth.[13]

In this Eustathius' doctrine of the Father and the Son appears to be thoroughly orthodox. Writing of the controversy between Eustathius and Eusebius of Caesarea in the years immediately following the Nicene Council, Socrates the historian confesses that he is mystified as to the point of conflict, for 'it is admitted on both sides that the Son of God has a distinct person and existence, and all acknowledged that there is one God in a trinity of Persons'.[14] Sellers, however, asserts[15] that the basis of

---

[1] See below, ch. 8. [2] PG, xviii, 681 c. [3] de Eng. 65, 4.
[4] Ibid. 40, 4.
[5] Eustathius of Antioch and his Place in the Early History of Christian Doctrine, Cambridge, 1928, p. 84. [6] de Eng. 56, 17.
[7] PG, xviii, 685 c; cf. John i. 1. [8] Idem. [9] PG, xviii, 677 A.
[10] PG, xviii, 693. Is this possibly a Latin translation of Heb. i. 3: χαρακτὴρ τῆς ὑποστάσεως αὐτοῦ?
[11] Idem. [12] PG, xviii, 677 A. [13] de Eng. 56, 19.
[14] Hist. Eccl. I, 23. [15] Eustathius of Antioch, p. 91.

Eustathius' teaching must be sought not in the Father–Son relationship but in the God–Logos relationship, which he interpreted in the light of the Hebraic Word-concept as the relationship between God and his impersonal or non-personal Word. Sellers quotes with approval Loofs' view that

Eustathius seems to think rather with 'Logos' of the Word through which God creates and carries out his will on earth, and so far as I can see there is no trace of the everlasting begetting... The Logos for Eustathius, the advocate of the μία οὐσία or ὑπόστασις of the Father and of the Son, has or is no proper *hypostasis*.[1]

If Sellers (and Loofs) is right Eusebius had some justification in accusing Eustathius of Sabellianism;[2] for him the pre-existent Logos is not *personally* distinct from God; he (or it) is an attribute of God, in God potentially (δυνάμει) but coming forth from God as an activity of the Godhead (θεότητος ἐνεργείᾳ),[3] i.e. the Logos, being in God ἐνδιάθετος comes forth προφορικός. In his more recent study, *Two Ancient Christologies*, Sellers asserts what he had previously denied, that the Son has his own hypostasis; 'Eustathius' teaching on the personal existence of the Son is not so definite as that of his successors simply because he, in his generation, was called upon to resist the subordinationism of the Lucianists. Consequently, as we would expect, he lays all the emphasis on the truth that *divinitatis una est substantia*.'[4]

The indefiniteness of Eustathius' teaching on the personal pre-existence of the Son is due even more to the fact that just as Tertullian and Novatian in the West and Origen and Dionysius in Alexandria were aware of the inadequacy of the philosophical Logos-concept as a basis for trinitarian and christological thinking, so also Eustathius is aware of the inadequacy of the Hebraic Word-concept and tries to substitute for it the more personal Son-concept. He stands 'at the parting

---

[1] *Paulus von Samosata*, pp. 296 f. (Sellers' translation, *op. cit.* p. 88).

[2] Cf. *Eustathius of Antioch*, pp. 88 ff.

[3] *de Eng.* 57, 3; cf. Sellers, *op. cit.* p. 90.

[4] *Two Ancient Christologies*, p. 123. Cf. *idem.* n. 6: 'Eustathius' determination to uphold the doctrine of the true divinity of the Son is seen, for instance, in his constant use of the expressions ὁ λόγος καὶ θεός or ὁ θεὸς καὶ λόγος; he adds the θεὸς καί (or the καὶ θεός...) to show that the Logos is truly God and not subordinate to the Father.'

of the ways',[1] or rather at the critical point where Antiochene theology must decide whether to go forward to a theology in which the Father–Son relationship is central or to hold fast to the old theology based on the God–Word relationship. Using another metaphor, Sellers says that 'the teaching of Eustathius contains within itself the plant of the new theological outlook which expressed itself in terms of Father and Son. In his teaching that plant seems to be struggling for existence; in that of the later Antiochenes it is bearing fruit.'[2]

Eustathius' theology, then, is a theology of transition, in which there is a conflict between the new awareness of the centrality of the Son-concept and the old Antiochene tradition in which the Old Testament Word-concept was central. This conflict is equally apparent in Eustathius' doctrine of the incarnation. Faithful to his tradition he emphasises the completeness of Christ's humanity; coupled with his indefiniteness concerning the pre-existent hypostasis of the Son this emphasis leads him towards a christology of the *Word–man* type. There are indications, however, that he is trying to think in terms of the fuller and more adequate *God–man* type of christology. For instance, he says that 'the soul (i.e. the human soul) of Christ really dwelt with the Word and God' (συνδιαιτωμένη ἡ ψυχὴ τοῦ Χριστοῦ τῷ λόγῳ καὶ θεῷ);[3] speaking of the temptations of Jesus, he says: 'The Devil, gazing into the face of Christ (τὸ τοῦ Χριστοῦ πρόσωπον)[4] saw, within, God in fact and operation and true Son of God by nature, beholding him clothed without with a Man, holy, undefiled, and spotless, even a most beautiful temple, consecrated, inviolate'.[5]

It appears legitimate, then, to conclude that Eustathius marks a turning-point in the Antiochene tradition. To the traditional emphasis on the oneness of God and his Word, he tries to add the other half of the Johannine paradox, the personal distinction between the Father and the Son. The prevalence in Antioch, the home of Lucian's school, of extreme subordinationism makes him hesitant to make the modification

---

[1] Sellers, *Eustathius*, p. 91. [2] *Ibid.* p. 97.
[3] *PG*, xviii, 689 D.
[4] Sellers translates this phrase 'the Person of Christ'. While it is certainly not impossible that this is Eustathius' meaning, the more primitive and less technical meaning 'face of Christ' appears more likely.
[5] *de Eng.* 40, 2.

more definite. At the same time he also tries to add to the traditional Antiochene emphasis on the completeness of Christ's humanity, the other half of the second Johannine paradox, the completeness of Christ's divinity. Again he hesitates because of the over-emphasis in subordinationist theology on the divinity at the expense of the humanity. These two modifications of Antiochene theology, tentative and hesitating though they may be, are accompanied by an increased emphasis on soteriology in the theology of Eustathius as compared with that of his predecessors, Paul of Samosata and Theophilus of Antioch. Eustathius' contemporary, Marcellus of Ancyra, as we shall see, refused to make the modifications required by the new theological outlook, taking refuge in the archaic Antiochene tradition, and so came into conflict with Eusebius of Caesarea and the Arians on the one hand, and with Athanasius (or, at least, with the author of the *Fourth Oration against the Arians*) on the other. While the Arian controversy itself was the battleground on which the three traditions met, it is in the sadly neglected side-skirmish of the Marcellan controversy that their conflict with each other is most discernible.

B. EUSEBIUS OF CAESAREA

At the outbreak of the Arian controversy, the old Alexandrian theological tradition was ably represented by Eusebius of Caesarea, who had inherited an Origenistic theology through Pierius and Pamphilus. As evidence of this theological position before the controversy broke out we may concentrate on his *Demonstratio Evangelica, Preparatio Evangelica,* and his *Ecclesiastical History,* with some reference to letters which he wrote during its opening stages.

Through his teacher Eusebius had inherited a theology set in a cosmological framework with a graded hierarchy of beings,[1] the highest place in which is occupied by 'the Creator of the universe' (ὁ δημιουργὸς τῶν ὅλων),[2] 'the first and eternal and alone unbegotten God, the transcendent cause of the universe and ruler and monarch of all'.[3] Eusebius is fond of piling up

---

[1] Cf. H. Berkhof, *Die Theologie des Eusebius von Caesarea* pp. 35 ff.
[2] *Dem. Ev.* I, 5, 12 a (*GCS*, VI, 22, 34).
[3] *Ibid.* IV, 1, 144 b (*GCS*, VI, 150, 5 f.).

adjectives and titles in order to stress the absolute transcendence of the supreme God:

There is one first cause of the universe, or rather, one even earlier than the first cause, born earlier than the first and more original than the Monad, and superior to every title, inexpressible, unutterable, incomprehensible, good, the cause of all, the maker, the bountiful, the provident, the saving, himself being the one and only God, from whom are all things and through whom are all things.

μία...τῶν ὅλων ἀρχή, μᾶλλον δὲ τὸ καὶ ἀρχῆς ἀνώτερον, καὶ πρώτου προγενέστερον καὶ μονάδος ἀρχηγονώτερον καὶ πάσης κρεῖττον προσηγορίας, ἄρρητον, ἀνέκφραστον, ἀπερινόητον, ἀγαθόν, τὸ πάντων αἴτιον, τὸ ποιητικόν, τὸ εὐεργετικόν, τὸ προνοητικόν, τὸ σωτήριον, αὐτὸς ὢν εἷς καὶ μόνος θεός, ἐξ οὗ τὰ πάντα, δι' ὃν τὰ παντ' ἐστίν.[1]

It has been necessary to quote the Greek of this passage in full, for it indicates how Eusebius prefers to speak of God in abstract, neuter, and negative terms. Having commenced with the feminine noun ἀρχή (beginning), Eusebius proceeds to apply to this ἀρχή a series of neuter adjectives, then a series of neuter nouns, finally identifying this 'beginning' thus qualified with 'the one and only God'. This indicates that Eusebius conceives God in the most abstract terms possible; God, for him, is the Absolute (ὁ ὤν or τὸ ὄν) of the Greek philosophers, removed into the sphere of the utmost transcendence which it is impossible for man even to conceive,[2] and not the living God of the Bible. His God is 'the first God' (ὁ πρῶτος θεός),[3] indeed even 'born earlier than the first and more original than the Monad'.[4] In this connection Eusebius frequently quotes John xvii. 3: ὁ μόνος ἀληθινὸς θεός.[5]

Next in the hierarchy, below the Supreme God is the Logos, who 'was not the transcendent God himself, but a second God' (μὴ ὁ ἐπὶ πάντων θεὸς οὗτος ἦν, ἀλλά τις δεύτερος)[6] who

---

[1] *Ibid.* IV, 1, 145 *b* (*GCS*, VI, 151, 7 ff.); cf. also *de Ecc. Theol.* II, 14, 6 (*GCS*, IV, 115, 15–19).

[2] For a discussion of Eusebius' doctrine of God as ἀρχή, cf. A. Weber, ΑΡΧΗ: *ein Beitrag zur Christologie des Eusebius von Cäsarea*, Rome, 1965, ch. 1.

[3] *Dem. Ev.* V, 4, 227 *b* (*GCS*, VI, 225, 30).

[4] Cf. p. 122, n. 3 above.

[5] *Dem. Ev.* V, 17, 244 *c* (*GCS*, VI, 240, 19); cf. *Letter to Euphration of Balanea* (Opitz, *Urk.* 3; p. 5, 10–16).

[6] *Dem. Ev.* I, 5, 10 *d* (*GCS*, VI, 21, 34 f.); cf. also *ibid.* IV, 6, 154 *d*; V, 3, 220 *a*; V, 30, 255 *b*; *Hist. Ecc.* I, 2, 5. This is a common designation of the

'stands midway between the unoriginated God and the things originated after him'.[1] The Logos is called 'Lord' and 'God' only in a secondary sense,[2] yet Eusebius denies that the Logos in any way resembles a human word; for him the Logos is always a personal being,[3] yet he is always a second God inferior to the transcendent God who says, 'I am the One-who-is' (ἐγώ εἰμι ὁ ὤν: Exod. iii. 14, LXX).[4]

Eusebius carries the subordination of the Logos to God farther than Origen did;[5] nevertheless he strives to keep the Logos on the divine side of the boundary between the godhead and the created order. He emphasises that the manner in which the Logos is generated differs from that in which other beings are created through the Logos: 'He is before all ages the creative Logos of God, co-existing with the Father, only-begotten Son of the God of the universe, and minister[6] and fellow-worker with the Father in calling the universe into being and establishing it.'[7] However, while keeping the distinction between the Logos and God quite clear, Eusebius is not quite as successful in keeping clear the distinction between the Logos and the creatures. Like Philo, he frequently calls the Logos an 'angel'. 'Sometimes he distinguishes Christ from the *geneta*, sometimes he includes him among them, sometimes he hesitates about the right method of classifying the Logos, or while calling him *genetos*, distinguishes him from the remaining *geneta*, which derived their existence out of the non-existent.'[8] Although he never calls the Logos κτίσμα or ποιητός, he uses terms which are almost synonymous with them, δημιούργημα and

Logos with Philo. Eusebius quotes with approval a passage from Philo's *Quaest. et Solut.* in which he calls the Logos ὁ δεύτερος θεός, and God ὁ πρὸ τοῦ λόγου θεός (*Prep. Ev.* VII, 13, 323a; *GCS*, VIII (2), 389, 5 ff.).

[1] *Dem. Ev.* IV, 10, 164d (*GCS*, VI, 167, 34 f.).

[2] *Ibid.* V, 6, 232a (*GCS*, VI, 230, 6).

[3] *Ibid.* V, 5, 230a (*GCS*, VI, 228, 15 ff.).

[4] *Ibid.* IV, 1, 145d (*GCS*, VI, 151, 25); cf. also *ibid.* V, 3, 223a (*GCS*, VI, 221, 34); V, 13, 239c and 240a (*GCS*, VI, 236, 13 and 28).

[5] Only once does Origen refer to the Logos as 'a second God'; *c. Cels.* V, 39; cf. Crouzel, *Théologie de l'image de Dieu*, 112, n. 197.

[6] Cf. *Dem. Ev.* V, 5, 229a (*GCS*, VI, 227, 18).

[7] *Ibid.* V, 1, 214c (*GCS*, VI, 212, 30 ff.).

[8] G. L. Prestige, *God in Patristic Thought*, p. 139; cf. Prestige, ''Αγέν[ν]ητος and γεν[ν]ητός and Kindred Words in Eusebius and the Early Arians', *JTS*, XXIV (1923), 486 ff.

ἀρχιτεκτόνημα, in a passage which makes quite clear the fundamentally cosmological nature of his theology:

Everything that has ever existed or now exists derives its being from the One who alone exists and pre-exists (ἐξ ἑνός τοῦ μόνου ὄντος καὶ προόντος), who also said, 'I am the One-who-is', because, you will see, as the only One-who-is and who is always, he himself is the cause of existence to all those to whom he has given existence from himself by his will and power, and has bestowed on all things their existence and powers and forms richly and ungrudgingly from himself. And then he establishes as the first of all things his offspring (γέννημα), the first-born Wisdom, completely intellectual and rational and all-wise, or rather, absolute Intelligence and absolute Reason and absolute Wisdom (αὐτόνουν καὶ αὐτόλογον καὶ αὐτοσοφίαν), and if it is right to conceive anything else among originated things that is absolute Beauty and absolute Goodness (αὐτόκαλον καὶ αὐτοάγαθον) he himself lays it as the first foundation of the things that are afterwards to be made. He is the perfect creation (δημιούργημα) of a perfect creator, the wise building (ἀρχιτεκτόνημα) of a wise builder, the good offspring (γέννημα) of a good Father, and to those who should afterwards receive existence through him he is certainly Friend and Guardian, Saviour and Physician and the Helmsman who holds the rudder-lines of the creation of the universe.[1]

Although he does not use the word κτίσμα, Eusebius makes it clear in his *Letter to Alexander of Alexandria*,[2] written shortly after the outbreak of the controversy, that he has no objection to applying it to the Son. He submits that Alexander has failed to understand what the Arians mean, when in their *Confessio Fidei* presented to Alexander, they had declared that the Son is 'a perfect creature, but not as one of the creatures' (κτίσμα τοῦ θεοῦ τέλειον, ἀλλ᾽ οὐχ ὡς ἓν τῶν κτισμάτων).[3]

In the long quotation above, as well as in those quoted earlier, the influence of Philo can be clearly seen. The extent of Eusebius' indebtedness to the Alexandrian Jew has never been fully assessed, but on almost every page of *Demonstratio Evangelica*, Philonic influence is unmistakable. Eusebius has modified the teaching of Origen by making his Logos-concept almost completely Philonic. By doing so Eusebius weakens Origen's doc-

---

[1] *Dem. Ev.* IV, 1–2, 145 d–146 b (*GCS*, VI, 151, 23–152, 7).
[2] Opitz. *Urk.* 7.
[3] *Urk.* 6 (12, 9 f.), quoted by Eusebius, *Urk.* 7 (14, 10 f.).

trine of eternal generation in which the Logos is acknowledged as co-eternal with God and as being continually generated by God. It is true that Eusebius declares the Logos to be eternal, but he thinks of eternity in temporal terms, in terms of 'before' and 'after'. Only once does he apply the adjective ἀΐδιος to the Logos (Son), reserving it elsewhere for God; he prefers to say that the Logos (Son) was 'begotten before all ages':

The Logos...did not co-exist unoriginately (ἀγενήτως) with the Father, but has been begotten from the Father as his only-begotten Son before all ages (πρὸ πάντων τῶν αἰωνίων)...For neither was he existent with the Father without beginning (ἀνάρχως), since the one is unbegotten and the other begotten, and one is Father and the other Son. All would agree that a father must exist before and precede his son.[1]

Similarly in his *Letter to Alexander*:

For if the One-who-is (ὁ ὤν) is one, it is plain that everything which is from him is also after him. If, however, he is not only One-who-is, but the Son also was One-who-is, how did the One-who-is beget the One-who-is, for then there would be Two-who-are?[2]

That is, the Logos is begotten 'before all ages' but he is not co-eternal with God. 'The eternity of the Son does not mean a co-eternity with the Father...The Father has eternity in the proper sense; the Son, as begotten, has it in a derivative sense.'[3] The Son's essence (οὐσία or ὑπόστασις), being derived from that of the Father, is both *inferior* and *posterior* to the Father's; so also the Son's eternity, being derivative, is *inferior* and *posterior* to that of the Father.

Eusebius identifies the Logos with the only-begotten Son of God, yet the regulative concept of his whole theology is the Logos-concept, the notion of an intermediate being between the Absolute and the created order. This comes out quite clearly in the Creed of Caesarea which he submitted to the Nicene Council as proof of his orthodoxy, the christological clause of which reads: 'And in one Lord Jesus Christ, the Logos of God, God from God, Light from Light, Life from Life, only-begotten Son, first-born of all creation, begotten from the Father before all ages, through whom all things came to be, etc.'[4] Here the

[1] *Dem. Ev.* v, 1, 215 b–c (*GCS*, VI, 213, 19–30).
[2] *Urk.* 7 (15, 3–6).   [3] Berkhof, *Eusebius von Caesarea*, pp. 75 f.
[4] *Urk.* 22 (43, 10 f.); cf. Ch. 7 below.

primary characterisation of Jesus Christ is Logos, followed by a number of phrases which were part of the common stock of phrases used to describe the relation of the Logos to God, which have their roots in the Logos-theology of the apologetic tradition from Justin Martyr onwards. It is only after this emphasis on the Logos that the title 'Son' is introduced, and then in a phrase which, in context, retains and strengthens the cosmological emphasis of the Creed: 'only-begotten Son, firstborn of all creation, begotten from the Father before all ages, through whom all things came to be'. The emphasis is on the temporal priority of the Logos-Son to the created order and his role as cosmological intermediary in God's activity of creation. The phrase 'begotten from the Father before all ages', which is Eusebius' stock phrase to describe the relation of God to the Logos, Father to Son, does not mean that the Logos-Son was eternally generated from the Father;[1] he did not understand it to mean that the Son is co-eternal with the Father. He assigned to the Son 'semi-eternity' as befitted 'his semi-divine being'.[2] The Creed contained in the Synodal Letter of Antioch avoided the phrase, asserting quite unequivocally the eternity of the Son 'who exists always and did not at one time not exist' (τὸν ἀεὶ ὄντα καὶ οὐ πρότερον οὐκ ὄντα).[3] Nevertheless the phrase 'begotten before all ages', being scriptural, was used universally before the Council of Nicaea, and was used by Alexander of Alexandria himself.[4] Both the Synod of Antioch and the Nicene Council however avoided it, almost certainly because the Arians, placing their own interpretation upon it, could accept it.[5]

[1] We shall see later that the Arians could equally assert that the Son was 'begotten before all ages', without denying their proposition that 'there was once when he was not'. In the *Confessio Fidei*, Arius and his followers say that 'the Son, generated outside of time (ἀχρόνως) by the Father, and created and established before time, did not exist before he was generated' (*Urk.* 6 (13, 8 ff.)). On the whole question cf. Simonetti, *Studi sull'Arianesimo*, pp. 32 ff. Further, for a discussion of Prov. viii. 22 ff. and its connection with Col. i. 13 ff. and Gen. i. 1, cf. W. D. Davies, *Paul and Rabbinic Judaism*, London, 1948, pp. 150 ff. [2] Berkhof, *Eusebius von Cäsarea*, p. 75.
[3] *Urk.* 18 (39, 1). [4] *Urk.* 14 (27, 20).
[5] For a more comprehensive analysis of the contrasting theological emphases of the creeds of Antioch, Caesarea and Nicaea, cf. my article, 'The Creeds of A.D. 325: Antioch, Caesarea, Nicaea', *SJT*, XIII (1960), 278 ff., and ch. 6 below.

An examination of his christology shows how all of Eusebius' thinking about the incarnation begins from the Logos and that for him the incarnation is little more than an appendix to the pedagogic work of the Logos throughout history. Both in *Demonstratio Evangelica* and *Historia Ecclesiastica* he deals with the divinity of Christ first, ascribing to him all the cosmological functions and attributes of the pre-existent Logos who makes his divinity known to men through his activity in creation, in the theophanies of the Old Testament and through the words of the prophets. This divine Logos 'descends to our world and takes possession of our rational nature' (τῆς λογικῆς φύσεως).[1]

Eusebius sets out his doctrine of the incarnation thus:

And since he (*sc.* the Logos) needed a human instrument (ὄργανον) in order to show himself to men and to give true teaching of the knowledge of the Father and of religion (εὐσεβείας) he did not even refuse this way (i.e. the way of incarnation); but presenting himself in our nature, he indeed came among men, showing to all the great wonder, God through a man (θεὸν δι' ἀνθρώπου)... Giving his teaching by tongue and articulate voice to the bodily ears (of men), he manifested himself to all...the Saviour and Benefactor;[2] God the Logos was called the Son of Man and was named Jesus, because he made his approach to us in order to cure and heal the souls of men[3]...And he led the life we lead, in no way forsaking the existence which he had before, preserving the God in the man (ἐν τῷ ἀνθρώπῳ...τὸν θεόν).[4]

The necessity of a human instrument (ὄργανον), mentioned at the beginning of this passage, applies to the whole activity of the Logos in showing himself to men, i.e. to the theophanies of the Old Testament and not specifically to the incarnation. Indeed the significance of the incarnation is almost entirely evaporated by its assimilation to a theory of general revelation. In the whole of *Demonstratio Evangelica* Eusebius refers to John i. 14 on only two occasions. Introducing a juxtaposition of John i. 1–3 and i. 14 he says that John 'sets forth his incarnate visitation to men at the same time as the doctrine of his

---

[1] *Dem. Ev.* IV, 10, 164 *d* (*GCS*, VI, 168, 8 f.).
[2] Cf. *ibid.*, where Eusebius refers to the Logos as σωτὴρ καὶ ἰατρός. On the meaning of σωτήρ for Eusebius, see below, p. 130.
[3] Cf. *Dem. Ev.* IV, 10, 164 *d* (*GCS*, VI, 168, 10).
[4] *Ibid.* IV, 10, 165 *a–c* (*GCS*, VI, 168, 15 ff.).

divinity'.[1] A little later in the same book he says 'the Logos became flesh and took and made divine him who was of David's seed'.[2] In his ante-Nicene writings his interest in christology is almost non-existent; in his more strictly theological post-Nicene writings it becomes clear that his christology belongs to the *Logos–Sarx* schema.[3] The Logos assumes flesh as an instrument through which he may continue his work of teaching men about God and true religion, which he accomplished in former generations in the patriarchs, Moses and the prophets.[4]

It is clear that the saving purpose of the incarnation has a very minor place in Eusebius' theology. For him the essence of Christianity is contained in the cosmological role of the Logos who mediates the creative activity of the supreme God, the Absolute, and in the pedagogical role of instructing men—in every age, even before the incarnation—in true religion and the knowledge of God. For Eusebius 'soteriology is a continuation and even a part of cosmology',[5] 'an appendage to the doctrine of creation'.[6] Discussing the title σωτήρ and its cognates σώзω and σωτηρία which Eusebius frequently uses to describe the relation of the Logos to mankind, Berkhof[7] has shown that for Eusebius σωτήρ denotes the Logos, not as the one who saves men from sin, but as 'the preserver and steersman of the world',[8] and that σωτηρία rarely means 'salvation', but is more frequently related to σύστασις (= stability), i.e. that 'salvation' refers to the Logos' providential care for creation, and is neither primarily concerned with sin nor connected specifically with the incarnation. The Logos may be called 'Saviour' and

[1] vii, 1, 309b (*GCS*, vi, 297, 17 ff.).
[2] vii, 3, 352d (*GCS*, vi, 339, 26 ff.). In *Hist. Ecc.* John i. 14 occurs only once (vii, 25, 18), and that in a quotation from Dionysius of Alexandria! In *c. Marc.* he does not quote John i. 14a at all, and 14b once (i, 32 (*GCS*, iv, 7, 34)). In *de Ecc. Theol.* John i. 14a is quoted only in two places (i, 20 (*GCS*, iv, 82, 11–23) and ii, 18 (*GCS*, iv, 122, 8 and 26)). It is clear that this most crucial christological text played little part in Eusebius' theology.
[3] See below, ch. 8, ii.
[4] For Eusebius' idea that the patriarchs, Moses and the prophets knew the whole truth about the Trinity, see below, ch. 8, ii.
[5] Berkhof, *Eusebius von Caesarea*, p. 115.   [6] *Ibid.* p. 35.
[7] *Ibid.* pp. 92 ff.
[8] Cf. quotation, p. 124, n. 8 above.

'Physician' (σωτὴρ καὶ ἰατρός)[1] because he promises to care for sick souls;[2] 'Saviour' and 'Physician' are synonymous.

In the face of the changing emphasis away from cosmology towards soteriology, Eusebius takes refuge in archaism and clings to a Logos-theology which is at many points more primitive than that of Origen. He makes the distinction between Father and Son so absolute that he loses entirely the conception of the unity of God, except in so far as the Logos, as a second God, is derived from the Absolute. It is significant that in the whole of the *Demonstratio* on no occasion does he quote John x. 30 or xiv. 10. The paradox of the Father–Son relationship within the unity of the godhead is lost in an extreme subordinationism which is almost ditheistic, while the paradox of the incarnation is evaporated by his emphasis on the Logos as the subject of the incarnate life in an extreme form of the *Logos–Sarx* christology. Thus, in the ante-Nicene theology of Eusebius, the inadequacy of the cosmological Logos-concept as the regulative concept of theology becomes quite clear, and it is but a short step to the doctrine of the Arians who severed the few remaining strands by which Eusebius connects the Son with the Father rather than with the creatures.

C. ATHANASIUS

When Peter of Alexandria denied Origen's doctrine of the pre-existence of the soul, theology was faced with two alternatives: *either*, it had to deny the co-eternity of the Son with the Father, *or*, it had to find other grounds on which to maintain the doctrine of eternal generation. Both Eusebius of Caesarea and the Arians chose the former alternative, while Alexander and Athanasius chose the latter, seeking to base the doctrine of eternal generation no longer on cosmology but on soteriology. Berkhof has pointed out[3] that the re-interpretation of the doctrine on this basis involved a radical alteration of the Logos-doctrine, for the Logos is now considered to be eternal and one with the Father for the reason that no incarnate demi-god can restore fallen creation to fellowship with God. Because of

---

[1] *Dem. Ev.* IV, 10, 164 *d* (*GCS*, VI, 168, 10 ff.).
[2] *Ibid.* IV, 10, 165 *a–c* (*GCS*, VI, 168, 15 ff.).
[3] *Eusebius von Caesarea*, p. 75.

this shift in emphasis there is a vast difference between the Logos-doctrine of Athanasius and that of Origen, a difference which involves a total re-orientation of the whole doctrine of God and of the person and work of Christ.

While Athanasius may be 'charmed with the depth of his thought',[1] and while he never openly criticises Origen, his basic approach, method and theology are different from those of Origen, even in his ante-Nicene writings.[2] Both writers make the Prologue of St John's Gospel their starting-point, but there is a vast difference between them in the content which they give to the Logos-concept, and therefore in their interpretation of the Prologue as a whole. Origen interprets the Prologue as cosmology, while Athanasius interprets it as a statement of the nature of God and of his activity towards mankind. They differ in their view of the relation of God to the world. For Origen, it belongs to God's nature to create; not only is the generation of the Logos an eternal process, but so also is the creation of spiritual beings. The life of God consists in the activity of creating. For Athanasius, on the other hand, God lives in himself, transcending his creatures of whom he has no need; 'his life surpasses them, and it is not the creation of the world but the begetting of the Logos which constitutes the divine life'.[3]

For Origen, to create is a necessity of God's being, but God is far removed from the world; therefore God needs an intermediary, the Logos, through whom to create the world of rational beings (λογικοί) who are necessary for his existence as God. For Origen, and for Eusebius of Caesarea, the Logos 'plays the part of a metaphysical hybrid, neither God nor man, but a little of each',[4] 'a mathematical mean (ratio)'[5] between

---

[1] J. B. Berchem, 'Le rôle du Verbe dans l'œuvre de la création et de la sanctification d'après saint Athanase', *Ang*, xv (1938), 204.

[2] It is assumed here that the *contra Gentes* and *de Incarnatione Verbi Dei* were written before the outbreak of the Arian controversy.

(Since the manuscript went to press, Père Charles Kannengiesser has drawn my attention to his arguments for a date *c.* A.D. 336–7 for these two treatises in his article, 'Le témoignage des *Lettres Festales* de saint Athanase sur la date de l'Apologie *Contre les païens, sur l'Incarnation du Verbe*', *RechSR* LII (1964), 91–100. While his arguments carry considerable weight, I am not completely convinced by them.)

[3] L. Bouyer, *L'incarnation et l'église-corps du Christ dans la théologie de saint Athanase*, Paris, 1943, p. 48.   [4] *Ibid.* p. 53.

[5] E. Evans, *Tertullian's Treatise against Praxeas*, pp. 32 ff.

God and the cosmos, an instrument (ὄργανον) which enables God to create the cosmos. For Athanasius, on the contrary, 'the position of the Logos becomes independent again, if one may put it thus, because the position of the Father has become independent again'.[1] The Logos is no longer an intermediate being who bridges a metaphysical gulf between God and his creatures, but the divine mediator who restores to fallen man the image of God[2] and brings men to participate with him in sonship of God through his incarnate activity in the life, death and resurrection of Jesus of Nazareth and through his continued presence in the church as its risen and exalted Lord.[3]

Athanasius rejects the idea that the generation of the Logos is an act of God's will. For him the generation of the Logos (or the begetting of the Son) is an eternal necessity of the life of the godhead irrespective of the divine intention to create other beings.

What, in fact, distinguishes the Athanasian Logos is that he is no longer an instrument, an agent, but an end in himself; and he is an end in himself because it is his generation, and no longer creation, that constitutes the life of God, as a result of Athanasius' deliberate return to the scriptural idea of the living God who has no need of his creatures.[4]

Or, as Loofs says,[5] 'He has overcome the philosophical Logos-doctrine in principle and argues on the basis of the doctrine of salvation (*Heilslehre*)'.

That Athanasius' theology is rooted in soteriology[6] is evident from his two ante-Nicene treatises, *contra Gentes* and *de Incarna-*

---

[1] Bouyer, *L'incarnation*, p. 57.

[2] Cf. R. Bernard, *L'image de Dieu d'après saint Athanase*, Paris, 1952, ch. 1; A. Gaudel, 'La théologie du Logos chez saint Athanase', *RevSR*, IX (1929) 524–39 and XI (1931) 1, 26 ff.

[3] Cf. D. Ritschl, *Memory and Hope: an Inquiry concerning the Presence of Christ*, New York and London, 1967, pp. 86 f.

[4] Bouyer, *L'incarnation*, p. 57.

[5] *Leitfaden*, §3 b.

[6] This assertion is not intended to be a contradiction of Dietrich Ritschl's criticisms of the emphasis on redemption by von Harnack and others. As I read Ritschl's *Athanasius* (*Theologische Studien*, 76), Zürich, 1964, what he rejects, and rightly so, is the equation of 'deification' with 'salvation', made by many previous interpreters of Athanasius' theology. Ritschl's promised 'longer study in English' is keenly awaited.

tione Verbi Dei.[1] He begins with a clear statement of his purpose; he is going to set forth:

a few points on the faith of Christ...namely, the faith of Christ the Saviour...the one fact of the cross of Christ which is the subject of scoffing among the Gentiles... which has not been a disaster but the healing of creation...He who ascended the cross is the Logos of God and the Saviour of the world.[2]

Like Paul he asserts that he is proclaiming 'Christ crucified' (1 Cor. i. 23; ii. 2); yet, like Paul also he includes within this proclamation the whole of the gospel: the incarnation, ministry, death, resurrection and exaltation of Christ. His primary interest, like that of Paul and John, is not cosmology but soteriology, the saving work of God in Christ. He does not argue from creation to salvation, but from man's need for salvation to the incarnation or, perhaps more correctly, he is going to argue the necessary connection between man's plight as a sinner and God's act in Christ to restore man in the image of God in which he was originally created.[3] Within this argument the doctrine of creation through the Logos–Son becomes but the first step in the mystery of the Gospel, but it is no longer the key to the gospel.[4]

Whereas Origen's attention seems to have been fixed on the first three verses of the Prologue of St John, and his doctrine of the Logos dominated by them, for Athanasius, on the other hand, it is verses 10–14 which are supremely important. His attention is riveted on Jesus Christ, the Logos who 'became flesh and dwelt among us' (i. 14) who gave 'to as many as welcomed him the power to become the children of God' (i. 13). His early treatises are in fact an expansion of the Prologue in the form of a spiritual history of mankind or of God's saving

[1] With Ritschl (*op. cit.* p. 21) and others I accept an ante-Nicene date for these treatises.

[2] *c. Gentes*, 1 (*PG*, xxv, 4–5).

[3] Cf. Ritschl, *Athanasius*, ch. II. I use 'salvation' in its widest sense in discussing Athanasius' theology to include all of the ideas the New Testament uses to describe 'salvation'—redemption, justification, adoption, reconciliation, the gift of eternal life, etc.

[4] On the relation between creation and redemption (or reconciliation) in the New Testament, and particularly in St Paul's letters (although the argument applies equally to St John), cf. Stig Hanson, *The Unity of the Church in the New Testament*, pp. 109 ff.

purpose throughout the ages culminating in his self-revelation in the Christ-event. He asserts the eternal unity of the Logos with God, while assuming always the distinction of the Logos from the Father as mediator of all the Father's activity towards mankind. He asserts the presence of the Logos in creation, yet is careful to distinguish his view both from the Stoic idea of the 'spermatic Logos' immanent in the minds of men as 'reason' and from the analogy of the Logos with a human word comprised of syllables and sounds. For Athanasius the Logos is 'the living and powerful Logos of the good God, the God of the universe, the very Logos which is God (John i. 1 c)'.[1] Made in the image of God, man is intended for knowledge of God and communion with him, but in perversity man has turned away from this knowledge and fallen into idolatry, lust and corruption. Although he nowhere quotes John i. 10 in these treatises, they read like a commentary on this verse in conjunction with Romans i. 18 ff. The Logos 'was in the world, and the world was made through him, and the world did not recognise him' (John i. 10); as a result man has fallen under the wrath of God, meriting the curse of death which is the punishment of apostasy. Yet God could not leave his creatures to perish. In mercy and goodness he has acted to re-create fallen man and to restore him to his original nature. The incarnation of the Logos is God's act to restore mankind to its true life of fellowship with himself.

One passage from the *de Incarnatione* is sufficient to show how closely Athanasius connects the incarnation and the atonement:

The Logos saw that the corruption of men could be undone in no other way than by death as a necessary condition. For this reason, while it was impossible for him to suffer death—for he is immortal and the Son of the Father—he takes to himself a body capable of death, so that, by participating in the Logos who is above all, it might be worthy to die instead of all and might remain incorruptible because of the Logos which had come to dwell in it, and that henceforth corruption might be stayed from all by the grace of the resurrection...For, being over all, the Logos of God naturally, by offering his own temple and corporeal instrument for the life of all, satisfied the debt by his death. And thus he...naturally clothed all with incorruption by the promise of the resurrection...Now that he has come to our realm and taken up his abode in one body

---

[1] *c. Gentes*, 40 (*PG*, xxv, 81).

among his equals, henceforth the whole conspiracy of the enemy against mankind is checked, and the corruption of death is destroyed which previously was prevailing against them. For the race of men would have gone to ruin, if the Lord and Saviour of all, the Son of God, had not come forth to put an end to death.[1]

The Logos became incarnate so that death's power over the human race might be broken. 'Now we die no longer as men under a sentence, but as men who rise from the dead we await the general resurrection of all...This, then, is the first reason for the Saviour's incarnation'.[2]

Athanasius sees, however, that payment of the debt and destruction of the power of death are negative rather than positive. Simple annulment of the sentence, even though it involve the death of the Son of God, does not in itself affect the sinful nature of man. Salvation involves something positive as well, a radical change in human nature. Man must receive again the capacity to know God which he has lost through his sin. This aspect of salvation Athanasius discusses in terms of the doctrine of the Image of God. Through the incarnation of the Logos who is 'the Image of God', 'the Image of the Father',[3] man is re-created or renewed in the Image of God so that he may be capable of perceiving the Logos, who *is* the Image of God, and through that Image come to know the Father whose Image he is. When he creates men, God, in his goodness gives them a share in his own Image, our Lord Jesus Christ, and makes them after his own Image and after his likeness, so that, through grace such as this, perceiving the Image, that is the Logos of the Father, they may be able to get an idea of the Father, and knowing their maker live the happy and truly blessed life.[4] By this gift of a share in the Image men were made λογικός, but they refused to acknowledge God and 'loaded themselves all the more with evils and sins, so that they no longer seemed λογικούς but from their manner of life are to be reckoned ἀλόγους'.[5] If man is to be enabled to know God again, he must be changed from ἄλογος to λογικός, that is, he must again share in the Logos, the Image of God. This could be achieved only by the presence among men of the very Image

---

[1] *de Inc.*, 9 (*PG*, xxv, 112). [2] *Ibid.* 10 (*PG*, xxv, 113).
[3] *c. Gentes*, 2 (*PG*, xxv, 6 f.). [4] *de Inc.* 11 (*PG*, xxv, 116).
[5] *Ibid.* 12 (*PG*, xxv, 117).

of God, Jesus Christ. 'Therefore the Logos came in his own person (δι' ἑαυτοῦ), so that, since he was the image of the Father, he might be able to create afresh the man made after his Image.'[1] When Jesus said to Nicodemus, 'Except a man be born again' (John iii. 3), he was speaking of 'the soul born again and created again in the likeness of God's Image'.[2] Therefore the Logos was born and seen as a man and died and rose again in order to recall men from their sin and 'teach them about his own true Father'.[3] By the life he lived and the deeds he did as a man he sought 'to persuade men that he is not a man only, but also God and the Logos and Wisdom of the true God'.[4]

Thus Athanasius emphasises the double aspect of the atonement wrought through the incarnate Logos, Jesus Christ, what he calls 'both his works of love: firstly, removing death from us and renewing us, and secondly, being unseen and invisible, in manifesting and making himself known by his works to be the Logos of the Father'.[5] After discussing the works of Jesus Christ—his miracles,[6] his death on the Cross,[7] his resurrection[8]—Athanasius goes on to refute Jewish[9] and Gentile objections.[10] At the end of the treatise he impresses on the reader the necessity of studying the scriptures, of being prepared for the second coming of Christ, 'no longer in lowliness, but in his own glory, no longer in humble guise, but in his own magnificence'.[11] Above all he emphasises that 'an honourable life is needed and a pure soul and that virtue which is according to Christ',[12] if one is to be able to search the scriptures and understand them rightly. Throughout the whole of both treatises, his interest is religious and evangelical.

Nowhere in these treatises does Athanasius argue either for the unity (and co-eternity) of the Son with the Father or for the distinction between them. He simply assumes both, for both are clearly implied throughout. There is no hint of

[1] Ibid. 13 (PG, xxv, 120).   [2] Ibid. 14 (PG, xxv, 120).
[3] Ibid. 15 (PG, xxv, 124).
[4] Ibid. 16 (PG, xxv, 124). For a full discussion of Athanasius' doctrine of the Imago Dei, cf. R. Bernard, L'image de Dieu.
[5] Ibid. 16 (PG, xxv, 124–5).   [6] Ibid. 18 f. (PG, xxv, 128 f.).
[7] Ibid. 20–5 (PG, xxv, 129–40).   [8] Ibid. 26–32 (PG, xxv, 140 ff.).
[9] Ibid. 33–40 (PG, xxv, 152 ff.).   [10] Ibid. 41–5 (PG, xxv, 168 ff.).
[11] Ibid. 56 (PG, xxv, 196).   [12] Ibid. 57 (PG, xxv, 197).

identification of the Son with the Father, as in Sabellianism, nor of the subordinationism found in Clement, Origen and Eusebius of Caesarea. That is, Athanasius, at this stage, simply accepts the first Johannine paradox as a presupposition of his thought demanded by his faith in Jesus Christ as Saviour and Lord.

In the same way, Athanasius presupposes the fact of the incarnation as a real incarnation of God in man. It may be true, as a number of scholars have argued,[1] that Athanasius uses language which implies an incomplete human psychology of Christ, at least until after the Synod of Alexandria in A.D. 362, but his preoccupation in the Arian controversy with the full divinity of the Son may have made him unaware of the importance of this question until then. Nevertheless, his understanding of the soteriological significance of the Christ-event points beyond the *Logos-Sarx* or *Logos-Soma* terminology which he uses towards a *God-man* christology.

He identifies the Logos with Jesus Christ, the Son of God and Saviour of men, and nowhere gives to the Logos-concept any content other than that given to it by St John. He does not interpret the Prologue either in the light of current philosophical speculations about a subordinate or second God, or in the light of the Old Testament concepts of personified Word and Wisdom, but rather in the light of the Son-concept of St John's Gospel and in the light of the gospel of salvation proclaimed in the whole New Testament.

At the beginning of the Arian controversy, then, Athanasius, who was to become the greatest antagonist of the Arians and the stoutest defender of the church's faith, has grasped more firmly than his contemporaries the New Testament witness to the person and work of Christ, and is well armed for the battle. The controversy, itself, sharpens his theological position, but does not alter his fundamental emphasis, and in the course of it he draws heavily on the armoury of St John's Gospel for the weapons with which to defeat his opponents.

[1] Notably M. Richard, 'Saint Athanase et la psychologie du Christ selon les Ariens', *MSR*, IV (1947), 5–54. Cf. also A. Grillmeier, *Christ in Christian Tradition*, pp. 193 ff.; Liébaert, *L'incarnation*, pp. 132 ff.

PART II

JOHANNINE CHRISTOLOGY AND THE ARIAN CONTROVERSY

CHAPTER 5

THE ARIAN CONTROVERSY
BEFORE NICAEA

There is no complete agreement about the theological antecedents of Arius. Recent articles...have not closed the debate whether Arianism can be explained as a derivative of Origenism, or whether some independent influence must be recognized.[1]

G. C. Stead has recently pointed out that the attempt to solve the problem of Arian origins is beset by two difficulties, both due to the paucity of the information available to us: (i) our knowledge of Lucian of Antioch and his theology is too limited for us to be able to estimate the extent of Arius' debt to him, and (ii) we have too little information about the philosophy current in Alexandria during this period.[2] Despite these limitations of our knowledge, and the further limitation indicated by M. F. Wiles[3] that 'our knowledge of the teaching of Arius is drawn for the most part from short doctrinal fragments chosen for polemical purposes by his opponents',[4] we are forced either to refuse to pass any judgment—and this is difficult to do because of the critical nature of the controversy which arose over Arius' teaching—or, on the basis of the fragmentary

[1] G. C. Stead, 'The Platonism of Arius', *JTS*, N.S. xv (1964), 16. This article is a response to my articles, 'Logos and Son in Origen, Arius and Athanasius', *SP*, II (*TU*, 64), 282–7, and 'The Origins of Arianism', *JTS*, N.S. IX (1958), 103–11, and to the criticism of them offered by M. F. Wiles, 'In Defence of Arius', *JTS*, N.S. XIII (1962), 339–47.

[2] *Loc. cit.*

[3] 'In Defence of Arius', p. 346.

[4] Wiles uses this fact to suggest that we thus get only an extremely biased view of Arius' teaching, and cites the parallel of the distorted view we get of Antiochene christology if we rely entirely on extracts quoted by their opponents. However, another parallel pointing in exactly the opposite direction may be used: recently discovered gnostic writings tend to demonstrate the fairness with which their opponents (Irenaeus, Tertullian, etc.) have outlined the main points of their teaching. In the absence of any complete Arian writings and until such writings are discovered we can do nothing other than use the little information we have, fragmentary though it may be.

evidence we have, to form the hypothesis which accounts most adequately for that evidence.

In two studies published some years ago[1] I put forward the hypothesis that there are some elements in Arian teaching whose derivation is difficult to trace to the Alexandrian tradition stemming from Origen, and that these elements are more probably derived from the Antiochene tradition, from Paul of Samosata through Lucian of Antioch. The arguments I adduced to support this hypothesis have been criticised by M. F. Wiles, who has argued that my 'claim that Arianism cannot be understood in terms of a purely Alexandrian heritage has not been established'.[2] He makes five main points against arguments which I used to support my hypothesis:

(i) Arius' literalistic exegesis could have been derived from Peter of Alexandria who, as we have seen already,[3] reacted strongly against Origen's allegorical exegesis.

This possibility, of course, must be admitted, yet there is no evidence that Arius received any theological education in Alexandria, while, on the other hand, it is certain that he was trained for the priesthood in Antioch under Lucian before going to minister in Alexandria. Further, the probability that Arius was excommunicated by Peter for his connection with the Melitian schism[4] after having been associated with him for some time tells us nothing at all about any possible theological connection between Arius and Peter.

(ii) My contrast between Arius' extreme monotheistic emphasis and the pluralism of Origen is misleading and unfair to Origen whose pluralism is balanced by an emphasis on the oneness and soleness of God, from which Arius could have derived his monotheistic emphasis.

Again it must be pointed out that the Antiochene tradition had refused to allow 'personal' distinctions within the godhead, setting forth an extreme monarchianism of the dynamic variety, and this had been strongly opposed by the Origenist bishops who had deposed Paul of Samosata in A.D. 268.[5]

---

[1] Articles cited in p. 141, n. 1.   [2] 'In Defence of Arius', p. 343.

[3] Cf. pp. 111 f. above.

[4] Which may help to explain the alliance between Arians and Melitians testified to in numerous places, e.g. Athanasius, *Hist. Ar.* 78–9.

[5] Cf. J. N. D. Kelly, *Early Christian Doctrines*, p. 158.

Arius' monotheism is closer to this monarchian tradition than to the pluralistic monotheism of Origen, and his 'subordinationism' is of an entirely different kind from that of Origen.

(iii) The Arian distinction between the Logos and the Son which I argued was fundamental to Arianism and foreign to the Alexandrian tradition is similarly only an extension of Origen's emphasis on 'the secondary derivative and subordinate nature of the Son'.[1]

The manner in which Wiles demonstrates his contention does not account for Arius' de-personalisation or de-hypostatisation of the Logos. On the other hand, in the Antiochene tradition the Logos was assumed to be impersonal as an attribute belonging to God. Arius said that the Son could only be said to be Logos 'in a lesser, relative sense (καταχρηστικῶς)'[2] or, as Kelly says, Logos was only 'a courtesy title' of the Son.[3] This is completely in line with the extreme monarchianism of Arius and in clear opposition to the pluralistic monotheism of Origen in which the Logos–Son is a personal being distinct from the Father and eternally generated by him, even though subordinate to him.

(iv) My agreement with Gwatkin's statement that Arianism is 'utterly illogical' does not do justice to the logic of Arius' argument.

This criticism I am prepared to accept without cavil, and indeed I am prepared to go farther than Wiles and say that in fact Arius tried to be too logical, and by doing so removed entirely the element of paradox and mystery which is inherent in Christian faith in Christ as Son of God and Word made flesh.

(v) Finally Wiles disputes my claim that the victory of Athanasius over Arius was a victory of soteriology over cosmology.

At this point I see the radical difference between Arius and Athanasius. Arius' theology is speculative and rationalistic. He uses a number of carefully selected biblical texts chosen to fit his philosophical presuppositions, and uses them as premises on which to develop his argument,[5] and it is only as a system built on extra-biblical foundations that Arianism can be

---

[1] Wiles, 'In Defence of Arius', p. 342.   [2] *Idem.*
[3] *Early Christian Doctrines*, p. 229.
[4] Cf. my article, 'The Exegesis of Scripture and the Arian Controversy', *BJRL*, XLI (1959), 415 f.

understood. His system allows little room for faith in the biblical and traditional sense of the word. S. Laeuchli[1] has demonstrated this clearly, pointing to the difference in terms used by Arius and Athanasius. Arius continually uses the verbs 'teach', 'say', 'think', and begins his creed 'we know' (οἴδαμεν); the terms Athanasius uses are on a different level: 'confess', 'receive', terms which, as Laeuchli points out[2] represent 'an involvement of faith'. Arius' doctrine is the product of a rationalistic philosophy; Athanasius' is derived from his existence as a Christian involved in faith in a relationship with God which can only be confessed and received. Athanasius, like Alexander before him, feels that in the controversy his whole existence as a Christian is at stake, that Arianism cuts away the foundations of all that he confesses as a Christian concerning God's saving, redeeming and reconciling act in Christ. Granted, some of Athanasius' arguments to support his soteriology may not convince us today, but beneath them lies the firm conviction that Arianism undermines the Gospel as 'the power of God unto salvation'.

G. C. Stead[3] has criticised my hypothesis from a different angle; he argues with Wiles that it is unnecessary to look beyond Alexandria for the parentage of Arianism, and postulates that it is to be found in the philosophical debates going on in Alexandria. That these may have played a part in the formation of Arius' teaching cannot be denied, but to acknowledge this does not rule out Lucianic influence. Both Stead and Wiles overlook a number of historical facts, and these, I believe, support my hypothesis rather than theirs:

(i) Arius appears to have gained little support for his doctrinal position within the Egyptian church. What support he did receive came from the schismatic Melitians, and that was given for political rather than theological reasons. Further it was, it appears, to the Melitians that Eusebius of Nicomedia appealed for support against Athanasius on a number of occasions.[4] Had Arius' theology been a natural and logical outgrowth from the

---

[1] 'The Case of Athanasius against Arius', *CTM*, xxx (1959), 403 ff.

[2] *Ibid.* pp. 405–6.   [3] 'The Platonism of Arius.'

[4] Socrates, *Hist. Eccl.* I, 29; Theodoret, *Hist. Eccl.* I, 25–6. On the possibility of Melitian support for the Arians, see H. Nordberg, *Athanasius and the Emperor*, Helsinki, 1963, pp. 10 ff.

Alexandrian tradition, some theological support from fellow Alexandrian presbyters and bishops could have been expected, but there is no evidence that there was any.

(ii) The theological support which Arius did receive came from his fellow *alumni* of the school of Lucian,[1] in particular from Eusebius of Nicomedia, Asterius the Sophist and Paulinus of Tyre; and after Arius' death it was his fellow Lucianists who carried on the battle. This fact, strongly attested by all the available evidence, points clearly to a common theological understanding which it is not unreasonable to trace to the influence of their teacher Lucian.

(iii) In all the troubles which were to befall Athanasius during his long episcopate, he had the greater part of his church loyally behind him. Intrigues against him within his see appear to have been instigated by 'foreign agents' sent in by Eusebius of Nicomedia who used the Melitian schismatics as his tools in fomenting trouble. Bishops sent in to take his place when he was sent into exile met with hostility, while Athanasius on his return was greeted with popular enthusiasm. In other words, internal opposition within Alexandria was political; theological opposition to Athanasius came from without and was led by the pupils of Lucian.

For these reasons, the probability that Arianism had its roots in the soil of Lucian's school in Antioch remains strong, and Arius' indebtedness to Lucian is the hypothesis which accounts most adequately for the available evidence. Yet this is not to say that Arius has close affinities with the traditional Antiochene theology. The opposition of Antiochene theologians like Eustathius of Antioch and Marcellus of Ancyra, as well as that of the Antiochene bishops who met at the Synod of Antioch in A.D. 325 a few months before the Council of Nicaea, makes it abundantly clear that the theology of the Arians and of their Lucianist leaders was out of step with the accepted theology of the Antiochene church.

Whatever may be the parentage of Arianism we have sufficient, though fragmentary, evidence of the grounds on which the opening skirmishes were fought between Arius and his supporters on the one side and Alexander of Alexandria and the

---

[1] In *Letter of Arius to Eusebius of Nicomedia* (*Urk.* 1), Arius addresses Eusebius as 'my fellow Lucianist' (συλλουκιανιστά) (p. 3, line 7).

Antiochene bishops on the other. Arius' doctrine aroused immediate opposition, not only from his bishop in Alexandria, but also from those who, like Marcellus, tried to remain faithful to the old Antiochene tradition, or who, like Eustathius, were endeavouring to re-orientate Antiochene theology towards the new emphasis on the Father–Son relationship. On the other hand, Arius received ardent support from Eusebius of Nicomedia, and in the initial stages from Eusebius of Caeasrea whose theology was an extreme form of the subordinationist strand in Origen's theology.[1]

The documents which come from the hand of Alexander, the *Depositio Arii* (*Urk.* 4*b*),[2] and his *Letter to Alexander of Thessalonica* (or Byzantium) (*Urk.* 14), give a clear indication of the theology on the basis of which the Alexandrian bishop opposed Arius,[3] and taken together with the documents which come from the hands of Arius and his supporters also give a reasonably clear picture of the theology which aroused the opposition of Alexander and of the Antiochene bishops. Further, the theology of Alexander is one in which the Johannine witness to the Father–Son relationship in the godhead is central and regulative.

From the very beginning of the controversy it was St John's Gospel, the pre-eminent New Testament witness to the divine Father–Son relationship, which provided Arius' opponents with their most powerful arguments. In the *Depositio Arii*, for instance, the chief arguments against Arian propositions take the form: 'What man who hears John saying..., does not condemn those who say...?' The Arian documents provide little evidence on Arian exegesis of St John's Gospel: only John viii. 42 is quoted. The short fragments of the letters of Eusebius of Caesarea con-

---

[1] It seems highly probable that the two main factors which have led to the supposition that Arianism was essentially a left-wing form of Origenism are (i) the fact that Arius was a presbyter of Alexandria (despite the fact that he had received his theological education in the school of Lucian of Antioch) and (ii) the fact that Arius, at least at the beginning of the controversy, received strong support from the left-wing Origenist, Eusebius of Caesarea.

[2] Robertson (*Athanasius*, *NPNF*, p. 68), following J. H. Newman, is inclined to accept the view that *Dep. Arii* was composed by Athanasius as secretary to Alexander.

[3] The best study of Alexander's theology is that by M. Simonetti, *Studi sull'Arianesimo*, ch. III.

tain three Johannine quotations: a conflation of John vi. 44 with xiv. 28, i. 1 and xvii. 3. The Alexandrian documents, on the other hand, contain twenty quotations and direct references to Johannine texts: John i. 1 (twice); i. 1–3; i. 3 (twice); i. 7; i. 18 (twice); v. 23; x. 15 (twice); x. 30 (twice); xiv. 8, 9; xiv. 9; xiv. 10; xiv. 23; xiv. 28 (twice); xvi. 23. In these early stages of the controversy, then, as indeed throughout the controversy, the evidence is very one-sided. In his letters Alexander opposes Johannine exegesis, not to Arian exegesis of the same texts, but to Arian theological propositions. The only satisfactory procedure, therefore, is to take the Arian propositions one by one, discussing Alexander's use of the Fourth Gospel in refuting them, and seeking, wherever possible, to deduce what the Arian interpretation must have been. Because of the interdependence of Arian propositions one with another, it is impossible to keep strictly to the refutation of any one particular proposition; the refutation of one proposition has implications in opposition to other propositions.

(i) ' *There was once when the Son was not* ' (ἦν ποτε ὅτε οὐκ ἦν ὁ υἱὸς τοῦ θεοῦ) (*Urk.* 14 (21, 8)).

' *He was not before he was begotten* ' (οὐκ ἦν πρὸ τοῦ γεννηθῆναι) (*Urk.* 6 (13, 9 f.)).

' *The Son has a beginning* ' (ἀρχὴν ἔχει ὁ υἱός) (*Urk.* 1 (3, 4)).

The strict monotheism from which the Arians started did not allow them to think of distinctions within the godhead; the Supreme God is alone unbegotten, alone eternal, alone without beginning (μόνον ἀγέννητον, μόνον ἀΐδιον, μόνον ἄναρχον).[1] If there is a Son of God he must be posterior to the Father, he must have a beginning, and therefore cannot be eternal.

Against this Arian doctrine Alexander sets John i. 1*a*: 'What man who hears John saying, "In the beginning was the Logos", does not condemn those who say, "There was once when he was not"?'[2] In view of Arius' distinction between the Logos and the Son, this argument does not directly refute his proposition. The possibility that Alexander has failed to understand the distinction is ruled out, however, for he explicitly refuses to accept it, setting forth his arguments on the basis of the identity of the Logos and the Son. He later asks, 'How, if the Son is the Logos and the Wisdom of God, was

---

[1] *Urk.* 6 (12, 4 f.).   [2] *Urk.* 4*b* (8, 18 ff.).

there once when he was not?', a question which he himself answers thus, 'That would be equal to saying that God was once without Logos and without Wisdom' (ἄλογος καὶ ἄσοφος).[1] For Alexander, John i. 1*a* testifies to the eternity of the Logos (Son), while for Arius this verse would refer only to God's own Logos, God's attribute of reason, and not to the Son, who is inaccurately (καταχρηστικῶς) called *Logos*.

Alexander also appeals to John i. 18 as an argument against this proposition which denies the eternity of the Son, and against the view that the Son was created out of nothing (ἐξ οὐκ ὄντων). Against these two views, John 'taught sufficiently when he wrote thus concerning him, "The only-begotten Son, who is in the bosom of the Father". This divine teacher, taking care to point to two things undivided from each other, the Father and the Son, especially mentioned him who is in the bosom of the Father.'[2] The phrase 'in the bosom of the Father' means that the Son is undivided from the Father, that he co-exists eternally with the Father, and that the Father was never without the Son.

Alexander again quotes John i. 1 in opposition to the Arian denial of the eternity of the Son, this time linking it with John i. 3: 'In the beginning was the Logos, and the Logos was with God, and the Logos was God...All things were made through him, and without him was made not even one thing.'[3] Alexander says that in these verses St John

is making plain the Son's own peculiar subsistence...For if all things were made through him, how is it that he who gave existence to all things that were made could ever at any time not exist himself? ...He shows that there is no interval between the Father and the Son, the mind being unable to imagine this even with some mental effort...The most pious John, having perceived further that the word 'was',[4] when applied to the Logos, goes far beyond the understanding of originate beings, did not consider himself worthy

---

[1] *Ibid.* (9, 4 ff.).   [2] *Urk.* 14 (22, 5 ff.).

[3] *Ibid.* (22, 10 ff.). In the first three centuries John i. 3 is always quoted as ending at οὐδε ἕν, and the ὃ γέγονεν is placed at the beginning of verse 4; the first quotation of verse 3 with the ending ὃ γέγονεν appears in Adamantius, *de Recta Fide* (*GCS*, ed. W. H. van den Sande Bakhuysen, 172, 18 f.) which was written *c.* A.D. 300 (cf. B. Altaner, *Patrologie*, 180). The best discussion of the punctuation is by B. F. Westcott, *The Gospel acc. to St John*, *in loc.* The punctuation is of no significance in the Arian controversy.

[4] I.e. in 'In the beginning *was* the Logos'.

to speak of his genesis or creation...; not that he was unbegotten (for one is the unbegotten, the Father), but that the inexpressible subsistence of the only-begotten God is beyond the keenest insight of the evangelists, and perhaps even of the angels.[1]

The Arians appear to have interpreted John i. 3 to mean that the Son was the only creature created directly by the hand of God, and that through him as an instrument God created all the rest of the creatures. To this Alexander replies that he who gave existence to all creatures, that is the Son through whom all things were created, must have always existed himself.

In the course of his argument against the Arian denial of the eternity of the Son, Alexander takes the opportunity to answer a charge which both Arius and Eusebius of Caesarea had levelled against him, namely that he had taught that 'the Son co-exists unbegottenly with God' (ἀγεννήτως τῷ θεῷ),[2] and that the Son 'is eternal or co-eternal or co-unbegotten with the Father' (ἀΐδιος ἢ συναΐδιος ἢ συναγέννητος τῷ πατρί).[3] Eusebius of Caesarea argued, and the Arians would have agreed most heartily, that if the Son and the Father co-exist and are co-eternal one cannot be Father and the other Son:

for two beings co-existing equally in the same way as each other are thought to be equal in honour, and...either both are unbegotten or both are begotten. But neither of these is true; for neither can the unbegotten be both nor the begotten be both (ἀγέννητα ἢ ἑκάτερα γεννητά. ἀλλ᾽ οὐδέτερον τούτων ἀληθές· οὔτε γὰρ τὸ ἀγέννητον οὔτε τὸ γεννητὸν ἀμφότερον ἂν εἴη).[4]

In reply Alexander insists that co-eternity does not imply that both are unbegotten or that both are begotten; the Father alone is unbegotten, while the Son is 'the only-begotten God' (John i. 18).[5] He interprets the phrase 'the only-begotten God' as indicating the uniqueness of the Son's generation by and from the Father; being unique, the generation of the Son defies description in human language and perhaps even in the language of the angels.

It appears that at first the Arians declared that there was

---

[1] *Urk.* 14 (22, 9 ff.).   [2] *Urk.* 1 (2, 1).
[3] *Urk.* 6 (13, 10 f.).   [4] *Urk.* 3 (4, 4 ff.).
[5] At the beginning of the fourth century, the variants ὁ μονογενὴς θεός and ὁ μονογενὴς υἱός occur frequently in quotations of John i. 18, even within the works of the same writer; cf. Hort, *Two Dissertations.*

a time when the Son was not, but under the pressure of the controversy withdrew the word χρόνος, and declared that the Son was created apart from time. Alexander points out that the withdrawal of this word makes no difference to their argument:

The phrase 'he was not' must either refer to time or to some interval of the ages. If then it is true that 'all things were made through him' (John i. 3 *a*), it is plain that every age and time and interval and the 'when' in which the 'was not' is found also were made through him. Is it not absurd to say that there was a time when he who created times and ages and seasons, with which the 'was not' has been confused, was not? For it would be stupid and the height of ignorance to say that the cause of any created thing can be posterior to the creation thereof.[1]

Alexander and the Arians, then, have a fundamentally different view of time and eternity; for the Arians, eternity is an infinite extension of time, so that it is possible to speak of 'before' and 'after' in the pre-temporal sphere of eternity. For Alexander, on the contrary, it is absurd to speak of 'before' and 'after' when referring to eternity; if time is one of the things created through the Son, the Son himself must be pre-temporal and therefore eternal; if the Son is eternal, he must be co-eternal with the Father, even though, as Son, he is said to be 'begotten' and the Father, as Father, is said to be 'unbegotten'.

(ii) '*The Son is not like the Father according to essence*' (οὔτε δὲ ὅμοιος κατ' οὐσίαν τῷ πατρί ἐστιν).[2]

'*The Logos is foreign and alien to and isolated from the essence of God*' (ξένος τε καὶ ἀλλότριος καὶ ἀπεσχοινισμένος ἐστιν ὁ λόγος τῆς τοῦ θεοῦ οὐσίας).[3]

The presupposition from which Arius commences, namely that the godhead is an indivisible unity which admits of no internal differentiation or distinction, forces him to argue not only that there was a time when the Son did not exist, but also that if there is a 'Son' of God he cannot be 'from God' or 'from the essence of God', for that would be to acknowledge that the godhead is divisible. Alexander's statement that 'the Son is from God himself' (ἐξ αὐτοῦ τοῦ θεοῦ ὁ υἱός)[4] savours too much of Valentinian gnosticism, which said that the Off-

[1] *Urk.* 14 (23, 14 ff.). [2] *Urk.* 4*b* (7, 21 f.).
[3] *Ibid.* (8, 3 f.). [4] *Urk.* 1 (2, 3).

spring of God was a projection (προβολή), or of Manichaeism which said that the Offspring is a part which is one in essence with the Father (μέρος ὁμοούσιον τοῦ πατρὸς τὸ γέννημα) or of Sabellianism which divided the Monad and spoke of the 'Son–Father' (τὴν μονάδα διαιρῶν υἱοπάτορα εἶπεν), or of the heresy of Hieracas who spoke of one torch lit from another or of a lamp divided into two; Arius says that he had heard Alexander himself condemn all these heresies;[1] but the language which Alexander uses implies that God is mutable and divisible. The essence of God is indivisible, asserts Arius; therefore the Son is not ἐκ τῆς τοῦ θεοῦ οὐσίας, nor is he ὅμοιος κατ' οὐσίαν τῷ πατρί.

This Arian argument brings us to the crux of the controversy. The Arians have asserted not only that the Son is posterior to the Father, but also that he is inferior to the Father according to essence. The Son is not God in the proper sense of the word; if he is God at all, he is an inferior God whose essence is completely other than the essence of the Supreme God. To say anything else is to assert that the essence of God is divisible. Two Old Testament texts which had traditionally been given a christological interpretation were: 'My heart hath uttered a good Logos' (Ps. xlv. 1–LXX: xliv. 1), and 'From the womb before the morning star have I begotten Thee' (Ps. cx. 3–LXX: cix. 3). Alexander appeals to them, arguing that 'womb' and 'heart' mean the same as 'bosom' (John i. 18) and that these terms mean that the Son partakes of the Father's essence.[2] Against this, Arius argues:

If the phrase 'from him' (ἐξ αὐτοῦ), 'from the womb' (ἐκ γαστρός), and 'I have proceeded from the Father and have come' (ἐξῆλθον ἐκ τοῦ πατρός, καὶ ἥκω: John viii. 42) are understood by some to imply a part of him, one in essence, and a projection, then according to them the Father is composite and divisible and mutable and corporeal, and... the incorporeal God suffering in a body (σύνθετος ἔσται ὁ πατὴρ καὶ διαιρετὸς καὶ τρεπτὸς καὶ σῶμα...καὶ σώματι πάσχων ὁ ἀσώματος θεός).[3]

Alexander was quick to perceive that the Arian denial of the Son's participation in the essence of the Father was a denial of the true divinity of the Son; any attempt to speak of the Son as

---

[1] *Urk.* 6 (12, 10—13, 4).   [2] *Urk.* 4*b* (9, 1 f.).
[3] *Urk.* 6 (13, 17 ff.).

God involves, according to Arian premisses, a denial of the oneness of God and leads to ditheism. According to Athanasius,
Arius was quite willing to say that the Logos (Son) is God:
'though he is called God, yet he is not true God'.[1] Similarly,
one of Arius' earliest supporters, Paulinus of Tyre, spoke of
'many Gods' (πολλοὺς θεούς), 'more recent Gods' (νεωτέρους
θεούς), and 'a more human God' (ἀνθρωπινώτερον θεόν).[2]

Alexander argues that the Arians cannot have it both ways:
either the Son is God, as being from the essence of God, *or* he is
not God at all. If the Son is not God in the proper sense of the
word, we have no right to worship him; it is because of his
difference from us men and because he is Son of God by
nature that 'he is worshipped by all'.[3] 'In Jewish fashion
they have organised a gang to fight against Christ, denying
the divinity of our Saviour and declaring him to be on a
level with all men.'[4]

Like Athanasius after him, Alexander constantly accuses the
Arians of selecting only those passages of scripture which suit
their presuppositions and ignoring those which are contrary to
them. He complains that they

pick out every passage which refers to the dispensation of salvation
and to his humiliation for our sakes... while they avoid all those
which declare his eternal divinity and the indescribable glory which
he possesses with the Father...[5]

By their hypothesis that he has been created out of nothing (ἐξ
οὐκ ὄντων), they overthrow the scriptures which say that he always
was, which declare the immutability of the Logos and the divinity
of the Wisdom of the Logos, which things Christ is.[6]

Later in the same letter, Alexander says that they bring forward
the passages which speak of

the sufferings of the Saviour, his humiliation, his self-emptying and
his so-called poverty, and everything else which the Saviour accepted

---

[1] *Or. c. Ar.* I, 6.   [2] *Urk.* 9 (18, 6 f.).
[3] *Urk.* 14 (24, 22). The importance of the *lex orandi*, the worship of
Christ, as an influence in the formulation of doctrine has been stressed by
M. F. Wiles, *The Making of Christian Doctrine*, ch. IV; H. E. W. Turner, *The
Pattern of Christian Truth*, *passim*. For its importance in Athanasius' opposition to the Arians, cf. Laeuchli, 'The case of Athanasius against the Arians',
pp. 416 ff.
[4] *Urk.* 14 (20, 6 ff.).   [5] *Ibid.* (20, 8 ff.).
[6] *Ibid.* (21, 12 ff.).

for our sakes...in order to disprove his divinity which is from above and from the beginning, and they have forgotten the words which indicate his natural glory and nobility and his abiding with the Father.[1]

One of the texts which the Arians consistently ignore is John x. 30: 'I and the Father are one',[2] and another is in John xiv. 8–9: 'Show us the Father...He that has seen me has seen the Father'. Quoting John x. 30, Alexander says:

In these words the Lord does not declare himself to be the Father,[3] neither does he claim that the two subsistent natures are one (τὰς τῇ ὑποστάσει δύο φύσεις μίαν), but that the Son of the Father in his very nature preserves accurately the likeness of the Father, in every way having taken his likeness as an impression of his nature (τὴν κατὰ πάντα ὁμοιότητα αὐτοῦ ἐκ φύσεως ἀπομαξάμενος), and being the exact image of the Father (ἀπαράλλακτος εἰκὼν τοῦ πατρός) and the distinct expression of the prototype (τοῦ πρωτοτύπου ἔκτυπος χαρακτήρ). When, then, Philip desired to see the Father, the Lord answered him with abundant clarity: Philip said, 'Show us the Father', and he answered, 'He that has seen me has seen the Father', as though the Father were seen in the spotless and living mirror of his divine image. The same idea is put forward in the Psalms (xxxv. 10), 'In thy light we shall see light'. It is for this reason that 'He that honoureth the Son honoureth the Father' (cf. John v. 23), and it is quite fitting; for every impious word which men dare to utter against the Son is also spoken against the Father.[4]

In accordance with a well-established tradition, Alexander interprets the unity of the Father and the Son in terms of the unity of the image with that of which it is the image. He interprets John x. 30 in terms of Col. i. 15 and Heb. i. 3; he had already made plain his interpretation of these two texts earlier in the same letter:

For to say that 'the reflection of the glory' (Heb. i. 3) did not exist, takes away also the prototypal light of which it is the glory. And if the image of God (Col. i. 15) did not always exist, it is plain that he whose image he is did not always exist either. Also when it is asserted that the expression of the substance of God did not exist, he also is taken away who is also expressed by him.[5]

[1] *Ibid.* (25, 17 ff.).
[2] Cf. my article, 'The Exegesis of John x. 30'.
[3] That would be Sabellianism.   [4] *Urk.* 14 (25, 22—26, 5).
[5] *Ibid.* (24, 3-6).

These metaphors are, for Alexander, attempts to express the oneness of the Father and the Son which John x. 30 and xiv. 9 set forth more explicitly. Just as light cannot exist without its glory and the model cannot exist without its image and the substance without its expression, so God cannot exist without the Son. Father and Son are one with each other and co-eternal with each other.

Alexander returns to this same theme in a later passage where he deals with it at greater length and makes use of the important text, John xiv. 28, 'My Father is greater than I', a text which favoured the Arian subordinationism but which, surprisingly, finds little place in the extant documents from either side of the controversy.[1] Alexander says that:

> this Being, the all-sufficient and perfect Son, who is immutable and unchangeable just as the Father is, is like the Father, falling short of the Father only with respect to the 'unbegotten'. For he is the Father's accurate and exact image. It is clear, therefore, that the image is full of all things on account of which the greater likeness exists, as the Lord himself taught saying, 'The Father is greater than I' (John xiv. 28). And in accordance with this, we also believe that the Son is always from the Father.[2]

He proceeds to argue that the words 'was', 'always', and 'before the ages' must not be taken to mean 'unbegotten',

> for these words appear to mean merely the extension of time (χρόνων παρέκτασις) and cannot indicate worthily the divinity of the Only-begotten, and, as it were, his primitive being (ἀρχαιότητα) ...Whatever may be the meaning of these words it is not the same

---

[1] In the early documents it appears only in this letter of Alexander (*Urk.* 14) and in the *Letter of Eus. Caes. to Euphration of Balanea* (*Urk.* 3), where it is quoted in the longer form. Commenting on one of the few fragments extant from Athanasius of Anazarbus, *Sermones Arianorum* (*PL*, XIII, 593), which gives a subordinationist interpretation of John xiv. 28, Bardy says, 'This text is rarely used in the Arian controversy. The known fragments of Arius, Asterius and Eusebius (of Nicomedia) do not comment on it; and St Athanasius himself, in the *Orations against the Arians*, finds few occasions to interpret it. It is only in the *Second Formula of Sirmium* in 357 that it is put in the foreground in a purely subordinationist sense. But we cannot doubt that it must have entered early into the exegetical arsenal of Arianism, and the passage of Athanasius (of Anazarbus) confirms on this point the letter of Eusebius of Caesarea to Euphration of Balanea' (*Recherches sur saint Lucien d'Antioche et son école*, p. 209).

[2] *Urk.* 14 (27, 13 ff.).

as 'unbegotten'. Therefore, his own dignity as Father must be reserved to the Unbegotten by our saying that there is no cause of his being (μηδένα τοῦ εἶναι αὐτῷ τὸν αἴτιον); to the Son likewise must be given the honour that is fitting to him by ascribing to him the birth (γέννησιν) from the Father which has no beginning. As we have already said, when we render worship to him it is only in a religious and pious way that we ascribe to him the words 'was' and 'always' and 'before the ages'. We do not reject his divinity, however, but we ascribe an accurate and complete likeness to the image and expression of the Father, but we hold that the property of unbegottenness belongs only to the Father (τὸ δὲ ἀγέννητον τῷ πατρὶ μόνον ἰδίωμα παρεῖναι), even as the Saviour says, 'My Father is greater than I' (John xiv. 28).[1]

While in opposition to Arian subordinationism Alexander affirms very strongly that the Son is from the Father and like the Father according to essence, he none the less strives to maintain the Son's distinction from the Father. The distinction is not one of *essential* difference, of *essential* inferiority and posteriority, as the Arians maintain, but a distinction of dignity; the distinction between the Unbegotten and the Only-begotten is that which the later trinitarians formulated in the phrases *ordo subsistendi* and *pater fons totius divinitatis*. The Arians could not understand this distinction; any being who is distinct from the Supreme God, the Father, must, they thought, be distinct from him according to essence and posterior to him. When Arius heard Alexander drawing a distinction between the Father and the Son he could think of the distinction only in terms of posteriority; in his *Confessio Fidei*, which he and his colleagues addressed to Alexander *c.* A.D. 320, he asserts: 'God is before all things as Monad and Source (ἀρχή) of all. Therefore he is also before the Son (πρὸ τοῦ υἱοῦ) as we have learned from your preaching in the midst of the Church.'[2]

Alexander, then, interprets John xiv. 28 to mean that the Father is greater than the Son in that he alone is Unbegotten and the Son alone Only-begotten: the Father is begotten by none, the Son is begotten by the Father; the Father has no source or beginning, but he is the source or beginning of the Son. Alexander has transposed Origen's insight into the eternity of the Son's generation as a continual begetting from the

[1] *Ibid.* (27, 24—28, 7).   [2] *Urk.* 6 (13, 12–14).

cosmological key into the religious and theological key. Temporal terms are inapplicable to the relationship of the Father to the Son which is an eternal relationship; 'greater' (John xiv. 28) cannot imply superiority or priority of essence. This same interpretation is set forth by Athanasius,[1] Basil,[2] and Gregory of Nazianzus.[3]

The subordinationist interpretation of John xiv. 28 is clear from the *Letter of Eusebius of Caesarea to Euphration of Balanea*:

However, the Son of God, himself being more accurately set over all, knowing himself to be other than the Father and less than and inferior to him (ἕτερον ἑαυτὸν εἰδὼς τοῦ πατρὸς καὶ μείω καὶ ὑποβεβηκότα), teaches this also much more piously when he says, 'The Father who sent me is greater than I'.[4]

The fragment from the *Sermones Arianorum* of Athanasius of Anazarbus[5] agrees with this subordinationist interpretation by Eusebius.

We have seen how Alexander combines Heb. i. 3, Col. i. 15 and John x. 30; in the *Depositio Arii* he combines John xiv. 9: 'He that has seen me has seen the Father' with the terms ἀπαύγασμα (Heb. i. 3) and εἰκών (Col. i. 15) in order to prove that the Son cannot be unlike the Father in essence. 'How is he who says, "He that has seen me has seen the Father" unlike the essence of the Father, who is the perfect image (εἰκών) and the reflection (ἀπαύγασμα) of the Father?'[6] Alexander's continual use of the metaphors 'image', 'reflection' and 'expression' in relation to the oneness of the Son with the Father is motivated by his acknowledgement that the revelation of the Father through the Son is a real revelation only if the Son is like the Father and from his essence.

The situation on this crucial Arian proposition may be summed up thus: the Arians, in asserting the Son's essential difference and distinction from the Father, ignore the strong Johannine emphasis on the essential identity of the Father and the Son. Alexander, on the contrary, takes seriously the Johannine paradox of the Son's unity with and distinction from the Father, for he knows that if the Son is not God in the proper

---

[1] *Or. c. Ar.* I, 58; see below, p. 217. [2] *c. Eunomium*, IV.
[3] *Or* xxx (*Theol. Or.* IV), 7 (ed. Mason, 118, 16 ff.).
[4] *Urk.* 3 (5, 1–3). [5] See above, p. 154, n. 1.
[6] *Urk.* 4b (9, 3 f.).

sense of the word, then the church has no right to worship him, and there is no real revelation of the Father through the Son. The nature of his opponents' teaching makes him emphasise the unity of the Father with the Son, but in doing so, he never loses sight of the distinction between them.

(iii) *'The Son is from nothing'* (ἐξ οὐκ ὄντων ἐστίν).[1] The Arians presupposed that in the beginning there was God, the Monad, alone, who admits of no internal differentiation or distinction; beside him there was nothing. The Son cannot be from God, argued Arius, for that implies that the Monad is divisible; if he is not from God, he cannot be like God in essence, and he must be 'from nothing'.

Opposing this proposition, Alexander sets forth the words of John i. 18, 'who is in the bosom of the Father', and proceeds to argue thus:

The Logos, the One who makes (τὸ ποιοῦν), is in no way to be defined as being of the same nature as originated things, if he was 'in the beginning' (John i. 1 a), and 'all things were made through him' (John i. 3 a), and he made them out of nothing. For that which is (τὸ ὄν) seems to be the opposite of and exceedingly far removed from the things that are made out of nothing. For he (John) shows that there is no interval (διάστημα) between the Father and the Son.[2]

Alexander interprets the word 'bosom' in the same way as he has already interpreted 'heart' (Ps. xlv. 1) and 'womb' (Ps. cx. 3); these three terms imply the unity of the Son with the Father and the Son's participation in the essence of the Father: 'there is no interval between the Father and the Son'. The term διάστημα may mean 'interval of time', or 'distance', or 'difference'; in the above context the most likely meaning appears to be 'distance'. The word 'bosom', then, implies essential unity. The Son belongs to the sphere of the uncreated godhead and not to the sphere of things created out of nothing.

A little later in the same letter Alexander uses the term διάστημα in the temporal sense, speaking of this 'interval during which they say that the Son was not created by the Father' (τὸ διάστημα ἐν ᾧ φασι μὴ γεγενῆσθαι τὸν υἱὸν ὑπὸ τοῦ πατρός),[3] and a little later he writes: 'Since the assumption

---

[1] *Urk.* 1 (3, 5); cf. *Urk.* 4b (7, 19; 9, 1) *inter alia.*
[2] *Urk.* 14 (22, 13–17).   [3] *Ibid.* (23, 21).

implied in the phrase "out of nothing" is plainly impious, the Father must always be Father, and he is Father because the Son, on account of whom he is designated Father, is always with him (ἀεὶ παρόντος).'[1]

(iv) A further consequence of the Arian doctrine that the Son is unlike the Father, and one which was to occupy the attention of Athanasius in later stages of the controversy, is contained in the proposition: *The Son is a creature and thing made ...one of things made and things originated*' (κτίσμα γάρ ἐστι καὶ ποίημα ὁ υἱός...εἷς τῶν ποιημάτων καὶ γενητῶν ἐστι).[2]

If the Son is unlike the Father in essence, foreign and alien to and isolated from it, then it follows that the Son, being derived from nothing, belongs to the sphere of the created.

Against this proposition Alexander sets forth an argument based on John i. 18; iii. 16, 18; 'Only-begotten Son', and John i. 3a: 'All things were made through him'. He asks: 'For how can he be one of the things which were made through himself, or how can he be "only-begotten" who is, according to these fellows, numbered with all things?'[3] This conjunction of John i. 18 and i. 3a provides the clue to a fundamental difference between Alexander and the Arians. The Arians, it is certain, interpreted μονογενής as meaning that the Son alone was created directly by God, while all the rest of the creatures were created through him.[4] Alexander, on the contrary, interprets μονογενής in its true meaning of 'unique' or 'only one of its kind'; the Son, being μονογενής, is essentially different from the creatures made through him.[5]

Later Arius, in view of the storm which he had aroused by calling the Son a creature, modified his language but not his opinion; in the *Confessio Fidei* addressed to Alexander, he and his supporters declared that the Son is 'a perfect creature of God, but not as one of the creatures, an offspring, but not as one of the beings that have been begotten' (κτίσμα τοῦ θεοῦ τέλειον, ἀλλ᾽ οὐχ ὡς ἓν τῶν κτισμάτων, γέννημα, ἀλλ᾽ οὐχ ὡς ἓν

---

[1] *Ibid.* (23, 28 f.).　　　　[2] *Urk.* 4b (7, 21–3).
[3] *Ibid.* (8, 21—9, 1).
[4] That this is the Arian view is confirmed by Athanasius, see below.
[5] Cf. D. Moody, ' "God's Only Son": The Translation of Jn. 3. 16 in the R.S.V.', in *JBL*, LXXII (1953), 213 ff.; P. Winter, 'Μονογενὴς παρὰ πατρός' in *ZRGG*, v (1953), 335–65; C. H. Turner, 'ὁ υἱός μου ὁ ἀγαπητός' in *JTS*, XXVII (1926), 113–29.

τῶν γεγεννημένων).[1] As we have already seen, Eusebius of Caesarea approved of this statement and wrote to Alexander criticising him for asserting that the Arians teach that the Son is a creature. He says, 'They do not say this, but they clearly declare that "he is not as one of the creatures".'[2] This Arian equivocation is matched by the strange exegesis which the Arians set forth in support of their view. Athanasius of Anazarbus, for example, writing to Alexander, argues on the basis of the Parable of the Lost Sheep (Luke 15. 4–7), thus:

Why blame the Arians if they say, 'The Son of God has been made a creature out of nothing and is one of all (the creatures)'? For since all things that are made are represented in the parable of the hundred sheep, even the Son is one of them. If then the hundred are not creatures and originate beings, or if there is something besides the hundred, it is clear that the Son may not be a creature or one of the creatures; but, if all the hundred are originate and there is nothing besides the hundred except God alone, what is absurd in what the Arians say, if comprehending Christ and numbering him as one of the hundred, they have said that he is one of all the creatures.[3]

Similarly, George of Laodicea, seeking to play the role of peacemaker, wrote letters to both Alexander and Arius. To Alexander he wrote:

Do not blame the Arians if they say, 'There was once when the Son of God was not', for Isaiah became the son of Amoz, and since Amoz was before Isaiah came to be, Isaiah was not before but came to be afterwards.[4]

To Arius he wrote:

Why do you blame Alexander the Pope for saying that the Son is from the Father (ἐκ τοῦ πατρός)? For you also need have no fear of saying too that the Son is from God. For, if the Apostle wrote, 'All things are from God' (I Cor. xi. 12), and it is plain that all things have been made out of nothing, then the Son also is a creature and one of the things that have been made. The Son may be said to be from God in the sense in which all things are said to be from God.[5]

---

[1] *Urk.* 6 (12, 9–10).   [2] *Urk.* 7 (14, 15—15, 1).
[3] *Urk.* 11 (18).   [4] *Urk.* 12 (19).
[5] *Urk.* 13 (19).

These Arian arguments which seek to assimilate the Son to the creatures lead on to a further Arian proposition:

(v) '*When at some time he did come into existence, he became such as every man is*' (τοιοῦτος γενόμενος ὅτε καί ποτε γέγονεν, οἶος καὶ πᾶς πέφυκεν ἄνθρωπος).[1]

Alexander does not quote St John's Gospel in refuting this view but quotes Rom. viii. 32; Matt. iii. 17; xvii. 5; Ps. ii. 1; cx. 3. He says, for example, that

Paul thus declared his true, peculiar, natural and special sonship (τὴν γνησίαν αὐτοῦ καὶ ἰδιότροπον καὶ φυσικήν καὶ κατ' ἐξαιρετὸν υἱότητα), saying of God, 'He did not spare his own Son (τοῦ ἰδίου υἱοῦ), but delivered him up for us all' who are plainly not sons by nature (τῶν μὴ φύσει υἱῶν).[2]

This Arian proposition does not occupy much of his attention; he concentrates rather on another proposition which is its corollary:

(vi) '*The Son is by nature mutable and changeable like all the rational beings*' (τρεπτός ἐστι καὶ ἀλλοιωτὸς τὴν φύσιν ὡς καὶ πάντα τὰ λογικά).[3]

Alexander relies on St John's Gospel to provide the main weapons for his attack on this doctrine. He asks: 'How can he be mutable and changeable who says concerning himself, "I in the Father and the Father in me" (John xiv. 10) and "I and the Father are one" (John x. 30)?'[4] and supports this argument with a quotation of Mal. iii. 6, 'Behold me that I am and I was not changed'; 'for', he says, 'the Son was not changed when he became man, but as the Apostle said, "Jesus Christ, the same yesterday, today and forever" (Heb. xiii. 8)'.[5]

Because the Arians placed the Son on the creaturely side of the Creator–creature dualism, they asserted that he was mutable like the rest of rational beings; because he places the Son on the divine side of the line which divides the divine from the human, Alexander declares that the Son, like the Father, is immutable. Alexander sees that the answer which one gives to the question whether the Son is mutable or immutable depends on the more fundamental question whether his sonship is unique

---

[1] *Urk.* 14 (21, 9 f.).
[2] *Urk.* 14 (24, 25–7).
[3] *Urk.* 4*b* (8, 2–3).
[4] *Ibid.* (9, 7 f.).
[5] *Ibid.* (9, 10 ff.).

and natural or only adoptive like ours. His answer to the latter question is that which the New Testament gives; he asserts:

The sonship of our Saviour has nothing in common with the sonship of the rest (of rational creatures). For just as his inexpressible subsistence (ὑπόστασις) can be shown to surpass by incomparable excellence all those to whom he has given existence, so also his sonship, which by nature shares the Father's godhead, differs by unspeakable excellence from (that of) those who have been adopted to sonship by adoption through him (τῶν δι' αὐτοῦ θέσει υἱοθετηθέντων). For he has an immutable nature, being perfect and in no way lacking in anything, while those who exist, each in the manner fitting to him, need his help (in order to become sons).[1]

The sonship which is natural to the Son is ours only by appointment or adoption. Thus Alexander reproduces the Pauline and Johannine doctrine of adoption, although he does not quote John i. 12, 13. The distinction between Christ's sonship and ours becomes even clearer in another passage:

Men and angels, who are his creatures, have received blessing, being enabled to advance in virtue so that in conformity with his commands they may avoid sin. It is on account of this that our Lord, being Son of the Father by nature (κατὰ φύσιν), is worshipped by all; and those who have cast off the spirit of bondage, and by brave deeds and progress in virtue have received the spirit of adoption, being dealt with kindly by him who is Son by nature (φύσει), have themselves become sons by adoption (θέσει).[2]

Alexander brings out more explicitly the general distinction between Christ's sonship and ours which is implicit in St John's reservation of the title *Son* for Jesus and in his emphasis that while Jesus *is* the Son of God, those who welcome him and believe in his name *become* children of God.[3]

It appears that the Arians interpreted the sonship of Christ in the light of sayings from the Old Testament which spoke of the Hebrews as 'sons of God'. Here we catch a glimpse of the selective use which the Arians made of scripture, picking out isolated texts or even parts of texts to quote in support of their arguments, and ignoring the context of the text.[4] Alexander

---

[1] *Urk.* 14 (24, 6–12).   [2] *Urk.* 14 (24, 19–24).
[3] See above, ch. 1.
[4] Cf. my article, 'The Exegesis of Scripture and the Arian Controversy', pp. 416 f.

quotes the Arians as saying, 'We also are able to become sons of God like him, for it has been written, "I have begotten and brought up sons" (Isa. i. 2).' Alexander says that they ignore the rest of the text which says, 'and they have rebelled against me', which is not fitting to the Son who is immutable by nature. When their attention is drawn to these words they reply that

God fore-knew and fore-saw that his Son would not rebel against him, and he chose him from all. For he was not chosen because he had by nature what other sons of God had by choice...He was chosen because, although he had a mutable nature, his painstaking character underwent no deterioration,

and Alexander adds,

as though even if a Paul or a Peter should make this effort, their sonship would differ in no way from his.[1]

For Arius, the Son has his sonship by adoption just as we have ours, except that in his case God knew and saw beforehand that he would not rebel and therefore adopted him to sonship in advance. The Arians' introduction of the concept of God's foreknowledge and foresight is necessitated by their reading back the distinction between the Logos and the Son from the incarnation to the beginning of creation. It is only this concept which separates the Arians from the adoptionism of Paul of Samosata, and Paul's view, heretical though it may have been, can lay more claim to being scriptural than that of the Arians.

(vii) '*The Father is invisible to the Son. For neither does the Logos know the Father perfectly and accurately, nor can he perfectly see him. For the Son does not even know what his own essence is*' (ἀόρατός ἐστιν ὁ πατὴρ τῷ υἱῷ. οὔτε γὰρ τελείως καὶ ἀκριβῶς γιγνώσκει ὁ λόγος τὸν πατέρα, οὔτε τελείως ὁρᾶν αὐτὸν δύναται. καὶ γὰρ καὶ ἑαυτοῦ τὴν οὐσίαν οὐκ οἶδεν ὁ υἱὸς ὡς ἔστι).[2]

This aspect of the Arian teaching plays little part in the initial stages of the controversy, and Athanasius pays little attention to it. It is a corollary of their doctrine that the Son was a creature, for they held that God is incomprehensible and invisible to the creatures. If for the most part it is ignored, it is because the refutation of the central Arian doctrine of the Son's creatureliness automatically demolishes this doctrine as well. If

---

[1] *Urk.* 14 (21, 15–24).　　　　　[2] *Urk.* 4*b* (8, 4–5).

it is proved that the Son is like the Father's essence or from the Father's essence, the question of his ability to know the Father perfectly is answered. The Arians arrived at this proposition by one of their typical syllogisms:

> No creature can know God,
> The Son is a creature,
> The Son cannot know God.

If the minor premiss is denied, as it was by Alexander, the conclusion is false.

In the *Depositio Arii* Alexander disposes of this Arian tenet with a short argument based on exegesis of John x. 15:

There is no need to be amazed at their blasphemous assertion that the Son does not know the Father perfectly. For, once having made up their minds to fight against Christ, they thrust away even the words of him who says, 'As the Father knows me, even so do I know the Father'. If therefore the Father knows the Son partially, it is evident that the Son does not know the Father perfectly. If it is not lawful to say this, however, and the Father knows the Son perfectly, it is evident that just as the Father knows his own Logos, so also the Logos knows his own Father, whose Logos he is.[1]

In the ante-Nicene documents we have in miniature the whole of the Arian controversy; the main Arian propositions became quite clear from the beginning, as also did the orthodox method of refuting them by appeal to scripture and exegesis of it. In this early stage the doctrine of the incarnation plays little part, for the controversy was focused on the question of the nature of the pre-existent Son; the orthodox theologians were faced with the task of throwing back a fresh attack on the first Johannine paradox, an attack which resolved the paradox by denying one side of it, the unity of the Son with the Father. Whether Alexander, in emphasising the unity, so diminishes the distinction that he comes near to Sabellianism is, on the evidence we have, an open question, but we have seen that he strives to maintain the distinction within the unity and that, for him, both are vital parts of any doctrine of the godhead which seeks to do justice to the witness of scripture and to the faith and worship of the church.

---

[1] *Urk.* 4*b* (9, 13–19). Athanasius reproduces the same argument in *ad Epp. Aeg.* 19 (*PG*, xxv, 576).

Just as Hippolytus and Tertullian had used St John's Gospel as their main weapon against Sabellianism, just as Novatian had used it against those who said that the Son is a mere man, so now Alexander uses it against the extreme subordinationism of Arius. If it is St John's Gospel which raises the questions which these heresies sought to solve, it is the same Gospel which provides the basis for the answers which the church gave to them.

The Sources of the Documents used in Chapter 5

In the text all references to the Documents have been given according to the numeration in *Urkunden zur Geschichte des arianischen Streites*, 318–328, which forms the first part of vol. iii of H. G. Opitz, *Athanasius Werke*, which is being published by *Der Kirchenväter-Kommission der preussischen Akademie der Wissenschaften*. The following list sets out the sources of the documents referred to in this chapter.

Urkunde 1. *Letter of Arius to Eusebius of Nicomedia, c.* A.D. 318, Epiphanius, *Haer.*, 69, 6; Theodoret, *H.E.*, i. 5.

Urkunde 3. *Letter of Eusebius of Caesarea to Euphration of Balanea, c.* A.D. 318, Second Nicene Council, Actio V; Mansi, 13, 176.

Urkunde 4b. *Letter of Alexander of Alexandria to All Bishops (Depositio Arii), c.* A.D. 319, Socrates, *H.E.*, i, 6, 4.

Urkunde 6. *Confession of Faith of Arius and his Colleagues to Alexander of Alexandria, c.* A.D. 320, Athanasius, *de Synodis*, 16.

Urkunde 7. *Letter of Eusebius of Caesarea to Alexander of Alexandria, c.* A.D. 320, Second Council of Nicaea, Mansi, 13, 316.

Urkunde 9. *Letter of Paulinus of Tyre, c.* A.D. 320/1, Eusebius *contra Marcellum*, i, 4, 18–20; i, 4, 49; i, 4, 50; i, 4, 51.

Urkunde 11. *Letter of Athanasius of Anazarbus to Alexander of Alexandria, c.* A.D. 322, Athanasius, *de Synodis*, 17.

Urkunde 12. *Letter of George the Presbyter to Alexander of Alexandria, c.* A.D. 322, Athanasius, *de Synodis* 17.

Urkunde 13. *Letter of George the Presbyter to the Arians in Alexandria, c.* A.D. 322, Athanasius, *de Synodis* 17.

Urkunde 14. *Letter of Alexander of Alexandria to Alexander of Thessalonica, c.* A.D. 324, Theodoret, *H.E.*, i, 4, 1.

Urkunde 18. *Letter of the Synod of Antioch*, early A.D. 325, *Codex Parisinus Syriacus* 62; Greek translation by E. Schwartz in *Nachrichten von der Kgl. Gesellschaft der W'schaften zu Göttingen*, 1905.

CHAPTER 6

THE CREEDS OF A.D. 325

The wide repercussions which the controversy between Arius and Alexander his bishop had beyond the borders of the arch-diocese of Alexandria, the resulting alignment of powerful bishops like Eusebius of Nicomedia and Eusebius of Caesarea on the side of Arius, and the disruption of the peace and unity of the church in the eastern empire, could not but become a matter of political concern for the Emperor Constantine. The Emperor, it appears, had looked to the church as the social cement which would bind a crumbling empire together,[1] but now the social cement itself was in danger of crumbling. When his letter to Alexander and Arius[2] (carried by Hosius, his ecclesiastical adviser) failed to heal the breach, he decided to call a synod of all bishops to deal with this and other problems which were dividing the church.

It is unnecessary for us to go into the details of the history of the months leading up to the assembling of the bishops at Nicaea, nor is it necessary to go into detailed discussion of the basic theologies of the three creeds which come to light in the discussion of the Arian controversy before and during the Nicene Synod.[3] It is important, however, that these creeds should be examined briefly in order to see what influence St John's Gospel had on their formulation.

[1] Cf. G. H. Williams, 'Christology and Church–State Relations in the Fourth Century', *CH*, xx (1951), no. 3, pp. 3–33; no. 4, pp. 3–26.

[2] *Urk.* 17; cf. Socrates, *Hist. Eccl.* I, 7.

[3] For a detailed discussion of the contrasting theological emphases of the creeds of Antioch, Caesarea and Nicaea, cf. my article, 'The Creeds of A.D. 325', *SJT*, xiii (1960), 278–300.

A. THE CREED OF THE SYNOD OF ANTIOCH
(*early* A.D. 325)

The Letter of the Synod of Antioch contained in a Syriac MS. of the eighth or ninth century (*Codex Parisinus Syriacus* 62)[1] contains an exceedingly involved and cumbersome credal statement.[2] Its cumbersomeness is due to the insertion within what is clearly a basic creed of passages of anti-Arian polemic and of explanatory notes on some of the phrases in the creed itself. When these insertions are removed, we are left with a concise creed which conforms to the usual pattern of other early tripartite creeds. The christological clause of the basic creed reads thus:

in one Lord Jesus Christ the only-begotten Son...God the Logos (θεὸν λόγον), true Light, Righteousness, Jesus Christ, Lord and Saviour of all...(who) having been born in flesh from Mary the Mother of God, and made incarnate, having suffered and died, rose again from the dead, and was taken up into heaven, and sits on the right hand of the Majesty most high, and will come to judge the living and the dead.[3]

The first and longest anti-Arian insertion follows the words *the only-begotten Son*, and consists of criticism of Arian interpretation of the phrase, together with a statement of what the Antiochene bishops understand by it:

begotten not from what is not but from the Father, not as made but as properly an offspring, but begotten in an ineffable, indescribable manner, because only the Father who begot and the Son who was begotten know (for 'no one knows the Father but the Son, nor the Son but the Father', Matt. xi. 27), who exists everlastingly and did not at one time not exist. For we have learned from the Holy

---

[1] First brought to notice by E. Schwartz in 1905. There was considerable controversy over its authenticity between Schwartz and A. von Harnack (cf. F. L. Cross, 'The Council of Antioch in 325 A.D.', *CQR*, cxxviii (1939), 49 ff.), but it is now generally accepted as genuine.

[2] J. N. D. Kelly calls it 'this tortuous compilation' (*Early Christian Creeds*, p. 210.)

[3] *Urk.* 18 (38, 17 f.; 39, 8 f.; 39, 11–13). (References are given to Schwartz' Greek translation.) I am grateful to my former fellow-students, President David Hubbard, of Fuller Theological Seminary, and Prof. R. B. Laurin, of California Baptist Seminary, for assistance in comparing Schwartz' translation with the Syriac text.

Scriptures that he alone is the express image, not, plainly, as if he might have remained unbegotten from the Father, nor by adoption (for it is impious and blasphemous to say this); but the scriptures describe him as validly and truly begotten as Son, so that we believe him to be immutable and unchangeable, and that he was not begotten and did not come to be by volition or by adoption, so as to appear to be from that which is not, but as it befits him to be begotten; not (a thing which it is unlawful to think) according to likeness or nature or commixture with any of the things which came to be through him, but in a way which passes all understanding or conception or reasoning we confess him to have been begotten of the unbegotten father...[1]

It is clear from this that the Antiochenes grasped clearly the import of Arian teaching and attacked it at its central point, namely the meaning of the word μονογενής, which is applied to Christ in scripture only in the Johannine writings (John i. 14, 18; iii. 16, 18; I John iv. 9).

The second anti-Arian insertion comes after the words *Lord and Saviour of all*: 'For he is the express image of the very substance of his Father, and not of his will or of anything else. This Son, the divine Logos...'[2]

The main points of the anti-Arian polemic of the credal statement are taken up again in the anathemas attached to the end of the creed:

We anathematize those who say or think or preach that the Son of God is a creature or has come into being or has been made and is not truly begotten, or that there was when he was not. For we believe that he was and is and that he is light. Furthermore we anathematize those who suppose that he is immutable by his own act of will, just as those who derive his birth from that which is not, and deny that he is immutable in the way the Father is. For just as our Saviour is the image of the Father in all things, so in this respect particularly he has been proclaimed the Father's image.[3]

It is clear from these insertions and anathemas that the Antiochenes were well informed on the nature of Arian teaching and definite in their opposition to it. Their letter is directed against the teaching that the Son has been generated from nothing (ἐκ τοῦ μὴ ὄντος), that there was once when he did not

---

[1] *Urk.* 18 (38, 18—39, 8). [2] *Ibid.* (39, 9–11).
[3] *Ibid.* (39, 16—40, 2).

exist (ἦν ὅτε οὐκ ἦν), and against the corollaries drawn from these positions, that the Son is distinct from the Father and therefore is not God.

The primary characterisation of the One Lord Jesus Christ in the basic creed itself is *only-begotten Son*; the attachment of the first anti-Arian insertion to this phrase shows that the Antiochene bishops recognised that the crux of the controversy lies in the word μονογενής. It has already been shown that Alexander of Alexandria had interpreted it in its proper sense of 'unique' or 'only one of its kind';[1] the Arians, on the other hand, interpreted it as though it were the equivalent of μονογέννητος, 'only-begotten', and it must be remembered that they drew no distinction between γεννητός and γενητός; for them it meant the same thing to say that the Son was begotten and that he was created or originated. They thought that the Son was the *only*-begotten because he alone was created by God himself; all other begotten or created beings were made through the Son as through an instrument. The Antiochenes agreed with Alexander and asserted the absolute uniqueness of the Son's generation from the Father. They interpreted the Person of Christ in the light of his being ὁ μονογενὴς υἱὸς τοῦ θεοῦ, the *only*, the *unique* Son of God, and they interpreted his generation in the light of the uniqueness of his relationship to the Father to which St John's Gospel bears pre-eminent witness in the New Testament. The regulative concept of the whole christological section of the creed of Antioch is that of sonship. 'Unique Son' (υἱὸν μονογενῆ) introduces this section of the creed, while 'divine Logos' (or 'God the Logos'-θεὸν λόγον appears as only one among a number of titles ascribed to the unique Son: 'divine Logos, true Light, Righteousness, Jesus Christ, Lord and Saviour of all'. Thus it keeps the titles 'unique Son' and Logos in the same relative perspective as St John does. Further, in opposition to the Arian distinction between the Logos and Son, the creed clearly identifies them: οὗτος δ' ὁ υἱὸς θεὸς λόγος.[2] The Antiochenes are emphatic that this Son of God 'was, and is, and is Light' and that 'this Son, the divine Logos, having been born of Mary the Mother of God, and made incarnate, suffered and died, etc.'.[3]

---

[1] See above, ch. 5. [2] Cf. p. 168, n. 2 above.
[3] Cf. p. 168, n. 3 above.

The anti-Arian insertions in the credal statement and the anathemas attached to it emphasise the uniqueness of the Son's generation, and the inadequacy of human language to describe it, except in a negative way by excluding the ideas that he is a creature (κτίσμα), a thing made (ποίημα or ποιητός) or a thing originated (γενητός), or that like created, made or originated beings he came forth 'out of nothing' (ἐκ τοῦ μὴ ὄντος or ἐξ οὐκ ὄντων). In opposition to this Arian teaching, the Antiochenes emphasise that the Son is 'from' or 'out of the Father' (ἐκ τοῦ πατρός).[1] The more usual Johannine expression is παρὰ τοῦ πατρός, but in the crucial verse, xvi. 28, ἐκ τοῦ πατρός occurs immediately after Jesus has said that he has come forth παρὰ τοῦ πατρός. Jesus says that the Father loves the disciples because they had loved the Son and have believed that he has come forth παρὰ τοῦ πατρός, that is, because they have believed in his divine origin. Jesus goes on to say that he has come forth ἐκ τοῦ πατρός and has come into the world and that he is leaving the world again and going πρὸς τὸν θεόν. The πρὸς τὸν θεόν is a clear echo of John i. 1b: ὁ λόγος ἦν πρὸς τὸν θεόν; when Jesus says that he is going πρὸς τὸν θεόν, he is asserting that he is returning to where he was 'in the beginning' (ἐν ἀρχῇ). The phrase ἐκ τοῦ πατρός is a closer definition of παρὰ τοῦ πατρός; Jesus says that he has come *from* the Father as well as *from beside* the Father. It is the Johannine phrase ἐκ τοῦ πατρός that the Antiochene bishops set over against the Arian ἐκ τοῦ μὴ ὄντος. While they do not make the meaning of ἐκ τοῦ πατρός more specific, as the Nicene Creed was to do some months later in the phrase ἐκ τῆς οὐσίας τοῦ πατρός, their second anti-Arian insertion makes the meaning of the phrase quite clear. It asserts that the Son 'is the express image, not of the will or of anything else, but of the Father's

---

[1] This phrase occurs only four times in the N.T., all in the Johannine writings: John viii. 42 (ἐκ τοῦ θεοῦ); xvi. 28; vi. 65; I John ii. 16. Of these only John viii. 42: ἐγὼ γὰρ ἐκ τοῦ θεοῦ ἐξῆλθον καὶ ἥκω, and xvi. 28: ἐξῆλθον ἐκ τοῦ πατρὸς καὶ ἐλήλυθα εἰς τὸν κόσμον are strictly relevant. In the passage John xvi. 27–32 in which the Johannine Jesus is speaking 'no longer in figures of speech, but plainly', John calls into service a wide variety of prepositions in order to indicate the relationship between the Father and the Son: xvi. 27: ἐγὼ παρὰ τοῦ θεοῦ (*v.l.* πατρός); xvi. 28: ἐξῆλθον ἐκ τοῦ πατρός (*v.l.* θεοῦ); xvi. 28: πορεύομαι πρὸς τὸν πατέρα; xvi. 30: πιστεύομεν ὅτι ἀπὸ θεοῦ ἐξῆλθες; xvi. 32: ὁ πατὴρ μετ' ἐμοῦ ἐστιν.

THE CREEDS OF A.D. 325

very substance' (εἰκὼν...αὐτῆς τῆς πατρικῆς ὑποστάσεως, which is a clear reference to Heb. i. 3: χαρακτὴρ τῆς ὑποστάσεως αὐτοῦ).

The image-concept plays a leading role in the Arian controversy and in the Marcellan controversy. Here it is interesting to notice that the creed of Antioch conflates Col. i. 15 with Heb. i. 3, replacing the word χαρακτήρ of Heb. i. 3 with εἰκών of Col. i. 15. It might be thought that this conflation has no doctrinal significance, but it is clear that the conflation is intentional, for instead of using ṣalmā by which the Syriac Version translates χαρακτήρ (Heb. i. 3), it has *yuʷḳnā*, a transliteration of the Greek εἰκών. This fact of transliteration suggests that some special meaning is intended by the phrase. In Col. i. 15 a the Son is asserted to be 'the image of the invisible God', the one, that is, through whom the invisible God becomes visible. Like John xiv. 9: 'He who has seen me has seen the Father', this phrase has a revelational significance, asserting the reality and authenticity of the revelation of God given in and through Jesus Christ the Son. Similarly, the opening words of the Epistle to the Hebrews are concerned with the reality and authenticity of the revelation of the Father in and through the Son, and Heb. i. 3 in particular emphasises that the Son, who is the agent of the Father in creation, by whom the Father made the worlds (Heb. i. 2), 'reflects the glory of God and bears the very stamp of his nature'; that is, the Son reveals to men the glory of God, which is God himself, and he is the outward expression of the nature of the godhead. By conflating Col. i. 15 and Heb. i. 3 the revelational emphasis, which is found in each, is made even more emphatic, and the revelation in and through the Son is asserted to be a revelation not of the will or of anything else, but of the Father's very nature or substance. Thus the Antiochene bishops would have had no hesitation in accepting the Nicene phrase ἐκ τῆς οὐσίας τοῦ πατρός, nor in agreeing wholeheartedly with the word ὁμοούσιος. They interpret the image-concept in the light of the Son-concept—the Son 'is the image of the Father, validly and truly begotten as Son'. The phrase ἐκ τοῦ πατρός refers to the generation of the Son from the Father's substance (ὑπόστασις) of which he is the εἰκών. It is by implication rather than by explicit statement that the Antiochenes give precision to the meaning of ἐκ τοῦ πατρός.

It is clear from a study of the *Letter of the Synod of Antioch* that the assembled bishops were strongly opposed to the doctrine of the Arians. The creed itself, the anti-Arian insertions and the anathemas combine to emphasise the real divinity of the Son of God, recognising clearly the Johannine paradox of distinction-within-unity within the godhead. Furthermore, the theology expressed in the letter directly contradicts the Arian distinction between the Logos and the Son, and passes beyond a Logos- or Word-christology to a Son-christology. One wonders how much the drafting of this letter owes to Eustathius, the most prominent Antiochene theologian of the period, whom the synod elected to fill the vacant see of Antioch.

When the Synod of Nicaea met a few months later, Alexander of Alexandria, following the Antiochene synod, could count on strong support from the Antiochene bishops who had already declared themselves so definitely against the theology of Arius.

B. THE CREED OF CAESAREA PRESENTED AT THE COUNCIL OF NICAEA BY EUSEBIUS OF CAESAREA

The decision of the Synod of Antioch must have been very disturbing to Eusebius of Caesarea. Its emphasis on the unity of the Son with the Father was completely contrary to his own emphasis on the distinction between them as one of posteriority and inferiority of essence. Early in the controversy, in a letter to Euphration of Balanea, he had emphasised this distinction by exegesis of one of his favourite texts, John xvii. 3: 'the only true God':

He (the Son) teaches that he (the Father) is the only true (God) in the place where he says, 'That they may know thee, the only true God', with the most necessary addition of the word 'true', since the Son also is God himself (αὐτὸς θεός) but not the 'true God' (ἀληθινὸς θεός). For there is only one true God, because he has no one prior to him. If the Son himself also is true, he would be God as the image of the true God, for 'the Logos was God' (John i. 1*c*), but not as being the only true God.[1]

The ditheistic tendency already noticed in the ante-Nicene theology of Eusebius is clear in this passage, and even more

[1] *Urk.* 3 (5, 5–10).

explicit in the *Letter of Narcissus of Neronias to Chrestus, Euphonius and Eusebius* (of Nicomedia?), which almost certainly refers to the debate in the Synod of Antioch. Narcissus says that Hosius asked him if he, like Eusebius of Palestine (Caesarea), would say that there are 'two essences' (δύο οὐσίαι).[1] Holding to his view of the distinction between Father and Son by which the Son is in effect an independent divine being beside the Father, Eusebius could not subscribe to the Antiochene letter which so strongly affirmed the unity of the Son with the Father. Accepting provisional excommunication along with Theodotus of Laodicea and Narcissus of Neronias who also refused to subscribe,[2] Eusebius was prepared to await the general council called by the Emperor, at which he could hope for a more sympathetic hearing than it was possible to get from a small strongly anti-Origenist local synod in Antioch.

There is general agreement that Eusebius submitted the Creed of Caesarea to the Council at Nicaea not, as he himself suggests in his *Letter to his Congregation*,[3] as an attempt to break the deadlock between Arius and Alexander, but rather as an attempt to demonstrate his own orthodoxy and to rehabilitate himself.[4]

The different theological outlook of Antioch and Caesarea is clear from a comparison of the two christological clauses of the two creeds. The christological clause of the Caesarean creed reads:

And in one Lord Jesus Christ, the Logos of God, God from God, Light from Light, Life from Life, Only-begotten Son, First-born of all creation begotten from the Father before all ages, through whom all things came to be, who, for our salvation, was incarnate and dwelt among men, and suffered, and rose again the third day...[5]

The primary description of Jesus Christ in the Antiochene creed was 'unique Son' (or 'Only-begotten Son'); in the Caesarean creed it is 'the Logos of God'. The emphasis in Antiochene theology, as far as we know it, had always been on Jesus the incarnate and had shunned cosmological speculation.

---

[1] *Urk.* 19 (41, 3). [2] *Urk.* 18 (40, 5 ff.).
[3] *Urk.* 22.
[4] Cf. Kelly, *Early Christian Creeds*, pp. 205–62; F. L. Cross, 'The Council of Antioch in 325 A.D.'; T. E. Pollard, 'The Creeds of A.D. 325'.
[5] *Urk.* 22 (43, 10 ff.).

Caesarean theology, as heir to the tradition of Origen and the apologists, emphasises primarily the cosmological role of the Logos, and this emphasis is continued and strengthened in the phrases which follow: 'God from God, Light from Light, Life from Life', the roots of which lie in the apologetic tradition. These same phrases will also be used in the Nicene Creed, but there they are severed from their roots in Logos-theology and are grafted on to the Son-concept. In the Caesarean Creed, however, they remain within the framework of the old Logos-theology.

It is only after this emphasis on Jesus Christ as the 'Logos of God', that the title Son is introduced: 'Only-begotten Son'. Even in this title the cosmological emphasis is retained, however, for it is coupled with another title: 'First-born of all creation', a quotation from Col. i. 15 b. The Antiochene Creed also quoted Col. i. 15, but focused attention on i. 15 a, 'image of the invisible God', which refers to the revelational significance of Jesus Christ. Col. i. 15 b, when removed from its context, assumes a cosmological significance;[1] it is as first-born of all creation that Jesus Christ is 'Only-begotten Son'. The addition of the former to the latter reduces the generic uniqueness which the term μονογενής implies to a mere priority in time and status of the Logos-Son to the rest of creation. The interpretation of these two terms in relation to each other becomes a burning question in the refutation of the Arians by Athanasius and also in the controversy which raged around the figure of Marcellus of Ancyra.[2]

That the Caesarean Creed does not move out of the realm of cosmology when it introduces the title Son is indicated by the section which follows: 'Begotten from the Father before all ages, through whom all things came into being'. The addition of these words to 'First-born of all creation' shows that the emphasis is on the temporal priority of the Logos–Son to the rest of creation and his role as cosmological intermediary in the activity of creation. The first of these phrases does not

---

[1] This is not to deny that St Paul intends this phrase in a cosmological sense, but the context in which the hymn in Col. i. 15 ff. occurs is soteriological. Cf. S. Hanson, *The Unity of the Church in the New Testament*, pp. 109 ff.; also ch. 4, p. 133, n. 4 above.

[2] Cf. ch. 8.

necessarily mean that the Logos–Son was eternally generated from the Father. The Arians could assert that the Son was begotten from the Father before all ages, without denying their proposition that 'there was once when he was not'. Eusebius, as we have seen, understood it to mean that the Son was not co-eternal with the Father; he assigned to the Son 'semi-eternity' as befitted his 'semi-divine being'.[1] The Antiochene Creed, on the other hand, asserts unequivocally that the Son is eternal (τὸν ἀεὶ ὄντα καὶ οὐ πρότερον οὐκ ὄντα). 'Begotten before all ages', however, being scriptural, was used universally before the Council of Nicaea, and was considered to be quite orthodox;[2] the Council of Nicaea was forced to avoid the phrase because of the fact that the Arians, placing their own interpretation on it, could accept it.

The remaining section of the christological clause of the Caesarean Creed deals with the incarnation. While it is orthodox in tone, it is inadequate in the face of the challenge which Arianism was making to the christology of the church. There is no mention of the Virgin Birth, a doctrine which was aimed at safeguarding both the real humanity and the real divinity of the Saviour. While it is asserted that the Logos–Son became flesh (σαρκωθέντα; cf. John i. 14: ὁ λόγος σάρξ ἐγένετο), it is not said that he *became man*, but only that he 'dwelt among men' (ἐν ἀνθρώποις πολιτευσάμενον). It is interesting that Eusebius, who was to object to the explicitly anti-Arian phrases of the Nicene Creed on the grounds that they were unscriptural, should propose a creed containing the word πολιτεύομαι, which is never used with Christ as subject in the New Testament; Eusebius himself was frequently guilty of the very things of which he accused his opponents. The terms which he uses in his creed to describe the incarnation, σαρκωθέντα καὶ ἐν ἀνθρώποις πολιτευσάμενον, do nothing to safeguard the church's faith in the reality and completeness of the manhood which the Son of God assumed; it does justice only to the old *Logos–Sarx* christology of the apologetic tradition. The Council was to make the completeness of the manhood of the Saviour more explicit by incorporating into its creed the word ἐνανθρωπήσαντα.

The theology implicit in the Caesarean Creed, then, pre-

---

[1] Berkhof, *Eusebius von Caesarea*, p. 75.
[2] Alexander himself used it, *Urk.* 14 (27, 20).

supposes a cosmological interpretation of the Christian faith; the regulative concept of its christological clause is 'the Logos of God', and the concept of sonship enters only as one among many of the titles of the Logos. There is no evidence which can be adduced to prove that the teaching of Origen had any direct influence on its formulation, but it is significant that such a creed as the Caesarean should belong to a church in which Origen had laboured for so long and whose bishop at the time of the Nicene Council was Eusebius, the last representative of the old Origenist tradition.

Eusebius produced this creed as proof of his orthodoxy. It is open to orthodox interpretation, and there is nothing explicitly Arian in it; the bishops assembled at Nicaea accepted it as orthodox and removed the ban of excommunication which the local Synod of Antioch had imposed. Recognising that such a creed was inadequate to exclude Arianism, the Council proceeded to produce a creed which would close once and for all any loopholes by which the Arians might escape to continue preaching their heresy in the name of the church. The creed which the Council produced was just as disconcerting to Eusebius as that which he had refused to sign at Antioch, and it was only after much hesitation that he signed the Nicene formulary.

C. THE CREED OF THE COUNCIL OF NICAEA

It is unnecessary to enter into detailed discussion of the debates within the Council of Nicaea or of the question of the provenance of the creed which was used as a basis for the Creed promulgated by the Council. What concerns us is the theology expressed in the christological clause of the creed and the comparison of it with the theology expressed in those of Antioch and Caesarea. It will be convenient to set out this section of the creed with the Greek text and English translation in parallel columns.[1]

(πιστεύομεν)	(we believe)
εἰς ἕνα κύριον Ἰησοῦν Χριστόν,	in one Lord Jesus Christ
τὸν υἱὸν τοῦ θεοῦ,[2]	the Son of God

[1] The Greek text is that given by Opitz, *Urk.* 24.

[2] Biblical references to the phrase 'Son of God' are too numerous to be listed. We have already pointed out that while the title 'Son of God' is

γεννηθέντα ἐκ τοῦ πατρὸς[1]	begotten from the Father
μονογενῆ,[2]	uniquely,
τουτέστιν ἐκ τῆς οὐσίας τοῦ	that is from the substance of the
πατρός,[3]	Father,
θεὸν ἐκ θεοῦ,[4] φῶς ἐκ φωτός,[5]	God from God, Light from Light,
θεὸν ἀληθινὸν ἐκ θεοῦ	true God from true God,
ἀληθινοῦ,[6]	
γεννηθέντα[7] οὐ ποιηθέντα,	begotten not made,
ὁμοούσιον τῷ πατρί,[8]	consubstantial with the Father
δι' οὗ τὰ πάντα ἐγένετο[9]	through whom all things were made
τά τε ἐν τῷ οὐρανῷ καὶ τὰ ἐν	both those in heaven and those
τῇ γῇ,[10]	on earth,
τὸν δι' ἡμᾶς[11] τοὺς ἀνθρώπους	who for us men and our
καὶ διὰ τὴν ἡμετέραν σωτηρίαν[12]	salvation
κατέλθοντα[13] καὶ σαρκωθέντα,	came down and was made flesh,
ἐνανθρωπήσαντα,[14] πάθοντα, κτλ.	became man, suffered, etc...

ascribed to Jesus in almost every New Testament writing it is in the Johannine literature that the concept of the sonship of Jesus occupies the central place.

[1] I John v. 18: ὁ γεννηθεὶς ἐκ τοῦ θεοῦ.

[2] John i. 14; iii. 16, 18; I John iv. 9: μονογενὴς υἱός; John i. 18: μονογενὴς θεός (v.l.).

[3] I John v. 18: ἐκ τοῦ θεοῦ; John viii. 42; xvi. 28: ἐξῆλθον ἐκ τοῦ θεοῦ; Heb. i. 3: χαρακτὴρ τῆς ὑποστάσεως αὐτοῦ.

[4] John i. 1c: θεὸς ἦν ὁ λόγος; John xx. 28: ὁ κύριός μου καὶ ὁ θεός μου. Cf. R. E. Brown, 'Does the New Testament call Jesus God?'.

[5] I John i. 5: ὁ θεὸς φῶς ἐστι; John i. 9: τὸ φῶς τὸ ἀληθινόν (cf. I John ii. 8). John viii. 12: ἐγώ εἰμι τὸ φῶς τοῦ κόσμου.

[6] John xvii. 3: τὸν μόνον ἀληθινὸν θεόν. The adjective ἀληθινός is applied to Jesus a number of times by St John: John i. 9: τὸ φῶς τὸ ἀληθινόν (cf. I John ii. 8); John vi. 32: τὸν ἄρτον...τὸν ἀληθινόν; John xv. 1: ἡ ἄμπελος ἡ ἀληθινή.

[7] See above, n. 1.

[8] The question whether ὁμοούσιος τῷ πατρί has any scriptural support for the meaning given to it by the Nicene party is one of the main points of argument in the continuing controversy for the next half-century.

[9] John i. 3; πάντα δι' αὐτοῦ ἐγένετο.

[10] Col. i. 16: ἐν αὐτῷ ἐκτίσθη τὰ πάντα, ἐν τοῖς οὐρανοῖς καὶ ἐπὶ τῆς γῆς.

[11] II Cor. viii. 9: δι' ὑμᾶς ἐπτώχευσε.

[12] σωτηρία occurs only once in the Johannine literature (John iv. 22).

[13] κατερχέσθαι is not a Johannine word: John uses καταβαίνω to describe the descent of the Son from heaven in iii. 17; v. 7; vi. 33, 38, 41, 42, 50, 51, 58.

[14] Neither σαρκόω nor ἐνανθρωπέω occurs in the New Testament.

The influence of Johannine language and thought on the Nicene Creed is quite evident. The Arians and Eusebius of Caesarea objected to the use of unscriptural words (ὁμοούσιον and ἐκ τῆς οὐσίας τοῦ πατρός in particular), while their opponents argued that even if these words are unscriptural, they embody the sense of scripture. Athanasius reports that no scripture words could be found which would not allow the Arians to place their own interpretation on them,[1] and that therefore it was necessary to look beyond the actual phraseology of scripture for words which would express the teaching of scripture as a whole. It seems likely that the term ὁμοούσιος was proposed by the Emperor himself at the suggestion of Hosius of Cordova, his ecclesiastical adviser, for its Latin equivalent, *consubstantialis*, was well established in Western theology.[2] *The Letter of Eusebius of Caesarea to his Congregation* makes it clear that it was not the fact that the terminology was unscriptural that worried him, but the theology of the Creed, which appeared to him to be a dangerous innovation.

The three creeds differ in the primary characterisation of 'one Lord Jesus Christ'. The Caesarean Creed has 'the Logos of God'; the Antiochene 'only-begotten Son'; the Nicene has 'the Son of God'. The last omits entirely the title 'Logos', and even avoids introducing the adjective μονογενής into the primary characterisation.

The Nicene Creed goes on to define more closely what it means by 'the Son of God', with the words 'begotten from the Father uniquely, that is from the substance of the Father'. The words 'begotten from the Father' are common to all three creeds. The Antiochene has them in the anti-Arian insertion: '*begotten* not from that which is not but *from the Father*',[3] the Caesarean modifies the phrase by adding 'before all ages', which excludes neither Arianism itself nor the near-Arianism of Eusebius. The Nicene Creed modifies it by adding 'uniquely'

[1] *de Decr.* 20 (*PG*, xxv, 449 f.).

[2] Athanasius (*Hist. Ar.* 42; *PG*, xxv, 744) says that it was Hosius who put forth the Nicene faith; Eusebius says that it was the Emperor who suggested the inclusion of ὁμοούσιον (*Urk.* 22).

[3] It appears to me that the basic Antiochene Creed contained the words 'begotten from the Father', and that the words 'not from that which is not but' were inserted between 'begotten' and 'from' in order to exclude the Arian doctrine of the Son's creation out of nothing.

(μονογενῆ), which it has separated from υἱόν and has placed in the midst of phrases concerning the begetting of the Son. By placing μονογενῆ after 'begotten from the Father', and by following it immediately with the explanatory phrase 'that is from the essence of the Father' the Creed emphasises that the Son's uniqueness lies in his relation to the Father, not simply as 'only-*begotten* Son' but as the Son who alone is begotten 'from the essence of the Father'.[1] Alexander of Alexandria had already emphasised this by insisting that Jesus Christ is the Son of God by nature (φύσει) while through faith in Christ men become God's children by adoption (θέσει). E. R. Hardy's translation of μονογενῆ by the adverb 'uniquely'[2] brings out the force of the word in its immediate context much better than the traditional, but erroneous, phrase 'only-begotten'. The Creed emphasises, not that the Son is the only-begotten from the Father, but that he is uniquely begotten from the Father, for he alone is begotten 'from the essence of the Father'.

The Nicene Creed proceeds with the phrases 'God from God, Light from Light', which also occur in that of Caesarea. In the latter, however, they are direct characterisations of 'the Logos of God', and therefore in the framework of the Logos-theology. Nicaea transfers them into the framework of the doctrine of the Son and goes on to add the further phrase 'true God from true God', which contradicts the idea of the inferiority of the Son to the Father (of the Logos to God) which both the Arians and Eusebius of Caesarea were insisting on. From the beginnings of the controversy Eusebius had interpreted John xvii. 3 to mean that the Father alone is 'true God', and that Jesus Christ, while being 'God', is not 'true God'. Eusebius would have agreed wholeheartedly with an expression such as 'God from true God' but, although he does not mention it in his *Letter to his Congregation*, he must have found the phrase '*true* God from true God' as difficult to accept as the phrases 'from the substance of the Father' and 'consubstantial with the Father'.

[1] It is likely that those drafting the Creed had in mind the fact that before St John speaks of Christ as μονογενής (i. 14), he already emphasises (i. 12, 13) that all who welcomed Christ and believed in his name were given power 'to become children of God' (τέκνα θεοῦ γενέσθαι), and describes them as those 'who were begotten from God' (ἐκ θεοῦ ἐγεννήθησαν).

[2] *Christology of the Later Fathers* (*LCC*, III), 338.

After distinguishing Christ's sonship from ours by asserting the uniqueness of his generation from the substance of the Father, Nicaea further distinguishes him from all created things by directly contradicting the Arian view that the Son is a κτίσμα, made ἐξ οὐκ ὄντων, with the assertion 'begotten, not made'. Then, in order to remove any possibility of equivocation, it proceeds to make the assertion of the reality of the Son's essential or substantial unity with the Father completely unmistakable by adding the phrase 'consubstantial with the Father' (ὁμοούσιον τῷ πατρί). It declares not only that the Son is 'from the substance of the Father' but that his 'substance' is the same as the substance of the Father. Thus, concisely, the Nicene Creed states the same basic doctrine as that which the Antiochene Letter had sought to state in a cumbersome way, when it said that the Son is 'begotten...from the Father, not as made but as properly an offspring, but begotten in an ineffable, indescribable manner...validly and truly begotten as Son...begotten of the unbegotten Father...the express image...of his Father's very substance'.

When we remember that at this time no distinction had been drawn between οὐσία and ὑπόστασις, it becomes evident that Antioch's phrase 'express image of his Father's very substance (ὑποστάσεως)', is very close to Nicaea's 'consubstantial with the Father'. On the other hand, Caesarea leaves the question of the οὐσία of the Son undefined and indefinite; Eusebius, however, followed his recital of his creed with the words: 'believing each of these (sc. Father, Logos, and Holy Spirit) to be and to exist, the Father truly Father, and the Son truly Son, and the Holy Spirit truly Holy Spirit'.[1] Nicaea is anxious to emphasise the essential oneness of the Father and the Son, while Eusebius and his creed seek to emphasise the distinction of the Son from the Father.

The *Letter of Narcissus of Neronias*, to which reference has already been made,[2] relates how Narcissus was asked by Hosius, apparently at the Synod of Antioch,[3] whether he, like Eusebius

[1] *Urk.* 22 (43, 15–17).   [2] *Urk.* 19; see above, pp. 173 f.

[3] The suggestion that the Synod of Antioch was the *locale* of this incident which Narcissus relates is made, with a great measure of plausibility by Opitz, 'Euseb von Caesarea als Theologe', in *ZNTW*, xxxiv (1935). Cf. also Berkhof, *Eusebius von Caesarea*, p. 176.

of Palestine, taught that there are 'two essences' (δύο οὐσίαι), to which Narcissus replied that according to the scriptures there are 'three essences' (τρεῖς οὐσίαι). For Eusebius the two essences were the Father and the Son; the Holy Spirit is the first creature created through the Logos;[1] the Logos–Son is a second independent divine being beside 'the only true God', a second οὐσία distinct from and inferior to the first divine οὐσία. In his letter to his congregation 'Eusebius does not commit himself to any positive sense in which the formula "of the essence" is to be understood, but only says what it does not mean'.[2] He writes:

We thought it good to assent to the sense of such religious doctrine, teaching as it did that the Son was from the Father, not however, as part of his essence. On this account we assented to the sense ourselves, without declining even the term ὁμοούσιος, peace being the object which we set before us, and steadfastness in the orthodox view.[3]

The assertion that the Son is ὁμοούσιος τῷ πατρί sums up the absolute uniqueness of the Son's relationship with the Father which the previous phrases of the creed emphasised by distinguishing between his sonship and ours, and between his origination and that of all the creatures. He is Son of God, begotten from the οὐσία of the Father; 'true God from true God', he is 'consubstantial with the Father'.

Having concentrated up to this point on the problem of safeguarding the divinity of Jesus Christ and the uniqueness of his relation to the Father, Nicaea turns its attention briefly to the cosmological role of the Son which it describes in words which conflate John i. 3a and Colossians i. 16: 'through whom all things were made, both things in heaven and things in

---

[1] Eusebius scarcely mentions the Holy Spirit in his writings. In *Dem. Ev.* and *Theophaneia* the Holy Spirit is ignored, while in *de. Ecc. Theol.*, in a section entitled 'How the Church of God Believes', he sets forth a curious 'trinity': 'Therefore for us there is one God, the Father, from whom are all things...and one Lord Jesus Christ, through whom are all things, who pre-exists only-begotten Son of God, and, thirdly, the Son of Man according to the flesh, which the Son of God assumed on our behalf' (I, 6; *GCS*, IV, 65, 3 ff.). Cf. Berkhof, *Eusebius von Caesarea*, 86 ff.

[2] Robertson, *Athanasius*, p. 75, note 5.

[3] *Urk.* 22 (45, 10–14).

earth'. The comparison of Nicaea and Caesarea at this point is again illuminating. The whole of the christological section of Caesarea from the primary characterisation of Christ as 'the Logos of God' is cosmological; the whole of the Nicene clause has been concerned with the Son's unique relation to the Father, and only now states his relationship to God's creative activity. Having stated it in brief scriptural terms, Nicaea moves on immediately to state the church's faith that this Son of God has become incarnate 'for us men and our salvation'.

The soteriological emphasis of the Nicene faith comes out clearly in the concluding section of the christological clause: 'who for us men and our salvation came down and was made flesh, became man, suffered, and rose again the third day, ascended into heaven, and is coming to judge the living and the dead'. The close similarity between this and the corresponding section of the Caesarean Creed must not be allowed to obscure the differences. The divine origin of the Son is emphasised in the words 'came down' which have no equivalent in either of the other two creeds. All three creeds assert that the Son 'was made flesh', but in order to emphasise the reality of the incarnation and the fullness of the manhood which the Son of God assumed it further defines 'was made flesh' by the phrase 'became man', a phrase with which the Antiochenes would be in full agreement with their traditional emphasis on the complete manhood of Christ. The Caesarean Creed, as we have already seen,[1] was content with the phrase 'and dwelt among men'. The emphasis on the full divinity of the Son (together with the omission of any reference to the Logos), coupled with the phrase 'became man' points to a God–Man christology in the Nicene Creed, a christology which avoids both the truncation of the humanity implicit in the *Logos–Sarx* christology of the apologetic and old Alexandrian tradition, represented by Eusebius of Caesarea, and the truncation of the divinity which is implicit in the *Word–Man* christology of the Antiochene tradition.

The Nicene formula is particularly significant beause it strives to do full justice to both of the Johannine paradoxes. For all of its emphasis on the co-eternity and consubstantiality of

---

[1] P. 175 above.

the Son with the Father, it still preserves the distinction between them, while for all its emphasis on the divinity of the Son, it preserves also the emphasis on his complete manhood. The transposition of theology from the cosmological key into a soteriological key has been made, but the debate on the trinitarian and christological implications of this transposition has only just begun.

CHAPTER 7

ATHANASIUS' REFUTATION OF
THE ARIANS

The Creed promulgated by the Nicene Council did not settle
the issue of Arianism; indeed, its definition of the relationship
of the Son to the Father served only to fan the fires of controversy which were to burn fiercely for the next fifty years. It
appears that Eustathius of Antioch, one of the signatories of the
Letter of the Synod of Antioch which had provisionally excommunicated Eusebius of Caesarea, was not convinced of the
latter's honesty and sincerity in subscribing his name, after a
day's delay, to the Nicene definition, and continued to charge
him with holding Arian views.[1] Eusebius counter-attacked by
charging Eustathius with Sabellianism. At a Synod held in
Antioch, shortly after the Arians regained favour with the
Emperor, Eustathius was deposed and exiled from Antioch.
The deposition, on whatever grounds it was achieved,[2] marked
the beginning of the Arian policy of forcing a reversal of the
decision of Nicaea by removing, one by one, the supporters of
the Nicene definition.

Having removed Eustathius, the Arians turned their attention to Athanasius who had succeeded to the see of Alexandria
a few months after the Council had ended, and in A.D. 335
Athanasius was exiled to Treveri in Gaul, after being found
guilty by an Arian Synod held at Tyre of murdering Arsenius,
a Melitian bishop, and of violently treating Ischyras, a Melitian presbyter, while the latter was in the very act of celebrating
the Eucharist.[3] It was possibly during this period of exile that
Athanasius composed his three *Orations against the Arians*,[4] which

[1] Socrates, *Hist. Eccl.* I, 23.
[2] Cf. R. V. Sellers, *Eustathius of Antioch*, ch. III.
[3] For Athanasius' own account, cf. *Apol. c. Ar.* 59–76.
[4] The question of the date of *Orations* has been the subject of considerable
discussion. A. Gaudel ('La théologie du Logos chez saint Athanase',
pp.524), gives a good summary of the debate up to 1929, and favours the
date 338–9 for their composition, as Loofs and Stülcken had done before

are the main source for the study of Athanasius' use of St John's Gospel in the refutation of the teachings of the Arians.

In these treatises Athanasius seeks to show that the Arian doctrine is absurd when it is taken to its logical conclusion, that it involves the denial of the fundamental teachings and practice of the church and, above all, that it is supported by a basically false method of interpreting the scriptures. He does not seek explicitly to defend the terminology in which the Nicene Council had stated the church's faith in Jesus Christ as the eternal Son of God; indeed, through respect for the many who felt that the insertion of non-scriptural terms into a creed was an innovation, he appears to avoid using ὁμοούσιος intentionally.[1] He is concerned not with arguments about words but with arguments about facts, and for him the facts are the faith of the church in the eternal divinity of the Son of God, Jesus Christ, the Saviour of the world, and the witness of scripture to this faith. After setting forth brief statements of Arian and Nicene doctrine[2] Athanasius asks, 'Which of the two theologies which have been set forth proclaims our Lord Jesus Christ as God and Son of the Father? This which you have vomited forth, or that which we have spoken and maintain from the scriptures?'[3] By far the larger part of the first three *Orations* consists of Athanasius' criticism of Arian exegesis of the texts which they used as supports for their teaching and, in contrast to it, his own exegesis of the same texts. His primary aim is to show that their teaching and their exegesis are 'alien to the divine oracles'.[4]

It has already been shown[5] how appeal to and exegesis of St John's Gospel played an important part in the ante-Nicene criticism of the teaching of Arius and his allies. This method of refutation is carried on by Athanasius and more fully developed by him; St John's Gospel provides him with his strongest argu-

---

him. D. Ritschl (*Athanasius*, p. 27) accepts a date 356–62, i.e. during Athanasius' third exile in the Egyptian desert, following W. Schneemelcher ('Athanasius von Alexandrien als Theologe und als Kirchenpolitiker', *ZNTW* (1950–1), p. 249). It is assumed here that the Fourth Oration is not by Athanasius, but cf. ch. 8 below.

[1] *Or. c. Ar.* I, 9 (*PG*, xxvi, 29) is the only passage in the *Orations* where he uses the term.

[2] *Idem* (*PG*, xxvi, 28–32).   [3] *Ibid.* I, 10 (*PG*, xxvi, 33).

[4] *Idem* (*PG*, xxvi, 33).   [5] See above, ch. 5.

ments against his opponents. Just as Hippolytus and Tertullian had accused their monarchian opponents of a 'piecemeal' use of scripture,[1] just as Novatian had argued that the only way in which his opponents could call their teaching scriptural was by cutting out of scripture all the passages which speak of Christ as divine,[2] so also Athanasius accuses his opponents of seizing on a few isolated texts, of lifting them out of their context, and interpreting them, not in the light of scripture as a whole, but in the light of their own presuppositions. Athanasius is more concerned with the sense of a passage than with its actual words, and he seeks to interpret individual texts in the light of the 'scope' (σκοπός)[3] of scripture as a whole. Indeed, it is the scope of scripture which forms the framework of his theology and the basis of his refutation of the Arians. He states what he means by the 'scope of scripture' thus:

Now the scope and character of holy scripture...is this: it contains a double account of the Saviour, that he was ever God and is the Son, being the Father's Logos and Radiance and Wisdom, and that afterwards for us he took flesh of a Virgin, Mary, Bearer of God, and was made man. This scope is to be found throughout inspired scripture.[4]

The thought of Athanasius revolves around two foci: the pre-existent divine Logos (John i. 1–3), and the Logos Incarnate (John i. 14). These foci are apparent in his basic equation: *Jesus Christ the Crucified = the Logos of God = the Saviour of the world*. This is the scope of faith and the scope of scripture, the Logos as God and the Logos as Man, Jesus Christ the God–Man.

As proof of this scope of scripture Athanasius quotes John i. 1–3 and i. 14: 'The Logos was God' and 'the Logos became flesh'. Beside these Johannine texts he sets Phil. ii. 6–8: 'Being in the form of God...taking the form of a servant... being found in human form'. He says:

---

[1] See above, pp. 53 ff. and 65 ff.   [2] See above, pp. 72 f.

[3] The word 'scope' is used here as a translation of σκοπός, but it must be borne in mind that σκοπός means more than 'scope' does. The meaning of σκοπός is 'the general drift of scripture doctrine' (Newman, in Robertson, *Athanasius*, 409, note 8). 'Scope' has been used because there is no other single word which is as suitable, however deficient it may be itself. Cf. my discussion in 'The Exegesis of Scripture and the Arian Controversy', *BJRL*, XLI (1959), 414 ff.

[4] *Or. c. Ar.* III, 29 (*PG*, XXVI, 385).

Anyone who begins with these passages and goes through the whole of scripture on the basis of the meaning which they suggest, will perceive how, in the beginning, the Father said to him, 'Let there be light', 'Let there be a firmament', and 'Let us make man' (Gen. i. 3, 6, 26), but, in the fullness of the ages, sent him into the world 'not that he might judge the world, but that the world might be saved through him' (John iii. 17).[1]

Jesus Christ is God *and* Man. To this both scripture and the faith of the church from the beginning bear witness; he who walked among men in Galilee and died on Calvary was in the beginning with God. This double scope of scripture provides Athanasius with the basis of his theology and, at the same time, with a court of appeal in criticising Arian exegesis.

The Arians fell into error because they ignored the scope of faith and of scripture, applying to the divinity of Christ what scripture attributes to his humanity. 'Being ignorant of this scope, they have wandered from the way of truth and have stumbled on a stone of stumbling (Rom. ix. 32), thinking otherwise than they ought to think.'[2] They do not interpret individual texts in the light of the whole of scripture. It is particularly when he comes to discuss the series of texts on the incarnation that Athanasius appeals to the scope of scripture,[3] but it lies behind the whole of his discussion of Arian doctrine, for his whole theology is built upon this principle as a foundation.

A. THE DOCTRINE OF THE ARIANS

The Arian propositions which Athanasius attacks in the *Orations* are basically the same as those which Alexander attacked at the beginning of the controversy; in the time that had elapsed, however, some of the Arian doctrines had undergone modification and clarification, mainly through the endeavours of Asterius the Sophist who appears to have become the main theological spokesman of the Arian party after Nicaea. In order that the Arian propositions which Athanasius attacks may be kept clearly in mind, they are set out below in words derived mainly from Athanasius' *Orations*:

(i) It has already been shown that the basis of Arianism was an abstract metaphysical monotheism. In their *Confessio Fidei*

---

[1] *Idem (PG, xxvi, 385 f.).*　　　　　　[2] *Ibid.* 28 *(PG, xxvi, 385).*
[3] *Ibid.* 26–58 *(PG, xxvi, 377–455).*

(*c.* A.D. 320) Arius and his colleagues made this plain: 'We know One God, alone unbegotten, alone eternal, alone without beginning, alone true, alone possessing immortality, alone wise, alone good, alone sovereign'.[1] On the basis of this extreme monotheism they argued:

(ii) If there is only one God, Jesus Christ the Son cannot be God in any real sense of the word.

(iii) If God alone is eternal, 'the Son of God did not always exist, and there was once when he was not' (οὐκ ἀεὶ ἦν ὁ υἱός... καὶ ἦν ποτε ὅτε οὐκ ἦν).[2]

(iv) If there is only one God, the Son cannot be from the essence of God, for that would mean that the essence of God is divisible.[3]

(v) If God alone is unbegotten (ἀγέννητος) or unoriginate (ἀγένητος) and without beginning (ἄναρχος), then the Son is originate (γενητός),[4] and has a beginning of being: 'He does not have his being at the same time as the Father, as some speak of relations, introducing two unbegotten beginnings' (οὐδε ἅμα τῷ πατρὶ τὸ εἶναι ἔχει, ὡς τινες λέγουσι τὰ πρός τι, δύο ἀγεννήτους ἀρχὰς εἰσηγούμενοι).[5]

(vi) If the Son is not from the essence of God, he must be from nothing (ἐξ οὐκ ὄντων),[6] and is therefore a creature and thing made (κτίσμα καὶ ποίημα).[7]

(vii) If God is unalterable and unchangeable (ἄτρεπτος καὶ ἀναλλοίωτος),[8] the Son, being a creature, is alterable by nature as all men are (τῇ φύσει, ὡς πάντες, οὕτω καὶ αὐτὸς ὁ λόγος ἐστι τρεπτός).[9]

These are the basic teachings which Athanasius attacks, but behind all his attacks on these tenets there lies an attack, sustained throughout his anti-Arian writings, on the very basis of the Arian structure, their philosophical conception of God. His attack on this emerges from the background and comes to the centre of the stage when Athanasius discusses the Arian view that God is unoriginate (ἀγέν[ν]ητος).

[1] Opitz, *Urk.* 6.
[2] *Or. c. Ar.* I, 5 (*PG*, XXVI, 21).
[3] *Urk.* 6.
[4] *Or. c. Ar.* I, 56 (*PG*, XXVI, 129).
[5] *Urk.* 6.
[6] *Or. c. Ar.* I, 5 (*PG*, XXVI, 21).
[7] *Ibid.* I, 9 (*PG*, XXVI, 28).
[8] *Urk.* 6.
[9] *Or. c. Ar.* I, 5 (*PG*, XXVI, 21). In their *Conf. Fid.* (Urk. 6), the Arians say that the Son also is ἄτρεπτος καὶ ἀναλλοίωτος; they would not have added the words τῇ φύσει however, for Athanasius (I, 5) shows that they taught that the Son was τρεπτός by nature, but ἄτρεπτος by grace.

B. THE IDEA OF GOD

R. Arnou makes the interesting suggestion that 'at the period when Arianism arose, recourse was had to the doctrine of relations in order to explain how the Father and the Son exist simultaneously from all eternity'.[1] It has already been pointed out that Tertullian makes use of the doctrine of relations to prove that the two *relata* in the Father–Son relationship cannot be identical,[2] and that Dionysius of Alexandria uses it to prove the co-eternity of the Father and the Son.[3] Arnou points to the statement in the Arians' *Confessio Fidei* that 'the Son is not eternal, nor co-eternal with the Father, nor co-unoriginate; he does not have his being at the same time as the Father, as some speak of relations, introducing two unbegotten (or unoriginate) beginnings',[4] and he concludes from that that 'the Arians no longer wish to regard the Father and the Son as the terms of a relation'.[5] He suggests that the Arians are attacking the view which Dionysius of Alexandria had proposed: 'Since the Father is eternal, the Son is eternal, being Light from Light; for if there is a parent, there is also a child. If there were not a child, how and of whom could there be a parent? But there are both, and they always exist.'[6] Arnou maintains that the Arians rejected the Aristotelian doctrine of relations because they thought that its application to the godhead destroys the 'monarchy' of the Father; if the Father and the Son exist simultaneously from eternity, then there must be two beginnings or first principles (ἀρχαί), which is impossible. Therefore they argue that the Son must have had a beginning, and there must have been once when he was not.

Arnou's suggestion is valuable in so far as it draws attention to the use made of the doctrine of relations; his main thesis, however, is false at this point for the Arians were not concerned to safeguard the monarchy of the Father *qua* Father, but rather the monarchy of God *qua* God. Arius says, 'God was not always a Father. Once God was alone and not yet a Father, but he

---

[1] 'Arius et la doctrine des relations trinitaires', *Greg*, xiv (1933), pp. 270 f.
[2] See above, pp. 64 f.   [3] See above, pp. 108 f.
[4] *Urk.* 6.
[5] 'Arius et la doctrine des relations trinitaires', p. 270.
[6] *Apud* Athanasius, *de Sent. Dion.* 15 (Feltoe, p. 186, 4–9).

became a Father afterwards',[1] thus accepting the doctrine of relations, but rejecting the idea that the Father–Son relationship in the godhead is eternal. The difference between the Arians and their opponents is at a deeper level by far than the acceptance or rejection of the doctrine of relations; it is a difference between fundamentally opposed conceptions of God.

In the face of the orthodox doctrine that the Son is co-eternal with the Father, the Arians ask, 'Is the Unoriginate one or two?'[2] In reply Athanasius argues:

(i) The Arians, who have criticised the Nicene bishops for introducing non-scriptural phrases, fall under the same accusation themselves; ἀγένητος is not to be found in scripture.[3]

(ii) They disagree among themselves on the exact meaning of the word.[4]

(iii) The introduction of this term is a subterfuge to deceive the simple now that they have been forbidden to use their other phrases, 'once he was not', and 'he was not before his generation'.[5]

(iv) Despite their denials, 'this term is not used in contrast with the Son but with originated things (τὰ γενητά)'.[6] That is, ἀγένητος does not distinguish the Father from the Son, but God from the creatures. If the Father rules over all things through his Logos (cf. John i. 3), then the Son is not to be counted as one of the 'all'. 'As the word "unoriginate" (ἀγένητος) is meant in relation to originated things (τὰ γενητά), so the word "Father" is indicative of the Son...He who calls God "Father", in doing so conceives and contemplates the Son.'[7]

(v) The Arians may think that by calling God 'unoriginate' they are preserving his honour and dignity; but they have not read the words of the Son of God himself, 'He who does not honour the Son, does not honour the Father who sent him' (John v. 23).[8]

(vi) Athanasius develops more fully the argument of (iv). When the Arians call God 'unoriginate', they are naming him from his relation to the things which he has made, thinking that

---

[1] *Or. c. Ar.* i, 5 (*PG*, xxvi, 21).
[2] *Ibid.* i, 30 (*PG*, xxvi, 73).
[3] *Idem.*
[4] *Ibid.* i, 30–1 (*PG*, xxvi, 73–7).
[5] *Ibid.* i, 32 (*PG*, xxvi, 77–80).
[6] *Ibid.* i, 33 (*PG*, xxvi, 80).
[7] *Idem.*
[8] *Idem.*

in this way they will be able to demonstrate that the Son is a ποίημα. Athanasius says: 'They do not know the Son any more than the Greeks do; but he who calls God "Father" names him from the Logos, and knowing the Logos, he acknowledges him to be fashioner of all, and understands that through him all things have been made (John i. 3)';[1] and 'The title "Father" has its significance and bearing only from the Son.'[2]

(vii) The term ἀγένητος is unscriptural and is to be suspected because of the wide variety of meanings which it has; on the other hand, 'the word "Father" is simple and scriptural and more accurate and alone implies the Son', and, furthermore, the name 'Father' is that which Jesus himself uses when speaking of God and to God.

For he, himself knowing whose Son he was, said, 'I am in the Father and the Father in me' (John x. 38; xiv. 10), and 'I and the Father are one' (John x. 30), and 'He who has seen me has seen the Father' (John xiv. 9); but nowhere is he found calling the Father 'Unoriginate'.[3]

Athanasius points out that the Lord's Prayer does not begin, 'O God Unoriginate', but 'Our Father', and Jesus does not command us to be baptised into the name of Unoriginate and Originate, but into the name of Father, Son and Holy Spirit. Therefore, says Athanasius, 'their argument about the term "unoriginate" is vain and nothing more than a fantasy'.[4]

For Athanasius, then, such metaphysical concepts as those which the Arians apply to the godhead have no connection with the Christian doctrine of God; for him the essence of the godhead is that it contains the Father–Son relationship within itself, it belongs to the essence of God that he is Father of an only Son, and it is the eternal process of the generation of the Son from the Father 'that constitutes the life of God'.[5] This is the Christian God, not the 'Unoriginate' but the Father of our Lord Jesus Christ; this is the centre of God's self-revelation in Christ, that he is Father of the only Son, and that through his goodness and grace men also may become his sons by adoption;

---

[1] *Ibid.* 1, 33 (*PG*, xxvi, 81).   [2] *Ibid.* 1, 34 (*PG*, xxvi, 81).
[3] *Idem.* John xiv. 10, xiv. 9, and x. 30 are a trilogy of texts to which Athanasius appeals continually.
[4] *Idem* (*PG*, xxvi, 84).
[5] L. Bouyer, *L'incarnation et l'Église-Corps du Christ*, p. 57.

this revelation is the surety of our hope of eternal life, of our restoration to fellowship with God, of our deliverance from the curse and sentence of death.

Over against the metaphysical monotheism of the Arians, for whom the essence of the godhead is to be without beginning and unoriginate, Athanasius sets the biblical concept of the living and loving God, the Father of Jesus Christ. Over against the concept of a God who is remote, inaccessible and incapable of entering into direct relations with the created world, Athanasius sets the church's faith in a God who condescends continually to man in creation, revelation, redemption and sanctification; who, in Jesus Christ his Son, becomes man for the salvation of men. The God of the Arians neither creates, nor reveals himself, nor redeems man. 'Arius never speaks of the love of God.'[1]

There is no room in Athanasius' conception of God for the lifeless, impersonal, privative attributes derived from extra-biblical sources, which the Arians ascribe to the godhead. The difference between Athanasius and Arius is the difference between a living religion and an intellectualistic philosophy, between salvation and speculation, between the evangelical faith in God who reveals himself as Father through his Son Jesus Christ and flights of metaphysical fancy into the realm of the unknown and unknowable. 'The sin of Arianism is that it shifts the centre of interest from the hope of salvation to the hope of explanation.'[2]

C. THE IDEA OF THE LOGOS

From the beginning of the controversy the Arians had drawn, as we have seen, a radical distinction between the Logos which, as an attribute, is proper to God and co-eternal with him, and the Son, who may be called 'Logos' by grace since he partakes of God's proper Logos;[3] indeed Arius says that he is only called 'Son' by grace.[4] Nowhere, however, in any of the extant fragments of the writings of Arius and Asterius the

---

[1] H. M. Gwatkin, quoted by D. M. Baillie, *God was in Christ*, London, 1948, p. 70.

[2] W. Temple, *Christus Veritas*, p. 131.   [3] See above, pp. 143 f.

[4] *Or. c. Ar.* I, 5 (*PG*, XXVI, 21).

Sophist and the other early Arians,[1] is any indication given who this Being is who receives the names 'Logos' and 'Son' by grace. Arius says, 'Wishing to form us, God thereupon made a certain one (ἕνα τινά), and named him Logos and Wisdom and Son, that he might form us by means of him.'[2] This Being is a 'certain one', made to be the instrument of God in the creation of all the rest of the creatures; he is a κτίσμα, ποίημα, γενητόν. Arius was forced to qualify this statement that the Son is a creature by adding 'but not as one of the creatures'.[3]

The Arians make an absolute distinction between the Logos and the Son. Athanasius assumes their identity; for him they are one and the same being, and the titles refer to the same being. But what does he mean by the title 'Logos'? Nowhere in his ante-Nicene writings does he make the content of his Logos-concept plain, and it is not until the middle of the second anti-Arian Oration that he states explicitly what he means by this term.[4]

Athanasius' starting-point is John i. 1–3. The Logos is necessary to God as mediator of his creative activity; 'the creatures could not have come into existence except through him'.[5] 'As by a hand, the Father accomplished all things by the Logos, and without him makes (or does?—ποιεῖ) nothing.'[6]

[1] The fragments of the writings of Arius, Asterius, and the other early Arians have been collected by G. Bardy in his invaluable study of the Collucianists, *Recherches sur saint Lucien d'Antioche et son école*. Those of Arius may be found in Bardy, 'La Thalie d'Arius', in *RPh*, LIII (1927), 211–33, and those of Asterius in Bardy, 'Asterius le Sophiste', in *RHE*, XXII (1926), 221–72. Asterius' *Homilies on the Psalms*, which have been falsely attributed hitherto to Asterius of Amaseia and John Chrysostom, have been published by Marcel Richard as *Fasciculus Suppletorius* XIV *Symbolae Osloenses*. A pre-history of this edition is to be found in Eiliv Skard, *Asterius von Amaseia und Asterios der Sophist*, in *SO*, fasc. 20 (1940), pp. 86–132, and M. Richard, *Une ancienne collection d'homélies grecques sur les Psaumes i–xv*, in *SO* fasc. 25 (1947), pp. 59 ff. Richard says of the task of editing these homilies, 'What makes it worth while, extremely worth while, is that it opens up to us completely new perspectives on the exegesis of the school of Lucian of Antioch and particularly on the pastoral theology of the Arians. I do not think that after reading the homilies of Asterius one can keep any great illusions on the pretended literalistic exegesis of the Collucianist party' ('Saint Athanase et la psychologie du Christ selon les Ariens', p. 72). These homilies, however, contain little trinitarian doctrine.

[2] *Or. c. Ar.* I, 5 (*PG*, XXVI, 21). [3] *Urk.* 6.
[4] *Or. c. Ar.* II, 31 ff. (*PG*, XXVI, 212 f.).
[5] *Ibid.* II, 31 (*PG*, XXVI, 212). [6] *Idem.*

This necessity, however, is not an external necessity; the Logos does not come into existence for the purpose of fulfilling God's creative will, but is proper to the essence of God. The activity of creation, like all the external activities of God, is an activity of the whole godhead, and not of only a part of the godhead. While Athanasius often ascribes the work of creation directly to God the Father,[1] his fuller teaching is that creation is the work of the whole trinity. The necessity of creating *through the Logos* is a necessity inherent in the very nature of the godhead. When God said, 'Let there be light', 'Let the waters be gathered together', 'Let the dry land appear', and 'Let us make man' (Gen. i. 3, 6, 9, 26)—and as the Psalmist says, 'He spake and they were made; he commanded and they were created' (Ps. xxxiii. 9—LXX, xxxii. 9)—God 'spoke, not, as in the case of men, in order that some under-worker might hear, and learning the will of him who spoke, go away and do it', but he spoke to his Logos 'who is the Fashioner and Maker and the Father's Will'. When God speaks to others—angels, Moses, the patriarchs and prophets—there is questioning and answering, but in the case of the Logos this is not so, for the Father is in him and he is in the Father (John xiv. 10).

It is sufficient (for God) to will and the work is done... 'God said' is explained in 'the Logos', for it says, 'Thou hast made all things in Wisdom' (Ps. civ. 24—LXX, ciii. 24), 'By the Logos of the Lord were the heavens made fast' (Ps. xxxiii. 6—LXX, xxxii. 6), and 'There is one Lord Jesus Christ through whom are all things and we through him' (I Cor. viii. 6).[2]

It is plain from this that the primary content of Athanasius' Logos-concept is the creative Word-concept of the Old Testament. God's Word, Will, and Act are one;[3] God's Word contains the Deed within itself.[4] Like St John, however, Athanasius cannot leave the matter there; the fact of the incarnation, of the identification of this creative Word with Jesus Christ, has

[1] E.g. in *c. Gentes*, 2, 3, 4, 6, 7, etc.; J. B. Berchem, 'Le rôle du Verbe dans l'œuvre de la création', *Ang.* xv (1938), 204.

[2] *Or. c. Ar.* II, 31 (*PG*, XXVI, 213). Athanasius misquotes I Cor. viii. 6: TR has ἐξ οὗ τὰ πάντα καὶ ἡμεῖς εἰς αὐτόν, whereas Athanasius says δι'οῦ... δι' αὐτοῦ.

[3] Cf. E. Stauffer, *N.T. Theology*, London, 1955, ch. 10.

[4] *Ibid.* p. 56, and note 110.

transformed the Hebraic Word-concept. The Logos, the Word of creation and revelation in the Old Testament, is the Son of God, Jesus Christ. The Arians, seeking to divide the Logos from the Son, ask, 'How can the Son be a Word, or the Word be God's Image? For the word of a man is composed of syllables and only signifies the speaker's will, and then is over and lost.'[1] Athanasius replies that we must not push the analogy between a human word and God's Word too far, for 'God is not as a man'.[2] Since a man 'has come into existence from nothing, his word also is over and does not continue (in existence). God, however, is not as a man, but continues to exist and is eternal; therefore, his Word also continues to exist and is eternally with the Father.'[3] A man's word is composed of syllables, it is significative of the speaker's meaning, but it is not living and effective; it is uttered, then disappears, for it did not exist in any way before it was spoken. On the other hand,

God's Word is not merely pronounced (προφορικός), as it were, nor is it a sound of spoken words, nor is 'the Son' this, namely God's act of commanding (τὸ προστάξαι θεόν); but as radiance from light so he is perfect offspring from the Perfect. Hence he is also God, as being God's Image; for 'the Word was God' (John i. 1 c).[4]

We must not ask, says Athanasius, why God's Word is different from ours, nor must we ask how the Word is from God, or how he begets the Word who is his Son. It is by seeking to answer such questions that the Arians fall into error, for they seek to know what is known to God alone, and to measure God by the yardstick of our human nature. Against them Athanasius emphasises that the Father–Son relationship within the godhead, the generation of the Son from the Father, the begetting of the Logos by the Father, are not facts reached by human reasoning, but facts given by God in his self-revelation.

[1] *Or. c. Ar.* II, 34 (*PG*, XXVI, 220). In the argument that follows it is necessary to translate λόγος as *Word* or *word*, rather than to transliterate it as hitherto.

[2] Num. xxiii. 19, a text which Athanasius quotes continually. While Athanasius understands the O.T. doctrine of the Word of God, the distinction which he draws between God's Word and a human word is not Hebraic. In Hebraic thought even a man's word has a concrete existence. This, however, does not affect his understanding of the *d^ebhar Yahweh*.

[3] *Or. c. Ar.* II, 35 (*PG*, XXVI, 221).   [4] *Idem.*

If we would take our human speech as an analogy of God's speaking, we must not press the analogy too far; the most that we can say that our words have in common with the Word of God is that they are 'proper to us, from us, and not a work external to us; so God's Word is proper to him, is from him, and is not a work'.[1] That is as far as the similarity goes. Men's words are many and various, they are spoken, then disappear:

God's Word is one and the same, and, as it is written, 'The Word of God endureth for ever' (Ps. cxix. 89—LXX, cxviii. 89), not changed, not before or after another, but existing the same always. For it was fitting, since God is one, that his Image should be one also, and his Word one and his Wisdom one.[2]

The Arians, however, insist on taking metaphors literally and on pushing analogies to extremes. 'The trouble with Arius was that he could not understand a metaphor';[3] he treats God's Word as if it were in every way similar to a human word. 'Many words does God speak; which of these then are we to call Son and Word, only-begotten of the Father?'[4]

The Arians deny the identity of the Logos and the Son: The Father's proper and natural Logos is other than the Son; he who is really Son is only notionally (κατ' ἐπίνοιαν μόνον) called Logos, in the same way as he is called Vine, and Way, and Door, and Tree of Life; he is also called Wisdom in name, the proper and true Wisdom of the Father which co-exists unoriginately (ἀγεν[ν]ήτως) with him being other than the Son, by which he even made the Son and named him Wisdom, as partaking of it.[5]

From this Athanasius concludes that the Arians teach that there are two *logoi* of God,[6] that which is proper to God as an attribute, and the Son who is Logos only nominally and notionally. Replying to this Arian distinction, Athanasius asks where in the scriptures they have found it written that there is another

---

[1] *Ibid.* II, 36 (*PG*, XXVI, 224–5).   [2] *Idem.*

[3] H. E. W. Turner, *The Pattern of Christian Truth*, p. 439.

[4] *Apud* Athanasius, *de Decr.* 16 (*PG*, XXV, 444).

[5] *Apud* Athanasius, *Or. c. Ar.* II, 37 (*PG*, XXVI, 225); cf. *Urk* 4 *b*.

[6] It is possible that Arius derived this idea from Origen's interpretation of John i. 1 *a*; Origen said that Wisdom is the ἀρχή of the Logos (*in Joh.* I, 22). The Arians have made the Logos, like Wisdom, an attribute of God, whose ἀρχή is God. The Son, who partakes of the Logos and Wisdom, is in the Logos which is his ἀρχή.

Logos and Wisdom beside the Son. Scripture certainly speaks of 'words' of God (Jer. xxiii. 29, Prov. i. 23, Ps. cxix. 101, etc.), but these are God's precepts and commands to men. The Son distinguishes himself from such 'words' of God when he says, 'The words which I have spoken to you' (John vi. 63). There was only one Word, that which became flesh (John i. 14), that through which all things were made (John i. 3). Athanasius continues:

Of him alone, our Lord Jesus Christ, and concerning his oneness with the Father (περὶ τῆς πρὸς τὸν πατέρα ἑνότητος αὐτοῦ) are the testimonies written and set forth, both those of the Father who signifies that the Son is one (Matt. iii. 17 and parallel, Matt. xvii. 5 and parallels), and of the saints, who are aware of this, that the Word is one and that he is unique (μονογενής, John i. 18; iii. 16, 17, I John iv. 9). And his works are set forth, for all things visible and invisible have been made through him (Col. i. 16) and 'without him not one thing was made' (John i. 3).[1]

The Arian distinction between the Logos and the Son, then, is contrary to the witness of scripture, which identifies the two:

The Word of God is one, being the only Son proper and genuine from his essence, who has with his Father the indivisible oneness of the godhead (ἀχώριστον ἔχων πρὸς τὸν πατέρα ἑαυτοῦ τὴν ἑνότητα τῆς θεότητος)...If it were not so, why does the Father create through him (Col. i. 16, John i. 3), and in him reveal himself to whom he wills (Matt. xi. 27), and illuminate them (John i. 9)?[2]

Just as Athanasius sets over against the Arian metaphysical conception of God the biblical idea of the living, creating, revealing and saving God of the Bible, so also, over against the Arian metaphysical distinction between the Logos and the Son, he sets the biblical identification of the two in Jesus Christ, the Son of God, the Word made flesh. Athanasius' concept of the Logos is Johannine, and he places the emphasis where St John places it, on the Logos Incarnate, Jesus Christ.

[1] *Or. c. Ar.* II, 39 (*PG*, XXVI, 229).
[2] *Ibid.* II, 41 (*PG*, XXVI, 233).

D. THE ETERNITY OF THE SON

The Arians' conception of God and the distinction which they drew between the Logos and the Son necessarily involve the denial of the Son's eternity: 'There was once when the Son was not'.[1]

Against this Arian doctrine, Athanasius sets many proofs from scripture, most of them drawn from the Fourth Gospel.

(i) Jesus says, 'I am the Truth' (John xiv. 6); he does not say, 'I became the Truth', but it is always '*I am*'—'I am the Shepherd' (John x. 14), 'the Light' (John viii. 12), and 'Teacher and Lord' (John xiii. 13). 'The words "I am" mean that the Son is eternal and without beginning before all time' (τὸ ἀΐδιον καὶ τὸ πρὸ παντὸς αἰῶνος τοῦ υἱοῦ).[2] Thus Athanasius does not hesitate to ascribe to the Son the property of being without beginning which the Arians would ascribe only to the God who is over all. He goes on to point out that Jesus implies his eternity when he says, 'If you loved me, you would have rejoiced because I said, I go to the Father, for my Father is greater than I' (John xiv. 28), and again when he says, 'Before Abraham was, I am' (John viii. 58).[3]

(ii) The Arians object that if the Son is co-eternal with the Father, he should not be called the Father's Son, but brother; Athanasius replies, 'How can he who is begotten be considered brother of him who begets?' The Father and the Son do not come from some pre-existing source (ἔκ τινος ἀρχῆς προϋπαρχούσης), as they would do if they were brothers. The Father is the source and begetter of the Son (ὁ πατὴρ ἀρχὴ τοῦ υἱοῦ καὶ γεννήτωρ ἐστί).[4] The error of the Arians lies

in considering the relations independently of the processions without which we could not know that there are relations in God. The Father and the Son, as terms of the same relation, exist simultaneously; yes, but as Father and Son, the one proceeding from the other. To

---

[1] *Or. c. Ar.* I, 5 (*PG*, XXVI, 21); cf. also *ibid.* I, 11, 14, 18; II, 33, 43; III, 59.

[2] *Ibid.* I, 12 (*PG*, XXVI, 37).

[3] *Ibid.* I, 13 (*PG*, XXVI, 37–40). Athanasius' point in quoting John xiv. 28 here is not clear unless we read into the quotation the meaning which he gives to it later.

[4] *Ibid.* I, 14 (*PG*, XXVI, 40–1).

consider them as 'two beginnings' because of the fact that they are correlative is to forget that in God the relation, as such, implies necessarily an order of origin.[1]

The difference between Athanasius and the Arians is the difference between opposed conceptions of the generation of the Son from the Father. For the Arians, the begetting of the Son is an *act* of God which takes place at a specific point of time like the begetting of a son from a human father, and it naturally involves the idea of the Son's posteriority to the Father. For Athanasius, on the other hand, the Son's begetting by and from the Father is an eternal *fact*,[2] an eternal *activity* within the godhead, just as it was for Origen.[3]

(iii) Athanasius asserts that the Logos = Wisdom = Jesus Christ on the basis of three texts:

Ps. civ. 24: 'In Wisdom thou has made them all'.

John i. 3: 'All things were made through' the Logos 'and without him was made not even one thing'.

I Cor. viii. 6: 'There is one God, the Father, from whom are all things... and one Lord, Jesus Christ. through whom are all things.'

Scripture ascribes the mediatorial work in creation to the Logos, to Wisdom, and to Jesus Christ. Over and over again Athanasius repeats the argument: 'If "all things are through him", he himself is not to be counted as one of the "all".[4] If he is not one of the "all", then he must be such as the Father is, and therefore he is eternal.'[5]

(iv) If the Son 'was not before his generation' (οὐκ ἦν ὁ υἱὸς πρὶν γεννηθῇ),[6] as the Arians assert, then Truth was not always in God, and that is blasphemous, 'for since the Father was, the Truth was always in him, and this Truth is the Son who says, "I am the Truth" (John xiv. 6)'.[7]

(v) Athanasius closely connects Col. i 15 with John xiv. 9. If the Son is 'the Image of the invisible God', then he must possess all the attributes of the Father, otherwise the words of

---

[1] R. Arnou, 'Arius', pp. 271 f.; cf. Ps.-Ath., *Or. c. Ar.* IV, I.

[2] Cf. Robertson, *Athanasius*, p. 314, note 4.

[3] See above, pp. 93 ff.   [4] *Or. c. Ar.* I, 19 (*PG*, XXVI, 52).

[5] *Idem.*

[6] *Ibid.* I, 11 (*PG*, XXVI, 33).

[7] *Ibid.* I, 20 (*PG*, XXVI, 55).

Jesus 'He who has seen me has seen the Father', are false. If the Son is not eternal, how can he be the Image of the Father?[1]

The Arians object that if the Son is the Image of the Father, he also, like the Father, ought to beget a Son and become a Father. Fatherhood, says Athanasius, is not an attribute of God; the Father–Son relation is not an accidental property of the godhead but the very life of the godhead. 'The Father is always Father, and the Son is always Son.'[2] While denying the propriety of using anthropomorphic language concerning God, Arius treats the Father–Son relationship in God as though it were in every way similar to the father–son relationship among men. Athanasius argues that it is not essential for a man to be a father, but God is always Father:

God is not as a man, for men beget passibly, having a fluctuating nature which has to wait for seasons because of the weakness of its own nature. This, however, cannot be said of God, for he is not composed of parts, but being impassible and simple, he is impassibly and indivisibly Father of the Son. There is strong evidence and proof of this from divine scripture. For the Logos of God is his Son, and the Son is the Father's Logos and Wisdom...Joining the two titles, scripture speaks of the 'Son', then, in order to proclaim the natural and true offspring of the Father's essence, and, on the other hand, in order that no one may think of the offspring in a human way, when signifying his essence it also calls him 'Logos', 'Wisdom' and 'Radiance', to teach us that the generation was impassible and eternal and worthy of God.[3]

(vi) One further argument on the eternity of the Son must be considered, not directly in connection with the use of St John's Gospel, but in connection with the central point of the controversy. Athanasius appeals to the doctrine of the trinity, which has been the framework of the church's catechetical instruction from the beginning: 'If the Son is not with the Father eternally, then the trinity is not eternal'. The Arians teach that first there was the Monad alone, and then, by a process of addition, the Monad becomes a Triad. A creature is added to the Creator and 'receives divine worship and glory with him who eternally existed'. The Arian trinity is a trinity-

---

[1] *Idem.*   [2] *Ibid.* I, 20 f. (*PG*, XXVI, 53–57).
[3] *Ibid.* I, 28 (*PG*, XXVI, 69).

by-addition, and there is no telling where the process will end.[1]
The Arians have opened the door to polytheism.

Athanasius asserts that if there were not a trinity eternally,
then there is never a trinity:

The faith of Christians acknowledges that the blessed trinity is
unalterable and perfect and ever what it was, neither adding to it
anything more, nor subtracting from it...and therefore it dissociates
it from all originated things, and it guards the unity of the godhead
itself as indivisible and worships it...And it confesses and acknowledges that the Son was always, for he is eternal like the Father
whose eternal Logos he is.[2]

Athanasius proclaims an eternal trinity, the Arians a trinity-
by-addition, and, as we shall see,[3] Marcellus a trinity-by-
expansion.

E. THE ESSENTIAL SONSHIP OF THE SON

Closely connected with the refutation of the Arian denial of the
Son's eternity is the refutation of their further denial that the
Son is the proper offspring of the Father's essence (τὸ δὲ εἶναι
τοῦτον τῆς οὐσίας τοῦ πατρὸς ἴδιον γέννημα ἀρνοῦνται).[4] They
argue that to say that the Son is ἐκ τῆς οὐσίας τοῦ πατρός
implies that the godhead is divisible and composed of parts; if
the essence of God is indivisible, then the Son cannot be from
that essence, but must be from nothing. Athanasius refutes this
argument by drawing out its implications. 'If then the Son is
from nothing, he, as well as others, must be called Son and God
and Wisdom by participation (κατὰ μετουσίαν).' Of what does
he partake then? Unlike all other created beings, he does not
partake of the Spirit, for the Spirit takes from the Son (John
xvi. 15). Therefore it must be of the Father that he partakes;
when the Son says that God is his own Father (John v. 18), it
follows that what is partaken is not something external to the
Father, but the essence of the Father. 'What is from the essence
of the Father and proper to him is altogether the Son; to say
that God is wholly participated is equal to saying that he begets,
and what does begetting signify but a Son?'[5]

[1] *Ibid.* I, 17 (*PG*, xxvi, 48).   [2] *Ibid.* I, 18 (*PG*, xxvi, 48–49).
[3] See below, pp. 248 ff.   [4] *Or. c. Ar.* I, 15 (*PG*, xxvi, 44).
[5] *Ibid.* I, 15 f. (*PG*, xxvi, 44 f.).

In a magnificent passage, Athanasius argues that revelation, creation, and salvation are all dependent upon the Son's being the proper offspring of the Father's essence:

Beholding the Son, we see the Father (John xiv. 9), for the thought and comprehension of the Son is knowledge of the Father (Matt. xi. 27), because he is his proper offspring from his essence...If, then, ...what is the offspring of the Father's essence is the Son...we cannot hesitate, indeed we are certain, that the same is the Wisdom (I Cor. i. 24, Prov. viii. 20 ff.), and Logos (John i. 1–3) of the Father, in and through whom he creates and makes all things (Col. i. 16, John i. 3), and his brightness also (Heb. i. 3) in whom he enlightens all things (John i. 9), and is revealed to whom he will (Matt. xi. 27), and his expression (Heb. i. 3) and image (Col. i. 15), in whom he is contemplated and known. Therefore he and the Father are one (John x. 30), and he who sees him sees the Father (John xiv. 9); and (he is) the Christ, in whom all things are redeemed (Gal. iii. 13), and the new creation wrought afresh (II Cor. v. 17).[1]

There is little direct argument against the Arian denial that the Son is from the essence of the Father, but indirectly, in all that he has to say about the distinction between Christ's sonship and ours, and in his refutation of the Arian doctrine that the Son is a creature, Athanasius is affirming the essential sonship of Jesus Christ.

F. THE SON OF GOD IS NOT A CREATURE

The Arian proposition, 'The Son is a creature', sums up in itself the whole of the Arian heresy, and it is to the refutation of this doctrine that Athanasius devotes his longest and most thorough argument. The Arians supported this proposition by a literal interpretation of Prov. viii. 22 (LXX),[2] a text which had from very early times been given a christological reference.

St Paul had called Jesus Christ 'the Wisdom of God' (I Cor. i. 24),[3] and from then onwards the early church had found in

---

[1] *Ibid.* 1, 16 (*PG*, xxvi, 45).

[2] Cf. Simonetti, *Studi sull'Arianesimo*, pp. 32 ff.

[3] Rendell Harris, in *The Origin of the Prologue to St John's Gospel*, claims that there is a Wisdom-christology even in the Synoptic Gospels and Acts, and argues that the Prologue of St John was originally a hymn of praise to Wisdom, in which λόγος was later substituted for σοφία.

the Old Testament figure of Wisdom a reference to Jesus Christ.[1] This verse (Prov. viii. 22), as it was translated in the LXX, provided the Arians with their most explicit scriptural proof that the Son was a creature: 'The Lord created (ἔκτισεν) me a beginning of his ways for his works'.

It may be regretted that Athanasius did not know Hebrew or, if he did, did not refer to the Hebrew text, but it must be remembered that very early in the history of the church the LXX had become the bible of the church and was regarded by all as inspired.[2] Eusebius of Caesarea, who had access to Origen's *Hexapla*, was the only writer of the immediate post-Nicene period to compare the LXX with the Hebrew and with the other Greek versions, and he discusses the question at great length.[3] He discusses the LXX reading first, and says that 'created' is said metaphorically for 'ordained' or 'appointed'.[4] Next he turns to the Hebrew text which has *qānāh*, and which the versions of Aquila, Symmachus and Theodotion translate by ἐκτήσατο ('possessed'); this reading is to be preferred to ἔκτισεν, for it can be taken literally, since the Son is the possession of the Father. Eusebius says:

There would be a great difference between 'created' and 'possessed'; the former indicates the creature according to the usual meaning of passing from non-existence into existence; the latter indicates the possession of the pre-existent one, as involving a peculiar relationship to him who possesses.[5]

The Arians, however, persisted in accepting the LXX reading[6] and it is on the basis of it that Athanasius attempts to refute them by applying to it, not very convincingly, his principle of appeal to the scope of scripture, and by arguing that 'created

---

[1] Justin, *Dial.* 61, 129; Athenagoras, *Leg.* 10; Clem. Alex. *Protr.* 8; Irenaeus, *adv. Haer.* IV, 20, 3; Tertullian, *adv. Prax.* 6; Origen, *in Joh.* I, 11, 17, 22, etc.

[2] Cf. G. A. F. Knight, *A Biblical Approach to the Doctrine of the Trinity* (*SJT* Occ. Paper, 1), pp. 1–8.

[3] *de Ecc. Theol.* III, 2, 1 (*GCS*, IV, 138, 31 ff.); cf. Simonetti, *Studi sull'Arianesimo* pp. 48 ff.

[4] *Ibid.* III, 2, 14 (*GCS*, IV, 141, 26 ff.).   [5] *Idem* (*GCS*, IV, 143).

[6] Epiphanius records (*Haer.* LXXIII, 29–33) that in 361, Emperor Constantius commanded a series of sermons to be delivered on Prov. viii. 22 (LXX) by Arianising Bishops assembled in Antioch for the purpose of electing a new bishop.

refers to the flesh which the Logos assumed at the incarnation.[1] Despite the weakness of this argument, however, Athanasius incorporates into the framework of his exegesis of Prov. viii. 22 a vast mass of exegesis of other scriptural passages, which in itself is sufficient refutation of the Arian doctrine.

(i) Athanasius opens his attack on the Arian doctrine of the creatureliness of the Son by criticising the chameleon-like changes of Arian terminology; they put their doctrine into 'various shapes, and turn the same errors to and fro, hoping that the changes will deceive some'.[2] Thus they qualify their original statement that the Son is a creature by adding 'but not as one of the creatures'. This qualification, says Athanasius, means nothing; if the Son is a creature, even though not like the rest of the creatures, his difference from the rest is only one of degree, and he is still a creature, no matter by how much he may excel the rest.

Quoting Ps. xix. 1, 'The heavens declare the glory of God and the firmament showeth his handiwork', and I Esdras iv. 26, 'All the earth calleth upon the truth', Athanasius argues that if the whole earth hymns the Creator and the Truth, and the Creator is the Logos who declares, 'I am the Truth' (John xiv. 6), it follows that

the Logos is not a creature, but alone is proper to the Father; for 'I was by him disposing' (Prov. viii. 30, LXX) and 'My Father works still, and I work' (John v. 17). The word 'still' demonstrates his eternal existence as Logos in the Father (τὸ ἀϊδίως ὡς λόγον ὑπάρχειν αὐτὸν ἐν τῷ πατρί), for it is proper to the Logos to work the Father's works (John ix. 4) and not to be external to him.[3]

If what the Father does, the Son does also (John v. 19), then it follows, says Athanasius, that what the Son creates is the creation of the Father; if, as the Arians assert, the Son is the Father's creature, then either he will create himself, which is absurd, or since he creates and works the things of the Father, he himself is not a work or a creature.[4] If God creates through

---

[1] Simonetti (*Studi sull'Arianesimo*, p. 56) says that we owe to Athanasius 'the most diffuse and exhaustive comment on this passage that has been handed down to us, even if it is not so satisfying in the eyes of the modern reader'.

[2] *Or. c. Ar.* II, 18 (*PG*, XXVI, 184).

[3] *Ibid.* II, 20 (*PG*, XXVI, 189).　　[4] *Ibid.* II, 21 (*PG*, XXVI, 189).

the Son (Col. i. 16, John i. 3), the Son cannot be a creature; rather, he is the Logos of God the Creator, and is recognised to be 'in the Father and the Father in him' (John xiv. 10), from the Father's works which he himself works (John v. 19). 'He who has seen him has seen the Father' (John xiv. 9), because the Son's essence is proper to the Father, and he is like the Father in every respect. The Logos differs from all created and originate things in that he alone knows (Matt. xi. 27), and he alone sees (John vi. 46) the Father. 'How did he alone know, except that he alone was proper to him? And how was he proper to him if he were a creature and not a true Son from him?' The difference between the Son and created things is qualitative and not merely one of degree, and the Arian assertion that he is 'a creature but not as one of the creatures' is blasphemy and nonsense.[1]

This argument, based on exegesis of John i. 3, v. 17, 19, leads Athanasius to assert that because the Father and the Son are united in their works, the Son cannot be a creature, but belongs to the godhead. It is not the Father alone, nor the Son alone, that is Creator, but 'the trinity is Creator and Fashioner'.[2] Later, in opposition to the *Tropici* who, while holding the orthodox view of the Son, maintained that the Holy Spirit is a creature, Athanasius develops the idea of the unity of the trinity in external operation, and states it in a formula which he repeats continually: 'The Father does all things *through* the Logos *in* the Spirit'.[3] On the basis of the same two Johannine texts (i. 3, v. 19), he asserts that 'the Son, like the Father, is Creator... The Father creates all things through the Logos in the Spirit.'[4] *Opera ad extra trinitatis indivisa sunt.* Therefore, if the Son and the Spirit are present in the divine work of creation, they cannot be creatures.

(ii) Athanasius, who was primarily a churchman and pastor, and only by force of circumstances a polemical theologian, saw that Arianism was more than an erroneous teaching; it was a threat to the very life of the church, its liturgy and its sacramental practice. In his refutation of Arianism his mind at no

---

[1] *Ibid.* ii, 22 (*PG*, xxvi, 192–3).   [2] *Ibid.* i, 18 (*PG*, xxvi, 49).

[3] *Ep. ad Serap.* i, 28 (*PG*, xxvi, 596); cf. *ibid.* iii, 5.

[4] *Ibid.* iii, 4–5 (*PG*, xxvi, 632); cf. J. McIntyre, 'The Holy Spirit in Greek Patristic Thought', in *SJT*, vii (1954), 353 ff.

time strays far from the practical issues involved in the controversy; if Arianism is true, then the church has no right to worship Jesus Christ the creature, men do not come to know God through him, men do not find salvation through him, and the sacrament of baptism is a farce.

From the argument that he through whom the Father creates cannot himself be a creature, Athanasius turns to these practical issues; if the Son is a creature, we have no right to worship him, for God alone is worthy to be worshipped. But Jesus Christ, the incarnate Son of God, accepts the worship of his disciples: 'You call me Lord and Master, and you are right, for so I am' (John xiii. 13). And when Thomas says, 'My Lord and my God' (John xx. 28), Jesus accepts his worship and does nothing to prevent him.[1]

He would not have been worshipped thus, nor spoken of in this way, if he had been merely a creature. But since he is not a creature, but the proper offspring of the essence of that God who is worshipped, and his Son by nature, therefore he is worshipped and believed to be God...as the Father is; for he said himself, 'All that the Father has is mine' (John xiv. 15). For it is proper to the Son to have the things of the Father, and to be such that the Father is seen in him (John xiv. 9), such that 'through him all things were made' (John i. 3), and such that the salvation of all comes to pass and consists in him.[2]

Arguing thus from the fact that the Son is worshipped and accepts the worship of men, Athanasius emphasises the dependence of revelation, creation and salvation on the godhead of the Son, who is the Father's mediator in all his works.

(iii) Athanasius brings the argument back to the question of creation through the Son in order to refute another Arian statement on the creatureliness of the Son. Scripture places the Son, not among the creatures, but beside the Father 'as him in whom providence and salvation are achieved and made effective for all'.[3] The Arians, having set the Son among the creatures, try to distinguish him from them as the only creature created directly by the hand of God, a distinction which, it has been pointed out, influences their interpretation of the word μονογενής.[4] They said:

---

[1] *Or. c. Ar.* II, 23 (*PG*, XXVI, 196–7).   [2] *Ibid.* II, 24 (*PG*, XXVI, 197).
[3] *Idem.*   [4] See above, pp. 158 f. and 168 ff.

When God willed to create originate nature, he saw that it could not endure the untempered hand of the Father and to be created by him; therefore, he makes and creates first and alone one only, and calls him *Son* and *Logos*, so that through him as a medium (τούτου μέσου γενομένου) all things might thereupon be made.[1]

This idea of the Arians, says Athanasius, suggests that God grew weary of commanding, or that his strength was not sufficient for the task of creating all things, for, according to them, he needed the help of the Son in the work of creation. They think that it is undignified for God to create originated things himself; but, if it is not undignified for him to exercise providential care over a hair of the head, a sparrow, and the grass of the field (Matt. x. 29 f., vi. 25 f.), it cannot be undignified for him to create them.[2]

This Arian doctrine involves an infinite hierarchy of intermediaries. If the Son, being a creature, could endure the untempered hand of the Father, all creatures could; if none of the creatures could endure it, the Son could not, and it is necessary to postulate an intermediary between the Father and the Son, and 'we shall have to invent a vast crowd of accumulating intermediaries'; the result will be that it will be impossible for creation to exist at all, 'for it will always be in need of an intermediary...For all the intermediaries will be of that originated nature which cannot endure to be made by God alone.'[3]

(iv) Another Arian doctrine is that the Son 'has learned to fashion as from a teacher and craftsman; in this way he ministered to God who taught him'.[4] This is absurd, answers Athanasius, for if fashioning and creating are arts to be learned, the Arians are in danger of saying that God himself has learned these arts, and that it is possible for him to lose the ability to create.[5]

Athanasius argues that if the ability to fashion is acquired by instruction, then we must ascribe jealousy and weakness to

---

[1] *Or. c. Ar.* II, 24 (*PG*, xxvi, 200).   [2] *Ibid.* II, 25 (*PG*, xxvi, 201).

[3] *Ibid.* II, 26 (*PG*, xxvi, 201). Cf. the more fully developed argument in *de Decr.* 8 (*PG*, xxv, 429–37). N.B. columns 425–56 in *PG* xxv should be numbered 417–48; cf. G. Müller, *Lexicon Athanasianum*.

[4] *Ibid.* II, 28 (*PG*, xxvi, 205).

[5] *Idem.*

God; jealousy, because he taught only one creature to create, and weakness, because he needed a fellow-worker or under-worker in order to be able to create:

The Logos did not become Fashioner by instruction, but being the Image and Wisdom of the Father, he does the works of the Father (John v. 36; ix. 4), and God has not made the Son in order to make originated things, for behold, although the Son exists, the Father is seen to be working still, as the Lord himself says, 'My Father works still, and I work' (John v. 17).[1]

If the Father has made the Son to be the fashioner of the rest of creation, and yet still continues to work after making him, then the making of the Son was superfluous.

(v) Athanasius points out that in reality the Arian teaching that the Son was created in order to be the instrument of God in creating the rest of the creatures means that he is inferior to the rest, and not, as they think, superior to them. 'We are brought into existence simply in order that we might exist, but he was made, not simply that he might exist, but to be an instrument through whom we might be created.'[2] The reverse is the case, says Athanasius, for the existence of the Logos does not depend on God's will to create us; rather, our existence depends on him:

Even if it had seemed good to God not to make originated things, still the Logos would no less have been 'with God' (John i. 1 *b*), and the Father in him (John xiv. 10)...For since the Logos is by nature the Son of God proper to his essence, and is from him (John xvi. 28) and in him (John x. 38; xiv. 10), as he himself says, the creatures could not have been made except through him...The Father wrought all things through the Logos and without him makes not even one thing (John i. 3).[3]

Thus Athanasius has broken through the old apologetic tradition that the existence of the Logos as a being distinct from the Father depends on God's will to create.[4] His existence is independent of creation; it is an internal necessity of the godhead.

(vi) Athanasius next turns to the Arian conception of the Son as an under-worker and, in opposition to it, sets forth his

---

[1] *Ibid.* II, 29 (*PG*, XXVI, 208).   [2] *Ibid.* II, 30 (*PG*, XXVI, 209).
[3] *Ibid.* II, 31 (*PG*, XXVI, 212).   [4] See above, pp. 131 ff.

doctrine of the Logos as God's creative Word, who is also the Wisdom and Will of the Father.

(vii) The practical issues at stake in the controversy come into the foreground of Athanasius' argument once again; he argues that 'if the Son is a creature, the naming of him in baptism is superfluous, for God who made him a Son is able to make us sons also'. The Son is named with the Father in baptism because he, being God's Logos, is ever with the Father (John i. 1 *b*), and

it is impossible, if the Father bestows grace, that he should not give it in the Son, for the Son is in the Father (John xiv. 10) as the radiance in the light... Where the Father is, there is the Son... and just as what the Father worketh, he worketh through the Son —the Lord himself says, 'What I see the Father doing, that I also do' (John v. 19, not quoted exactly)—so also when baptism is given, him whom the Father baptises, the Son baptises, and he whom the Son baptises is consecrated in the Holy Spirit.[1]

Baptism is the gift, not of the Father only, but of the Father, Son and Holy Spirit, and is a witness to the unity of the godhead in external operation.[2] If the Arians refuse to acknowledge God to be a true Father and the Son to be a true Son, their baptism is invalid.[3] 'The water which they administer is unprofitable, as lacking in holiness, so that he who is sprinkled by them is polluted by irreligion rather than redeemed.'[4]

(viii) The Arians fall into the error of calling the Son a creature because they ignore the scope of scripture, and apply to his godhead what scripture says concerning his manhood.[5] Athanasius argues that Prov. viii. 22 refers to the manhood and not the godhead, and on this basis he interprets 'the works' for which the Lord created Wisdom, not as the creation of origi- nated things, but as 'such things as already existed and needed restoration'.[6] ' "Created" does not denote the beginning of

---

[1] *Or. c. Ar.* II, 41 (*PG*, xxvi, 233 f.).

[2] *Idem.* Cf. also *Ep. ad Serap.* I, 30 (*PG*, xxvi, 600): 'This grace and gift (i.e. baptism) is given in the Triad, from the Father, through the Son, in the Holy Spirit'; see above, p. 205.

[3] *Or. c. Ar.* II, 42 (*PG*, xxvi, 236).   [4] *Ibid.* II, 43 (*PG*, xxvi, 237).

[5] For a discussion of this 'two-nature' exegesis cf. M. F. Wiles, *The Spiritual Gospel*, ch. VII.

[6] *Ibid.* II, 52 (*PG*, xxvi, 257).

his being...but his beneficent (work of) renewal (ἀνανέωσιν) which took place for us.'[1]

In conjunction with the appeal to the scope of scripture, Athanasius appeals to the 'custom' (ἔθος) of scripture:

This is the custom of scripture: when it indicates the fleshly origination (γένεσιν) of the Logos, it also adds the reason for his becoming man; but when he says, or any of his servants declare anything concerning his godhead, it is all said in simple language, with an absolute sense and with no reason added...Thus it is written, 'In the beginning was the Logos, and the Logos was with God, and the Logos was God' (John i. 1), and no reason is given; but when 'the Logos became flesh' (John i. 14), then it gives the reason why he has become, saying, 'and dwelt among us'.[2]

When Jesus speaks about himself as Son of God, he speaks absolutely: 'I am in the Father and the Father in me' (John xiv. 10), 'I and the Father are one' (John x. 30), 'He who has seen me has seen the Father' (John xiv. 9), 'I am the light of the world' (John viii. 12), and 'I am the Truth' (John xiv. 6). His existence as the Son of God is not subordinate to any reason other than that he is the Father's offspring; a reason is given only for his becoming flesh; apart from man's need for renewal and restoration he would not have become man:

What the need was for which he became man he himself tells us: 'I have come down from heaven, not to do my own will, but the will of him who sent me, that I should lose nothing of all that he has given me, but raise it up at the last day. For this is the will of my Father, that everyone who sees the Son and believes in him should have eternal life' (John vi. 38–40), and again, 'I have come as light into the world, that whoever believes in me may not remain in darkness' (John xii. 46). And again he says, 'For this was I born and for this I have come into the world, to bear witness to the truth' (John xviii. 37). And, as St John says, 'The reason the Son of God appeared was to destroy the works of the devil' (I John iii. 8).[3]

The Saviour came then to give a witness, to undergo death for us, to raise man up, and to destroy the works of the devil; this is the reason for his incarnate presence.[4]

Continuing the same argument, Athanasius quotes John iii. 17 and ix. 39, and concludes:

[1] *Ibid.* II, 53 (*PG*, XXVI, 260).   [2] *Idem.*
[3] *Ibid.* II, 54 (*PG*, XXVI, 261).   [4] *Ibid.* II, 55 (*PG*, XXVI, 261 f.).

Not for himself then, but for our salvation...has he come; but if not for himself, but for us, then consequently not for himself, but for us is he created. But if he is created not for himself, but for us, then he is not himself a creature, but he uses such language as having put on our flesh.[1]

Athanasius applies the same principle, that when he is referred to as Son of God no reason is given, to John i. 1:

For even if no works had been created, still 'the Logos of God was', and 'the Logos was God'. His incarnation would not have taken place if the need of man had not been a cause. The Son then is not a creature.[2]

He compares John i. 1 with Gen. i. 1. The creatures had a beginning of being made, but the Logos had no beginning, for 'in the beginning' he 'was'.

The Logos has his being in no other beginning (ἀρχή) than the Father, whom they (the Arians) allow to be without beginning, so that he too exists without beginning in the Father, since he is his offspring and not his creature.[3]

John did not say, 'In the beginning he has become' (γέγονεν), or 'has been made' (πεποίηται), but 'was' (ἦν), so that by the 'was' we may understand 'offspring'.[4]

(ix) Athanasius appeals to another 'custom' of scripture: 'Generally when scripture wishes to signify a son, it does so, not by the word "created" but by the word "begat".' St John maintains this 'cautious distinction' in John i. 12–13: 'He gave to them power to become children of God, even to those who believed in his name; who were begotten, not of blood, nor of the will of the flesh, nor of the will of man, but of God':[5]

First he says 'to become' (γενέσθαι), because they are not called sons by nature, but by adoption (μὴ φύσει, ἀλλὰ θέσει); then he says 'were begotten' (ἐγεννήθησαν), because they too had at least received the name of son.[6]

Thus Athanasius asserts the generic difference between Christ's sonship and ours, a point which had been made central by Alexander in his ante-Nicene attacks on the Arians, and which the Antiochene and Nicene Creeds had strongly emphasised.

[1] *Ibid.* II, 55 (*PG*, XXVI, 264).   [2] *Ibid.* II, 56 (*PG*, XXVI, 268).
[3] *Ibid.* II, 57 (*PG*, XXVI, 269).   [4] *Ibid.* II, 58 (*PG*, XXVI, 269).
[5] *Ibid.* II, 59 (*PG*, XXVI, 272).   [6] *Idem.*

Continuing to argue on the basis of John i. 12–13, Athanasius clearly delineates the difference; we are first created by God, and then begotten as sons when we receive the Logos, 'for those who were by nature creatures could not become sons except by receiving the Spirit of him who is Son in nature and in truth'. Therefore, 'the Logos became flesh' (John i. 14) in order that men might become capable of receiving divinity (δεκτικὸν θεότητος):

It is not we who are sons by nature, but the Son who is in us; and again, God is not by nature the Father of us but of that Logos which is in us, in whom and because of whom we cry, 'Abba, Father' (Gal. iv. 6)...We are not begotten first, but made.[1]

The reverse, however, is true of the Logos; God is not *first* his creator, *then* his Father, but he is his Father by nature, and then becomes his creator

when the Logos puts on that flesh which was created and made, and becomes man...his flesh, before all others, was saved and liberated, since it was the body of the Logos; and henceforth we, becoming incorporated with it (σύσσωμοι, Eph. iii. 6), are saved after its pattern.[2]

In this created flesh Christ becomes

our guide to the kingdom of heaven and to his own Father, saying, 'I am the Way' (John xiv. 6), and 'the door' (John x. 7), and 'through me all must enter' (John x. 9). Hence he is also called 'First-born from the dead' (Col. i. 18, Rev. i. 5), not that he died before us, for we had died first, but because, having undergone death for us and abolished it, he was the first to rise, as man, for our sakes raising his own body. Henceforth, since he has risen, we too, from him and because of him, rise in due course from the dead.[3]

This discussion of the difference between Christ's sonship and ours leads Athanasius to a discussion of the titles 'First-born of all creation' (Col. i. 15) and 'Only(-begotten)' (John i. 18 etc.). The Arians interpreted both these titles by referring them to the Son's creation by the Father and, apparently, interpreted the latter in the light of the former. Asterius equated the two titles, saying, 'The Father is different, to be sure, who has

---

[1] *Ibid.* II, 59 (*PG*, XXVI, 272–3).   [2] *Ibid.* II, 61 (*PG*, XXVI, 277).
[3] *Idem.*

begotten from himself the Only-begotten Logos and Firstborn of all creation.'[1] Arius argued that 'if he is firstborn of all creation, it is plain that he too is one of the creatures'[2] and he interpreted μονογενής in the sense of 'the only creature created directly by the hand of God'.[3] According to the Arians, then, the Son, as a creature, is 'Only-begotten' in that he alone is created directly by the hand of God, and 'Firstborn' in that, after he is created, God creates all the rest through him.

Athanasius asserts that there is a contradiction between these two titles:

The term μονογενής is used where there are no brethren, and πρωτότοκος because there are brethren...If then he is μονογενής, as indeed he is, πρωτότοκος needs some explanation; if, on the other hand, he is really πρωτότοκος, then he is not μονογενής. For the same cannot be both μονογενής and πρωτότοκος, except in different relations.[4]

He says that the Son is called μονογενής because of his generation from the Father, and πρωτότοκος

because of his condescension to creation and because of his making the many his brethren. Certainly, since these two terms are inconsistent with each other, we should say that the attribute of being μονογενής rightly has preference in the case of the Logos, since there is no other Logos, nor any other Wisdom, but he alone is true Son of the Father. Moreover...it is said of him absolutely, 'the only Son who is in the bosom of the Father' (John i. 18). But the word πρωτότοκος again has the creation connected with it as a reason, 'for in him all things were created' (Col. i. 16). But if all the creatures were created in him, he is other than the creatures, and he is not a creature but the creator of the creatures.[5]

It is his coming into the world that makes him to be called 'Firstborn of all'; he is the Father's 'only' Son, because he alone is from the Father, and he is 'Firstborn' because of the adoption of all as sons. These two titles, then, express the generic difference between his sonship and ours.

[1] *Apud* Marcellus, Fr. 3 (Eusebius, *GCS*, IV, 186, 4–10).
[2] *Or. c. Ar.* II, 63 (*PG*, XXVI, 280). [3] See above, pp. 204 ff.
[4] *Or. c. Ar.* II, 62 (*PG*, XXVI, 277).
[5] *Ibid.* II, 62 (*PG*, XXVI, 277–80). In *de Decr.* 6 ff., Athanasius deals with the double sense of the word 'son' in scripture, as (*a*) adoptive and (*b*) essential, and develops the distinction more clearly, without, however, introducing any Johannine exegesis.

(x) Athanasius always shifts the emphasis from the cosmological level, where the Arians' argument moves, to the soteriological and religious level. Asking how the Son is 'a beginning of ways' (Prov. viii. 22), he argues that

> when the first way, which was through Adam, was lost, and instead of living in paradise we wandered into death...the Logos of God, who loves man, puts on created flesh at the Father's will...If a new creation has taken place, someone must be the first of this creation. Now a mere man, made only of earth, such as we have become through the transgression, he could not be. For in the first creation men had become unfaithful, and through them that first creation had been lost, and there was need of someone else to renew the first creation and to preserve the new creation which had come to be. Therefore, out of love to man, none other than the Lord, the 'beginning' of the new creation, is created as 'the Way' (John xiv. 6).[1]

Because of the sin of man, the first creation had become a way of death, and 'death, to Athanasius, is a condition, and not an occasion'.[2] Through the incarnation of the Logos, however, the renewal of creation has been effected and its restoration accomplished; death is vanquished and the fear of death removed:

> No more shall we hear, 'In the day that thou eatest thereof thou shalt surely die' (Gen. ii. 17), but, 'Where I am, there ye [shall] 'be also' (John xiv. 3)...The perfect Logos of God puts around him an imperfect body and is said to be 'created for the works' (Prov. viii. 22), in order that, paying the debt in our stead, he might, by himself, perfect what was lacking in man. Now what man lacked was immortality and the way to paradise. This is what the Saviour says, 'I glorified thee on earth, having perfected the work which thou gavest me to do' (John xvii. 4), and 'The works which the Father has granted me to perfect, these very works which I am doing, bear witness to me' (John v. 36); but 'the works' which he here says that the Father has given him to perfect are those for which he is created.[3]

The work of renewing and restoring man could not be accomplished by a creature, for the creatures could not be united to

---

[1] *Ibid.* II, 65 (*PG*, xxvi, 285).
[2] H. A. Blair, *A Creed before the Creeds*, London, 1955, p. 30.
[3] *Or. c. Ar.* II, 66 (*PG*, xxvi, 288).

the Creator by a creature; a creature could not undo the death-sentence and remit sins, for 'this is God's doing' (Micah vii. 18):

It is the Lord who has undone it, and he himself says, 'Unless the Son shall make you free' (John viii. 36), and the Son who has made man free has shown in truth that he is no creature, nor one of the originated things, but the proper Logos and Image of the essence of the Father who at the beginning condemned man and alone remits sins.[1]

A creature cannot re-create or redeem fallen man.

Similarly Athanasius argues that a creature cannot make men immortal or save them; a part of creation cannot be the means of salvation to creation, for it is in need of salvation itself.[2]

To provide against this also, God sends his own Son (John iii. 16), and he becomes Son of man by taking created flesh, so that, since all were under the sentence of death, he, being other than them all, might himself offer his own body to death for all...so that all through him might become free from sin and from the curse that came upon it, and might truly abide for ever risen from the dead and clothed in immortality and incorruption...Being joined to God, we no longer abide upon earth, but, as he himself has said, we shall be where he is (John xiv. 3).[3]

So, too, if the Son had been a creature, the devil would not have been overcome, for the warfare would have been an endless battle between creature and creature; as a result, man would not have been saved. 'Therefore the union was of such a kind that he might unite what is man by nature to him who is according to the nature of the godhead (τῷ κατὰ φύσιν τῆς θεότητος), and that his salvation and deification might be sure'. If he had not been Son of God by nature, and had not assumed 'true human flesh from Mary, Ever-Virgin', the incarnation and atonement would not have profited us men.[4]

(xi) Finally, having shown that, if the Son is a creature, God

---

[1] *Ibid.* ii, 67 (*PG*, xxvi, 289–92).

[2] Cf. *Ep. ad Adelphium*, 8 (*PG*, xxvi, 1081): 'What help can creatures derive from a creature that itself needs salvation?'

[3] *Or. c. Ar.* ii, 69 (*PG*, xxvi, 293).

[4] *Ibid.* ii, 70 (*PG*, xxvi, 296).

did not create through him, he cannot be worshipped, the naming of him in baptism is superfluous, the devil could not have been overcome, and mankind could not have been renewed, restored, saved, delivered, made immortal and deified, Athanasius emphasises the reality of the self-revelation of God through the incarnate Logos. The *heilsgeschichtlich* framework of his theology, which is so apparent in his ante-Nicene treatises, makes itself apparent continually in his refutation of the Arians. He emphasises the identity of the incarnate Logos with the Logos and Wisdom of God and the continuity of God's activity of self-revelation through his Logos:

No longer, as in former times, has God willed to be known by an image and shadow of Wisdom, that namely which is in the creatures, but he has made the true Wisdom himself to take flesh and become man and to undergo the death of the Cross, in order that, through faith in him, henceforth all that believe may obtain salvation. However, it is the same Wisdom of God, who through his own image in the creatures (whence also he is said to be created) first manifested himself, and through himself his own Father; and afterwards, being himself the Logos, has 'become flesh' (John i. 14)...and after abolishing death and saving our race, revealed himself still more and through his own Father, saying, 'Grant that they may know thee, the only true God, and Jesus Christ whom thou has sent' (John xvii. 3). Hence the whole earth is filled with the knowledge of him (Hab. ii. 14); for the knowledge of the Father through the Son and of the Son through the Father is one and the same.[1]

Within the framework of his exegesis of Prov. viii. 22, then, and largely on the basis of exegesis of and appeal to St John's Gospel, Athanasius refutes the Arian contention that the Son is a creature. Behind all his arguments is the firm conviction that the sonship of Christ is generically different from ours, and that the works which the Son accomplishes are not the works of a creature but those of God himself. The Father and the Son are united in all God's activity towards the created world, in creation, baptism, salvation, restoration, renewal, deification and revelation. It is God, Father, Son and Holy Spirit, who creates, redeems and sanctifies; if the trinity is worthy of our worship, it must be an essential trinity and not one formed by the addition of creatures to the Creator. If the Son is a creature,

---

[1] *Ibid.* II, 81–2 (*PG*, xxvi, 320).

the incarnation is purposeless and the death on the cross is futile, accomplishing nothing.

(xii) The Arians also used Heb. i. 4, 'Being made so much better than the angels, etc.' to prove that the Son is a creature. Athanasius argues that these words are not a comparison of the Son with originated beings, as though he were of the same nature and *genus* as they, but rather a contrast between the new dispensation and the old.[1] The dispensation through the Son is superior to that through the angels, patriarchs and prophets, who are all creatures. The world was formerly under the judgment of the law, but now the Logos has taken the judgment upon himself. This is what St John meant when he said, 'The Law was given through Moses, but grace and truth came by Jesus Christ' (John i. 17). 'Better is grace than the Law, and truth than the shadow.'[2]

If 'better' is used to contrast beings belonging to different *genera*, 'greater' in 'My Father is greater than I' (John xiv. 28), is used to compare beings belonging to the same *genus*. Athanasius says that the Son does not say, 'My Father is *better* than I',

lest we should think him to be foreign to the Father's nature, but 'greater', not in size, nor in time, but because of his generation from the Father himself; indeed in saying 'He is greater', he again shows that he is proper to the essence of God.[3]

That is, while 'better' is used to contrast two different *genera*, 'greater' is used to compare two beings of the same *genus*. The Son belongs to the godhead, and not to the sphere of the creatures.

G. THE SON IS NOT ALTERABLE

The Arians said, 'By nature the Logos, like all others, is alterable, and remains good by his own free will, while he chooses to do so; when, however, he wills, he can alter as we can, since he is of alterable nature.'[4] It appears that, when they were challenged about this teaching in the early stages of the controversy, they modified their original statement with equivocation similar to that with which they modified their original statement that the Son is a creature:

[1] *Ibid.* 1, 64 (*PG*, xxvi, 145).   [2] *Ibid.* 1, 60 (*PG*, xxvi, 137 f.).
[3] *Ibid.* 1, 58 (*PG*, xxvi, 133).   [4] *Ibid.* 1, 5 (*PG*, xxvi, 21).

Therefore, since he foreknew that he would be good, God, in anticipation, bestowed upon him this glory (of unalterability) which afterwards as man he attained from virtue. Thus in consequence of his works which God foreknew, God brought it to pass that he should become such (a good man) (ὥστε ἐξ ἔργων αὐτοῦ, ὧν προέγνω ὁ θεός, τοιοῦτον αὐτὸν νῦν γεγονέναι πεποίηκε).[1]

By nature the Son is alterable, but since God foreknew that he would always choose what is good, he bestowed upon him the gift of unalterability beforehand. Thus, in their *Confessio Fidei* Arius and his supporters could state that the Son is 'unalterable and unchangeable (ἄτρεπτος καὶ ἀναλλοίωτος)'.[2]

Athanasius ignores this Arian modification for what it is, an attempt to cloud the issue. The modification does not change the fact that the Arians state that the Son is alterable 'by nature'. His main argument against this Arian doctrine is that if the Son is alterable, then he can in no way be the revelation of the Father.

(i) Athanasius argues that the assertion that the Son is alterable is a denial of the Son's own words, 'He who has seen me has seen the Father' (John xiv. 9):

If the Logos is alterable and changing, where will he stop and what will be the end of his development? How can what is alterable be like what is unalterable? How can he who has seen the alterable be considered to have seen the unalterable? At what stage must he arrive for us to be able to see the Father in the Son, because the Son is ever altering and is of a changing nature...How can one who is alterable be the Image of one who is unalterable? How can he be really 'in the Father' (John xiv. 10) if his will is ambiguous (ἀμφί-βολον)?...Must not he who is one with the Father (John x. 30) be unalterable...This is why 'He who has seen' the Son 'has seen the Father' (John xiv. 9), and why the knowledge of the Son is the knowledge of the Father (Matt. xi. 27).[3]

What exactly do the words 'unalterable' and 'alterable' mean in this argument? Athanasius makes it plain that he is not thinking in metaphysical terms, but rather in terms of moral perfection. Discussing Heb. iii. 2, 'who was faithful to him that made him', a text to which the Arians appealed for

---

[1] *Idem.*
[2] *Urk.* 6 (12, 9); cf. Ath. *Or. c. Ar.* I, 35 (*PG*, xxvi, 84).
[3] *Ibid.* I, 35 (*PG*, xxvi, 85–8).

support of their idea of the Son's alterability, Athanasius argues that it does not imply any parallel with others; it does not mean that

by having faith, he became well-pleasing, but, being Son of the true God, he too is faithful and ought to be believed in all he says and does, since he himself remains unalterable and not changed (ἄτρεπτος καὶ μὴ ἀλλοιούμενος) in his human economy and fleshly presence.[1]

He compares the faithfulness of Christ with the Greek gods who are 'faithful neither in essence nor in their promises'.[2] The unalterability of the Son consists in his faithfulness to his own nature as Son of God, and in the fact that he is true in all that he says and does. Because he is 'faithful', he is worthy of our faith.[3] The unalterability which Athanasius has in mind is the moral perfection of one who is sinless by nature.

(ii) It is mainly on the basis of two texts that the Arians argued for the alterability of the Son:

(a) Phil. ii. 9–10: 'Therefore (διό) God has highly exalted him and bestowed on him the name which is above every name, that at the name of Jesus every knee should bow, in heaven and on earth and under the earth.'

(b) Ps. xlv. 7 (LXX, xliv. 7): 'Therefore (διὰ τοῦτο) God, even thy God, has anointed thee with the oil of gladness above thy fellows.'

They argued:

If he was exalted and received a favour (χάριν) for a reason (διό) and for a reason (διὰ τοῦτο) he was anointed, he received a reward for his deliberate choice; and having acted from choice, he is wholly of an alterable nature.[4]

(a) Concerning Phil. ii. 9–10, Athanasius says that the Arians' argument is true of those who are sons of God 'from

---

[1] *Ibid.* ii, 6 (*PG*, xxvi, 160). [2] *Ibid.* ii, 9–10 (*PG*, xxvi, 164–8).

[3] The criticism which I have made of Athanasius' view of impassibility in my article, 'The Impassibility of God' in *SJT*, viii (1955), 360 ff., needs some modification. Athanasius' conception of God is that of the Living God. Athanasius does attribute impassibility to the divine in Christ, but this is an example of the persistence of Greek metaphysical concepts which had become part of the common stock of Christian thought from the moment it entered the hellenistic world. Athanasius' return to the biblical view of God has not been quite complete; Greek metaphysical elements which are irreconcilable with it persist on the fringe of his thought.

[4] *Or. c. Ar.* i, 37 (*PG*, xxvi, 88).

virtue and grace'.[1] If, however, they say this of the Saviour, it follows that he is neither 'true, nor God, nor Son, nor like the Father', but is only Son by grace, and has received the name 'Son' as a reward for virtue.[2] In this interpretation the Arians ignore both the context of the passage and the scope of scripture. The exaltation does not refer to the essence of the Son, but to the manhood which he assumed. 'If, because of his assuming flesh, the word "humbled" is written, it is clear that "highly exalted" is also said because of it.'[3]

Similarly the words 'bestowed on him' are not written for his sake but for ours:

For as Christ died and was exalted as man, so, as man, he is said to receive what, as God, he always had, in order that even such a gift of grace might come to us...The Logos' becoming flesh and undergoing death in the flesh has not happened for the degradation of his godhead, but 'to the glory of the Father'. For it is the Father's glory that men, made, then lost, should be found again, and when dead should be made alive and should become God's temple.[4]

Athanasius also suggests that these words from the Epistle to the Philippians may be interpreted in connection with the resurrection of Christ. 'The "therefore" (διό) signifies not a reward for virtue but the reason why the resurrection takes place.'[5]

Within the framework of this exegesis, Athanasius comments on John xvii. 5, 'Father, glorify thou me with the glory which I had with thee before the world was'. The 'highly exalted' cannot refer to the divinity of the Son, for he had the glory with the Father before the incarnation; they must therefore refer to the manhood:

If even before the world was made, the Son had that glory...and is ever to be worshipped, it follows that he was not improved on account of his descent, but rather himself improved the things which needed improvement...Therefore he did not receive the name 'Son' and 'God' in reward, but rather he himself has made

[1] *Idem.*　　　　　　　　　　　　　[2] *Ibid.* I, 38 (*PG*, xxvi, 89–92).
[3] *Ibid.* I, 41 (*PG*, xxvi, 96).
[4] *Ibid.* I, 42 (*PG*, xxvi, 100).
[5] *Ibid.* I, 44 (*PG*, xxvi, 101–4).

us sons of the Father and deified men by himself becoming man. Thus he was not man and then became God, but he was God and then became man, and he did this to deify us.[1]

(b) Just as the Son is 'highly exalted' for our sakes, so also he is 'anointed' (Ps. xlv. 7) for us. Neither of these passages implies any alteration in the Son of God:

The Saviour, being God...and being himself the one who supplied the Holy Spirit, is nevertheless said here to be anointed, so that, as before, being said to be anointed, as man, with the Holy Spirit, he might provide for us men not only exaltation and resurrection, but also the indwelling and intimacy of the Holy Spirit.[2]

By 'anointing' Athanasius understands the gift of the Holy Spirit, and he proceeds to set forth the Johannine texts which refer to sanctification and Christ's gift of the Holy Spirit to his disciples.

Jesus says, 'I have sent them into the world, and for their sakes I sanctify myself that they also may be sanctified in truth' (John xvii. 18–19); thus Jesus shows that 'he is not the sanctified but the sanctifier', for 'he who sanctifies himself is the Lord of sanctification'.[3] This self-sanctification takes place when the Son of God becomes man:

If it is for our sake that he sanctifies himself, and he does this when he has become man, it is very plain that the Spirit's descent on him in Jordan was a descent upon us, because of his bearing our body. And it did not take place for the improvement of the Logos, but, again, for our sanctification, that we might share his anointing.[4]

When, as man, the Lord was washed in Jordan, we were washed in him and by him, and when he received the Spirit, we were made recipients of it through him.

Of the Holy Spirit Jesus says, 'The Spirit shall take of mine' (John xvi. 14), and 'I will send him' (John xvi. 7), and 'Receive the Holy Spirit' (John xx. 22). Athanasius proceeds to argue:

If, as the Lord himself has said, the Spirit is his, and takes of his, and he sends him, it is no longer the Logos, considered as Logos and Wisdom, who is anointed with the Spirit which he himself gives, but

---

[1] *Ibid.* I, 38–9 (*PG*, xxvi, 92).   [2] *Ibid.* I, 46 (*PG*, xxvi, 108).
[3] *Idem.*   [4] *Ibid.* I, 47 (*PG*, xxvi, 108).

the flesh assumed by him, which is anointed in him and by him; that the sanctification which comes to the Lord as man may come to all men from him.[1]

When the Son is said to be anointed as man, it is we who are anointed in him, and when he is baptised, it is we who are baptised in him. This is what Jesus means when he says, 'The glory which thou hast given me, I have given to them, that they may be one even as we are one' (John xvii. 22).[2]

Jesus shows his disciples that he is the equal of the Holy Spirit, for he gave them the Spirit, and he said, 'Receive the Holy Spirit' (John xx. 22), 'I send him' (John xv. 26, xvi. 7), 'He shall glorify me' (John xvi. 16), and 'Whatever he hears he will speak' (John xvi. 13).[3]

Thus when Jesus is said to be 'highly exalted' and 'anointed' it is as man, and not as Son of God, and it is for our sakes and not for his own. As Logos and Son of God he is not alterable, but is always faithful to his own nature as God and to the promises which he makes to men. It is by interpreting these phrases in the light of St John's account of the gift of the Holy Spirit and in the light of Jesus' sayings concerning his self-sanctification, that Athanasius refutes the Arian doctrine of the alterability of the Son.

H. EXEGESIS OF SPECIFIC JOHANNINE TEXTS

A lengthy part of the *Oratio III* is devoted to criticism of Arian exegesis of texts from St John's Gospel.[4] 'Refutation does not stop them', says Athanasius, 'nor perplexity abash them'; they have even 'proceeded next to disparage our Lord's sayings'.[5]

(i) John xiv. 10: 'I in the Father and the Father in me'.[6]

The Arians asked:

How can the one be contained in the other, and the other in the one? or How can the Father, who is greater, be contained at all in

---

[1] *Ibid.* 1, 47 (*PG*, xxvi, 109).

[2] *Ibid.* 1, 48 (*PG*, xxvi, 112–13); for Athanasius' exegesis of John xvii. 22 ff., see below, pp. 227 ff.

[3] *Ibid.* 1, 50 (*PG*, xxvi, 116–17).

[4] *Ibid.* iii, 1–25 (*PG*, xxvi, 321–77).

[5] *Ibid.* iii, 1 (*PG*, xxvi, 321).   [6] *Ibid.* iii, 1–6 (*PG*, xxvi, 321 ff.).

the Son who is less? or What marvel is there if the Son is in the Father, seeing that it is written even of us, 'In him we live and move and have our being' (Acts xvii. 28)?[1]

Athanasius answers that John xiv. 10 does not mean that the Father and the Son are poured into each other, the one filling the other as in the case of empty vessels; this would mean that each is imperfect and incomplete. 'The Father is full and perfect and the Son is the fullness of the godhead.'[2] Neither is the Son in the Father in the sense of Acts xvii. 28,

For he, as from the fountain of the Father, is the Life (John xiv. 6), in which all things are endued with life and consist; for (he who is) the Life does not live in life, else he would not be Life; but rather he endues all things with life.[3]

Athanasius spends little time over the variety of interpretations which the Arians suggest for this saying of Jesus, but turns to a passage where Asterius the Sophist expounds it:

It is very plain that he has said that he is in the Father and the Father again in him for this reason, that neither the discourse which he was going through was his own, as he says, but the Father's (John xiv. 24), nor do the works belong to him, but to the Father (John ix. 4) who had given him the power.[4]

(a) Athanasius first criticises this interpretation on the grounds that if it is correct, then all men can say, equally with Jesus, 'I am in the Father and the Father in me'. If so, then Jesus Christ is not the only Son of God but only one among many.[5] But if Jesus had meant this he would not have said, 'I in the Father and the Father in me', but 'I *too* am in the Father and the Father is in me too'. As it stands, the saying of Jesus means that the Son is in the Father

because his whole being is proper to the Father's essence...so that whoever sees the Son, sees what is proper to the Father, and knows that the Son's being, since it is from the Father, is therefore in the Father...Since the form and the godhead of the Father is the being of the Son, it follows that the Son is in the Father and the Father in the Son.[6]

---

[1] *Ibid.* III, 1 (*PG*, XXVI, 321).
[2] *Idem* (*PG*, XXVI, 324).
[3] *Idem.*
[4] *Ibid.* III, 2 (*PG*, XXVI, 324 f.).
[5] *Ibid.* III, 2 (*PG*, XXVI, 325 f.).
[6] *Ibid.* III, 3 (*PG*, XXVI, 328); a reference to ἐν μορφῇ θεοῦ, Phil. ii. 6?

Jesus has already said, 'I and the Father are one' (John x. 30); he now adds these words 'in order to show, on the one hand, the identity of the godhead and, on the other, the unity of essence (ἵνα τὴν μὲν ταὐτότητα τῆς θεότητος, τὴν δὲ ἑνότητα τῆς οὐσίας δείξῃ).[1] The Father and the Son are two, because the Father is Father and not also Son, and the Son is Son and not also Father,[2] but the nature is one, for the offspring is not unlike its parent, since it is his image, and all that is the Father's is the Son's (John xvi. 15).[3] The Son is not another God; he and the Father are one 'in propriety and peculiarity of nature (τῇ ἰδιότητι καὶ οἰκειότητι τῆς φύσεως)' and 'in the identity of the one godhead (τῇ ταὐτότητι τῆς μιᾶς θεότητος)'.[4] The godhead of the Son is the godhead of the Father and it is indivisible. Since they are one, the same things are said of the Son which are said of the Father, except his being called 'Father'. For the Son himself claims that 'All that the Father has is mine' (John xvi. 15) and 'All mine are thine' (John xvii. 10).[5]

(b) Secondly, Athanasius develops the idea of the community of attributes; it is proper that the genuine offspring should have the same attributes as his Father. It is reasonable, then, that the Son, as the proper offspring of the Father's essence, says that the Father's attributes are his as well. He says, 'I and the Father are one' (John x. 30), then adds, 'that you may know that I am in the Father and the Father in me' (John x. 38); then, later, he adds, 'He who has seen me has seen the Father' (John xiv. 9): 'He who understands that the Son and the Father are one in this sense, knows that he is in the Father and the Father in the Son...and is convinced that he who has seen the Son has seen the Father, for in the Son is contemplated the Father's godhead.'[6]

(c) Like Eusebius of Caesarea,[7] but not so frequently, Athanasius uses the illustration of the Emperor's image, and

---

[1] *Ibid.* III, 4 (*PG*, XXVI, 328).　　[2] Cf. also III, 11 (*PG*, XXVI, 344–5).

[3] For fuller exposition of John xvi. 15, cf. *in Illud: Omnia...* 4 ff.

[4] *Ibid.* III, 3 (*PG*, XXVI, 328).

[5] *Ibid.* III, 4 (*PG*, XXVI, 328–9).

[6] *Ibid.* III, 5 (*PG*, XXVI, 329–32). The conjunction of John x. 30, xiv. 10, and xiv. 9 occurs repeatedly; e.g. *Or. c. Ar.* II, 54; III, 16, 67; *Ep. ad Serap.* II, 9.

[7] See below, pp. 278 ff.

from the illustration concludes that 'he who worships the image, worships the Emperor also; for the image is his form and appearance. Since then the Son too is the Father's Image, it must necessarily be understood that the godhead and propriety of the Father is the being of the Son (ἡ θεότης καὶ ἡ ἰδιότης τοῦ πατρὸς τὸ εἶναι τοῦ υἱοῦ ἐστι)'.[1] Athanasius then couples Phil. ii. 6, 'who being in the form of God', and John xiv. 10, 'The Father in me'. This form of the godhead, in which the Son is, is not partial and incomplete, for 'the Son is whole God (ὅλος θεός ἐστιν ὁ υἱός)'. He also quotes II Cor. v. 19, 'God was in Christ reconciling the world unto himself', as showing that the work of reconciliation which the Son achieved is also the Father's work. The Son and the Father have the same essence, possess the same attributes, and do the same works:

For the Son is such as the Father is, because he has all that is the Father's (John xvi. 15). Therefore he is implied together with the Father...When we call God 'Father', at once with the Father we signify the Son's existence. Therefore, also, he who believes in the Son believes in the Father also (John xii. 44), for he believes in what is proper to the Father's essence; thus the faith in the one God is one. He who worships and honours the Son, in the Son worships and honours the Father (John v. 23), for the godhead is one, and therefore one is the honour and one the worship which is paid to the Father in and through the Son.[2]

By developing the idea of community of essence, of attributes, and of works in this way, Athanasius is striving to avoid Sabellianism, on the one hand, which would be strengthened by over-emphasis on John x. 30, and ditheism, on the other hand, which Asterius' subordinationist interpretation of John xiv. 10 supports. The Father and the Son are two, and yet they are one in essence, in attributes and works.

(ii) John xvii. 3: 'That they may know thee, the only true God'.

The Arians say:

Behold God is said to be One and Only and First; how do you say that the Son is God? For if he (the Son) were God, he (God) would not have said 'I alone' and 'God is one'.[3]

---

[1] *Or. c. Ar.* III, 5 (*PG*, xxvi, 332).   [2] *Ibid.* III, 6 (*PG*, xxvi, 332–3).
[3] *Ibid.* III, 7 (*PG*, xxvi, 333).

The Arians suggest, says Athanasius, that there is rivalry of the Son towards the Father like that of Adonijah and Absalom towards their father David (II Sam. xv. 13; I Kings i. 11). He then sets forth a *florilegium* of sayings of the Son—Matt. xi. 27; John xiv. 9; Luke xviii. 19; Mark xii. 29; John vi. 38, xiv. 28, v. 23, xiii. 20—in which the Son acknowledges both his distinction from the Father and his unity with him. There is no difficulty, such as the Arians find, for the sayings 'God is one' and 'the only true God' are not said with reference to the Son as a denial of his essential godhead, but 'as a denial of those who are falsely called gods, invented by men'.[1] It is those who are devoted to the falsely called gods who revolt against the true God.[2] When God said, 'I am the only God', he said it through his Logos (Word); 'there is nothing that God says or does, but he says and does it in the Logos'. These sayings, which emphasise the oneness of God, being said through his Logos, are not intended as a denial of the Logos.[3] If the Father is called 'the only true God', it is not said in denial of him who said 'I am the truth' (John xiv. 6), but of those gods 'who by nature are not true, as the Father and his Logos are true'.[4]

If Jesus had intended by this saying to deny that he is true God, he would not have added immediately 'and Jesus Christ whom thou hast sent'. If he had been a creature, he would not have added these words, nor would he have ranked himself with the Father in this way:

For what fellowship is there between the True and the not-True? By adding himself to the Father, however, he has shown that he is of the Father's nature, and he has let us know that he is the true offspring of the true Father.[5]

This is what St John teaches when he says, 'And we are in him who is true, in his Son Jesus Christ. This is the true God and eternal life' (I John v. 20).[6]

Thus Athanasius, by quoting the complete saying (John xvii. 3), turns the argument against the Arians who, seeking to support their extreme monotheism, denied that the Son was God and, at the same time, against the extreme Origenism of

---

[1] *Ibid.* III, 7 (*PG*, XXVI, 336).

[2] *Ibid.* III, 8 (*PG*, XXVI, 336).

[3] *Ibid.* III, 8 (*PG*, XXVI, 337).

[4] *Ibid.* III, 9 (*PG*, XXVI, 337).

[5] *Ibid.* III, 9 (*PG*, XXVI, 337–40).

[6] *Idem* (*PG*, XXVI, 340).

Eusebius, who argued that the Son was true God, but not the *only* true God, being inferior to the true God who is over all.[1]

(iii) John x. 30: 'I and the Father are one.'

John xvii. 11: 'That they may be one, even as we are one.'

In opposition to the Arians and Eusebius of Caesarea, who interpret John x. 30 in the light of John xvii. 11, that is, the oneness of the Father and the Son in the light of oneness which we have through the Son,[2] Athanasius insists that John xvii. 11 must be interpreted in the light of John x. 30. Before demonstrating the falseness of Arian exegesis of these two verses taken in conjunction however, Athanasius discusses the Arian interpretation of John x. 30 when taken by itself.

(*a*) The Arians say:

Since the Son also wills what the Father wills and is not contrary in what he thinks or in what he judges, but is in all respects in agreement with him, declaring doctrines which are the same and a word which is consistent and united with the Father's teaching, therefore it is that he and the Father are one.[3]

In opposition to this Athanasius sets forth the following arguments:

(α) If the Arians' interpretation is correct, then angels, powers, authorities, sun, moon and stars should be sons, and it should be said of them too that they and the Father are one.[4] Even among men there will be found many who are like the Father and in agreement with him—martyrs, apostles, prophets, and patriarchs—yet none of these has dared to claim 'I and the Father are one' (John x. 30), or 'I in the Father and the Father in me' (John xiv. 10).[5]

(β) The likeness and oneness must be referred to the essence of the Son; if it is not understood in this way, he will not be shown to have anything more than the creatures, and he will not be like the Father. The Father and the Son are one, so that when the Son works, the Father is the worker, and when the Son comes to the saints, it is the Father that comes in the Son, as he promised when he said, 'I and my Father will come, and will make

---

[1] See above, pp. 124 ff. [2] See below, pp. 295 ff.

[3] *Or. c. Ar.* iii, 10 (*PG*, xxvi, 341).

[4] Cf. *de Syn.* 48 (*PG*, xxvi, 777–80).

[5] *Or. c. Ar.* iii, 10 (*PG*, xxvi, 341–4).

our abode with him' (John xiv. 23)...When the Father gives grace and peace, the Son also gives it (Rom. i. 7)...For one and the same grace is from the Father in the Son.[1]

If the Father and the Son were not one, and the Son were distinct from the Father in nature, then it would be sufficient that the Father alone should give, since no creature is a partner with God in his activity of giving. The fact that the Father gives in and through the Son shows the oneness of the Father and the Son. 'No one would pray to receive from God and the angels...but from Father and Son, because of their oneness and the oneness of their giving.'[2]

(γ) Developing still further the argument from the unity of operation, Athanasius emphasises the oneness of Father and Son in revelation:

What God speaks, he speaks through the Logos (Word), and not through another. And since the Word is not separate from the Father, nor unlike and foreign to the Father's essence, what he works, those are the Father's works (John v. 19), and his fashioning of all things is one with his, and what the Son gives, that is the Father's gift. And he who has seen the Son knows that, in seeing him, he has seen, not an angel, nor one merely greater than the angels, nor, in short, any creature, but the Father himself (John xiv. 9). And he who hears the Word knows that he hears the Father, just as he who is irradiated by the radiance knows that he is enlightened by the sun.[3]

(δ) Athanasius denies that his doctrine of the Father and the Son, distinct from each other in that the Father is always Father and the Son always Son, yet united in essence and activity, implies a multiplicity of gods.[4] Indeed he turns the accusation against the Arians themselves, for their doctrine of the Father (Creator) and Son (creature) is ditheism, and its ultimate outcome is polytheism.[5] 'There is one God and not many, and his Logos is one and not many, for the Logos is God (John i. 1c) and he alone has the form of the Father'.[6] Jesus himself puts the Jews out of countenance when he says, 'And the Father who sent me has himself borne witness to me. His voice you

---

[1] *Ibid.* iii, 11 (*PG*, xxvi, 345); cf. iii, 13 (*PG*, xxvi, 349).
[2] *Ibid.* iii, 12 (*PG*, xxvi, 345–8).   [3] *Ibid.* iii, 14 (*PG*, xxvi, 352).
[4] *Ibid.* iii, 15 (*PG*, xxvi, 352–3).   [5] *Ibid.* iii, 16 (*PG*, xxvi, 353).
[6] *Ibid.* iii, 16 (*PG*, xxvi, 356).

have never heard, his form you have never seen; and you do not have his Word (τὸν λόγον) abiding in you, for you do not believe him whom he has sent' (John v. 37–8). Athanasius takes τὸν λόγον here to refer to the Logos,[1] and argues that Jesus

has suitably connected the 'Logos' and the 'Form' of God in order to show that the Logos of God is himself the Image and Expression and Form of his Father...It is he who said John xiv. 9, xiv. 10 and x. 30, for thus God is one and one is the faith in the Father and the Son; for though the Logos is God, the Lord our God is one Lord; for the Son is proper to that one, and inseparable according to the propriety and peculiarity of his essence.[2]

(*b*) Having disposed of the Arian interpretation of John x. 30, Athanasius turns his attention to their attempt to reduce its significance to a oneness similar to that which we can have with each other through the Son, by interpreting it in the light of John xvii. 11, 20–3.

The Arians say:

If, as we become one in the Father, so also he and the Father are one, and thus also he is in the Father, how do you pretend from his saying, 'I and the Father are one', and 'I in the Father and the Father in me', that he is proper to and like the Father's essence? For it follows either that we also are proper to the Father's essence, or that he is foreign to it as we are foreign to it.[3]

To this teaching, Athanasius replies with a criticism which recurs like a refrain:

What is given to men by grace, this they would make equal to the godhead of the Giver. Thus hearing that men are called sons, they thought themselves to be equal to the true Son who is such by nature.[4]

He offers the following criticisms:

(α) He appeals again to the 'custom' of scripture: it is the custom of scripture 'to take patterns for man from divine

---

[1] Cf. C. K. Barrett (*The Gospel According to St John*, p. 222): 'The thought was probably not absent from John's mind that the true Word of God was Jesus.'

[2] *Or. c. Ar.* III, 16 (*PG*, XXVI, 356–7).

[3] *Ibid.* III, 17 (*PG*, XXVI, 357–60).   [4] *Idem* (*PG*, XXVI, 360).

things'.[1] Thus Jesus says, 'Be merciful, as your Father...' (Luke vi. 36), and 'Be perfect as your Father...' (Matt v. 48). He does not mean that we are to become as the Father is, for this is impossible for creatures, but that 'looking at his beneficent acts, we may do what we do, not for men's sakes, but for his sake, so that we may have the reward from him and not from men'.[2] Just as there is one who is Son by nature, and yet we too become sons, not by nature, but by grace, so also 'we become merciful as God is merciful, not by being made equal to God...but in order that we may impart to others without distinction what has happened to us from God himself through his grace'.[3] John does not say that we may come to be in the Father in the same way as the Son is, but that we may become virtuous and sons by imitation.[4] Therefore, says Athanasius,

Jesus did not say, 'That they may be one as we are one', with the meaning that we may become such as he is, but that just as he, who is the Logos, is in his own Father, we too, taking him as a pattern and looking at him, may become one towards each other in concord and unity of spirit...(and) mind the same thing like those five thousand in Acts who were as one (Acts iv. 4, 32).[5]

Jesus says, 'that they may be one as we are' whose nature is indivisible; that is, that they, learning from us about that indivisible nature, may preserve in like manner agreement one with another.[6]

(β) Similarly the words 'that they may be one in us' (John xvii. 21: ἵνα καὶ αὐτοὶ ἐν ἡμῖν ἓν ὦσιν)[7] have an orthodox sense. If it were possible for us to become sons in the same way as he is Son, he would have said, 'that they may be one in Thee, as the Son is in the Father':

By saying 'in us' he has emphasised the distance and the difference, because he alone, as only Logos and Wisdom, is in the Father alone, but we are in the Son and through him in the Father. When he spoke in this way, he meant only this: 'By our unity may they also be one with each other, as we are one in nature and truth; for they could not be one except by learning in us what the unity is.[8]

---

[1] *Ibid.* III, 19 (*PG*, XXVI, 361).   [2] *Idem.*
[3] *Idem* (*PG*, XXVI, 364).   [4] *Idem*; a reference to John i. 12–13.
[5] *Ibid.* III, 20 (*PG*, XXVI, 364).   [6] *Idem* (*PG*, XXVI, 365).
[7] Ath. reads ἐν ἡμῖν ἓν ὦσιν with ℵ Θ Ω vg sin pesh boh; ἐν is omitted by B C D it; cf. Barrett, *St John*, p. 427.
[8] *Or. c. Ar.* III, 21 (*PG*, XXVI, 365–8).

(γ) In the same way, Jesus said, 'that they may be one as we are' (John xvii. 23), and not 'that they may be one in thee as I am': 'The word "as" signifies, not identity, but an image and example of the subject being discussed.'[1]

(δ) Athanasius goes on to the words 'I in them and thou in me, that they may be made perfect in one' (John xvii. 23):

It is plain that the Logos has come to be in us, for he has put on our body. 'And thou, Father, in me', for I am thy Logos; and since thou art in me because I am thy Logos, and I in them because of the body, and the salvation of men is perfected in me because of thee, therefore I ask that they also may become one, according to the body that is in me and according to its perfection, that they may become perfect, having oneness with it, and having become one in it; that, as if all were borne by me, all may be one body and one spirit and may grow into a perfect man (Eph. iv. 13).[2]

(ε) Athanasius sums up his interpretation of John x. 30, xvii. 11, 20–3 in a passage which demonstrates the centrality of the incarnation and atonement in his theology:

The Son himself is simply and unconditionally 'in the Father' (John xvii. 21; cf. x. 38; xiv. 10), for he has this by nature; but for us who do not have it by nature, there is needed an image and example, so that he may say concerning us 'As thou in me and I in thee' (John xvii. 21). And when they shall be thus made perfect, he says, then the world knows that thou hast sent me; for if I had not come and borne this body of theirs, not one of them would have been made perfect, but one and all would have remained corruptible. Work thou in them, O Father, and as thou has given me to bear this, grant to them thy Spirit, so that they too may become one in him, and may be made perfect in me. For their being made perfect shows that thy Logos has sojourned among them, and the world, seeing them perfect and bearing God within themselves (θεοφορου-μένους), will completely believe that thou hast sent me and I have sojourned here. For whence is this being made perfect, except that I, thy Logos, having borne their body and become man, have perfected the work which thou didst give me, O Father (John xvii. 4)? And the work is perfected because men, redeemed from sin, no longer remain dead, but being deified, have in each other, by looking at us, the bond of love.[3]

[1] *Ibid.* III, 21 (*PG*, XXVI, 368); cf. III, 22 (*PG*, XXVI, 369).
[2] *Ibid.* III, 22 (*PG*, XXVI, 368 f.).   [3] *Ibid.* III, 23 (*PG*, XXVI, 372).

(3) As he concludes his exegesis of John x. 30; xvii. 11, 20–3, Athanasius turns to I John iv. 13 for further light: 'By this we know that we abide in him and he in us, because he has given us of his own Spirit'. He says that the Spirit does not unite the Son with the Father, for the Spirit receives from the Son (John xvi. 14–15); but on the other hand, we apart from the Spirit are foreign to God and distant from him. It is by partaking of the Spirit that we are joined to the godhead:

Our being in the Father is not ours but the Spirit's which is in us and abides in us so long as we preserve it in us by the true confession. John again says, 'Whoever confesses that Jesus is the Son of God, God abides in him and he in God' (I John iv. 15)...the Son is in the Father in one way, and we come to be in him in another.[1]

The prayer of Jesus (John xvii. 20–3) does not mean that he is asking that we should have identity with the Son, but that he wants us to receive through the Spirit what he himself has by nature, that we may become sons and gods, that we may be in the Son and in the Father, that we may be reckoned 'to have become one in the Son and in the Father, because that Spirit is in us which is in the Logos which is in the Father'.[2]

In his exegesis of the Johannine texts which the Arians had interpreted in the light of their basic presuppositions of the essential undifferentiated unity of God and the essential createdness of the Son, Athanasius shows that he has grasped the meaning intended by St John much more clearly than those whom he opposed. He has grasped clearly the relationship in which the evangelist sets the Logos-concept and the Son-concept, the centrality of the Father–Son relationship, the unity of the Son with the Father and the distinction between them, the distinction between Christ's sonship and ours, and the emphasis on the mediatorship of the Son in the divine activities of creation, revelation and redemption.

I. CHRISTOLOGY

It is beyond our scope to enter in depth into the current debate on whether or not Athanasius believed that the incarnate Son had a human soul, important though that question may be for the understanding of christology in the fourth century. M.

---

[1] *Ibid.* III, 24 (*PG*, XXVI, 373).   [2] *Ibid.* III, 25 (*PG*, XXVI, 376).

Richard[1] has reopened the question with a painstaking analysis of *Oratio III*, 35–7, in which Athanasius attacks the Arian view of the incarnation that the Logos (Son) was the subject of the passions, weaknesses, fears, ignorance, etc., which the gospels attribute to Jesus Christ. Whether the Arians originally explicitly denied a human soul in Christ, or whether, believing the Logos to be a creature, they thought of the Logos as being in fact the human soul of Christ, is impossible to judge on the basis of the information preserved for us. It is possible that they had asserted that the Logos took the place of the human soul; that is at least implied by the Arian texts which Athanasius criticises in *Oratio III*.[2] Richard has shown clearly that at no point in his lengthy refutation of Arian christology does Athanasius criticise the Arians for ignoring or denying the human soul of Christ. 'Nor does he ever resort to the expedient of giving Christ a human soul in order to solve the great difficulties raised by the Arians. So he knows nothing of one. His Christ is only Logos and sarx.'[3]

A. Grillmeier has taken Richard's arguments considerably farther. Richard's conclusion is based on an argument from silence, and so cannot be completely conclusive; 'positive proof must be added to a negative argument if the question of the soul of Christ in Athanasius is to be decided'.[4] From an investigation of Athanasius' teaching on the activity of the Logos in Christ's humanity, on the death of Christ as a separation of the Logos from the flesh or body, and on the body as an instrument (ὄργανον), Grillmeier concludes that, at least until A.D. 362 when he wrote the *Tomus ad Antiochenos*, the human soul of Christ was neither a theological nor a physical factor in Athanasius' christology, and that even after A.D. 362 it was nothing more than a physical factor. Further, he concludes that Athanasius' christology never moved outside the *Logos–sarx* framework.[5] A study of Arian exegesis and Athanasian counter-

---

[1] 'Saint Athanase et la psychologie du Christ selon les Ariens', *MSR*, IV (1947), 5–54.

[2] Cf. Grillmeier, *Christ in Christian Tradition*, pp. 195 f.; J. Liébaert, *L'incarnation*, pp. 113 ff.

[3] Grillmeier, *op. cit.* p. 196, summarising Richard's conclusion.

[4] *Idem.*

[5] Liébaert (*L'incarnation*, pp. 134 ff.) suggests that Athanasius was bound to this framework by his suspicion of the *Word-man* christology of Antioch.

exegesis of specific biblical texts may throw some further light on this question.

In opposition to the Nicene doctrine of the essential divinity of Jesus Christ as Son of God the Arians quoted texts from the gospels which specifically refer to the human attributes (τὰ ἀνθρώπινα) of Christ. By doing so, says Athanasius, 'like the Samosatene' they completely forget 'the Son's paternal godhead'.[1] The Arians set out these texts in four groups as evidence supporting their contentions that:

(i) *the Son is not from the Father by essence* (Matt. xi. 27; xxviii. 18; John iii. 35, 36; v. 22; vi. 37);

(ii) *the Son is not the natural and true power of the Father* (John xii. 27; xii. 28; xiii. 21);

(iii) *the Son is not the true and proper Wisdom of the Father* (Matt. xvi. 53; Mark vi. 38; Luke ii. 52; John xi. 34);

(iv) *the Son is not the Father's proper Logos* (Matt. xxvi. 41, xxvii. 46; Mark xiii. 32; John xii. 28; xvii. 5).

Athanasius compares their teaching with that of the Jews; both Jews and Arians 'deny the eternity and godhead of the Logos because of those human attributes which the Saviour took on him by reason of that flesh which he bore'.[2] He says, 'Let the Arians openly confess themselves to be pupils of Caiaphas and Herod, instead of cloaking Judaism with the name of Christianity'.[3]

---

[1] *Or. c. Ar.* iii, 26 (*PG*, xxvi, 377).   [2] *Ibid.* iii, 27 (*PG*, xxvi, 381).

[3] *Ibid.* iii, 28 (*PG*, xxvi, 381). Matthew Black ('The Pauline Doctrine of the Second Adam', in *SJT*, vii (1954), 177 f.) draws attention to a reference by the Islamic writer, Shahristani (*ob.* A.D. 1153), who, drawing on the work of a ninth-century Islamic historian, Isa al-Warrak, mentions a Jewish sect called *Maghariya*, or 'Cave-people', who flourished about 50 B.C. Shahristani tells us that Arius had been influenced by this sect in his doctrine of God and the Messiah. The Maghariya, he says, believed in a divine-human mediator, described as a 'god' or 'angel', but having the appearance of Adam. It is interesting to speculate on the possible identification of the Maghariya with the Covenanters of the Dead Sea Scrolls—as yet it can only be speculation, for none of the Scrolls published so far has any reference to the Messiah as divine, as an angel or a god. That the Arians called the Son 'God' is certain, and that they looked upon him as an angel is probable in the light of their exegesis of Heb. i. 4. Earlier it has been argued that the Dead Sea Scrolls are the background for the dualism and anti-Jewish polemic of the Fourth Gospel; Antioch, a centre in which Jewish influence was particularly strong, was a place where the Logos of the Prologue of the Fourth Gospel continued to be interpreted in the light of the

Before criticising the Arian exegesis of these texts in detail, Athanasius sets forth his most complete statement of the scope of scripture[1] which leads on to a discussion of the incarnation which is, in effect, exegesis of John i. 14. 'The Lord becomes man', he says, 'and did not come into a man.'[2] If he had only come to a man in the same way as that in which he came to the prophets of old, he would not have shocked the Jews sufficiently to make them ask, 'Wherefore dost thou, being a man, make thyself God?' (John x. 33).

But now, since the Logos of God, through whom all things have been made (John i. 3), endured to become Son of man as well, and humbled himself, taking a servant's form (Phil. ii. 7, 8), therefore,

Hebraic Word-concept right up to the time of the Arian controversy. Antioch was a city in which Jews and Christians mingled more freely and with less bitterness than elsewhere; cf. John Chrysostom, adv. Judaeos, and C. J. Kraeling, 'The Jewish Community of Antioch', JBL, LIV (1932), 130–60. Is it possible that the school of Lucian at Antioch, to which Arius belonged, had some connection with a form of Judaism which was in lineal descent from the Dead Sea Covenanters? Athanasius repeatedly tells the Arians to remove the cloak of Christianity from their Judaism, and Arius found support from the Jews in Alexandria. It has been argued above that the presuppositions of Arianism come from pagan metaphysics; it is possible however, that they were derived from a Judaism which had been strongly influenced by the metaphysical monotheism of Greek philosophy. It is possible that some slight evidence in support of Shahristani's connection of the theological views of Arius with the Jewish Maghariya may be present in the recently published *Melchizedek Scroll* (11Q Melchizedek), in which Melchizedek appears to resemble the angelic mediator of the Maghariya. See M. de Jonge and A. S. van der Woude, '11Q Melchizedek and the New Testament', *NTS* XII (1965/6), 301 ff.

[1] *Or. c. Ar.* III, 28–9 (*PG*, XXVI, 385); cf. my article, 'The Exegesis of Scripture'.

[2] *Ibid.* III, 30 (*PG*, XXVI, 388). It is difficult to know whether ἄνθρωπος γέγονε should be translated 'He became man' or 'He became a man'. Athanasius' doctrine of recapitulation implies that the manhood which the Logos assumed is such that in it the whole human race is represented, and that the very assumption of this flesh is the redemption of mankind.

He emphasises equally, however, the individuality of the manhood of the Saviour. It seems that both ideas are in the mind of Athanasius. The manhood of Jesus Christ is manhood such as ours, so that it is possible to say that Jesus Christ is *a* man, and yet he is not a man like other men, but 'God bearing flesh' (III, 51), 'for when he became a man, he did not cease to be God' (III, 38), and his manhood is representative of all humanity, so that we all participate in it, being baptised in his baptism, killed in his death, and raised again in his resurrection.

to the Jews the cross of Christ is a scandal, but to us Christ is 'God's Power' and 'God's Wisdom' (I Cor. i. 24), for as John says, 'the Logos became flesh', it being the custom of scripture to call man by the name of flesh.[1]

Thus when he dwelt among us,

it is said that he took flesh and became man and in that flesh suffered for us, in order that it might be shown and that all might believe that, whereas he was ever God...afterwards for our sakes he became man.[2]

From these passages it appears that Athanasius is clearly asserting the equivalence of the terms 'flesh' and 'man' and that the Logos in taking 'flesh' became 'man' or 'a man'. If this interpretation is correct, then he has broken through the *Logos–sarx* framework and is asserting a *Logos-man* or, since he is so emphatic that the Logos is God, a *God-man* christology. Whether, as he develops his argument, he is able to remain within this christological framework or falls back into the *Logos–sarx* framework is a question to which we shall have to return.

Having asserted the reality of the humanity which the Logos takes, the reality and integrity of the man that the Logos becomes, Athanasius resorts to the idea of *communicatio idiomatum*. Because the Logos becomes man, the properties of the flesh are said to be his, while the works which properly belong to the Logos himself he did through his own body: 'The Logos bore the infirmities of the flesh as his own, for his was the flesh; and the flesh ministered to the works of the godhead, because the godhead was in it, for the body was God's.'[3] When he did his Father's works as divine (θεϊκῶς), the flesh was not external to him or separate from him; he did them in the body. Therefore when he was made man he said, 'If I do not do the works of the Father, believe me not; but if I do, though you do not believe me, believe the works, that you may know that the Father is in me and I in him' (John x. 37–8). Further it was appropriate that when he put on human flesh he should put it on 'whole', with all the affections (πάθη) which properly belong

---

[1] *Or. c. Ar.* III, 30 (*PG*, XXVI, 388); cf. *ad. Epict.* 8 (*PG*, XXVI, 1064).

[2] *Or. c. Ar.* III, 31 (*PG*, XXVI, 388–9).

[3] *Idem* (*PG*, XXVI, 389).

to the human flesh: 'The affections of the body were proper to him alone, although they did not touch him according to his godhead.'[1] The 'body' or the 'flesh' did not belong to another but to the Logos and so the affections of the body are ascribed to him 'whose the flesh is'. The affections of the body are ascribed to the Lord 'so that grace also may be from him'.[2] In this way, through the idea of *communicatio idiomatum* Athanasius is struggling to express the belief embodied in the later formula, 'what he did not assume he did not redeem'. He argues that if the works of the godhead had not been done through the body, we would not have been deified, nor would we have been delivered from bondage to the flesh with its affections, sufferings and weaknesses. The Son of God transferred to himself all the affections of human nature,[3] in order that we, no longer as men but as those who belong to the Logos, may share in eternal life:

No longer according to our former origin in Adam do we die. But henceforth, our origin and all infirmity of the flesh being transferred to the Logos, we rise from the earth, the curse of sin being removed, because of him who is in us and who has become a curse for us. And with reason, for as we are all from earth and die in Adam, so being born again from above of water and Spirit (John iii. 5), in Christ we are made alive, the flesh no longer being earthly, but henceforth made 'Logos' (λογωθείσης τῆς σαρκός), by reason of God's Logos who for our sake became flesh.[4]

In *de Incarnatione* Athanasius had asserted, 'He was made man that we might be made God';[5] here he makes the same assertion in a different way, 'the Logos was made flesh that flesh may be made Logos'.

Athanasius emphasises the two natures of Christ as Logos and flesh or as God and man, which he asserts belongs to the 'scope' both of faith and of scripture; yet at the same time he is careful to make it plain that while we can distinguish between what belongs to the manhood and what belongs to the godhead, we must not divide the Son of God: 'If we recognise what belongs to each and see and understand that both these things and

---

[1] *Ibid.* III, 32 (*PG*, XXVI, 392).   [2] *Idem.*

[3] *Ibid.* III, 33 (*PG*, XXVI, 393); cf. Athanasius' emphasis on the word 'carried' in Is. liii. 4: 'He carried our infirmities' (*ibid.* III, 31 *fin*).

[4] *Ibid.* III, 33 (*PG*, XXVI, 393–6).   [5] *de Inc.* 54 (*PG*, XXV, 192).

those are done by *One*, we are right in our faith and shall never go astray.'[1] The Arians go astray because looking at 'what is human (τὰ ἀνθρώπινα) in the Saviour', they conclude that he is wholly a creature, and do not understand that it is the Logos, the Son of God, who has 'become flesh'.

By his emphasis on the scope of both faith and scripture Athanasius seeks to preserve the paradox which is implicit in St John's Gospel: The Logos who was in the beginning, who was with God, and who was God, has become flesh and dwelt among us as the man Jesus Christ for us men and for our salvation. 'He did not cease to be God when he became man...but rather, being God, he has assumed the flesh and being in the flesh deified the flesh.'[2]

When he turns from his statement of the teaching of the traditional faith of the church and the teaching of scripture as a whole[3] to the exegesis of specific texts which the Arians adduce in support of their doctrine of the createdness of the Son of God, Athanasius does not criticise their denial of a human soul in Christ as might be expected.[4] Instead, he proceeds to counter their exegesis with what M. F. Wiles calls 'two-nature exegesis,'[5] which was to become a standard method of interpreting the great christological texts of the gospels in the controversies of the fifth century: 'the clear differentiation between those things which referred to Christ's manhood and those which referred to his godhead'.[6] He criticises the Arians' interpretation in the following way:

(i) Concentrating their attention on the human attributes (τὰ ἀνθρώπινα) of Christ, they ask:

How can the Son be from the Father by nature and be like him in essence, who says...'The Father judges no man, but has committed all judgment to the Son' (John v. 22), and 'The Father loves the Son, and has given all things into his hand' (John vi. 37).[7]

---

[1] *Or. c. Ar.* III, 35 (*PG*, xxvi, 397).

[2] *Ibid.* III, 38 (*PG*, xxvi, 404–5).

[3] I.e. what he calls the σκοπός of faith and the σκοπός of scripture; cf. my article, 'The Exegesis of Scripture and the Arian Controversy', pp. 422 ff.

[4] Richard, Grillmeier and Liébaert base their argument that Athanasius finds no real place for a human soul in Christ on his failure to criticise the Arians in this way.

[5] *The Spiritual Gospel*, ch. VIII.   [6] *Ibid.* p. 129.

[7] *Or. c. Ar.* III, 26 (*PG*, xxvi, 377).

and

If he was, as you say, Son by nature, he had no need to receive, but he had by nature as a Son.[1]

In reply Athanasius argues that these passages 'do not show that once the Son did not possess these prerogatives, for he has always possessed what the Father has, who says, "All that the Father has are mine" (John xvi. 15), and what are mine are the Father's (John xvii. 10)'.[2] These sayings do not mean that the Son acknowledges that he was once without these things, but rather that 'whereas the Son eternally has what he has, still he has them from the Father.'[3] Athanasius says that the Son's purpose in saying these words was to distinguish himself from the Father, lest anyone be led to draw Sabellian conclusions from the exact likeness and identity of his attributes to those of the Father. On the other hand, these words which refer to the Son's receiving gifts do not diminish his godhead, as the Arians conclude from them, but

show him to be really Son...For if all things were delivered to him (Matt. xi. 27), first, he is other than the 'all things' which he has received, and next, being 'heir of all things' (Heb. i. 2), he alone is Son and proper to the essence of the Father.[4]

Similarly, Athanasius appeals to John v. 26: 'As the Father has life in himself, so he has given also to the Son to have life in himself':

By the words 'has given' he signifies that he is not the Father, but in saying 'so' he shows the Son's natural likeness and propriety towards the Father.[5]

In the short treatise on Luke x. 22 (= Matthew xi. 27), *in Illud: Omnia mihi tradita sunt*, Athanasius interprets the words, 'All things were delivered to me by my Father' in the light of John xvi. 15, 'All that the Father has is mine'. He says that

All things were delivered to the Son when he became man. The Arians argue that 'if all things have been delivered to the Son, then the Father has ceased to have power over what is delivered, having appointed the Son in his place'.[6]

[1] *Idem* (PG, xxvi, 377).   [2] *Ibid.* iii, 35 (PG, xxvi, 400).
[3] *Idem.*   [4] *Ibid.* iii, 36 (PG, xxvi, 400–1).
[5] *Idem.*   [6] *in Illud: Omnia*, 3 (PG, xxv, 213).

Again Athanasius replies that when Jesus says, 'All that the Father has is mine', he shows that he is ever with the Father:

For 'what he has' shows that the Father exercises the Lordship, while 'are mine' indicates the inseparable union...What belongs to the Father, belongs to the Son...As, then, the Father is not a creature, so neither is the Son...From this passage at one and the same time the delusion of Sabellius can be upset, and it will expose the folly of our modern Jews. For this is why the only (Son), having life in himself as the Father has (John v. 26), also knows alone who the Father is (Luke x. 22 = Matt. xi. 27), because he is in the Father and the Father in him (John xiv. 10 *et al.*). For he is his Image (Col. i. 15), and consequently, because he is his Image, all that belongs to the Father is in him. He is the exact seal, showing in himself the Father (John xiv. 9): the living and true Word, Power, Wisdom, our sanctification and redemption (I Cor. i. 30).[1]

Just as Jesus is said to be 'highly exalted' (Phil. ii. 10) for our sakes,[2] so also it is for our sakes that he is said to receive what, as God, he possesses eternally. These texts—John iii. 35–6; v. 22; vi. 37; Luke x. 22 (Matt. xi. 27) must be interpreted in the light of the scope of scripture, and in the light of John xvi. 15.

Athanasius' discussion of this Arian argument shows that he is still primarily concerned to demonstrate the falseness of the Arians' attempt to deny the essential unity of the Son with the Father. Therefore he ignores the psychological or anthropological question of the relation of the Logos to the 'flesh' or 'body' which the Logos assumed at the incarnation.

(ii) The Arians ask: 'How is he Wisdom, who increased in wisdom (Luke ii. 52), and was ignorant of what he asked of others?'[3]

Athanasius asks them why they consider him to be ignorant, for to ask a question does not necessarily mean ignorance of the answer. He conflates the accounts of the feeding of the five thousand in Mark vi. 38 and John vi. 6. In Mark vi. 38 Jesus asks, 'How many loaves have you?', but John vi. 6

---

[1] *Ibid.* 4–5 (*PG*, xxv, 216–17).

[2] See above, pp. 217 ff.

[3] *Or. c. Ar.* iii, 26 (*PG*, xxvi, 377). For the ignorance of Christ the Arians quoted Luke ii. 52; Matt. xvi. 13; John xi. 34; Mark vi. 38; cf. *Or. c. Ar.* iii, 37.

indicates that Jesus was not ignorant of the answer: 'This he said to test him, for he himself knew what he would do'.[1]

The ignorance must be ascribed to the flesh, says Athanasius, for the Logos, as Logos, knows all things:

When he became man, he did not cease to be God...The all-holy Logos of God, who endured all things for our sakes, did this [i.e. asked where Lazarus lay, John xi. 34] in order that, bearing our ignorance, he might grant us the grace of knowing his own only and true Father, and himself, sent because of us for the salvation of all; no grace could be greater than this.[2]

If the Logos has not become man, then ascribe to the Logos, as you would have it, to receive, and to need glory, and to be ignorant; but if he has become man, as indeed he has, and it belongs to man to receive, and to need, and to be ignorant, why do we consider the Giver to be receiver, and why do we suspect the Dispenser to others to be in need, and divide the Logos from the Father as imperfect and needy, while we strip human nature of grace.[3]

Again Athanasius appeals to the 'two-nature exegesis'. If the Logos had not become man, then these sayings must have been said about his divinity, but since he has become man they are said about his manhood. The affections, weaknesses and ignorance belong to the flesh, while the grace and power belong to the Logos:

He was real God in the flesh, and he was true flesh in the Logos. Therefore, by his deeds he revealed both himself as Son of God, and his own Father, and from the affections of the flesh he showed that he bore a body and that it was his own.[4]

The Arians naturally appealed to Mark xiii. 32 where Jesus explicitly acknowledges his ignorance of 'that hour and that day'. Again Athanasius replied by using two-nature exegesis, setting over against this text John xvii. 1: 'Father, the hour has come':

It is plain that he knows also the hour of the end of all things as the Logos, though as man he is ignorant of it, for ignorance is proper to man, especially ignorance of these things. Moreover, this is proper to the Saviour's life for man; for since he was made man, he

---

[1] *Ibid.* iii, 37 (*PG*, xxvi, 401–4).   [2] *Ibid.* iii, 38 (*PG*, xxvi, 404–5).
[3] *Ibid.* iii, 39 (*PG*, xxvi, 405).   [4] *Ibid.* iii, 41 (*PG*, xxvi, 412).

is not ashamed, because of the flesh which is ignorant, to say, 'know not', in order that he may show that, knowing as God, he is but ignorant according to the flesh.[1]

(iii) The Arians continue their argument for the alterability of the Son and his distinction from the true Wisdom of God by adducing Luke ii. 52: 'Jesus advanced in wisdom'. They asked, 'How is he Wisdom who increased in wisdom?'[2]

Athanasius asserts that here the question at issue is this: Is Jesus Christ a man like all other men, or is he God bearing flesh? If he is an ordinary man like the rest, then let him advance as a man; this, however, is the opinion of the Samosatene, which you virtually entertain also, although in name you deny it because of men. But, if he is God bearing flesh, as he truly is, and 'the Logos became flesh' (John i. 14), and being God descended upon earth, what advance had he who existed equal to God? Or how did the Son increase, being ever in the Father?[3]

At first glance, it appears that the assertion that Jesus is not 'a man like all other men, but God bearing flesh' indeed implies the denial of complete humanity to Jesus, i.e. the denial of a human soul in Christ. C. E. Raven[4] uses this passage as more or less explicit proof that Athanasius was in fact an Apollinarian before Apollinarius. He says that 'fear of Paul's heresy, the dread of any suggestion of humanity lest it would impair the godhead of Christ, constrains him to explain away the scripture and assert that the manhood...is confined to the assumption of a human body, that in Jesus there is no room for a human soul'.[5] The context of the passage, however, and the general drift of Athanasius' argument is against such an interpretation. If Athanasius had any fear of Paul's heresy it was fear of reduction of the pre-existent Logos to a mere attribute of God, which Athanasius equates with the Arian denial of the eternity and essential divinity of the Logos. Indeed Athanasius appears to anticipate the very objection which Raven raises, for a few lines after the passage Raven quotes,[6] he says:

---

[1] *Ibid.* III, 43 (*PG*, XXVI, 413–16).   [2] *Ibid.* III, 26 (*PG*, XXVI, 377).

[3] *Ibid.* III, 51 (*PG*, XXVI, 429).   [4] *Apollinarianism*, Cambridge, 1923.

[5] *Ibid.* p. 93. Richard, Grillmeier and Liébaert reach a very similar conclusion, although they would distinguish Athanasius' neglect of the human soul of Christ from Apollinarius' explicit denial of it.

[6] *Or. c. Ar.* III, 51 (*PG*, XXVI, 429).

It was not the Logos considered as Logos who advanced, who is perfect from the perfect Father... but humanly he is said to advance here, since advance belongs to man.[1]

Again a little later he says,

The evangelist did not say, 'The Logos advanced', but 'Jesus', by which name the Lord was called when he became man; thus, the advance is of the human nature.[2]

Yet again,

When the flesh advanced, he is said to have advanced, because the body was his own.[3]

Raven has been led by Athanasius' use of the *Logos–sarx* terminology into thinking that his christology remains strictly within the *Logos–sarx* framework; he ignores Athanasius' use of other terminology belonging to the *God–man* framework which points beyond the *Logos–sarx* schema.

Earlier Raven had argued that the dominant motive in Athanasius' christology was fear of falling into the heresy of Paul of Samosata:

Athanasius must vitiate his logic if he would escape heresy. He did so by accepting the gnosticism of Alexandria by making the godhead the centre of Christ's personality and by denying tacitly but indubitably his possession of a human soul. There was no other means of escape open to him... Clearly the conception of a perfect manhood and a human soul was not needed so long as the idea of godhead expressed by the term 'Logos' prevailed. It would seem to lead to the Samosatene heresy. So Athanasius at this time of his life (A.D. 318) definitely rejected it and persisted in so doing at least until his last years.[4]

If as we have argued[5] there is a fundamental difference between Athanasius' doctrine of God and of the Logos and that of what Raven calls 'the gnosticism of Alexandria', then Raven's argument is based on the false assumption that Athanasius' Logos-doctrine is identical with the old Alexandrian doctrine.[6] While the force of the arguments adduced by Richard

---

[1] *Ibid.* III, 52 (*PG*, XXVI, 432).   [2] *Ibid.* III, 53 (*PG*, XXVI, 433).
[3] *Idem.*   [4] *Apollinarianism*, pp. 83 f.
[5] See above, pp. 130 ff.
[6] Cf. L. Bouyer, *L'incarnation et l'église-corps du Christ*, pp. 101 ff.

and others concerning the weakness of Athanasius' christology, due to his failure to acknowledge the human soul of Christ as a theological factor, must be acknowledged, his use of two-nature exegesis, strange and forced though it may appear to twentieth-century theologians, implies that the manhood in Christ is complete. As God, the Logos cannot suffer, be ignorant, or advance in wisdom, for Athanasius holds fast to the idea of the immutability of God and therefore of the Logos. If these things belong to the man, then it is the man who suffers, is ignorant and advances in wisdom. That point Athanasius repeats over and over again. These things can be said of the Logos only by *communicatio idiomatum*. His retention of the *Logos–sarx* terminology may make it appear that he is tacitly denying or giving no theological importance to the human soul of Christ, but his exegesis of the relevant scriptural texts makes it clear that he is trying to assert the full manhood of Christ. It may be true that, as Grillmeier and Richard have argued, he could most easily have attacked Arian exegesis by asserting that Christ had a human soul, but the exigencies of the controversy made him concentrate all his attention on Arian denial of the eternity of the Son and of his being from the Father's essence. Therefore he answers their objections based on texts from the gospels by remaining within the universe of discourse in which the Arians posed the problem. This may mean that Athanasius' views on the relation of godhead to manhood in Christ are not completely clear, but it is because, within the controversy itself, clarification at this point was not demanded. He sees Arianism as an attack on the divinity of the Son, and it is within this limited sector of the theological front that he counter-attacks, using as his weapons the scope of faith, the scope of scripture and constant appeal to the witness of St John to Jesus Christ as the Son of God, the Word made flesh.

J. SUMMARY

In opposition to the metaphysical monotheism of the Arians Athanasius sets as the foundation of his theology the New Testament revelation of God as the Father of our Lord and Saviour Jesus Christ, a doctrine which finds its clearest expression and fullest development in St John's Gospel.

In opposition to the metaphysical dualism of the Arians, the dualism of Creator–creature, or Uncreated–created, Athanasius sets the biblical moral dualism of God–world, where 'world' is the mass of sinful men.

In opposition to the cosmological concept of the Logos as an intermediary and intermediate being between the uncreated transcendent God, the Absolute, and the created order, Athanasius sets the biblical concept of the Word of God, who is the Son of God, united to the Father yet distinct from him, who is present with the Father and the Holy Spirit in all the activities of God towards men. He alone is Son of God by nature, but by his grace men may be adopted to sonship of God, and indeed may be made 'gods'.

The Arian system had only a cosmological interest, whereas Athanasius grasps the threefold emphasis of St John on the mediatorial work of Jesus Christ in creation, revelation and salvation. As with St John, it is the last of these which is the dominant motif of Athanasius' theology.

Athanasius emphasises the Father–Son relationship, maintaining the paradox of the Son's unity with and distinction from the Father, and, at the same time, striving to preserve the unity of Jesus Christ as true God and true man.

In the theology of Athanasius the common faith by which the church had lived from the beginning, and which found its expression in the scriptures of the New Testament and the rule of faith, namely faith in Jesus Christ as Son of God and Saviour of men, finds its first full development in the Eastern church. This common faith was the faith which Athanasius spent his life in defending against the powerful attacks of a highly speculative theology which found strong support from the imperial court, and it was St John's Gospel which provided him with his most effective and devastating weapons.

CHAPTER 8

THE CONTROVERSY OVER
MARCELLUS OF ANCYRA

When the Arians had succeeded in having Eustathius deposed from Antioch and Athanasius from Alexandria, they turned their attention to Marcellus, bishop of Ancyra. Although less important as an ecclesiastic than the others, for his see was by no means as important as Antioch or Alexandria, Marcellus was important to the Arians as their most outspoken opponent; therefore he must be silenced as quickly as possible. In a lengthy treatise in reply to a *Syntagma* written by Asterius the Sophist, who had become the theological mouthpiece of the Arian party, Marcellus attacked the Arians—Eusebius of Nicomedia, Narcissus of Neronias, Paulinus of Tyre and, of course, Asterius himself—as well as Eusebius of Caesarea and Origen. Accused of Sabellianism at a synod at Constantinople in A.D. 336, Marcellus was deposed and went into exile in Rome. It appears that the synod deputed Eusebius of Caesarea to reply to Marcellus' views, which he did in two treatises, *contra Marcellum* and *de Ecclesiastica Theologia*.[1]

Until very recently these treatises and Marcellus' place in the Arian controversy had received little notice. In 1902 F. Loofs drew attention to Marcellus as 'one of the most interesting and instructive figures of the Arian controversy'.[2] In 1939 H. Berkhof paid considerable attention to these treatises in his study of Eusebius' theology,[3] and in 1940 the first full-scale monograph on Marcellus, by W. Gericke, was published.[4] In *Christ in Christian Tradition* (1965), A. Grillmeier remedies a

---

[1] F. C. Conybeare, in 'The Authorship of the *contra Marcellum*', *ZNTW*, IV (1903), 330 ff. and VI (1905), 250 ff., argues that these treatises were written by Eusebius of Emesa. E. Klostermann (*Eusebius Werke, GCS*, IV, ix–xvi) refutes Conybeare's arguments and establishes the traditional authorship by Eusebius of Caesarea.

[2] 'Die Trinitätslehre Marcell's von Ancyra und ihr Verhältniss zur älteren Tradition', *SAB* (1902), erster Halbband, p. 764.

[3] *Die Theologie des Eusebius von Caesarea*, Amsterdam, 1939.

[4] *Marcell von Ancyra, der Logos-Christologe und Biblizist*, Halle, 1940.

defect in his earlier German study of the history of christology[1] in which he ignored Marcellus, by devoting a separate short section to his christology,[2] as also does J. Liébaert (1966).[3] Marcellus and his christology have also been placed in their proper perspective by A. Weber,[4] and by M. Simonetti.[5] Finally, M. Tetz has written two lengthy articles in which he seeks, first, to demonstrate that the Pseudo-Athanasian *de Incarnatione et contra Arianos* was written by Marcellus,[6] and then, on the basis of this work and the fragments of Marcellus' writings collected by Klostermann, to link Marcellus' christology with the Pseudo-Clementine tradition of the true teacher and prophet.[7]

Marcellus, and Eusebius' criticism of him in the two treatises, are important for the purposes of this study because in the controversy which his views aroused, which has usually been treated as no more than a side-skirmish in the larger Arian conflict, there converge four distinct lines of approach to the doctrine of the trinity, each of which involves a different method of interpreting St John's Gospel: the Arian, the Antiochene, the apologetic Alexandrian, and the neo-Alexandrian with its close affinities with the western tradition.

Parallel with Eusebius' refutation of Marcellus from the apologetic Alexandrian position is the criticism from the point

---

[1] *Das Konzil von Chalkedon*, i, pp. 1 ff.

[2] *Christ in Christian Tradition*, pp. 249 f.   [3] *L'incarnation*, pp. 123 ff.

[4] APXH, pp. 83 ff., 132 ff.

[5] *Studi sull'Arianesimo*, pp. 38 ff. and pp. 135 ff. I have not had access to a Spanish study which appeared in 1953: J. Fondevila, *Ideas trinitarias y christologicas de Marcelo de Ancyra*, Madrid.

[6] 'Zur Theologie des Markell von Ankyra I. Eine Markellische Schrift *de Incarnatione et contra Arianos*', *ZKG*, LXXV (1964), 217-70.

[7] 'Zur Theologie des Markell von Ankyra II. Markells Lehre von der Adamssohnschaft Christi und eine pseudoklementinische Tradition über die wahren Lehrer und Propheten', *ZKG*, LXXIX (1968), 3-42. Tetz' hypothesis is attractive for, when taken in conjunction with Cullmann's hypothesis of a connection between the Pseudo-Clementine tradition and the Essene writings from Qumran (cf. 'Die neuentdeckten Qumrantexte und das Judenchristentum der Pseudoklementinen', *Theologische Studien für Rudolf Bultmann*, Berlin, 1954, pp. 35 ff.), it adds substantiation to my argument that Marcellus' christology seeks to preserve the old Antiochene tradition which contained a strong Hebraic influence. However, in dealing with Marcellus' christology here, attention will be concentrated on the fragments collected by Klostermann.

of view of Athanasian (neo-Alexandrian) theology contained in *Oratio IV contra Arianos* traditionally ascribed to Athanasius himself, but generally recognised as pseudo-Athanasian. Thus the controversy over Marcellus may be divided into three separate acts: (i) Marcellus *versus* the Arians; (ii) Eusebius of Caesarea *versus* Marcellus; (iii) Ps.-Athanasius *versus* Marcellus. Here, as nowhere else, we get a cross-sectional view of the varied theological traditions which were involved in the Arian controversy.

A. MARCELLUS OF ANCYRA VERSUS THE ARIANS

Loofs gives two reasons for his judgment concerning Marcellus:[1] the archaic character of Marcellus' theology[2] and the persistent refusal of Athanasius and the western church to repudiate him. He demonstrates the relationship between Marcellus and the earlier Antiochene tradition. Gericke seeks to be more specific by making a detailed comparison between the Antiochene tradition, as Loofs outlines it in his study of Theophilus of Antioch,[3] and the theology of Marcellus; he analyses the characteristic theology of second-century Antioch as follows:[4]

1. Consistent monotheism.
2. An outlook determined by the idea of *Heilsgeschichte* and economic trinitarianism.
3. A metaphysical, if unphilosophical, Logos-doctrine.
4. The metaphysical dualism: *Logos* and *Sophia*.
5. Bi-personal (dyo-prosopic) Christology.
6. An energetic relation between the divine and the human in Christ.
7. The limitation of the title 'Son' to the historical Jesus.
8. The slow education of the human race towards fellowship with God.

From his comparison of this Antiochene theology with that of Marcellus Gericke shows that the latter deviates from the

---

[1] 'Die Trinitätslehre Marcell's von Ancyra und ihr Verhältniss zur älteren Tradition', *SAB* (1902).
[2] Cf. Gericke (*Marcell von Ancyra*, p. 187), 'With him, as nowhere else, do we still have (in the fourth century!) a cross-section of the whole ante-Nicene history of dogma'.
[3] *Theophilus von Antiochien adversus Marcionem* (*TU*, XLVI, 2, 1930).
[4] *Op. cit.* pp. 85 ff.

tradition in (4) and (5), that we have no evidence on which to decide about (8), but that on the rest of the points there is either complete agreement or general agreement with occasional exceptions. Somehow, however, Marcellus has mingled with this Antiochene tradition some elements from the apologetic Alexandrian tradition. That is, like the Arians, Marcellus has tried to amalgamate elements from two divergent traditions into a theological system, and both, each in his own way, fail to produce a coherent theological system. In Marcellus' system the Antiochene tradition remains dominant and with it a strongly religious and biblical emphasis which the Arians lost in their rationalism.

It has already been argued that the Antiochene tradition was one in which the Logos-concept was interpreted in the light of the Hebraic concept of the $d^e bhar\ Yahweh$, the creative and revealing Word of God, which it made regulative for its theology. This interpretation was closely linked with, or a corollary of, a strong emphasis on biblical monotheism. God and his Word are revelationally identical. Because of this monotheistic emphasis, the Antiochene tradition had difficulty in ascribing any distinct hypostasis to the Word, at least prior to the incarnation. Whatever his faults may have been, Paul of Samosata sought to preserve this monotheism in the face of the pluralism of the Origenistic tradition; in the fourth century Eustathius seeks to do the same in the face of the pluralism of the Arians and of Eusebius of Caesarea. Further, its emphasis on the full humanity of Jesus Christ led it to give a larger place to history as the sphere of God's activity, and thus to emphasise *Heilsgeschichte*, which sees in the history of Israel, in the historical life of Jesus, and in the life of the church, not the earthly shadows of some heavenly reality, but God's activity of self-revelation in history for the salvation of mankind. This interest in *Heilsgeschichte* tended to produce another characteristic mark of Antiochene theology, an economic trinitarianism which argues back, as it were, from the stages or dispensations of *Heilsgeschichte* to a self-differentiation within the being of the one God, while at the same time maintaining that it is this one God who is at work in all the dispensations of *Heilsgeschichte*.

It is clear from the surviving fragments of Marcellus' writings that he belongs to this Antiochene tradition. Because of the centrality of its *heilsgeschichtlich* interest his theology can be adequately set forth only as the 'history' of a movement within the life of the godhead which is parallel to the movement of God's activity in the history of mankind.

1. In the beginning, before the creation of the world, there was no one else except God, the Monad (οὐδὲν ἕτερον ἦν πλὴν θεοῦ);[1] because God had not yet spoken the creative Word (Logos) there was silence, and the Logos was in God (πρὸ γὰρ δημιουργίας ἁπάσης ἡσυχία τις ἦν, ὡς εἰκός, ὄντος ἐν τῷ θεῷ τοῦ λόγου)[2] as the δύναμις,[3] and the σοφία[4] of God.

2. When God planned to create the world this operation demanded an 'efficacious activity' (δραστικὴ ἐνέργεια):

Therefore, there being no one else except God,...then the Logos came forth and became maker of the world (διὰ τοῦτο, μηδενὸς ὄντος ἑτέρου πλὴν θεοῦ...τότε ὁ λόγος προελθὼν ἐγένετο τοῦ κόσμου ποιητής).[5]

Thus the Monad was differentiated within itself into Father and Logos. While the 'coming forth' of the Logos from the Father took place at the time of the creation of the world and for the purpose of creating, it also took place for the purpose of revealing the Father to men:

for just as all things that have been made by the Father have been made through the Logos (John i. 3), so also all things that are said by the Father are said through the Logos,[6]

and

everything that the Father says he appears to say through the Logos.[7]

3. At the incarnation, the Logos, assuming human flesh, becomes the Son of God, Jesus Christ; before the incarnation he was nothing but the Logos.[8]

4. Before the ascension, the Son of God 'breathes' on the disciples and the third dispensation, that of the Holy Spirit,

---

[1] Fr. 60; cf. Fr. 63; 103; 104; 121; all references to fragments of Marcellus are according to the numbering in the collection of fragments at the end of Klostermann's edition of Eusebius' anti-Marcellan treatises, *GCS*, IV.

[2] Fr. 103; (cf. Ignatius of Antioch, pp. 27 ff. above).

[3] Fr. 52; 73; 129.   [4] Fr. 129.

[5] Fr. 60.   [6] Fr. 61.

[7] Fr. 62.   [8] Fr. 41; 42; 43; 48.

commences. The Holy Spirit proceeds from the Father through the Son.[1] Thus

The Monad which is indivisible, appears to be expanded into a Triad (ἡ μονὰς φαίνεται πλατυνομένη μὲν εἰς τριάδα, διαιρεῖσθαι δὲ μηδαμῶς ὑπομένουσα).[2]

5. At the end of the dispensation of the Holy Spirit, the Son will hand over his kingdom to the Father, as St Paul asserts in I Cor. xv. 24 ff., and the Logos will be absorbed into the Monad and will be in God, as he was formerly, so that God may be all in all.[3]

This system, based on *Heilsgeschichte*, appears at first glance to be in no way different from Sabellianism, and it is understandable that an Origenist like Eusebius (who may have been a good historian but was certainly a bad theologian) should have made the mistake of concluding that Marcellus was a Sabellian. Marcellus, however, tries to guard himself against Sabellianism by denying that God successively shows the 'faces' of Father–Creator, Son and Holy Spirit; the one God, ἡ τῆς θεότητος μονάς[4] is ἓν πρόσωπον,[5] who expands himself into a Dyad at the incarnation (or is it at the creation?), and then into a Triad at the breathing of the Holy Spirit, while still remaining essentially a unity. It is the one God who reveals himself in the three dispensations, and the movement of self-revelation in history has its supra-historical counterpart in the movement of self-differentiation within the Monad of the godhead. This differentiation, however, is not a division of the godhead into three distinct οὐσίαι or ὑποστάσεις or πρόσωπα; there is no division of essence, but only a division of activity. Marcellus says:

If we should make an examination of the Spirit (i.e. in the incarnate Son) alone, the Logos appears fittingly to be identical with God (ἓν καὶ ταὐτὸν...τῷ θεῷ). But if the fleshly supplement of the Saviour should be examined, the godhead seems to be expanded in activity alone (ἐνεργείᾳ ἡ θεότης μόνη πλατύνεσθαι δοκεῖ), so that fittingly it really is an indivisible Monad (ὥστε εἰκότως μονὰς ὄντως ἐστιν ἀδιαίρετος).[6]

That is, the Monad expands in activity into a Triad, while remaining *essentially* a Monad.

---

[1] Fr. 67. [2] *Idem.* [3] Fr. 117; 119; 120; 121; 127.
[4] Fr. 76. [5] Fr. 78. [6] Fr. 71.

If the fragments which Eusebius has preserved are a fair sample of his thought, Marcellus was an exceptionally muddled thinker. He does not make clear what the three dispensations are, and is particularly vague as to when the second dispensation begins. When the Monad speaks the Word (Logos) of creation, it expands into the Dyad of Father and Logos; is this the beginning of the dispensation of the Father, or of the Word, or of both? Marcellus nowhere calls the Monad *Father*; therefore it would seem to be the beginning of the dispensation of the Father. If so, we are entitled to ask whose Father God is. If God is Father of the Logos, then the Logos must be the Son of God; but Marcellus will not allow that, for he insists that before the incarnation the Word was nothing but Word. The first dispensation then appears to be the dispensation of the Father and the Logos, for the Logos proceeds from the Father when the Word (Logos) of creation is spoken. But Marcellus would insist that the second dispensation begins when the Logos becomes Son; if this is so, however, the beginning of the second dispensation has no corresponding expansion of the Monad, for the expansion into a Dyad has already taken place at the creation and the expansion into a Triad does not take place until the breathing of the Holy Spirit.

This confusion concerning the correspondence between the dispensations of God's activity in history and the movement of expansion within the godhead is due to the fact that Marcellus wavers between the Antiochene tradition in which the Logos is interpreted as a 'power' (δύναμις) or attribute of God with no separate personal existence of its own, and the Alexandrian tradition in which the Logos is a personal being, distinct and separate from God. It is the former which is dominant in his mind when he is thinking of the trinity, and the latter when he is thinking of the incarnate existence of the Logos as the Son.

Like the Arians, Marcellus draws a distinction between the Logos and the Son. He recognises that they draw a distinction, but he does not seem to be aware that their distinction differs from his. He argues that the Logos is 'genuinely and truly Logos' and not, as the Arians assert, 'called Logos inaccurately'.[1] The Arians, as we have seen, denied that the Son is 'God's proper Logos', but they did not say that the Logos was in-

[1] Fr. 45; 46.

accurately called Logos. For Marcellus the Son is the Logos joined to human flesh, while for the Arians he is the pre-existent first creature of God, created by God to be his instrument in the creation of the rest, and he is distinct from the Logos which is an attribute of God. Marcellus does not understand their distinction for he treats it as if it were the same as his own.[1] He repeatedly insists that before the assumption of the flesh the Logos was nothing but Logos, and that 'Son', 'Jesus', 'Christ', 'Life', 'Resurrection', and the rest are titles which are properly applicable to the Logos only after the incarnation.[2] Indeed, he goes so far as to say that 'if anyone should claim that the title "Christ" or "Jesus" is a designation of him who was Logos alone before the New Testament, he will discover that this is meant to be understood as a prophecy'.[3]

Marcellus says that in the beginning (ἐν ἀρχῇ, John i. 1 a)[4] the Logos was in God,[5] eternal,[6] and without any origin.[7] In his *Confessio Fidei* in the *Letter to Julius of Rome*, Marcellus says that the Logos 'never had a beginning of existence' (μηδεπώποτε ἀρχὴν τοῦ εἶναι ἐσχηκώς),[8] and he refuses to apply either γένεσις or γεγεννῆσθαι to the pre-existent Logos.[9] Any biblical passage which speaks of 'begetting' or 'first-born' (Prov. viii. 22 ff., Col. i. 15 ff., etc.) refers to the beginning according to the flesh (γένεσις κατὰ σάρκα)'.[10] This rejection of any idea of generation of the Logos is due to his opposition to the Arians' anthropomorphic treatment of the Father–Son relationship in the godhead. He complains that Asterius 'says more humanly to us that the Father is a father and the Son a son' (τόν τε πατέρα πατέρα λέγῃ καὶ τὸν υἱὸν υἱόν).[11]

Gericke describes Marcellus' Logos-concept as 'metaphysical, but unphilosophical'[12] like that of Theophilus of Antioch. The Logos is primarily God's Word of creation and revelation, eternally in God as δύναμις but coming forth from God as ἐνέργεια δραστική, a conception similar to Theophilus' use of λόγος ἐνδιάθετος and λόγος προφορικός,[13] and to Tertullian's

---

[1] See below, pp. 261 f.
[2] Fr. 42; 43; 48.
[3] Fr. 42.
[4] Fr. 33; 43; 51; 52; 53.
[5] Fr. 103.
[6] Fr. 38; 43; 51; 53 (3 times); 70.
[7] Fr. 33.
[8] Fr. 129 (215, 5).
[9] Cf. especially Fr. 32.
[10] Fr. 5; 24; 29.
[11] Fr. 65.
[12] *Marcell von Ancyra*, p. 85.
[13] See above, pp. 40 ff.

use of *ratio* and *sermo*.[1] Discussing Gen. i. 26, 'Let us make man', Marcellus says that the Father said this to the Logos,

since there is no other God who is able to co-operate with him in the task of creating. For he says, 'I am the first God and I am thereafter, and beside me there is no other God' (Is. xliv. 6). Therefore there is no God more recent nor is there any other God thereafter who was able to co-operate with God. For one may make use of a small example from our human sphere, examining the divine activity, as it were, through a figure of speech. A clever sculptor, who wishes to fashion a statue, first looks at the shape and features of the man as he is, then considers a suitable breadth and length and contemplates the proportion of the whole to each part in turn. Then when he has prepared brass and suitable materials and constructed the proposed statue in his mind, and when he has contemplated it in his imagination and acknowledged that he has the co-operation of the Reason (Logos) by which he calculates and is accustomed to do everything (for nothing is made beautiful except by Reason) he starts the actual work which may be perceived by the senses, saying to himself as if exhorting some one else, 'Come on! Let us make! Come on! Let us mould a statue!' So also God, the ruler of the universe, making the living man from earth, exhorts, not someone else, but his own Reason (Logos), saying, 'Let us make man!', yet in the same way as the rest; for by the Logos every creature was made.[2]

In another Fragment Marcellus says that the Logos can no more be separated from God than it is possible 'to separate Reason from a man by power and subsistence (δυνάμει καὶ ὑποστάσει), for the Logos is identical with the man, and is separated from him by nothing other than the activity of the deed alone (οὐδενὶ χωριζόμενος ἑτέρῳ ἢ μόνῃ τῇ πράξεως ἐνεργείᾳ)'.[3] Just as we do everything through our reason, so also does God.[4]

In these passages it is quite clear that Marcellus is thinking of the Logos which is in God as δύναμις, in the same way as that in which Theophilus thought of the λόγος ἐνδιάθετος, and Tertullian of the *ratio*. Nowhere in the extant fragments does

---

[1] See above, pp. 61 ff.

[2] Fr. 58. For earlier patristic interpretations of the plural 'let us make', see R. McL. Wilson, 'The Early History of the Exegesis of Gen. i. 26', *SP*, 1, pp. 420 ff.

[3] Fr. 61.   [4] Fr. 62.

Marcellus use the Stoic terms which Theophilus had used; he prefers to speak in terms of δύναμις and ἐνέργεια δραστική although he intends the same meaning as Theophilus did. Eusebius frequently accuses Marcellus of thinking in these Stoic terms,[1] so that it is possible that Marcellus had used them; his discussion of δύναμις and ἐνέργεια δραστική, however, makes it evident that, if he used them, like Theophilus he used only the language and not the conception of a radical distinction between the λόγος ἐνδιάθετος and the λόγος προφορικός, which the terms imply in Stoic thought. For Marcellus, as for Theophilus, 'God does not lose his Word when he sends him forth'.[2] The Logos does not cease to be in God δυνάμει after he has come forth from God ἐνεργείᾳ δραστικῇ; it is one and the same Logos who is δύναμις and ἐνέργεια. Eusebius treats Marcellus' view as if it were in fact the Stoic distinction, which it is not.[3]

One of the characteristic points of the Antiochene theology, according to Gericke, was a bi-personal or dyo-prosopic christology,[4]

a christology which sharply distinguishes between the human and divine in Christ, a christology which grants a certain independence to the human side, which, as it were, allows the human side its full rights, a christology which does not one-sidedly regard the divine as the subject of the human life of Jesus and is just as far from a denial of the 'Man' as it is from an absorption and deification of the flesh.[5]

In some of the fragments Marcellus appears to follow this tradition, accepting the Pauline distinction κατὰ σάρκα—κατὰ πνεῦμα. As Loofs says,[6]

Certainly he could distinguish continually in the historical Christ between the Logos and ὁ τῷ λόγῳ ἐνωθεὶς ἄνθρωπος,[7] the ἀγαπηθεὶς ὑπὸ θεοῦ ἄνθρωπος whom God τῷ ἑαυτοῦ συνῆψεν λόγῳ; the ἄνθρωπος has become διὰ τὴν πρὸς αὐτὸν (i.e. τὸν λόγον) κοινωνίαν θέσει υἱός,[8] and since the ascension is σύνθρονος ἐν οὐρανοῖς

---

[1] de Ecc. Theol. I, 17 (GCS, IV, 78, 16; cf. also 112, 20; 117, 34; 118, 30; 119, 4. 26; 121, 10).
[2] Gericke, Marcell von Ancyra, p. 136.
[3] See below, pp. 289 ff.
[4] See above, p. 248.
[5] Gericke, Marcell von Ancyra, pp. 153 f.
[6] Paulus von Samosata, p. 258.
[7] Fr. 42, 109.
[8] Fr. 41.

τῷ θεῷ.[1] His βασιλεία received its beginning 'not more than four hundred years ago',[2] and will find its end in days to come (I Cor. xv. 28).[3]

Marcellus' dyo-prosopic christology is one in which the Logos, not as a separate personal being, but as God himself in his activity, is joined to a man.

Marcellus, however, appears to have come under the influence of the Alexandrian type of christology which thought in uni-personal or heno-prosopic fashion of the Logos as 'the proper subject of the human life of Jesus',[4] a christology, that is, of the *Logos–sarx* type, which is also the type of christology which the Arians and Eusebius of Caesarea set forth. Gericke sets out a list of fifteen points[5] which indicate that Marcellus held this heno-prosopic christology along with but predominating over the Antiochene dyo-prosopic view. From the evidence which he sets forth, Gericke draws the conclusion that 'the Logos is, for Marcellus, predominantly the determining subject in the historical Jesus',[6] and that Marcellus 'has no sense that God has revealed himself humanly in Jesus Christ'.[7] The heno-prosopic christological schema, *Logos–sarx*, has gained predominance in his system over the dyo-prosopic schema *Word–Man*.

---

[1] Fr. 110.   [2] Fr. 115; 116.

[3] Fr. 113–15; 117.   [4] Gericke, *Marcell von Ancyra*, p. 154.

[5] *Ibid.* pp. 154 ff. They are: (1) The Logos 'descends' and therefore is an independent subject (Fr. 48; 49; 54; 101). (2) The Logos, as an independent active being, assumes flesh from the Virgin (Fr. 8; 11; 16; 43; 48; 49; 56; 63; 74; 76; 91; 92; 94; 108; 109; 110; 116; 117; 119). (3) The Logos was born (!) (Fr. 16; 29; 31; 48; 110). (4) The Logos 'becomes' 'flesh' (Fr. 16; or 'man' (Fr. 105; 106). (5) After the descent the Logos assumes another name (Fr. 41). (6) The Logos calls himself 'Son of Man' (Fr. 41). (7) The Logos, in his fleshly economy, is called 'Jesus', 'Christ', 'Life', 'Resurrection', etc. (Fr. 42; 43). (8) The Logos, in his human economy, can be called 'Son' (Fr. 20; 41; 44; 67; 68; 73; 74). (9) Marcellus designates the Logos, not the historical Jesus, as δεσπότης (Fr. 14; 43; 24; 31; 74), as σωτήρ (Fr. 9; 14; 15; 67; 73; 74; 77; 79; 100; 107), as κύριος (Fr. 80). (10) The Father is in the Logos, not in the historical Jesus (Fr. 55; 73). (11) The Logos, not the historical Jesus, reveals the Father (Fr. 44). (12) The Logos speaks in Gethsemane (Fr. 73). (13) The Spirit proceeds from the Logos (Fr. 67; 68). (14) The Logos, not the man Jesus, is exalted and made King (Fr. 111), and sits at the right hand of God (Fr. 117; 127). (15) The Logos will at the last day be subjected to God (Fr. 41; 121; 116).

[6] *Marcell von Ancyra*, p. 162.   [7] *Ibid.* p. 163.

If Gericke's analysis is correct, then despite his denial that there are two οὐσίαι, two ὑποστάσεις, or two πρόσωπα, Marcellus appears to think of the Logos which has proceeded from God as an independent being separate from God the Father, and that it is this hypostatised Logos of God that has become incarnate. That Marcellus does sometimes think of the Logos as an independent being beside the Father is borne out by Fragment 58 where he says that the Father spoke to the Logos when he said, 'Let us make man'.[1] Marcellus' theology, then, is a curious mixture of the two ancient traditions, an attempt to combine an economic view of the trinity with a christology which has its roots in a pluralist view of the godhead; that is, he has tried to combine two incompatible and irreconcilable views of the Logos. When he is discussing the doctrine of the godhead, he interprets ὁ λόγος as God's creative and revealing Word which is in God as a power and proceeds forth from God as an activity. When he is discussing christology, however, the Logos appears to be the hypostatised Reason of God joined to human flesh. Like the theologians of the *Logos–sarx* tradition, Clement and Origen, for example, he is not certain what to make of the humanity of Christ, for he takes a derogatory view of the flesh which the Logos assumed; when the Son (= Logos *plus* flesh) hands over his kingdom to the Father at the last day, the Logos is re-absorbed into the Monad but, Marcellus says, we do not know what happens to the flesh of the Son for scripture does not tell us;[2] all that we do know is that the flesh cannot be absorbed into the godhead because 'the flesh is of no avail' (John vi. 63).[3]

It is evident, then, that for Marcellus the regulative concept for both trinitarian thought and christological thought is the Logos–concept, interpreted sometimes as the Word and sometimes as the Logos of metaphysics. The Father–Son relationship plays little part in his system, owing probably to his reaction against the Arian's anthropomorphic treatment of it. The Johannine exegesis contained in the surviving fragments of his treatise bears witness to the primacy of the Logos-concept in his thought and to the confusion in his mind as to its content.

(i) Marcellus sets forth his view that before the incarnation

---

[1] See above, p. 254, n. 2. [2] Fr. 121.
[3] Fr. 117; 118.

the Logos was nothing but Logos and that all the other titles which scripture gives to the Logos are properly applicable to the Logos only when united to the flesh, by setting together John i. 1 a and i. 14:

For the Logos 'was in the beginning', being nothing but Logos. But the man who was united to the Logos, but did not exist beforehand, came into existence, as St John teaches us, saying, 'and the Logos became flesh'. For that reason, then, he seems to mention only the Logos; for when the divine scripture mentions the name 'Jesus' or 'Christ', it appears to mean by this the Logos of God existing with the human flesh.[1]

No other name but 'Logos' is fitting for the eternal being of the Logos; therefore,

mentioning the beginning from above and nothing more recent, (John) said, 'In the beginning was the Logos, and the Logos was with God, and the Logos was God' (John i. 1), so that he might show that if there is any new and more recent name, this began afresh from the new economy according to the flesh.[2]

(ii) Similarly by exegesis of John i. 1, 3, Marcellus sets forth his view of the Logos as δύναμις and ἐνέργεια δραστική:

In order that, in the statement 'In the beginning was the Logos', he might show that the Logos is in the Father δυνάμει—for God, 'from whom are all things' (I Cor. viii. 6, 12), is the beginning (ἀρχή) of all things that have been made; in the statement, 'and the Logos was with God', that the Logos was with God ἐνεργείᾳ— for 'all things were made through him and without him was not even one thing'; and in the statement that 'the Logos was God' that he might not divide the godhead, since the Logos is in him and he is in the Logos; for he says, 'The Father is in me and I am in the Father' (John x. 38).[3]

While Marcellus would refuse to refer statements about the pre-incarnate Logos (John i. 1–14a) to the Son of God, he has no hesitation in referring statements about the Son of God to the Logos. John i. 1–3 refers to him who was nothing but Logos; John x. 38, however, which refers to the Son of God, is referred by Marcellus to the Logos, confirmation of Gericke's conclusion that the Logos is the subject of the human life of Jesus.

[1] Fr. 42.   [2] Fr. 43.   [3] Fr. 52.

(iii) The application of the adjective μονογενής to the Son of God in John i. 18, iii. 16–18 creates difficulties for Marcellus. It has already been pointed out that he refuses to apply any reference to begetting or origin to the Logos and, as a result, he is forced to apply this adjective to the incarnate Son. Apart from his *Confessio Fidei* in his letter to Julius of Rome,[1] the only occurrence of the word in the fragments is in quotations which he has made from Asterius and his criticism of them.[2] In two fragments he quotes Asterius as saying, 'Certainly the Father, who has begotten from himself the only-begotten Logos and first-born of all creation is different. (ἄλλος μὲν γάρ ἐστιν ὁ πατήρ, ὁ γεννήσας ἐξ αὐτοῦ τὸν μονογενῆ λόγον καὶ πρωτό-τοκον πάσης κτίσεως).'[3] On Marcellus' principles both μονογενής and πρωτότοκος would have to refer to the incarnate, to the flesh which the Logos assumed. Like Athanasius,[4] Marcellus acknowledges that there is a contradiction between these terms: 'There is a great contradiction in these titles, as even the most stupid may easily see. For it is clear that the Only-begotten, if he is really Only-begotten, cannot be First-born as well, and the First-born, if he is really First-born, cannot also be Only-begotten'.[5] Unlike Athanasius, however, he does not seek to discover a way out of the difficulty by apply-ing μονογενής to the pre-existent (his principles will not allow that), and πρωτότοκος to the incarnate. Instead, he appears to reject the adjective μονογενής altogether, and to concentrate his attention on πρωτότοκος. In Fragments 4–9 he expounds the phrase πρωτότοκος πάσης κτίσεως as referring to the incarnate; in Fragment 6, for example, he says:

This most holy Logos, then, was not named 'first-born of all creation' before the incarnation—for how is it possible for that which always exists to be first-born of everything?—but the holy scriptures name him 'first-born of all creation' who is the first 'new man' (Eph. ii. 15) in whom God planned 'to sum up all things' (Eph. i. 10).

In Fragment 96 Marcellus gives a fuller quotation from Asterius, continuing the previous one:

Certainly the Father, who has begotten from himself the only-begotten Logos and First-born of all creation, is different, Sole

---

[1] Fr. 129.   [2] Fr. 3; 96.   [3] Fr. 3; 96.
[4] See above, pp. 213 f.   [5] Fr. 3.

(begetting) Sole, Perfect Perfect, King King, Lord Lord, God God, the unchangeable Image of (his) essence and will and glory and power.

Marcellus asks how the Lord can be begotten, and how God can be the Image of God,

for the Image of God is one thing and God is another; so that, if he is the Image, then he is neither Lord nor God, but Image of the Lord and God; if, on the other hand, he is really Lord and God, then it is possible no longer for the Lord and God to be the Image of the Lord and God.[1]

For Marcellus, the idea of the Logos' being μονογενής implies that he is begotten, while for Asterius there is no contradiction between μονογενής and πρωτότοκος; for the latter the Logos (Son) is only-*begotten* as the only creature created directly by God, but as such he can also be 'first-born of all creation'. Marcellus' rejection of the idea of the generation of the Logos involves the rejection of the title μονογενής. Like the exegesis of the Arians, that of Marcellus is highly selective, and Eusebius' criticism of Marcellus' view of the contradiction between μονογενής and πρωτότοκος is extremely apposite: 'Not in Asterius, but in the divine scriptures, do the sayings occur which, on one occasion, state that the Son is μονογενής, and, on another, that he is πρωτότοκος πάσης κτίσεως.'[2]

(iv) When expounding Prov. viii. 22 (LXX), 'He created me a beginning of his ways for his works', Marcellus, referring like Athanasius to the incarnate, asks, 'What kind of works does it mean?', and answers, 'Those concerning which the Saviour says, "My Father worketh hitherto and I work" (John v. 17), and "I perfected the work which thou hast given me to do" (John xvii. 4).'[3]

(v) Fragments 54–99 are concerned with the Arian doctrine that the Father and the Son are two distinct hypostases (δύο ὑποστάσεις)[4] or two essences (δύο οὐσίαι),[5] or that Father, Son and Holy Spirit are three hypostases (τρεῖς ὑποστάσεις)[6] or three essences (τρεῖς οὐσίαι).[7] Marcellus' main attack on this doctrine is directed at Asterius' exegesis of John x. 30, 'I

---

[1] Fr. 96.　　　　[2] *c. Marc.* I, 4 (*GCS*, IV, 20, 8 ff.).
[3] Fr. 15; cf. Simonetti, *Studi sull'Arianesimo*, pp. 38 ff.
[4] Fr. 63; 74.　　[5] Fr. 82; 83.　　[6] Fr. 66; 69.　　　　[7] Fr. 81.

and the Father are one'. He says that Asterius has fallen into error because, fixing his attention on

the human flesh which the Logos of God assumed and through which he thus manifests himself, he said that there are two hypostases, that of the Father and that of the Son; thus he separates the Son of God from the Father, as someone may separate the son of a man from his natural father.[1]

Because he concentrates on 'the second economy' (τῇ δευτέρᾳ οἰκονομίᾳ),[2] Asterius interprets John x. 30 to mean that there is complete agreement (συμφωνία) between the Son's will and that of the Father:

The Father and the Son are one and the same only in so far as they agree in all things; and on account of the complete agreement in words and actions, 'I and the Father are one'.[3]

Athanasius has preserved a longer fragment from Asterius on the exegesis of John x. 30:

Since what the Father wills, the Son wills also, and is not contrary in what he thinks or in what he judges, but is in all respects in agreement (σύμφωνος) with him, declaring doctrines which are the same, and a word consistent and united with the Father's teaching, therefore it is that he and the Father are one.[4]

From the beginning of his criticism of Asterius' exegesis of John x. 30 Marcellus falls into the error of interpreting the Arians' distinction between the Logos and the Son as if it were the same as his own. Because Asterius is speaking of the Son, Marcellus jumps to the conclusion that he is speaking of the incarnate, but what Asterius has to say about the agreement of the Father and the Son is intended to apply to the pre-existent as well as to the incarnate. Asterius has not concentrated on the 'flesh which the Logos assumed', and he does not have the 'second economy' particularly in mind; his starting point has not been the incarnation, but his view of the Logos–Son as a created intermediary between God and the world, as a being completely distinct from the Father. His presupposition that the Father and the Son are utterly distinct from each other

---

[1] Fr. 63.   [2] Fr. 73.
[3] Asterius, *apud Marcellus*, Fr. 72.
[4] *Or. c. Ar.* III, 10 (*PG*, XXVI, 341).

prevents him from interpreting John x. 30 in any other way than as implying agreement of wills. Athanasius' criticism of Asterius' exegesis[1] is more to the point than that of Marcellus, for Athanasius has understood the basis of the distinction which Asterius has made.

In criticising Asterius, Marcellus sets forth his own exegesis, supporting it with other sayings from St John's Gospel:

If then he says these things—'I came forth from the Father and have come' (John viii. 42), and again, 'And the Word which you hear is not mine but the Father's who sent me' (John xiv. 24), and 'All that the Father has is mine' (John xiv. 15)—it is clear that it is fitting for him to say, 'The Father is in me, and I am in the Father' (John x. 38), so that the Logos who says this may be in God and the Father in the Logos, because the Logos is the power (δύναμις) of the Father. For a trustworthy witness has said that he is 'the power of God and the wisdom of God' (I Cor. i. 24). Therefore it is not as Asterius said, 'because of the close agreement in all words and actions' that the Saviour says, 'I and the Father are one', but because it is impossible for the Logos to be separated from God or for God to be separated from his own Logos.[2]

He proceeds to deny Asterius' view that the Father and the Son agree in all words and actions, for this, he says, is contrary to the witness of the gospels; Asterius overlooks 'the evident disagreement'[3] between the will of the Father and that of the Son which is to be seen, for example, in the prayer of Jesus in Gethsemane (Matt. xxvi. 39), which Marcellus asserts is proof of an 'evident disagreement between him who is willing and him who is not willing'.[4] As further proof of the disagreement Marcellus quotes John v. 30, 'I seek not my own will but the will of him who sent me'.

Marcellus' anxiety to refute the Arian distinction between the Father and the Son as two hypostases or essences is the key to the involved argument and confused exegesis in Fragment 74. The 'one' in 'I and the Father are one' does not refer to agreement of wills but to identity of hypostasis or essence. If Asterius were right, Jesus would not have said, 'All that the Father has is mine' (John xvi. 15), but rather, 'All that the Father has is common'. Marcellus proceeds to discuss what this last saying

---

[1] See above, pp. 227 ff.   [2] Fr. 73.
[3] τὸ φαινόμενον ἀσυμφωνίαν , Fr. 73.   [4] *Idem.*

would have meant if Jesus had said it by referring to Acts iv. 32, 'All things were common to them', that is, to the early Christians in Jerusalem: 'If all things ought to be considered as common possessions with men who can agree with each other, how much more ought the Father and the Son to share in common, since they have been separated into two hypostases?' But, says Marcellus, the Father and the Son do not share all things in common, for Jesus says, 'All that the Father has is mine'; 'this was said by the Son who was undisguisedly enriching himself at the Father's expense'. The Son, however, also says that 'He is not the Lord of his own word, but that the Father is Lord of this, for he says, "The word which you hear is not mine but his who sent me" (John xiv. 24)'; thus 'he shows that the Father takes for himself the things which properly belong to the Son'.

Having shown, as he thinks, that there is not complete agreement between the Father and the Son, Marcellus appears to think that he has refuted the view that the Father and the Son are two hypostases. If Asterius' view rested on his exegesis of John x. 30, Marcellus' criticism would have some point against him; it is evident, however, that the reverse is the case: Asterius' interpretation of John x. 30 is an attempt to explain this text in the light of his presupposition that the Father and the Son are distinct and that the Son is *essentially* inferior and posterior to the Father.

Marcellus goes on to assert that while there is disagreement between the Father and the Son there is none between the Father and the Logos, for how can the Father and the Logos, who are identical (ἓν καὶ ταὐτόν) disagree? The disagreement must be referred 'to the weakness of the flesh which the Logos did not have formerly, but which he assumed'. When Jesus said, 'I and the Father are one'. he was not referring to 'the man which he assumed but to the Logos which proceeded from the Father'.

Continuing his commentary on John x. 30, Marcellus says that it is fitting that the Saviour said not only this but also, 'Am I with you so long, Philip, and you say, Show us the Father (John xiv. 9)?'. The rest of Fragment 74 depends on the words, 'He who has seen me has seen the Father', which it does not quote. Marcellus says:

Clearly he is not referring to these eyes of flesh but to the eyes of the mind which are able to see intelligible things (τὰ νοητά). For both the Father and the Logos are invisible to the eyes of the flesh. Therefore he did not say this to Philip on account of the agreement in all things.

It appears certain that, like Alexander[1] and Athanasius,[2] Marcellus connected John xiv. 9 with Col. i. 15, 'the image of the invisible God'; unlike the two Alexandrians, however, who interpreted the former in the light of the latter, Marcellus appears to have drawn a distinction between the two. For him John xiv. 9 does not refer to the Son, the incarnate Logos, but to the Logos who is invisible to the eyes of flesh just as the Father is. In Fragments 90–7 he argues that the Image must be visible and therefore Col. i. 15 cannot refer to the Logos; he insists that it refers to the flesh which the Logos assumed:[3]

It is quite clear, then, that before the assumption of our body, the Logos was not in himself the Image of the invisible God, for it is fitting that an image should be seen so that through the image that which has hitherto been unseen may be seen.[4]

If, since God is invisible, the Logos also happens to be invisible, how can the Logos in himself be the Image of the invisible God, and himself be invisible?[5]

When the Logos assumed the flesh which was made according to the image of God, he became the true Image of God. For if through this Image we were deemed worthy to know the Logos of God, we ought to trust the Logos himself who says through the Image, 'I and the Father are one' (John x. 30). For neither the Logos nor the Father can be seen apart from this Image.[6]

Throughout this exegesis of John x. 30, the conflict within the mind of Marcellus between the idea of the Logos as the impersonal Word and the idea of the Logos as personal is quite apparent. The Father and the Logos (Word) are one because they are identical and there is no personal distinction between them, yet it is the Logos who says, 'I and the Father are one', and 'He that hath seen me hath seen the Father'. If, as appears from so many of the Fragments, the Logos is the subject of the

---

[1] See above, pp. 153 ff. [2] See above, pp. 199 ff.

[3] Fr. 94. Marcellus is in striking opposition to the Alexandrian tradition in which it was argued that the Image of the invisible God must himself be invisible; cf. Crouzel, *Théologie de l'image de Dieu*, pp. 76 ff.

[4] Fr. 92. [5] Fr. 94. [6] Fr. 93.

human life of Jesus, then that life is not truly human, for the humanity is truncated just as it is in the christology of Arius, of Eusebius of Caesarea and of Apollinarius.

(vi) If the dispensation of the Son begins when the Logos assumes human flesh from the Virgin, it lasts on beyond the crucifixion until the day of judgment; Marcellus teaches that when on the last day the Son shall hand over the Kingdom to his Father, the Logos who has remained united to the flesh until then—for the Son equals Logos *plus* flesh—is re-absorbed into the Monad, so that God shall be all in all (I Cor. xv. 24–8). Because the flesh has survived beyond the death on the cross, says Marcellus, it has been made immortal through its fellowship with the Logos.[1] If, however, it is asked what happens to this immortalised flesh when the Logos is absorbed again into the Monad, Marcellus confesses that he does not know the answer: 'We do not think it safe to dogmatise about those things which we have not learned exactly from the scriptures.'[2] He is certain, however, that the flesh, even though immortalised, cannot be absorbed into the godhead along with the Logos, for scripture says that 'the flesh is of no avail' (John vi. 63). He asks: 'How is it possible that that which is from the earth and which is of no avail should be united with the Logos in the ages to come as being of avail to him?'[3]

Ultimately, then, for Marcellus, the Father–Son relationship is only a temporary manifestation of the being of God; it begins at the incarnation and ends on the last day. What distinguishes the Son from the Father is the flesh which the Logos assumes, and there is no real distinction between the Father and the eternal Logos, for they are identical. Despite the fact that the second dispensation of *Heilsgeschichte* is the dispensation of the Son of God, the conception of sonship means little or nothing to Marcellus. It is the Logos-concept which is regulative in his system and in his exegesis of St John's Gospel, a Logos-concept whose content is a confusion of the Hebraic Word of creation and revelation with the metaphysical Logos, the intermediary between the one God and the world.

Marcellus interprets the Prologue of St John in the light of the Hebraic Word-concept and the rest of the Gospel in the light of the metaphysical Logos-concept. It is the Logos who is

---

[1] Fr. 117.   [2] Fr. 121.   [3] Fr. 117.

the real subject of the whole of St John's Gospel, and as a result the role of the flesh in God's activity of self-revelation and redemption in Christ is treated as being merely incidental.

Marcellus' doctrine of the trinity is thus an economic doctrine, a transcription into the internal being of the godhead of the stages of the expansion of the godhead in *Heilsgeschichte*. It is not the simple or successive modalism of Sabellius, although Eusebius may perhaps be excused for confusing it with Sabellianism. It is rather 'expansionistic' modalism. The Monad does not change successively from one mode to another, but expands first into a Dyad and then into a Triad. It was inadequate as an answer to Arianism, for the trinity which it presents—Father, Son and Holy Spirit—is no more eternal than the Arian trinity—Father, Creature–Son, and Creature–Spirit. If the God of Sabellianism was, as St Basil says,[1] 'metamorphosed to meet the changing needs of the world', Marcellus' God was expanded to meet the changing needs of the world. H. E. W. Turner's remark applies equally to both: 'The motive of Modalism was better than its result. An unfolding purpose does not imply an unfolding essence. The eternal God may intervene in history; he cannot be said to have a history.'[2]

B. EUSEBIUS OF CAESAREA VERSUS MARCELLUS

Replying to the treatise of Marcellus, Eusebius of Caesarea thought that 'it would be sufficient for its refutation to set out side by side the sayings of Marcellus',[3] but later, fearing lest some might be caused to stumble by the voluminous work which Marcellus had written, he wrote a further three books, *de Ecclesiastica Theologia*, in which he pointed out the errors of Marcellus, and set beside them 'the incorruptible teaching of the Church of God which she has preserved, having received it from the beginning from those who saw with their own eyes and heard with their own ears the Logos from above'.[4]

---

[1] *Epistle*, ccx, 5.

[2] *The Pattern of Christian Truth*, p. 138. Cf. Gericke, *Marcell von Ancyra*, pp. 163 ff.: 'He has no concrete idea of history...he sublimates history... The subject of *Heilsgeschichte* is the Logos...*Heilsgeschichte* takes place not on earth but in the pre-existent and metaphysical sphere.'

[3] *de Ecc. Theol.* i, proem, i (*GCS*, iv, 62, 5 f.).

[4] *Ibid.* i, *proem*, 2 (*GCS*, iv, 62, 19 ff.).

In the first treatise, *contra Marcellum*, he is content to let Marcellus be his own accuser, and uses the scissors-and-paste method; 'to the end of his life Eusebius loved nothing better than to wield the scissors and make extracts'.[1] The quotations from Marcellus are interspersed with ridicule, sarcasm and vituperation;[2] after a particularly vituperative introduction he makes a brief general criticism of Marcellus' theology and then proceeds to attack it at the following specific points:

1. Marcellus is ignorant of the scriptures.[3]
2. Marcellus uses Greek proverbs as if they were holy scripture.[4]
3. He tries 'to contradict what has been written correctly and ecclesiastically'.[5] The 'ecclesiastical' writers whom Eusebius defends against the attacks of Marcellus are Narcissus of Neronias who, like himself, had come under the ban of the Synod of Antioch (A.D. 325), Asterius the Sophist, Eusebius of Nicomedia ('the Great'),[6] Paulinus of Tyre ('truly thrice-blessed'),[7] himself,[8] and Origen, to whom Marcellus traced the roots of Arianism.[9]

In the remaining part of the treatise he takes the main points of Marcellus' theology one by one and contradicts them rather than refutes them:

1. Marcellus' doctrine of the Logos denies 'alike the divinity and the humanty of the Son of God';[10] 'he dares to sin alike against the beginning and the end of the Son of God'.[11]
2. His view that the Logos was nothing but Logos before the incarnation is 'a bare-faced denial of the Son of God'.[12]
3. By ascribing all scriptural titles other than Logos, together with all references to the γένεσις or γεννηθῆναι of the Son or

---

[1] A. Puech, *Histoire de la littérature grecque chrétienne*, III, 203.

[2] He describes Marcellus as 'the noble fellow' (*c. Marc.* I, 2, 30), 'this amazing author' (*ibid.* I, 4, 3); he says that Marcellus 'talks a tremendous amount of utter nonsense' (*ibid.* I, 4, 47), and that 'he is absolutely pleased with no one but himself alone' (*ibid.* I, 4, 3).

[3] *c. Marc.* I, 2 (*GCS*, IV, 9 ff.).   [4] *Ibid.* I, 3 (*GCS*, IV, 14 ff.).

[5] *Ibid.* I, 4, 1 (*GCS*, IV, 17, 30 f.).

[6] *Ibid.* I, 4, 1 (*GCS*, IV, 17, 33), *et alia.*

[7] *Ibid.* I, 4, 2 (*GCS*, IV, 18, 2).   [8] *Ibid.* I, 4, 3 (*GCS*, IV, 18, 10).

[9] *Ibid.* I, 4, 3 (*GCS*, IV, 18, 8 f.).

[10] *Ibid.* II, 1, 8 (*GCS*, IV, 33, 9 ff.).

[11] *Ibid.* II, 1, 12 (*GCS*, IV, 34, 4).   [12] *Ibid.* II, 2, 41 (*GCS*, IV, 43, 7 f.).

Logos, to the flesh which the Logos assumed, Marcellus shows that he has not understood the meaning of scripture; 'having turned aside from the straight way, he contrived for himself a road which is no road at all'.[1]

4. Eusebius attacks Marcellus' view of the end of the Kingdom of Christ and of the flesh of the Son of God by persisting in asking the question to which Marcellus admits that he has no answer: 'What will happen to the flesh of the Son when the Logos is re-absorbed into the Monad?'[2]

The argument of the *contra Marcellum* is negative; Eusebius' method of attack is that of blunt denial of Marcellus' fundamental doctrines. There is little positive exposition of Eusebius' own theology and almost no exegesis of scripture. These defects are remedied in the *de Ecclesiastica Theologia*. One important positive result emerges from the negative argument of the first treatise, however: Eusebius sees clearly that the focal point of Marcellus' theology is his Logos-concept, which differs from his own philosophical concept which he has inherited from Origen. Eusebius continually refers to Marcellus' concept as a 'mere word' (ψιλὸς λόγος),[3] a 'significant' (σημαντικός),[4] or an 'imperative' (προστακτικός)[5] word. It is around the question of the content of the Logos-concept that Eusebius' argument in the second treatise revolves, and his criticism of Marcellus' doctrine consists for the most part of exegesis of St John's Gospel.

1. *The Pre-existence of the Son*

Eusebius attacks first of all Marcellus' view that 'before he was born of the Virgin, the Son of God was not called by any other name than "Logos" '.[6] Eusebius demonstrates the falseness of this view at great length by exegesis of scripture, and his starting-point is the Prologue of St John where alone in scripture the Son is called 'Logos'. At the very beginning of his gospel St John calls the Logos 'God' (John i. 1c), 'thus

[1] *Ibid.* II, 3, 10 (*GCS*, IV, 46, 10 f.).   [2] *Idem*; cf. Fr. 121.
[3] *c. Marc. GCS*, IV, 6, 28; 29, 32; 30, 33; *de Ecc. Theol. GCS*, IV, 60, 33; 65, 16; 88, 4. 20.
[4] *c. Marc. GCS*, IV, 32, 3; *de Ecc. Theol. GCS*, IV, 77, 17. 22; 78,2.17; 82, 24; 85, 12; 87,3.15; 88, 23; 97, 1; 106, 27; 112, 17; 135, 20.
[5] *c. Marc.* 36,10.24; *de Ecc. Theol.* 106, 27.
[6] *de Ecc. Theol.* I, 19, 2 (*GCS*, IV, 80, 21 f.).

showing the marvellous nature of his God-befitting dignity'.[1] Moreover, in John i. 8–11 St John calls him 'Light' and asserts the identity of the Light and the Logos, for 'all things were made through' the Logos (John i. 3), and 'the word was made through' the Light (John i. 10b). Therefore, says Eusebius, St John proclaims at the beginning of his gospel three names of the Son of God—'Logos', 'God' and 'Light'.[2]

When St John said, 'And the Logos became flesh and dwelt among us, and we beheld his glory, glory as of the only-begotten of the Father, full of grace and truth' (John i. 14), he was also calling the Logos 'only-begotten' before the incarnation.[3] This is proved by John i. 15, 16: 'John bare witness to him and cried, This was he of whom I said, He who comes after me ranks before me, for he was before me, because of his fullness have we all received and grace upon grace'. Eusebius asserts that 'the new Sabellius' could not have heard St John say this, for the Saviour was born after John the Baptist. It was as only-begotten Son that he was before John. Eusebius asks whether Marcellus claims that these words refer to the Father and God of the universe or to the non-substantial and non-subsisting (ἀνούσιον καὶ ἀνυπόστατον) Logos who is in God. He concludes that he who was before John the Baptist was not only Logos, but also God and Light and Only-begotten before the incarnation.[4]

It was in order to guard against such errors as that of Marcellus that St John, having acknowledged the Logos to be the Son of God, no longer calls him 'Logos' , but 'Son', 'Only-begotten', 'Life', 'Light', etc. In John x. 34–6 Jesus asserts that he is the Son of God and criticises those who accuse him of blasphemy; if men who are mortal by nature were called not only 'sons of God' but 'gods' by the Psalmist (lxxxii. 6), it is not blasphemy to acknowledge as Son of God and God 'him whom the Father consecrated and sent into the world' (John x. 36). Therefore Marcellus is wrong when he says 'He was Logos and nothing else'.[5]

Similarly, too, when Jesus says that he is the 'Light of the

---

[1] *Ibid.* I, 20, 1 (*GCS*, IV, 81, 2 f.).   [2] *Ibid.* I, 20, 2 (*GCS*, IV, 82, 6 ff.).
[3] *Ibid.* I, 20, 10 (*GCS*, IV, 82, 14 f.).
[4] *Ibid.* I, 20, 13 (*GCS*, IV, 82, 32 ff.).
[5] *Ibid.* I, 20, 22 (*GCS*, 84, 12 ff.).

World' (John viii. 12; iii. 19; xiv. 6),[1] he bears witness that he has come 'from above' (John iii. 31) and 'from heaven' (John iii. 32). It could not have been the flesh which said this, for the flesh did not come from above; it was the Logos, the Son of God, the Only-begotten.

Eusebius returns to John iii: 'The Father loves the Son and has given all things into his hand' (John iii. 35). What are the 'all things'? he asks, and he replies, 'the existence of all originate things (τῆς τῶν γενητῶν ἁπάντων ὑπάρξεως)',[2] both in heaven and on earth. The fact that the Son grasps all these things *in one hand* (!) shows 'the excellence of his tremendous power'.[3] God gave all things to the Son 'for their improvement and benefit',[4] 'for he made the delivery to the Preserver, Healer and Governor of the universe (σωτῆρι καὶ ἰατρῷ καὶ κυβερνήτῃ τῶν ὅλων)'.[5]

The next title which the Son of God applies to himself in the gospel is 'Bread of Life' (John vi. 48), 'the living bread which came down from heaven' (John vi. 51). Jesus makes it clear 'in what way he existed as living' (ὅπως ὑπῆρχε ζῶν) in the words, 'As the living Father hath sent me, and I live through the Father, so he who eats me will live through me' (John vi. 37), and also, 'For as the Father has life in himself, so has he granted the Son also to have life in himself' (John v. 26). From these texts Eusebius draws the conclusion: 'So then he was also "Bread of Life" and existed in heaven, feeding and nourishing the heavenly powers by the power of his divinity, and he was such before he came to earth, and he was the Son who has life "in himself" like the Father who has life "in himself"'.[6]

Thus, from St John's Gospel, Eusebius has demonstrated that before the incarnation the Logos was also 'God', 'Light', 'Son', 'Only-begotten', and 'Bread of Life'. Marcellus was mistaken when he said that he was Logos and nothing else. If Marcellus should say that these things are said in the New Testament, so

---

[1] Eusebius quotes John xiv. 6 as 'I am the *light*, the truth and the life', thus laying himself open to the accusation which he frequently levels at Marcellus, ignorance of scripture.

[2] *Ibid.* 1, 20, 26 (*GCS*, IV, 85, 17).

[3] *Ibid.* 1, 20, 27 (*GCS*, IV, 85, 25 ff.).

[4] *Ibid.* 1, 20, 30 (*GCS*, IV, 86, 5).   [5] *Idem* (*GCS*, IV, 85, 6 f.).

[6] *Ibid.* 1, 20, 32 (*GCS*, IV, 86, 17 ff.).

also were the words, 'In the beginning was the Logos' (John
i. 1*a*). Eusebius proceeds to show that St Paul asserts that
before the incarnation he was 'Son of God' (I Cor. viii. 6),
'Rock' (I Cor. x. 4), 'in the form of God' (Phil. ii. 6), 'Mediator
of the Law' (Gal. iii. 19, 20), 'Great High Priest' (Heb. iv. 14),
and so on. Similarly in the Old Testament he was called
'Fountain of Life', 'Truth', 'River', 'Righteousness' and a
host of other names.[1] Eusebius proves his point against Marcellus and, at the same time, makes the primacy of the cosmological interest in his theology quite plain.

2. *The Independent Hypostasis of the Son*

Closely connected with the foregoing argument is Eusebius'
criticism of Marcellus' denial of the pre-existent hypostasis of
the Logos and of his assertion that the Logos is identical with
God.

When he is discussing John i. 10*b*, 'the world was made
through him',[2] Eusebius allows himself to be diverted from his
main argument on the pre-existence of the Son by the words
that follow, 'and the world knew him not' (John i. 10*c*). His
comment on them makes his philosophical presuppositions
clear: 'All men instinctively acknowledge the God who is over
all.'[3] 'Therefore this God and Logos whom the world did not
know is a different being; he exists as Light and has been
called "Light".'[4]

The knowledge of the pre-existence of the Logos as 'Only-
begotten Son', which Eusebius finds implied in John i. 15, 16,
was given to the evangelist by none other than 'the only-
begotten Son who is in the bosom of the Father' who 'has
declared it' (John i. 18). It was not the invisible God who
declared it, but the visible Only-begotten Son 'who is clearly
another beside the invisible God' (ἕτερος ὢν δηλαδὴ παρὰ τὸν
ἀόρατον θεόν).[5] He did not pre-exist in the mind of the Father,
as Marcellus holds, but in his bosom. Now Jesus teaches that

---

[1] Cf. the summary in *ibid*. 1, 20, 90–2 (*GCS*, IV, 96, 25 ff.); cf. Origen,
in Joh. 1, 24.
[2] See above, p. 269.   [3] *de Ecc. Theol*. 1, 20, 6 (*GCS*, IV, 81, 22 f.).
[4] *Ibid*. 1, 20, 7 (*GCS*, IV, 81, 25 f.).
[5] *Ibid*. 1, 20, 17 (*GCS*, IV, 83, 26 f.).

we shall rest awhile in the bosom of Abraham, Isaac and Jacob (Matt. viii. 11 = Luke xiii. 28), but this does not mean that we shall become identical with them. Therefore, says Eusebius, the words 'the only-begotten Son who is in the bosom of the Father', do not mean that the Son (Logos) is identical with the Father.[1]

In John iii. 16–18 Jesus teaches that God 'gave' and 'sent' his Son (cf. also I John iv. 14). Eusebius says: 'He who has been sent is quite clearly another beside him who sends' (ὁ δὲ ἀπεστέλλετο ἕτερος ὢν δηλαδὴ παρὰ τὸν ἀποστέλλοντα).[2] In John iii. 31, 32 Jesus claims to have come 'from above' and 'from heaven'; it could not have been the flesh that said this for the flesh did not come from above; it was the Logos, the Son, and 'He bears witness to what he has seen and heard' (John iii. 32). The Son, then, saw and heard in heaven, and what he saw and heard was the Father. Therefore, says Eusebius, Jesus himself 'teaches that he is not a significant Logos, but the truly living and subsisting Son (οὐ λόγον σημαντικόν, ἀλλ' υἱὸν ἀληθῶς ζῶντα καὶ ὑφεστῶτα)'.[3]

When commenting on John iii. 35, 'The Father loves the Son and has given all things into his hand',[4] Eusebius says that the Son 'received the gift and cared for it like a trusty guardian, not as a non-substantial and non-subsisting Logos, but truly as Only-begotten Son and beloved of the Father'.[5]

Turning next to John v. 26, 'For as the Father has life in himself, so has he granted the Son also to have life in himself', Eusebius says:

The one gave and the other received, and the Son alone received this gift of life, not from outside like the rest of living beings, but he has it springing up in himself. Therefore the Son is the source of life to all other beings.

The Father has given this to the Son

for the benefit of those who are going to be made alive through him.[6]

The Son also teaches that he is 'the Bread which came down from heaven' (John vi. 58); Eusebius comments:

---

[1] *Idem* (*GCS*, IV, 83, 28 ff.).
[2] *Ibid.* I, 20, 19 (*GCS*, IV, 84, 11 ff.).
[3] *Ibid.* I, 20, 24 f. (*GCS*, IV, 85, 12 ff.).   [4] See above, p. 270.
[5] *de Ecc. Theol.* I, 20, 30 (*GCS*, IV, 86, 6 f.).
[6] *Ibid.* I, 20, 34 (*GCS*, IV, 86, 26 ff.).

Before he was sent by the Father, he was in heaven and lived through the Father, not as a significant Logos, nor as identical with God, but as subsisting and having his own life which the Father had given him.[1]

When the Son says, 'As the Father has taught me I speak these things. And he who sent me is with me; he has not left me alone, because I always do what is pleasing to him' (John viii. 28 f.), the Son is declaring 'the superiority of the Father's glory'.[2] Eusebius says that 'always' means not only now in the flesh but also before the incarnation. Jesus acknowledges the Father as his teacher, and therefore as another beside himself. Thus Marcellus is refuted by the Son's own words, for how, if the Father has the Logos in himself as Reason, could he be his own teacher? How if he is identical with God does he say that he does what is pleasing to God? If Marcellus would answer that it was the flesh that said these things, how was he in the flesh? If he was subsisting outside the Father, what was the Father, then, during the incarnation who did not possess his own Logos (Reason) in himself, but existed without it?

The Logos, however, if he was outside the Father when he was occupied with affairs on earth, was dwelling in the flesh, living and subsisting and moving the flesh after the manner of a soul;[3] it is clear, then, that he was another beside the Father (ἕτερος παρὰ τὸν πατέρα), and that he and the Father were two hypostases (δύο ὑποστάσεις).[4]

Furthermore it is nonsense to say that it was the flesh that said, 'As the Father taught me, I speak these things' (John viii. 28); God is not Father of the flesh but 'rather of him who inhabits it and acts in it...the living and subsisting only-begotten Son of God'.[5]

All these sayings of the Son of God which are recorded by St John, says Eusebius, are explicitly sayings of the subsisting and living Son who, through the whole gospel, prays to the Father, glorifies the Father, is worthy to be glorified with the Father, and so on. Thus he shows himself to be a hypostasis

[1] *Ibid.* I, 20, 36 (*GCS*, IV, 87, 2 ff.).
[2] *Ibid.* I, 20, 37 (*GCS*, IV, 87, 5 f.).   [3] See below, pp. 293 f.
[4] *de Ecc. Theol.* I, 20, 40 (*GCS*, IV, 87, 24 f.).
[5] *Ibid.* I, 20, 44 (*GCS*, IV, 88, 16 ff.).

distinct and separate from the Father. This is especially true
when he says, 'The witness of two men is true. I bear witness
of myself and the Father who sent me bears witness to me'
(John viii. 17 f.). Jesus never calls himself 'Logos', but 'Son',
'Only-begotten', etc.; he teaches, however, that he has the
Logos when he says, 'If anyone loves me, he will keep my
Logos' (John xiv. 23).[1]

At the beginning of his discussion of the nature of the Logos,
commenting on John i. 3 a, 'All things were made through
him', Eusebius points out that St John does not say 'by (ὑπό)
him' or 'out of (ἐξ) him', but 'through (διά) him'. He says
that 'the preposition "through" (διά) signifies someone who
performs a service'.[2] In order to discover what διά means here
Eusebius turns to John i. 17: 'The law was given through (διά)
Moses, but grace and truth came through (διά) Jesus Christ.'
The law was not a human invention; it came from God:
'Therefore St John describes Moses as the servant and assistant
in the act of giving the law to men. So also "grace came through
Jesus Christ" since the Father was bringing it to pass *through*
him.'[3] It is in this way that we must understand the διά in
John i. 3: 'another made, but the Logos assisted (ἑτέρου μὲν
πεποιηκότος, αὐτοῦ δὲ διακονησαμένου)'.[4] Therefore, we must
look for some other being who is the creator of the universe
whom this verse asserts to be established over all. Marcellus
cannot say who this being is; indeed, he would deny that there
is such a being. Eusebius says that this being is 'the only-
begotten Son of God...truly Son, living and subsisting, who is
in the beginning, who is with God and who is God (John i. 1),
through whom God creates all things (John i. 3)'.[5]

Thus Eusebius, mainly on the basis of sayings of Jesus
recorded by St John, proves that the pre-existent Son (Logos)
is a hypostasis distinct and separate from the Father, in opposition to Marcellus' view that the Logos is identical with the
Father. Marcellus emphasises the unity of the Logos with the
Father, while Eusebius emphasises the distinction between

---

[1] *Ibid.* 1, 20, 45 ff. (*GCS*, IV, 88, 22 ff.).
[2] *Ibid.* II, 14, 9 (*GCS*, IV, 116, 2).
[3] *Idem* (*GCS*, IV, 116, 6).
[4] *Ibid.* II, 14, 10 (*GCS*, IV, 116, 10).
[5] *Ibid.* II, 14, 11 (*GCS*, IV, 116, 14 ff.).

them. The conflict between Eusebius and Marcellus is, then, a conflict between the two sides of the Johannine paradox of the Father–Son relationship.

3. *The Monarchy of the Father and the Inferiority of the Son*

Having distinguished and separated the Logos–Son from the Father, Eusebius continually emphasises the monarchy of the Father and the inferiority of the Son. When discussing John i. 10*b*, 'the world was made through him' (i.e. through 'the Light'),[1] Eusebius asks what it means to say that the Logos is 'Light'; he answers that he is not a sensible light like the sun in which the 'irrational animals' (ἄλογα ζῷα) partake, for St John says, 'He was the true light which lightens every man coming into the world' (John i. 9): 'He alone was the rational light (τὸ λογικὸν φῶς) of men. Therefore, by intellectual and rational power (δυνάμει νοερᾷ καὶ λογικῇ) he makes the souls which have been made according to his image and likeness intellectual and rational.'[2] This Logos who was in the world as the rational light of men is inferior to the God 'who is beyond the universe', for the latter is Light (I John i. 5) and 'dwells in unapproachable light, whom no man has seen or can see' (I Tim. vi. 16).[3]

When discussing John i. 14, 'The Logos became flesh and dwelt among us, and we beheld his glory, glory as of the only-begotten of the Father',[4] Eusebius asserts:

If it was for our sakes that he says, 'The Logos became flesh', but we, whom he considered worthy to receive the revelation of his own divinity, looking not at the flesh—for it was 'the form of a servant' (Phil. ii. 7)—but at his glory, which is seen beyond the body by the pure mind,[5] 'beheld his glory', the glory which is ineffable and beyond all reckoning of mortals, it may be asked of what kind the glory of the only-begotten Son may be thought to be. It was glory 'of (or from) the Father'.[6]

---

[1] See above, pp. 270 f. 　　[2] *Ibid.* I, 20, 7 f. (*GCS*, IV, 81, 30 ff.).
[3] *Ibid.* I, 20, 8 f. (*GCS*, IV, 81, 34 ff.).
[4] See below, pp. 291 ff.
[5] Eusebius has Matt. v. 8 in mind; cf. *de Ecc. Theol.* III, 21 (*GCS*, IV, 181, 13 ff.). See below, p. 296, n. 4.
[6] *Ibid.* I, 20, 10 (*GCS*, IV, 82, 14 ff.).

St John does not say 'glory as of the Logos', but he had to call him 'only-begotten'

in order that he might teach us what kind of a Logos he was setting forth. It was not a significant Logos, for how and in what fashion could such a Logos become flesh? He teaches that his glory is that by which he is perceived to be only-begotten Son.[1]

Eusebius connects the word 'glory' with 'from the Father' instead of with 'as of an only-begotten Son'. He says that St John is asserting that the glory originates from the Father and that the Son did not have it 'without origin, without beginning or as a private possession (οὐ ἀγένητον οὐδὲ ἄναρχον οὐδὲ ἰδιόκτητον)' but received it from the Father.[2] He argues that the Son himself demonstrated this when he prayed, 'O Father, glorify me with the glory which I had with thee before the world was' (John xvii. 5) and the Father answered this request by saying, 'I glorified and I shall glorify' (John xii. 28). Here Eusebius has confused the prayer of John xvii. 1 ff. with that of John xii. 27 ff.: 'Father, glorify thy name'. The confusion is an easy one to make for there was a strong tendency to equate the Son with 'the Name of God' which is the central concept in the High-Priestly Prayer of John xvii.[3] The concept of 'the Name of God', however, appears nowhere else in Eusebius' anti-Marcellan writings, so there is no need for speculation on the possibility that he has this concept in mind; he has simply confused the two prayers of Jesus, thus laying himself open once again to the same accusation which he loves to hurl at Marcellus—ignorance of the scriptures.

[1] *Ibid.* I, 20, 11 f. (*GCS*, IV, 82, 23 f.).
[2] *Ibid.* I, 20, 12 (*GCS*, IV, 82, 28 ff.).
[3] G. Quispel, in a paper delivered at the 2nd International Conference on Patristic Studies (Sept. 1955) on 'The Johannine Logos and the Gospel of Truth', pointed out that, for the Valentinian gnostics, *Logos* and *Onoma* are designations of Jesus Christ the Saviour; that the *Gospel of Truth* has a long passage on Jesus as the *Name of God* which leaves no doubt that the background is judaistic; that Philo sometimes makes the identification of *Logos* and *Onoma*; and that esoteric Judaism (e.g. III Enoch) speculates about the *Name of God*. Of John xvii Quispel said, 'The *Name* of God and the *Logos* of God are correlated and convey practically the same meaning'. The identification was probably in Eusebius' mind, for he was by no means ignorant of the speculations of Valentinus and Philo, and he was possibly familiar with those of esoteric Judaism.

Discussing John v. 26, 'As the Father has life in himself, so has he given the Son also to have life in himself', Eusebius says:

Only the Son may have a share in the peculiar nature of the divine life of the unoriginate Father; for this reason the divine apostle said, 'He only has immortality' (I Tim. vi. 16), in so far as he is the image of the Father. He has this life which St John mentions, not without beginning or without origin or as a private possession, in the way in which the Father has it, but he received it from the Father.[1]

When Eusebius faces the criticism that the assertion that there are two hypostases means that there are two gods, he tries to show that his assertion of the *monarchy* of the Father has safeguarded him against such criticism. He says that while the church acknowledges two hypostases it does not acknowledge two Fathers or two Sons; it does not define Father and Son as equal in honour or as both without beginning or unoriginate. The Son himself teaches this when he says, 'I ascend to my Father and your Father, and my God and your God' (John xx. 17), thus showing that the God and Father is also God of his Son.[2]

The Son confesses that he lives 'through the Father' (John vi. 57), that he does not do his own will, but that of him who sent him (John vi. 38), that he can do nothing by himself (John v. 30). He acknowledges that he who sent him is another beside himself (John v. 37), and that his Father is greater than he is (John xiv. 28). He proves 'the superiority of the Father's glory'[3] by saying that the Father has sent him, but that he himself has been sent to do not his own will but that of him who sent him (John vi. 38). These sayings make sense, says Eusebius, only if they are said by the Son of God; through them

the Son of God proves his own reverence for the Father; and since he is author of all begotten things which have been made through him, being the Preserver and Lord and Creator of all—for 'all things were made through him and without him was made not even one thing' (John i. 3)—then he may also be called 'God', and 'Lord' (δεσπότης), and 'Preserver' and 'King'. Therefore his church has been taught to worship and honour him as God, having learned to do this from him.[4]

---

[1] *de Ecc. Theol.* I, 20, 31 ff. (*GCS*, IV, 86, 10 ff.).
[2] *Ibid.* II, 7, 1 ff. (*GCS*, IV, 104, 3 ff.).
[3] *Ibid.* II, 7, 8 (*GCS*, IV, 105, 7).
[4] *Ibid.* II, 7, 11 ff. (*GCS*, IV, 105, 28 ff.).

When Jesus said, 'For the Father judges no one, but has given all judgment to the Son so that all may honour the Son just as they honour the Father' (John v. 22 f.), he was 'explicitly exhorting us to honour him...almost as the Father himself (αὐτῷ τῷ πατρὶ παραπλησίως)'.[1] Thomas understood this, says Eusebius, when he said, 'My Lord and my God (John xx. 28)'. Therefore it is fitting that we should worship with divine honour the Son alone and no other, just as we honour the Father, for 'He who honours the Son honours the Father who sent him (John v. 23)'.[2]

H. Berkhof points out that the 'most frequent, and at the same time most characteristic term for Eusebius' understanding of God, is the name "Emperor" (βασιλεύς) or "Emperor of all" (παμβασιλεύς)'.[3] He is so obsessed with the thought of the power and magnificence of the first Christian Emperor and with the benefits which he has brought to mankind and to the church that his respect often approaches religious worship.[4] This obsession with the thought of the Emperor is reflected in his continual use of the analogy of the Emperor and his image to describe the relation of God and the Logos. He says:

Just as when we pay homage to the image sent out by the Emperor, we pay homage to the Emperor who is himself the prototype of the image, so also, in the same way, the Father would be honoured through the Son, as also being seen through him, for 'he who has seen' the Son 'has seen the Father' (John xiv. 9), seeing the unbegotten godhead which is expressed, as it were, in an image and mirror.[5]

He quotes Wisdom vii. 36: 'For he is the reflection of eternal light and the spotless mirror of the activity of God and the image of his goodness'. Since the Son has received all these things from the Father, he has also received from him the glory of the godhead as a genuine only-begotten Son. 'The Father, however, has not received them from any one, but since he is the beginning and fountain and root of all good things, he is

[1] *Ibid.* II, 7, 14 (*GCS*, IV, 106, 2 ff.).
[2] *Ibid.* II, 7, 16 (*GCS*, IV, 106, 12 ff.).
[3] *Op. cit.* p. 66.
[4] Cf. *Laus Constantini*, and G. H. Williams, 'Christology and Church-State Relations in the Fourth Century', *CH*, xx (1951), 15 ff.
[5] *de Ecc. Theol.* II, 7, 16 (*GCS*, IV, 106, 13 ff.).

fittingly declared to be the one and only God (εἶς καὶ μόνος θεός).'[1]

Eusebius returns to this same argument later in Book II, Chapter 23, whose central theme is the *Image of God*. He reiterates that the church does not preach 'two Gods', but 'one Beginning (ἀρχή) and God, and teaches the same to be the Father of the only-begotten and beloved Son',[2] who, he says, do not 'contend with each other for equal honour'.[3] The Son himself acknowledges the Father to be 'the only true God' (John xvii. 3), but we need have no hesitation in acknowledging the Son to be 'true God', for he possesses this also in an image 'so that the addition of the word "only" is fitting to the Father alone as the archetype of the Image'.[4] Again Eusebius introduces his favourite analogy:

Just as since the Emperor rules and one image of him is displayed everywhere on earth, no sane person would say that there are two rulers, but one who is honoured through the image, so also...the church of God, having received (the command) to worship one God, continues to worship him also through the Son as through an image.[5]

Both by this analogy and by exegesis of selected texts from St John's Gospel, Eusebius establishes the distinction between the Father and the Son. He over-emphasises the distinction at the expense of their unity to which St John bears eloquent testimony also and, as a result, the criticism against which he seeks to safeguard himself by emphasising the monarchy of the Father is still valid; the Father and the Son are so distinguished from each other that they are in fact 'two Gods'.

[1] *Ibid.* II, 7, 17 (*GCS*, IV, 106, 22 ff.).
[2] *Ibid.* II, 23, 1 (*GCS*, IV, 133, 11).
[3] *Idem* (*GCS*, IV, 133, 13).
[4] *Ibid.* II, 23, 2 (*GCS*, IV, 133, 29).
[5] *Ibid.* II, 23, 3 (*GCS*, IV, 133, 34 ff.). Eusebius does not see the weaknesses of his analogy, which could be used with equal force and validity to deny the divinity of the Son, thus: Just as since the Emperor rules and one image of him is displayed everywhere, no sane person would say that the image is an emperor, in the same way, the church of God, having received the command to believe in one God, continues to believe him alone and does not call his image, the Son, *God!*

4. The Ineffability of the Son's Generation

Eusebius asserts that John iii. 35, 'The Father...has given all things into his hand', which he parallels with Matt. xi. 27, declares the ineffability both of the Son's generation from the Father and of his substance.[1] Elsewhere in the *de Ecclesiastica Theologia* he says:

The church preaches the one God, teaching him to be both Father and Almighty, Father of only one being, Christ, but God and Creator and Lord of all the rest. Thus it teaches also the only-begotten Son of God, Jesus Christ, begotten from the Father before all ages, who is not the same as the Father, but is and subsists and co-exists (with him) truly as Son, God from God, Light from Light, Life from Life; who, in unspeakable and inexpressible and, for us, unknown and inconceivable fashion, is begotten from the Father for the salvation (preservation?—σωτηρίαν)[2] of the universe; who does not exist like the rest of begotten things, nor has a life similar to that of those who are begotten through him, but who alone was brought forth from the Father himself and exists as Life in himself.[3]

Thus Eusebius, having distinguished the Son from the Father, is anxious also to distinguish the Son, as only-begotten, from the creatures who were created through him. The manner of his begetting is beyond every human analogy, and defies definition. By his strong emphasis on the ineffability of the Son's generation from the Father, Eusebius is attacking Marcellus' view of the generation of the Logos as the utterance of a word. Berkhof points out[4] that before Nicaea Eusebius had no hesitation in using language which implied that the Father had created the Logos–Son,[5] but after the Council had laid it down that the Son was 'begotten, not made' he avoided such language. In *de Ecclesiastica Theologia* he explicitly criticises the Arian view that the Son was created or generated 'out of nothing': 'They dare to make him appear to be a creature (κτίσμα) made out of nothing like the rest of the creatures; this would make him a brother of the latter and not Son of God.'[6]

---

[1] *Ibid.* i, 20, 29 (*GCS*, iv, 85, 32 ff.).
[2] See above, pp. 129 f.
[3] *de Ecc. Theol.* i, 8, 2 (*GCS*, iv, 66, 14 ff.).
[4] *Eusebius von Caesarea*, p. 71.
[5] *Letter to Alexander of Alexandria* (Opitz, *Urk.* 8).
[6] *de Ecc. Theol.* i, 19, 11 (*GCS*, iv, 67, 4 ff.).

By emphasising the ineffability of the Son's generation and his distinction from the creatures, Eusebius strives to keep the Son on the divine side of the God–World dualism and thus to avoid the extreme position which Arianism had taken up; however, although he keeps the Son on the divine side of the dualism, his view of the godhead is hierarchical, and the Son is an intermediate being between God and created beings. In Eusebius' thought Christian monotheism is endangered by left-wing Origenism 'with its cascade of decreasingly divine potencies from the Supreme, impassible, transcendent One, through the Logos–Son and Holy Spirit, the chief of spirits, to angels and men.[1]

5. *The Nature of the Logos*

(a) *Eusebius' doctrine of the Logos.* Eusebius is aware that the central point of difference between himself and Marcellus lies in their conceptions of the nature of the Logos; both of them use the term ὁ λόγος, but they fill it with vastly different content. Eusebius begins his discussion of the Logos by setting forth five possible meanings of the term:[2]

(a) Reason, that is, the foundation in the rational soul (ἐν τῇ λογικῇ ψυχῇ) which makes human thought possible.

(b) A word which, when spoken, signifies something (σημαίνων τι).

(c) A treatise composed by a writer.

(d) A seminal *logos* (σπερματικὸς λόγος); what is stored up potentially (δυνάμει) in seeds and is going to come to light, but does not yet exist in actuality (ἐνεργείᾳ).

(e) The capacity for knowledge of some art or science.

The evangelist, however, said, 'In the beginning was the Logos, and the Logos was with God, and the Logos was God' (John i. 1) *absolutely*, (ἀπολύτως), i.e. without any qualification,[3] and in doing so introduces 'some strange usage' of the term,[4] different from the five usual meanings; thus he emphasises 'the strange and marvellous nature of the power that is peculiar to him'.[5] All the other usages of the term are seen to involve some

---

[1] G. H. Williams, 'Christology and Church-State Relations', p. 16.
[2] *de Ecc. Theol.* II, 13 (*GCS*, IV, 114, 10 ff.).
[3] *Ibid.* II, 14, 1 (*GCS*, 114, 23 ff.). [4] *Idem* (*GCS*, IV, 114, 25).
[5] *Idem* (*GCS*, IV, 114, 27).

pre-existing substance as a substratum (ἐν ἑτέρα προϋποκειμένη οὐσίᾳ).¹

'God the Logos did not need another pre-existing substance in order that he might come into existence and subsist in himself, but he is himself living and subsisting inasmuch as he is God, for "the Logos was God" (John i. 1c).'² Nevertheless, we must not suppose that he is without beginning or unoriginate like his Father; this God, the Logos, 'was in the beginning'.³

Eusebius asks what this beginning (ἀρχή) is in which the Logos was, but leaves the question unanswered except by the implication that it is the 'God who is over all'. He goes on immediately to make use of Origen's distinction between ὁ θεός and θεός.⁴ He says that St John did not say that the Logos was ὁ θεός 'with the addition of the article' for he had no intention of defining the Logos as 'the One over all' (τὸν ἐπὶ πάντων).⁵ Neither did St John say that the Logos is 'in God', for he wished to avoid all anthropomorphic language.⁶ Therefore he said, 'the Logos was *with* God'. To say that the Logos was 'in God' would mean that God is composite (σύνθετον),⁷ that he is an οὐσία apart from the Logos, and has the Logos as a property which is accidental to his οὐσία.⁸ Marcellus, says Eusebius, believes in an 'irrational God' (θεὸν ἄλογον),⁹ who has the Logos himself as an accidental property and is not himself λόγος.¹⁰

Eusebius states what he considers must be believed about God and his Logos thus:

It is necessary to acknowledge that that which is beyond the universe (τὸ ἐπέκεινα τῶν ὅλων) is something which is one, divine, ineffable, good, simple, uncompounded, who is himself absolute God,¹¹ absolute Mind, absolute Reason, absolute Wisdom, absolute Light, absolute Life, absolute Beauty, absolute Goodness, and superior to

---

¹ *Ibid.* II, 14, 2 (*GCS*, IV, 114, 32).
² *Ibid.* II, 14, 2 (*GCS*, IV, 114, 33 ff.).
³ *Ibid.* II, 14, 3 (*GCS*, IV, 114, 35 ff.).
⁴ *in Joh.* II, 2 ff. (*GCS*, IV, 54, 12 ff.).
⁵ *de Ecc. Theol.* II, 14, 3 (*GCS*, IV, 115, 4).
⁶ *Idem* (*GCS*, IV, 115, 5).   ⁷ *Ibid.* II, 14, 4 (*GCS*, IV, 115, 7).
⁸ *Idem* (*GCS*, IV, 115, 9).   ⁹ *Ibid.* II, 14, 5 (*GCS*, IV, 115, 13).
¹⁰ *Idem* (*GCS*, IV, 115, 14).
¹¹ αὐτοθεός; all the words in the above translation which are preceded by 'abolute' are prefixed with αὐτο-.

anything that one may conceive, and, further, Mind over all and beyond all thought and desire. We must acknowledge also the only-begotten Son of this God, as an image which has sprung from him, who is in every way and in every respect most like him who has begotten him, that he is himself God and Mind and Reason and Life and Light and Image of the Beautiful and Good himself; but that he is not himself the Father, nor himself unbegotten and unbegun, but is one who has sprung from him, for he who has begotten him is described as the Beginning (ἀρχή). If, however, Marcellus would contradict these statements and say that God and the Logos which is in him are identical, defining God as uncompounded and simple, it is time to confess that he is neither Father nor Son, and to bring forward openly the Jew or to introduce Sabellius who says that the same being is Father and Son; so that, according to him, the statement 'In the beginning was the Logos' is equal to 'In the beginning was God'; and 'and the Logos was with God' is equal to 'and God was with God'; and similarly the third also is the same as 'and God was God'. This, then, would be approaching the most irrational meaninglessness.[1]

Eusebius thus interprets John i. 1 as setting forth a distinct and separate divine being, the Logos, beside the one true God, one who possesses all that the Father has, only in a derivative manner.

He proceeds next to a discussion of John i. 3, 'All things were made through him'. He says that this is meaningless if the 'underlying being (τὸν ὑποκείμενον)' is one.[2] The fact that St John uses the preposition διά, and not ὑπό or ἐξ, implies that there are two beings;[3] we must look for some other being who is creator of the universe, whom this verse asserts to be established over all. Marcellus, who denies any hypostatic pre-existence of the Logos (Son) could not say who this being is; 'we must confess', says Eusebius, 'that he whom the evangelist asserts to be divine (John i. 1c) is not the God over all nor the Father, but that he is the only-begotten Son of this God, who is not an accidental property of the Father, nor in him as in an underlying substance, nor identical with him, but truly Son, living and subsisting.[4] Eusebius concludes this section of

---

[1] de Ecc. Theol. II, 14, 6–9 (GCS, IV, 115, 15 ff.); cf. Weber, ΑΡΧΗ, pp. 82 ff.
[2] Ibid. II, 14, 9 (GCS, IV, 115, 35).
[3] See above, p. 274, for Eusebius' discussion of διά.
[4] de Ecc. Theol. II, 14, 11 (GCS, IV, 116, 14 ff.).

his argument by suggesting that in John i. 1 we may substitute
'Son' for 'Logos' without altering the evangelist's meaning
at all.

In the foregoing exegesis of John i. 1, 3 Eusebius has been
striving to clarify the novelty of St John's usage of the term
'Logos'; for St John the Logos is a divine being subsisting
beside the Father. None of the usual meanings of the term is
applicable. In this exegesis Eusebius started from John i. 1*c*:
'The Logos was God'; now he takes up the verse again, commencing from the first clause, 'In the beginning was the
Logos': 'It is fitting, therefore, that the divine evangelist said
that he was "in the beginning", ascribing to him a beginning
which is clearly his birth from the Father.'[1] Despite all his
criticism of Marcellus' use of human analogies and his emphasis on their inadequacy, Eusebius cannot avoid them himself, for he goes on to say, 'for everything that was born of
someone else has, as a beginning, him who has begotten him'.[2]
Eusebius answers the question which he had asked several
pages earlier;[3] it is the Father who is the ἀρχή in which the
Logos was. He does not realise how near he is to agreement
with Marcellus; if the Father is the ἀρχή and the Logos is in
the ἀρχή, then Eusebius should go on to say that the Logos is
ἐν τῷ πατρί. He hastens to point out, however, that St John
does not say '*in* God', but '*with* God'; the preposition 'with'
teaches us that the one who was begotten and who possessed
the Father as his ἀρχή 'was not somewhere far from the
Father...but was present with him and was with him'.[4] He
quotes Prov. viii. 25, 27 in support of this, and concludes that
'the Logos, that is, the only-begotten Son, was with God, his
own Father, being united to him and present with him at all
times; this the evangelist demonstrates when he says "the
Logos was with God".'[5]

When the evangelist says, 'The Logos was God' (John i. 1*c*),
he is pointing out what his rank is:

How could he, who was begotten from the one and only unbegotten
God, not be God? For if 'what is begotten of the flesh is flesh and

---

[1] *Ibid.* II, 14, 13 (*GCS*, IV, 116, 25 f.).
[2] *Idem* (*GCS*, IV, 116, 26).   [3] See above, p. 282.
[4] *de Ecc. Theol.* II, 14, 3 (*GCS*, IV, 116, 31).
[5] *Ibid.* II, 14, 14 (*GCS*, IV, 116, 34 ff.).

what is begotten of the Spirit is Spirit' (John iii. 6), it follows also that what is begotten of God is God. Therefore also 'the Logos was God', and a God who is maker and creator of all.[1]

'The tutorial Law' (ὁ παιδαγωγὸς νόμος—Gal. iii. 24)[2] in Gen. i. 1 announces to all men through Moses that God is Creator of the world and that the world is a creature, so that the Jews may not 'worship the creature rather than the Creator' (Rom. i. 25); but the way in which God created the world and the intermediary through whom he created it was kept secret from the Jews, although Moses and the prophets knew it:

'Grace and truth' proclaims 'through Jesus Christ' (John i. 17) the mystery which Moses kept secret; it inaugurates a newer and mystic teaching by the church of God, and it shouts to all without distinction so that they may hear, 'In the beginning was the Logos, and the Logos was with God, and the Logos was God...All things were made through him' (John i. 1, 3); through these words it makes known the Son of God and the special facts (τὰ ἐξαίρετα) of the divine light and life which are in him, and how all things which were said through him by Moses and those still further beyond these are held together.[3]

Eusebius accuses Marcellus of both 'judaising' and 'sabellianising'; he 'judaises' when he says that before the creation there was nothing but God alone, whereas the church confesses that there were Father and Son; he 'sabellianises' when he says that the Father and the Logos are identical, and introduces the Logos as, first, the Logos-immanent (λόγος ἐνδιάθετος), and then the Logos-expressed (λόγος προφορικός). He says that Marcellus has made the mistake of giving to the term ὁ λόγος one of its human meanings. Eusebius says:

At any rate the divine evangelist did not establish that he whom he asserts to be God is the Logos in any of the ways we have set forth, but in a way in which it is fitting to think about the only-begotten Son of God, who is the Logos through whom all things that exist

[1] *Ibid.* II, 14, 15 (*GCS*, IV, 117, 4 ff.).
[2] *Ibid.* II, 14, 16 (*GCS*, IV, 117, 10 f.); this is a phrase of which Clement and Origen were extremely fond; cf. E. Molland, *The Conception of the Gospel in Alexandrian Theology, passim.*
[3] *Ibid.* II, 14, 18 f. (*GCS*, IV, 117, 17 ff.).

were made and God and only-begotten, because he alone was truly the Son of God who is over all, really the genuine beloved Son who has been made like his Father in every way. Therefore he was also 'True Light', because the intellectual and rational light shine in the souls which have been made according to his image.[1]

In the same way 'he was truly "Life", for out of the abundance of his own life he supplies life to all living things; in every respect also the Son of God was "Truth", for he proves this by saying, "I am the Truth" (John xiv. 6)'.[2]

What, then, is the content of Eusebius' Logos-concept which he opposes to that of Marcellus? At first sight it seems that he has fulfilled the task which Origen bequeathed to his successors, for he appears to have made the Son-concept regulative instead of the cosmological Logos-concept. Throughout these anti-Marcellan treatises he appears to be making the concept of 'the only-begotten Son' (John i. 18, iii. 16, 18) the centre of his thought and to be equating this Son with the Logos of the Prologue of St John. When we ask, however, what is the content of this Son-concept, we have to admit that, like his master Origen, Eusebius, because of his cosmological presuppositions, because of the demands of his Middle-Platonist cosmology, could not make the transposition from cosmology to biblical theology. The only-begotten Son of God is, for Eusebius, none other than the cosmological Logos; the content of his Son-concept is nothing more than the old cosmological Logos-doctrine under a different and more biblical name.

Berkhof has demonstrated[3] that the theology of Eusebius is a Logos-theology derived from that of Origen and, like the latter, dependent on a Middle-Platonist cosmology, the basis of which was the dualism between God and the cosmos of spiritual beings with the consequent necessity for an intermediary between the two if there is to be any intercourse between them. 'The existence of the Logos is (for Eusebius) a cosmological postulate, or more precisely, the postulate of a Platonist cosmology which recognises higher and lower grades of being.'[4] That this is Eusebius' position is clear from the following passage:

---

[1] *Ibid.* II, 14, 21 f. (*GCS*, IV, 118, 4 ff.).
[2] *Ibid.* II, 14, 22 (*GCS*, IV, 118, 14 ff.).
[3] *Eusebius von Caesarea.* [4] Berkhof, *op. cit.* pp. 67 f.

For it is the nature of created things, which possess the difference between bodies and bodiless beings, between beings which have souls and those which have not, between mortals and immortals, that they are unable to draw near to the God who is beyond all and to share the flashings of his divinity because they have fallen far from what is better, but have slipped farther and still farther through their natural weakness, unless they received God the Saviour as an ally. Therefore it is appropriate that the Father, in his love for men, should establish his only-begotten child over all, who spreads among all and presides over all and distributes wealth from himself.[1]

The existence of the only-begotten Son, like that of the Logos in Middle-Platonism, is dependent on God's 'philanthropy'; 'God caused him to subsist for the sake of the salvation (= preservation?) of and provision for all originate things.[2]

Origen's doctrine of the eternal generation of the Logos (Son) was dependent on his view that the cosmos of spiritual beings was eternal.[3] When the latter view was abandoned the eternity of the Logos–Son once again became a matter for debate. If it was to be retained, it could only be on soteriological grounds.[4] Nowhere in his anti-Marcellan treatises does Eusebius ascribe eternity to the world of spiritual beings, yet he still strives to hold on to a doctrine of pre-temporal generation on cosmological grounds. In the face of the disintegration of Origen's cosmology he takes refuge in archaism.[5] He says that the Logos-Son was begotten 'before the ages' (πρὸ τῶν αἰώνων).[6] What he means by this phrase may best be understood from his exegesis of Prov. viii. 23, 'Before the ages he established me'. This means, he says, that the Logos 'was and pre-existed and existed before the whole world (ἦν καὶ προῆν καὶ τοῦ σύμπαντος κόσμου προϋπῆρχεν)'.[7] He does not describe the generation of the Logos–Son as eternal, for to do so would endanger the monarchy of the Father and the position of the Logos–Son, by placing the latter too completely on the side of the God 'who

---

[1] de Ecc. Theol. I, 13, 1 (GCS, IV, 73, 1, ff.).
[2] Ibid. I, 12, 10 (GCS, IV, 72, 36 f.).
[3] See above, pp. 89 ff.
[4] See above, p. 112.
[5] Cf. Arnold Toynbee, A Study of History, VI, 49 ff.
[6] c. Marc. I, 4, 29 (GCS, IV, 24, 1); cf. de Ecc. Theol. (GCS, IV, 63, 21; 66, 18; etc.).
[7] de Ecc. Theol. III, 2, 25 f. (GCS, IV, 143, 21 ff.).

is over all'. As 'Mediator' (μεσίτης)[1] between God and men, the Logos–Son 'stood in the middle of the two (δυεῖν δ' ἄρα μέσος ἔστηκεν)'.[2] The 'eternity' of the Logos–Son is not a co-eternity with the Father, for that would be to assert that there are two who are unoriginate and without beginning.[3] Eusebius prefers to leave the definition of the Logos' eternity as vague as possible; if he had followed his argument to its logical conclusion he would have had to postulate a special category for the eternity of the Logos–Son, 'a semi-eternal state as befits a semi-divine being. The Father has eternity in the proper sense; the Son, as begotten, has it in a derivative sense.'[4]

Eusebius' opposition to the view of Sabellius and of Marcellus makes him emphasise almost on every page of the anti-Marcellan treatises that the Logos–Son has a separate and distinct hypostasis from that of the 'only true God'. It is not primarily a religious interest which motivates him here; if the Logos–Son had no separate subsistence he could not fill his function as an intermediary. He can maintain the distinction between the Father and the Son only in terms of the Son's inferiority to the Father. 'He ventured right up to the borders of Arianism... but nowhere does he step across them.'[5] In seeking to avoid the Arian doctrine of the createdness of the Son, yet at the same time, to preserve the distinction of the Son from the Father, he loosens his grip on monotheism, despite his strong denial that his view implies belief in 'two Gods'. He is constantly drawn in the direction of ditheism, for his view of the godhead is that there is a graded hierarchy of divine beings. He can maintain the monarchy of the Father only by making the Son a secondary, derivative and inferior being. Not only that, but also his view of the monarchy of the Father endangers the divinity of the Son, for if the essence of the only true God is to be ἀγέννητος καὶ ἄναρχος,[6] and the Son is begotten and has a beginning in the sense in which he asserts that he has, then the Son cannot be God.

[1] Cf. Eusebius' exegesis of Gal. iii. 19 f. and I Tim. ii, 5 in *c. Marc.* I, 1, 29 ff. (*GCS*, IV, 7, 17 ff.).

[2] *c. Marc.* I, 1, 31 (*GCS*, IV, 7, 27).

[3] *de Ecc. Theol.* II, 23, 1 (*GCS*, IV, 133, 12).

[4] Berkhof, *Eusebius von Caesarea*, p. 75.   [5] Berkhof, *op. cit.* p. 80.

[6] *de Ecc. Theol.* I, 5, 2 (*GCS*, IV, 64, 26); cf. Opitz, *Urk.* 3.

Eusebius' Son-concept, then, has the content of the cosmological Logos-concept. The Logos–Son is the intermediary between the transcendent and ineffable God and the world, the one through whom God creates, preserves and sustains the universe. This cosmological emphasis and particularly the emphasis on the inferiority of the Son to the Father precludes any possibility of an authentic self-revelation of God in Christ; indeed, there is no need for a revelation of the Father, the only true God, for all men instinctively know him. All that the Son reveals is that he himself exists.[1] Nor is there any possibility of a genuine reconciliation of sinful men with God for, according to Eusebius' theology, it is not true that *God* was in Christ, but rather that a demi-god was in Christ. 'Only God himself can reveal God and reconcile us with God.'[2] This is the truth which Marcellus was trying, however inadequately, to preserve, the truth which the Western Church tried to preserve in the face of gnosticism and Marcionism, the truth which Athanasius made the centre of his polemic against the Arians; it is a truth which Eusebius cannot grasp and which, in the last analysis, his theology denies.

(b) *Eusebius' criticism of Marcellus' Logos-doctrine.* Having stated what he means by the *Logos*, Eusebius goes on to criticise Marcellus' doctrine. He has made the mistake of interpreting the term ὁ λόγος of John i. 1 ff. as if it were a combination of the first two of the five usual meanings of the term, that is, as Reason by which God thinks, and as a word which when spoken signifies something.[3] Eusebius says that Marcellus has mistakenly argued from the analogy of the λόγος ἐνδιάθετος and the λόγος προφορικός in man:

Since he used the λόγος in man as an example, it must be pointed out that not every man has a son, although he is λογικός and possesses the λόγος innate in himself. Therefore a son is something other than the λόγος...The λόγος which is innate in the mind is far different from him who has been begotten from someone.[4]

[1] *de Ecc. Theol.* I, 20, 7 (*GCS*, IV, 81, 25 f.).
[2] Berkhof, *Eusebius von Caesarea*, p. 83; cf. E. Brunner, *The Mediator*, p. 21: 'Through God alone can God be Known'.
[3] See above, p. 281.
[4] *de Ecc. Theol.* II, 16, 1 f. (*GCS*, IV, 119, 34 ff.).

If St John had wished to set forth what Marcellus interprets him to say, he would not have said καὶ θεὸς ἦν ὁ λόγος (John i. 1c), but καὶ ὁ θεὸς ἦν ὁ λόγος or καὶ θεοῦ ἦν ὁ λόγος. Also the conjunction καί is important for it unites the divinity of the Son to the Father.[1]

Since Marcellus thought it sound to draw an analogy between the *Logos* of God and the *logos* of man, Eusebius asks if there is any analogy between them. He says that the mind is the 'father' of the *logos* in the case of men, being another beside the *logos*, and no one knows what Mind is, for its essence is incomprehensible.[2] He then turns to his favourite analogy, the Emperor:

An Emperor, living in the secrecy of his apartments, plans what is to be done. The *logos* from him, inasmuch as it has been begotten out of the innermost recesses of the father, makes him known to all who are without, and they then share in the benefits of his *logos*. In the same way, but rather beyond every simile and metaphor, the perfect *logos* of God, the Emperor of the universe, who is not composed of syllables and verbs and nouns in the same way as a human *logos* which is spoken (λόγος προφορικός), but, inasmuch as he is the living and subsisting only-begotten Son of God, comes forth from the Father's divinity and kingdom, and irrigates the whole world with abundant (water) from himself, flooding all originate things with life and *logos* and wisdom and light and every good possession.[3]

The Father, like the unseen and invisible mind, is incomprehensible, but through his Logos he permeates everything and is in everything by his watchful providence. This comparison alone is fitting.[4] Having rejected Marcellus' use of the analogy of human speech, Eusebius thus sets forth an analogy which is fundamentally the same as the Stoic concept of the σπερματικὸς λόγος, the *logos* which pervades the universe, the *logos* in which men participate.

It is doubtful whether Eusebius has understood Marcellus' analogy; as we have seen there is no evidence in the surviving fragments which Eusebius has quoted that Marcellus used the Stoic distinction between λόγος ἐνδιάθετος and λόγος προφορικός. If Marcellus used these terms, it is certain that he was not thereby borrowing the distinction which they expressed

---

[1] *Ibid.* II, 17, 1 ff. (*GCS*, IV, 120, 12 ff.).
[2] *Ibid.* II, 17, 4 (*GCS*, IV, 120, 33 ff.).
[3] *Ibid.* II, 17, 4 ff. (*GCS*, IV, 121, 3 ff.).
[4] *Ibid.* II, 17, 6 (*GCS*, IV, 121, 15 ff.).

in Stoic philosophy; for him, as for Theophilus, there is no distinction between the Logos which is immanent in God and the Logos when it is expressed by God. For Marcellus God's Logos is not composed of syllables and nouns and verbs, as Eusebius supposes, but he is God himself expressing himself in speech and action, yet, while speaking and acting in self-revelation and salvation, he does not cease to be God.

Furthermore, Eusebius' attempt to combine the analogy of the human *logos* with the analogy of the Emperor adds nothing to the understanding of the former analogy; it only serves to emphasise Eusebius' conception of God as an oriental potentate whose satrap the Logos is. Eusebius realises that one of the fundamental points of difference between himself and Marcellus is the content of the term *logos*, but he fails to recognise that he is opposing an unbiblical metaphysical Logos-concept to a concept which has its roots deep in the thought of the Old Testament and which was the primary concept in the mind of St John when he wrote his Prologue.

6. *The Incarnation and Heilsgeschichte*

Marcellus' view of the incarnation of the Logos, it has been pointed out,[1] can be understood only against the background of his view of *Heilsgeschichte*; the same is true of Eusebius. When the latter asks why St John, at the beginning of his Gospel, calls the Son 'Logos',[2] he goes back to Old Testament sayings which tell how 'the Word of the Lord' came to the prophets; e.g. Jonah i. 1: ἐγένετο λόγος κυρίου πρὸς Ἰωνᾶν. The Logos, he says, was not *in* any of the prophets, but 'came down' to each of them. St John, on the other hand, was going to proclaim

the intellectual economy of the Logos (νοερὰν τοῦ λόγου οἰκονομίαν); therefore, he no longer teaches that the Logos was coming to some one else as he did to the men of old, but that he has assumed flesh and has become man...Since he was going to proclaim to all his saving approach (τὴν σωτήριον πάροδον), he said next, 'And the Logos became flesh and dwelt among us' (John i. 14), going back of necessity to the beginning, to the Logos who has just recently been made flesh.[3]

[1] See above, pp. 250 ff.   [2] *de Ecc. Theol.* II, 18, 1 (*GCS*, IV, 121, 27 ff.).
[3] *Ibid.* II, 18, 2 f. (*GCS*, IV, 122, 3 ff.).

St John proclaims 'his more divine and singular beginning' which none of the prophets had preached openly; therefore he delivers to all 'the forgotten and hidden mystery concerning the Logos', saying, 'In the beginning was the Logos, and the Logos was with God, and the Logos was God...All things were made through him and without him was made not even one thing' (John i. 1, 3).

If, being taught by the Old Testament, you have previously learned that the Logos of the Lord came to this prophet and to that...now it is necessary to proclaim to all men, not that he came, but that he 'was in the beginning', and that he 'was God', and that 'all things were made through him'...and that this very Logos of God... through the love of the Father 'became flesh and dwelt among us'.[1]

A little later Eusebius develops the theme of St John's proclamation to all men of the mystery which Moses and the prophets knew secretly but did not proclaim to the Jewish people because of their hardness of heart,[2] because they were imperfect,[3] because they were continually being led away into the error of polytheism and were not able to receive the grace of the gospel.[4] The patriarchs openly practised the pure religion and knew that God had a Son; Moses and the prophets practised the pure religion in secret and knew in secret that God had a Son, but they kept it to themselves.[5] Instead, they proclaimed that 'God is one' for fear that the Jews might be further tempted into polytheism.

What of the theophanies of the Old Testament?[6] How was the invisible God seen in human form by Abraham and the rest of the patriarchs? The invisible God cannot become visible; therefore, it was the Logos, the Son of God, who appeared in human form, and the Son himself proves this when he says, 'Abraham your father rejoiced that he was to see my day, and he saw and rejoiced' (John viii. 58), most clearly demonstrating his pre-existence.[7]

---

[1] *Ibid.* II, 18, 5 f. (*GCS*, IV, 122, 19 ff.).

[2] *Ibid.* II, 20, 1 (*GCS*, IV, 127, 9).   [3] *Idem* (*GCS*, IV, 127, 11).

[4] *Ibid.* II, 20, 3 (*GCS*, IV, 127, 23 f.).

[5] Cf. D. S. Wallace Hadrill, 'A Fourth-Century View of the Origins of Christianity', *ExpT*, LXVII (1955), 53 ff.

[6] *de Ecc. Theol.* II, 21 (*GCS*, IV, 130, 3 ff.).

[7] *Ibid.* II, 21, 1 f. (*GCS*, IV, 130, 3 ff.).

The purpose of the incarnation of the Logos, then, is that the Logos, by coming in human form, may reaffirm the pure religion and make known to all men that there is only one true God and that he has an only-begotten Son.[1] The Logos is the bringer of eternal truth to men, formerly through the prophets, and now in these latter days by coming and dwelling among men. The secret which the prophets knew but did not divulge, namely that God has an only-begotten Son, has been unlocked to all through the incarnation and through the preaching of the church, and today, since the Empire has become Christian under the rule of a Christian Emperor, the pure religion is being practised everywhere. The universal religion of the patriarchs has now become the universal religion of the Roman Empire.

On the strictly christological question, the relationship of the divine to the human in the historical Jesus, Eusebius has little to say; what he does say, however, is clear and unequivocal: *The Logos dwells in the flesh, moving it in the manner of a soul.* When criticising Marcellus' view that the Son, as Son, did not exist before the incarnation, that the Logos, as pre-existent, had no separate hypostasis, and that in the incarnate life it was the Logos that was the ἐνέργεια, the active principle, Eusebius says:

The Logos, who was dwelling in the flesh, when he was busy with affairs on earth, if he was outside the Father, living and subsisting and moving the flesh in the manner of a soul, clearly it was as another beside the Father; and then again he and the Father must have been two hypostases.[2]

Throughout his exegesis of St John's Gospel, Eusebius has interpreted the sayings of Jesus as sayings of the Logos, and nowhere does he ascribe to the historical Jesus a human soul; indeed, to do so would be to make him a 'mere man' (ψιλὸς ἄνθρωπος).[3] The Logos takes the place of the human soul. The purpose of the conjunction of the Logos with human flesh in Jesus Christ was, as we have seen, that it might be made plain to all men that God has a Son, that is to impart information to men. This may be demonstrated from Eusebius' criticism

---

[1] Wallace Hadrill, 'The Origins of Christianity'.
[2] *de Ecc. Theol.* I, 20, 40 (*GCS*, IV, 87, 24 ff.).
[3] *c. Marc.* I, 4, 59 (*GCS*, IV, 29, 32).

of Marcellus' exegesis of John vi. 63, 'It is the Spirit that gives life, the flesh is of no avail'.[1] Marcellus said that Jesus is referring to the flesh which he had assumed. Eusebius replies by pointing out that Marcellus has ignored the context where Jesus is speaking of the eating of his flesh and the drinking of his blood. He says that Jesus is, in fact, referring to the 'mystic body and blood'; he is teaching his disciples to hear spiritually what had been said concerning his flesh and blood,

for, he says, do not think that I am saying that you must eat the flesh with which I am clad, nor suppose that I am commanding you to drink my sensible and physical blood, but know that 'the words which I have spoken to you are spirit and life' (John vi. 63), so that these are the words and these words are the flesh and blood of which he who partakes always, as if fed with heavenly bread, will partake of the heavenly life.[2]

For Eusebius the 'mystic body and blood' are the teaching of the Son of God about himself, the mystery which, before the incarnation, was hidden from all but Moses and the prophets, but is now proclaimed to all.[3]

To Eusebius, with his Greek conception of God as the One who is beyond the universe, invisible and unknowable, any assertion that God has circumscribed himself in a body by assuming flesh, any assertion, indeed, that GOD was in Christ, is Sabellianism. For him, it is not God who was in Christ, but the Logos. It was a demi-god who was joined to human flesh in order to teach men the truth that God has a Son. In Eusebius' system there is no real need for an incarnation, for all that Jesus Christ makes known was already known to the prophets and the patriarchs.

If his anti-Marcellan treatises show little interest in the

---

[1] de Ecc. Theol. III, 11 ff. (GCS, IV, 167, 21 ff.).

[2] Ibid. III, 12, 5 (GCS, IV, 169, 29 ff.).

[3] Often Eusebius loses the thread of his argument and sometimes contradicts what he is trying to prove. If Jesus is not referring here to the flesh that he assumed, but to the 'mystic body and blood', then the mystic body and blood is of no avail, and the whole of Eusebius' theology is an attempt to establish something which is valueless. The point of Jesus' saying is that the eating and drinking of his flesh and blood in themselves are valueless; it is only when the Spirit is in the heart and mind of the eater and drinker that the act of eating and drinking has any value. Eusebius, like Marcellus, misses the point; in doing so, Eusebius contradicts his whole theology.

incarnation and none whatever in redemption, his criticism of Marcellus' view of the last things reveals that he has no understanding of the end of *Heilsgeschichte*. This becomes plain in his criticism of Marcellus' exegesis of I Cor. xv. 28, in opposition to which he sets forth his own exegesis of the High-Priestly prayer of Jesus (John xvii). Jesus prays:

That they may all be one, just as thou, O Father, art in me and I in thee, so that they may also be one in order that the world may know that thou hast sent me. And I have given them the glory which thou hast given me, so that they may be one as we are one, I in them and thou in me, so that they may be made perfect in one, so that the world may know that thou didst send me and didst love them just as thou didst love me. Father, I desire that they also, whom thou hast given me, may be with me where I am to behold my glory which thou hast given me in thy love for me before the foundation of the world. (John xvii. 21–4).

Eusebius says that this is the great plea of the Saviour for us, that we may be with him and behold his glory, that he might give us his glory

so that we may no longer be many but one, being united with him by the divinity and glory of the Kingdom, not by amalgamation of substance, but by the perfection of virtue to its highest point; for he prayed 'that they may be made perfect'.[1]

The 'end' of *Heilsgeschichte*, both in the sense of its purpose and of its result, is the perfection of men in virture.

Eusebius asserts that it is in the light of John xvii that we must interpret those sayings from the Fourth Gospel which Marcellus quotes as proof of the identity of the Father and the Son.[2] John x. 30, 'I and the Father are one', must be interpreted in the light of John xvii. 22, 23, 'That they may be one even as we are one, I in them and thou in me, so that they may be perfectly one'. John x. 38, 'The Father is in me, and I in the Father' (cf. John xiv. 10) must be interpreted in the light of John xvii. 21, 22, 'Just as thou, O Father, art in me and I in thee, so that they may also be one in us, and I have given them the glory which thou hast given me'. In these sayings, says Eusebius, the Son clearly shows that the Father is in him

---

[1] *de Ecc. Theol.* III, 18, 3 (*GCS*, IV, 179, 21 ff.).
[2] *Ibid.* III, 19 (*GCS*, IV, 180, 1 ff.).

in the same way as he wishes to be in us. 'The Father and the Son are one according to their sharing in the glory which he shares with his disciples, esteeming them to be worthy of the same oneness (τῆς αὐτῆς ἑνώσεως).'[1] Having started with the presupposition of the absolute distinction between the Father and the Son, Eusebius explains away the other side of the Johannine paradox by reducing the unity of the Son with the Father to the same level as our unity with him.

The final chapter of *de Ecclesiastica Theologia* is devoted to a discussion of 'How the words, "He who has seen me has seen the Father" (John xiv. 9) are to be understood'.[2] Eusebius maintains that these words of the Son of God show that 'he alone and no other is "the image of the invisible God" (Col. i. 15) and "the brightness of his glory and expression of his substance" (Heb. i. 3) and that he is "in the form of God" (Phil. ii. 6)'.[3] Once again Eusebius resorts to the analogy of the Emperor and his image:

For just as he who has gazed at the imperial image which was made as an accurate likeness of the Emperor by stamping out copies of his form and making images of him, in the same way, yet rather beyond all description and comparison, he shines through the mind. He who, with the eyes of his understanding purified and enlightened by the Holy Spirit, gazes at the greatness of the power of the only-begotten Son of God and perceives how 'in him dwells all the fullness of the (paternal) godhead' (Col. ii. 9), and how 'All things were made through him' (John i. 3), and 'In him were created all things which are in heaven and on earth, visible and invisible' (Col. i. 16), and considers that the Father begat him alone as only-begotten Son, made like him in all things—he too will see the Father potentially (δυνάμει) through the Son, who is beheld by those who are purified in mind, of whom it has been said, 'Blessed are the pure in heart, for they shall see God' (Matt. v. 8).[4]

Thus Eusebius allows no real knowledge of the Father through the Son; our vision of God through Jesus Christ is only 'poten-

---

[1] *Ibid.* III, 19, 4 (*GCS*, IV, 180, 30 ff.).

[2] *Ibid.* III, 21 (*GCS*, IV, 181, 13 ff.); chapter heading.

[3] *Ibid.* III, 21, 1 (*GCS*, IV, 181, 13 ff.). A comparison of the exegesis of Phil. ii. 6 ff. by the Fathers would make an interesting study.

[4] *Idem* (*GCS*, IV, 181, 17 ff.). It seems that Eusebius would say that the 'God' of Matt. v. 8 is not the Father but the Logos.

tial' (δυνάμει); the most that we can ever see is the Son, the Image, and not the Father whose Image he is.

The failure of Eusebius to give an adequate place in his system to the incarnation, redemption and eschatology reveals the inadequacy of the cosmological Logos-doctrine as a basis for Christian theology. The incarnation is only a 'passing phase in God's solicitude for men and providential care of them'. The cross and resurrection occupy no place at all in 'the ecclesiastical theology', and the last day is not to be looked for in the future, for it is already here now that the pure religion of the patriarchal age has been re-established, first by the declaration of the fact that God has an only-begotten Son, and now by the establishment of peace and stability under the rule of the Logos through the first Christian Emperor.

Historian though he was, he was unable to make either the incarnation or the crucifixion central in his theology. He was philosophically unprepared to construe history as a primary vehicle of Eternal Truth. History was for him, rather, the area in which Eternal Truth has been confirmed and, to be sure, vindicated in the extraordinary expansion of the church as the bearer of truth. In robbing Bethlehem and Calvary of their primacy, Eusebius greatly enhanced the relative significance of the Milvian Bridge and the New Rome for the salvation of mankind...Salvation was understood as coming through the might of a godly ruler. It was a recovery of truth and order.[1]

The conflict between Eusebius and Marcellus is, therefore, a conflict between two fundamentally opposed interpretations of the Logos-concept of St John's Prologue, a conflict between two opposed methods of interpreting St John's Gospel, both of which made their interpretation of the Prologue determinative for their exegesis of the whole gospel and the foundation-stone of their theological systems. Marcellus has it in his favour that his Logos-doctrine is derived from the Old Testament and similar to that which St John had in mind when he composed the Prologue, while Eusebius has imported his Logos-doctrine from extra-biblical sources. Eusebius may be able to show that Marcellus is erratic in his use of scripture, but he does not escape completely from the same accusation himself. He may

[1] G. H. Williams, 'Christology and Church–State Relations' *CH*, xx (1951), 17 f.

be able to point out the difficulties which the Hebraic Word-concept, as he misunderstands it in Marcellus' theology, raises but does not solve, but his own Logos–Son-concept is just as inadequate, if not more so, for it removes the incarnation and the atonement from the centre of Christian faith, and precludes any possibility of a genuine self-revelation of God in Jesus Christ and of an effective reconciliation of men with God through Christ.

The conflict between the two bishops is a conflict between two ancient traditions, both of which have been taken to extremes, and in their conflict with each other the weaknesses of both are laid bare. The two opposing traditions of theology, the Alexandrian and the Antiochene, together with the opposing methods of interpreting St John's Gospel on which they are based, come to grips with each other; 'Here are two worlds: the Alexandrian world of Origen *versus* the (Asia Minor?) world of Irenaeus; and fundamentally this means: the Greek world versus the biblical world.'[1]

The stage is set for one to appear who has a more adequate understanding of the purpose of the Prologue of St John's Gospel and of its relation to the gospel as a whole and, beyond that, to the whole of scripture. That one is the author of the treatise which is traditionally ascribed to Athanasius as the fourth of his *Orations* against the Arians, a writer who criticises the theology of Marcellus from the point of view of the biblical theology of Athanasius.

C. PSEUDO-ATHANASIUS AGAINST MARCELLUS

After the chaotic treatises of Eusebius against Marcellus, with their muddled thinking and even more muddled exegesis, with their long and involved sentences and monotonous repetitions, it is pleasant to turn to the treatise against Marcellus which is usually ascribed to Athanasius as his fourth *Oration against the Arians*. Its clear style and terse argument, the absence of lengthy digressions to disturb the smoothness or diminish the force of its arguments, set it in welcome contrast to the treatises of Eusebius. It seems probable that it was not intended to be circulated in its present form; rather it appears to be a collec-

[1] Berkhof, *Eusebius von Caesarea*, p. 202.

tion of notes on various heresies and of notes against them: e.g. Chapters 6 and 7 are directed against Arianism. For the most part, however, the heresies which it criticises are those of Marcellus and of theologians like Photinus who composed variations on Marcellus' central theme.

It is unnecessary to enter into a detailed discussion of the question of the authorship of this treatise. If it was not written by Athanasius, it was written by someone who was thoroughly conversant with Athanasius' theology and with the arguments which he had used in the refutation of Arianism; the standpoint from which it attacks Marcellus is the Nicene theology as expounded by Athanasius. It is evident that it was written at a time when the Marcellan question was still a living issue, and therefore before the Council of Constantinople (A.D. 381) which explicitly condemned Marcellanism along with its offshoot, Photinianism, all shades of Arianism and also Apollinarianism, the first strictly christological heresy.[1] It excluded Marcellus' view of the end of the Kingdom of the Son by inserting into its creed the words 'of whose kingdom there shall be no end'.[2] The most probable date for the composition of the notes which form the basis of the treatise appears to be c. A.D. 360, following the Homoiousian Synod of Ancyra (358), which marked the beginning of the rapprochement between the Nicene theologians and the Homoiousians led by Basil of Caesarea who found the continued refusal of the Western church and of Athanasius to condemn Marcellus a stumbling-block in the way of their accepting the Nicene faith and, in particular, the word ὁμοούσιος.[3] If this is so, the treatise, or at least the notes which it embodies, must have been written during the lifetime of Athanasius. The influence of his thought, language, polemic and exegesis is so apparent that if the treatise did not come from his own hand, it must have come from that of one of his close associates. It seems most likely that the notes which form its basis were written by Athanasius himself and edited into their present form by one of his friends.

What is important here is the fact that in this treatise we have the refutation of Marcellus from the point of view of

[1] Canon I; text in W. Bright, *The Canons of the First Four General Councils* 2nd ed.), p. xxi.
[2] *Ibid.* p. xix.   [3] Basil, *Epistle*, LXIX.

Athanasian orthodoxy; thus it provides an illuminating contrast to that which Eusebius of Caesarea had set out on the basis of a subordinationism which was perilously close to Arianism. The author, Pseudo-Athanasius, states his theological position quite clearly at the beginning and end of the treatise. He commences:

The Logos is God from God; for 'the Logos was God' (John i. 1), and again, 'Of whom are the fathers, and of whom Christ, who is God over all, blessed for ever. Amen' (Rom. ix. 5). And since Christ is God from God, and God's Logos, Wisdom, Son, and Power, therefore but one God is declared in the divine scriptures. For the Logos, being Son of the one God, is referred to him whose he is; so that the Father and the Son are two, yet the monad of the godhead is indivisible and inseparable (ὥστε δύο μὲν εἶναι πατέρα καὶ υἱόν, μονάδα δὲ θεότητος ἀδιαίρετον καὶ ἄσχιστον.[1]

The treatise ends with these words:

Therefore God the Logos himself is Christ from Mary, the God–Man (θεὸς ἄνθρωπος); not some other Christ, but one and the same; he is before the ages from the Father, he is, too, in the last times from the Virgin; invisible before even to the holy powers of heaven, visible now because of his being one with the Man who is visible; seen, I say, not in his invisible godhead but in the activity of the godhead through the human body and whole Man (διὰ τοῦ ἀνθρωπίνου σώματος καὶ ὅλου ἀνθρώπου), which he has renewed by appropriating it to himself.[2]

Many of the statements which Ps.-Athanasius makes could easily have been made by Eusebius, for both equally insist on the equation of the Logos with the Son, on the Logos as an existing and subsisting being beside the Father, and on the pre-existence of the Son. The difference between them, however, is very great. Whereas Eusebius fills the Son-concept with all the content of the cosmological Logos–concept, Ps.-Athanasius makes the Son-concept determinative, and for him the Son is Jesus Christ,[3] the God–Man;[4] whereas Eusebius asserts the distinction of the Logos–Son from the Father ὑποστάσει καὶ οὐσίᾳ, Ps.-Athanasius insists on their 'one essence and subsistence', on their oneness θεότητι;[5] whereas for Eusebius

[1] Or. c. Ar. IV, 1 (PG, XXVI, 468).　[2] Ibid. 36 (PG, XXVI, 524).
[3] Ibid. 1 (PG, XXVI, 468).　[4] Ibid. 36 (PG, XXVI, 524).
[5] Ibid. 1 (PG, XXVI, 468).

the function of the Logos–Son is to be a cosmological inter-mediary between God and the world, for Ps.-Athanasius his function is to be Saviour,[1] the mediator between God and man,[2] who for our sakes became man,[3] who passes on to men the gifts of God,[4] who highly exalts man,[5] who, 'as long as he was on earth during the incarnation, was Light in the world',[6] through whom we receive God his Father to be our Father also,[7] 'whose name means Saviour, not because of anything else, but because of the Man's being made one with God the Logos',[8] 'who has renewed the human body and the whole Man by appropriating it to himself'.[9]

The focal point of Ps.-Athanasius' theology is Jesus Christ: 'Our Lord being Logos and Son, bore a body and became Son of Man, so that, having become mediator between God and man, he might minister the things of God to us and ours to God.'[10] The emphasis is on soteriology and not on cosmology; the Son is the mediator, not between Spirit and matter, nor between the Absolute God and the created world, but between God the Father and men for their salvation. The very act of the incarnation is in itself mankind's redemption; by uniting himself to human flesh or to man the Son has exalted and renewed man.

'After taking him (the Man) in his corrupted state (σαθρωθέντα) into himself, he renews him again through that sure renewal into endless permanence, and therefore is made one with him in order to raise him to a diviner lot.'[11]

'The Logos being in the flesh, man himself was exalted and received power.'[12]

The Logos-concept is stripped of all its cosmological associa-tions and becomes but another designation of Jesus Christ, the Son of God, and on the same level as 'Wisdom' and 'Power'. Although Ps.-Athanasius explicitly denies that the Logos is a 'significant sound (φωνὴ σημαντική)',[13] nowhere in this treatise does he state what he means by the term ὁ λόγος;

---

[1] *Ibid.* 36 (*PG*, xxvi, 524).
[2] *Ibid.* 6 (*PG*, xxvi, 476).
[3] *Ibid.* 7 (*PG*, xxvi, 477).
[4] *Ibid.* 6 (*PG*, xxvi, 477).
[5] *Idem* (*PG*, xxvi, 476).
[6] *Ibid.* 18 (*PG*, xxvi, 493).
[7] *Ibid.* 22 (*PG*, xxvi, 500 f.).
[8] *Ibid.* 36 (*PG*, xxvi, 524).
[9] *Idem* (*PG*, xxvi, 524).
[10] *Ibid.* 6 (*PG*, xxvi, 476).
[11] *Ibid.* 33 (*PG*, xxvi, 520).
[12] *Ibid.* 6 (*PG*, xxvi, 476).
[13] *Ibid.* 1 (*PG*, xxvi, 468).

it is a reasonable surmise that it means for him what it meant for Athanasius, God's Word of revelation and creation who in Jesus Christ is also his Word of salvation.[1]

Marcellus formulated the greater part of his doctrinal system by exegesis of St John's Gospel; Eusebius based his refutation of Marcellus and his formulation of his own 'ecclesiastical theology' similarly on exposition of Johannine texts. The same is true, too, of Ps.-Athanasius' refutation of Marcellus. As an indication of the importance which the Fourth Gospel had for him, the following figures are interesting. He has 55 quotations from John, three from I John, one from Revelation, and 65 from the Old Testament and the rest of the New Testament.

The point at which Ps.-Athanasius attacks Marcellus first is his doctrine of the insubstantiality of the Logos: 'The Logos is God from God, for "the Logos was God" (John i. 1)...and since Christ is God from God...therefore but one God is declared in the divine scriptures... so that the Father and the Son are two, yet the monad of the godhead is indivisible and inseparable'.[2] The church asserts one ἀρχή of the godhead and not two, and of this ἀρχή the Logos is Son by nature (φύσει).

'For according to John (i. 1), "in" that "beginning was the Logos and the Logos was with God", for the beginning was God; and since he is from it, therefore also "the Logos was God".'[3] Therefore there is one God, 'one essence and substance (οὐσία καὶ ὑπόστασις μία)',[4] who said, 'I am the One-who-is' (Exod. iii. 14), and not two. The Logos who is from the One is an essential Logos (οὐσιώδης), who is truly Son of God:

for, as he is God from God, and Wisdom from the Wise, and Logos from the Rational (ἐκ λογικοῦ λόγος), and Son from the Father, so he is from substance substantial and from essence essential and actual (ἐξ οὐσίας οὐσιώδης καὶ ἐνούσιος) and is from the One-who-is (ἐξ ὄντος ὤν).[5]

Ps.-Athanasius then, agrees with Eusebius in asserting, in opposition to Marcellus, the distinct substantial pre-existence of

---

[1] See above, pp. 192 ff.   [2] Or. c. Ar. IV, 1 (PG, XXVI, 468).
[3] Idem.
[4] The context demands that ὑπόστασις be translated by 'substance', i.e. almost as a synonym of οὐσία. Ps.-Athanasius would not deny that Father and Son are two hypostases in the later sense of the word.
[5] Or. c. Ar. IV, 1 (PG, XXIV, 469).

the Logos-Son; he disagrees with Eusebius, however, for he asserts that the essence and substance of the Father and the Son are one, and not two as Eusebius holds.

Ps.-Athanasius proceeds to show that the Logos and Wisdom are not in God as a quality or attribute (ποιότης), for that would mean that 'God is compounded of essence and quality' (σύνθετος ὁ θεὸς ἐξ οὐσίας καὶ ποιότητος), that God can be 'cut up into essence and accident (τεμνομένη εἰς οὐσίαν καὶ συμβεβηκός)'.[1] He says:

The monad remains undivided and whole...As the Father truly exists, so also Wisdom truly exists, and in this respect they are two...because the Father is Father and the Son Son; and they are one, because he is Son of the essence of the Father by nature, existing as his own Logos. For the Lord said, 'I and the Father are one' (John x. 30); for the Logos is not separated from the Father, and the Father never was or is without Logos (ἄλογος), and for this reason he says, 'I in the Father and the Father in me' (John xiv. 10).[2]

The Father and the Son must be two; and they are one, because the Son is not from without, but begotten from God.[3]

Here the different points of view of Asterius, Marcellus, Eusebius and Ps.-Athanasius become evident. Asterius says that the Father and the Son are one because of their complete harmony of will;[4] Marcellus says that it is 'because it is impossible for the Logos to be separated from God or for God to be separated from his own Logos';[5] Eusebius says that it is because the Father and the Son 'share the glory, which the Son shares with the disciples' who will be made one with him and the Father;[6] Ps.-Athanasius says that the Father and Son are one because 'the Son is from the essence of the Father by nature', and the Father and the Son participate in the same essence, in the one godhead.[7]

After a digression[8] in which he attacks the Arians and shows

---

[1] *Ibid.* 2 (*PG*, xxvi, 469). Cf. Eusebius, *de Ecc. Theol.* ii, 14, 5 (*GCS*, iv, 115, 14).
[2] *Idem.* [3] *Ibid.* 3 (*PG*, xxvi, 472).
[4] Marcellus, Fr. 72–5; see above, pp. 260 f.
[5] Marcellus, Fr. 73; see above, p. 261.
[6] *de Ecc. Theol.* iii, 20 (*GCS*, iv, 180, 30–2).
[7] *Or. c. Ar.* iv, 2 (*PG*, xxvi, 469).
[8] In chs. 4–8, Ps.-Ath. turns his attention to the Arian distinction between the Logos and the Son which, he shows, has similarities with, as well as

how Marcellus, despite his denials to the contrary, holds views akin to and even worse than theirs, Ps.-Athanasius returns to the text, 'I and the Father are one' (John x. 30).[1] He says that Marcellus and his friends say either (a) that the two are one, or (b) that the one has two names, or (c) that the one is divided into two. He dismisses (c) because it implies that God is corporeal, and that neither part is perfect; he dismisses (b) because it is the view of Sabellius. Marcellus would hold (a); against this Ps.-Athanasius argues:

If the two are one, then of necessity they are two, but one according to the godhead and according to the Son's co-essentiality with the Father (κατὰ τὸ ὁμοούσιον εἶναι τὸν υἱὸν τῷ πατρί), and the Logos' being from the Father himself; so that there are two, because there is Father and Son, who is the Logos; and one, because one God. For if not, he would have said, 'I am the Father', or 'I and the Father am'; but, in fact, by the 'I' he means the Son, and by the 'and the Father' him who begat him; and by the 'one', the one godhead and his co-essentiality.[2]

He answers those who would say, as they said to Eusebius, that this implies two Gods; whereas Eusebius answers this accusation by asserting that the Father is 'the only true God',[3] Ps.-Athanasius says that just as in saying that the Father and the Son are two the church still confesses One God, so also, in saying that there is One God, the church considers the Father and the Son to be two; they are one in godhead (τῇ θεότητι) and in the Father's Logos being inseparable from him.

The next point to be attacked is Marcellus' view that the Logos was in God δυνάμει when God was silent, but came forth δραστικῇ ἐνεργείᾳ when God spake the Word of creation. Ps.-Athanasius says:

If the Logos was in God before he was begotten, then, being begotten, he is without and external to him. But if so, how does he

differences from, that which Marcellus draws. In ch. 8, Ps.-Ath. draws a neat distinction between the Arians and Marcellus: 'Eusebius and his fellows, confessing a Son, deny that he is Logos by nature, and would have the Son called Logos notionally; and the others, confessing him to be Logos, deny him to be Son, and would have the Logos called Son notionally. Both are equally void of footing.'

[1] *Or. c. Ar.* IV, 9 (*PG*, XXVI, 480).   [2] *Idem.*
[3] *de Ecc. Theol.* II, 23 (*GCS*, IV, 133 ff.); see above, pp. 279 f.

now say, 'I in the Father and the Father in me' (John xiv. 10)?
But if he is now in the Father, then always was he in the Father as
he is now.[1]

This leads on to an attack on Marcellus' view of the expansion
of the Monad into a Triad, in which Ps.-Athanasius makes no
use of exegesis of St John's Gospel.

When he discusses Marcellus' distinction between the Logos
and the Son, Ps.-Athanasius says that this distinction takes
three different forms: (a) the man whom the Saviour assumed
is the Son, (b) the man and the Logos became Son when they
were united, and (c) the Logos himself became Son when he
became man; from being Logos he has become Son, not being
Son before, but only Logos. He points out that both the doctrine
of the expansion of the monad and the denial of the Son are
Stoic doctrines, but 'it is especially absurd to name the Logos
and yet deny that he is the Son'. If the Logos is not from God,
he argues, then it would be quite legitimate to deny that he is
Son; if, however, the Logos is from God, then he must be Son
of him from whom he is. 'If God is Father of the Logos, why
is not the Logos Son of his own Father?'[2] If the Logos is not
Son of God, then Marcellus must hold either that the Logos is
the Father, or that the Son is superior to the Logos. The Son
is 'in the bosom of the Father' (John i. 18); nothing can be
prior to him who is in the bosom of the Father; therefore the
Logos is not before the Son or the Logos must be the Father in
whom the Son is. If the Logos is not the Son, then he is not in
the bosom of the Father, and he must be external to God.[3]

If the Logos and the Son are different beings, the Son is superior
to the Logos, for 'no one knows the Father except the Son' (Matt.
xi. 27), not even the Logos. The same is true of such sayings as
'He that hath seen me hath seen the Father' (John xiv. 9), and
'I and the Father are one' (John x. 30), for it was the Son and
not the Logos who uttered these words. Ps.-Athanasius quotes
in full the argument between Jesus and the Jews (John x. 32–8)
which followed his claim, 'I and the Father are one' (John
x. 30).[4] When the Jews heard Jesus say this word 'one', they
thought that he was claiming that he was the Father; to make

---

[1] *Or. c. Ar.* IV, 12 (*PG*, XXVI, 484).   [2] *Ibid.* 15 (*PG*, XXVI, 488).
[3] *Ibid.* 16 (*PG*, XXVI, 489).
[4] *Idem* (*PG*, XXVI, 489).

plain what he meant, Jesus explained the Son's oneness with the Father in the words, 'Because I said, I am the Son of God' (John x. 36). He has referred the sense of the words 'are one' to the Son, and adds, 'That you may know that I am in the Father and the Father in me' (John x. 38). He said that the oneness lay 'not in this being that' (οὐκ ἐν τῷ αὐτὸ εἶναι ἐκεῖνο) with which it was one, that is, that the oneness did not consist in identity, but in his being in the Father and the Father in him. 'Thus', says Ps.-Athanasius, 'he overthrows both Sabellius, in saying "I am", not the Father, but "the Son of God", and Arius, in saying, "are one".'[1]

If the Son and the Logos are not the same, then the Logos is not one with the Father, but the Son is; and it is not 'he that hath seen' the Logos, but 'he that hath seen' the Son, that 'hath seen the Father' (John xiv. 9). Therefore, either the Son is greater than the Logos, or the Logos has nothing beyond the Son:

For what can be greater or more perfect than 'one', and 'I in the Father and the Father in me' (John xiv. 10), and 'He that hath seen me hath seen the Father' (John xiv. 9), sayings which come, not from the lips of the Logos, but from those of the Son, as also do, 'He that hath seen me hath seen him that sent me' (John. xii. 45), and 'I am come as light into the world, that whoever believes in me may not remain in darkness. If any one hears my sayings and does not keep them, I do not judge him; for I have not come to judge the world but to save the world. He who rejects me and does not receive my sayings has a judge; the word that I have spoken will be his judge on the last day' (John xii. 46–8). His preaching, he says, judges him who has not observed his words, 'for if I had not come and spoken to them, they would not have sin, but now they have no excuse' (John xv. 22), for they have heard his words through which those who observe them shall reap salvation.[2]

Marcellus might object that this saying belongs to the Logos and not to the Son, but the context makes it plain that the Son was the speaker, for he who says here, 'I came not to judge the world but to save it' (John xii. 47) is shown to be no other than the only-begotten Son of God by the saying, 'For God so loved the world that he gave his only-begotten Son, that whoever believes in him should not perish but have everlasting life,

---

[1] *Ibid.* 17 (*PG*, xxvi, 492).　　　　[2] *Idem.*

etc...' (John iii. 16–19). If it is the same speaker who says John xii. 47 and John xii. 45, and if he who came not to judge the world but to save it is the only-begotten Son, it is clear that it is the same Son who says, 'He who sees me sees him who sent me' (John xii. 45). He who says, 'He who believes in me' (John xii. 46; cf. vi. 35; vii. 38; xi. 26; xiv. 12), and 'If any man hears my words I judge him not' (John xii. 47), is the Son himself of whom scripture says, 'He who believes on him is not condemned, but he who believes not is condemned already, because he has not believed in the name of the only-begotten Son of God' (John iii. 18). 'This is the judgment' of him who does not believe in the Son, 'that light has come into the world' and they did not believe in him, for he is 'the light that enlightens every man coming into the world' (John i. 9). 'As long as he was incarnate (κατὰ τὴν ἐνανθρώπησιν) on earth, he was light in the world, as he said himself, "while you have light, believe in the light, that you may be children of the light" (John xii. 36), for he says, "I have come as a light into the world" (John xii. 46).'[1]

From this exegesis Ps.-Athanasius concludes that the Logos is the Son, and proceeds to demonstrate the truth of his conclusion by further exegesis of St John's Gospel. If the Son is the light which has come into the world (John xii. 46), then the world was made through the Son, for St John says of John the Baptist, 'He was not the light, but came to bear witness to the light' (John i. 8), for Christ 'was the true light which enlightens every man coming into the world' (John i. 9). If 'he was in the world, and the world was made through him' (John i. 10), then the Son is the Logos, 'through whom all things were made' (John i. 3). If Marcellus wishes to maintain that the Logos is different from the Son, then there must be two worlds, one created through the Son and the other through the Logos; if, on the other hand, there is only one world, then the Logos and the Son must be identical before all creation, for through him the world was made (John i. 3; i. 10).

Ps.-Athanasius, like Eusebius,[2] asserts that it is equally true to say, 'In the beginning was the Son', and 'In the beginning was the Logos' (John i. 1). Marcellus and his friends might

---

[1] *Ibid.* 18 (*PG*, xxvi, 493).
[2] *de Ecc. Theol.* ii, 14, 12 (*GCS*, iv, 116, 19 ff.); see above, pp. 284 ff.

answer, however, that St John did not say, 'In the beginning was the Son', and therefore that the attributes of the Logos (τὰ τοῦ λόγου) are not fitting to the Son; they ought also to draw the conclusion which follows equally that the attributes of the Son are not fitting to the Logos. It is, however, the Son who says John x. 30 and xii. 45; it is he who 'is in the bosom of the Father' (John i. 18). That the world was brought into existence through him is asserted of both the Logos and the Son (John i. 3; i. 10); therefore the Son existed before the world. What is said to Philip (John xiv. 9–13) is also said by the Son. If the Father is glorified in the Son (John xiv. 13), it must also be the Son who says, 'I in the Father and the Father in me' (John xiv. 10), and 'He who has seen me has seen the Father' (John xiv. 9). For he who says these things shows that he is the Son by adding 'that the Father may be glorified in the Son' (John xiv. 13).[1]

Having demonstrated that the Logos is the Son, Ps.-Athanasius then asks what relation the Logos–Son bears to the Man whom the Saviour assumed,[2] and takes up in turn the various positions which his opponents have held:[3]

(a) *The Man whom the Logos wore, and not the Logos, is the only-begotten Son.* He points out the absurdities which this view entails: the Man must be the one who is in the Father (John xiv. 10), in whom the Father is (John xiv. 10), who is one with the Father (John x. 30), who is in the bosom of the Father (John i. 18), and who is the true light (John i. 9). Thus they will be forced to say that it was through the Man that the world was made (John i. 10), and that this Man was he who came not to judge the world but to save it (John xii. 47; cf. iii. 17), and that the Man was in existence before Abraham, whose offspring he was (John viii. 58). They would have to say that the flesh which was born of Mary was that through which the world was made (John i. 10).[4] What meaning could they give to 'He was in the world' (John i. 10), which St John says to signify the Son's existence before the incarnation? Ps.-Athanasius asks:

How, if it is not the Logos but the Man who is the Son, can he save the world, since he is himself one of the world (εἶς ὢν καὶ

---

[1] *Or. c. Ar.* IV, 19 (*PG*, XXVI, 496).   [2] *Ibid.* 20–5.
[3] Cf. *ibid.* 15; see above, pp. 305 ff.   [4] *Ibid.* 20 (*PG*, XXVI, 497).

αὐτὸς τοῦ κόσμου)?...What relationship will the Logos have to the Father, since the Man and the Father are one? If the Man is the only-begotten, what will be the place of the Logos? Either it must be said that he comes second, or, if he is above the only-begotten, he must be the Father himself...What more does the Logos have than the Man, if the Logos is not the Son?[1]

Scripture says that through the Logos and the Son the world has been made, yet it goes on to place the seeing of the Father, not in the Logos, but in the Son, and to attribute the saving of the world, not to the Logos, but to the only-begotten Son; moreover, it does not say that the Logos knows the Father, but that the Son knows him.[2]

Ps.-Athanasius asks what the Logos can contribute to our salvation over and above what the Son contributes, for we are commanded to believe on the Son, not on the Logos (John iii. 36): 'Holy baptism, on which the substance of our whole faith is anchored, is administered, not in the name of the Logos, but in the name of the Father, Son, and Holy Spirit.'[3] If the Logos is not the Son, then baptism has no connection with the Logos. 'How are they able to hold that the Logos is with the Father, when he is not with him in the giving of baptism?' Perhaps they will say that the Logos is included in the name of the Father; if so, then the Monad expands, not into a Triad, but into a Tetrad—Father, Logos, Son, and Holy Spirit.[4]

Ps.-Athanasius says that when his opponents are refuted on their first explanation of the relation of the Logos to the Man, that is, of the divine to the human in Jesus Christ, they have recourse to a second explanation:

(b) *Not the Man by himself whom the Lord bore, but both together, the Logos and the Man, are the Son.* He asks them (i) if the Logos is a Son because of the flesh, (ii) if the flesh is Son because of the Logos, or (iii) if, neither the Logos nor the flesh being the cause, it is the concurrence of the two that constitutes the Son.

He dismisses (i) by saying that if the Logos is a Son because of the flesh, then the flesh is Son, and they have returned to their previous position. He proceeds to discuss (ii). If the flesh is called Son because of the Logos, then the Logos must have been Son before the incarnation:

---

[1] *Idem.*   [2] *Idem.*   [3] *Ibid.* 21 (*PG*, xxvi, 500).   [4] *Idem.*

How could a being who is not himself a Son make others sons, especially when there is a Father? If then, he makes sons for himself, then he himself is Father; but if for the Father, then he must be Son, or rather, that Son on account of whom the rest are made sons.[1]

If while the Logos is not Son, we are sons, then God is our Father and not his. How then does he claim that God is his own Father rather than ours, when he says, 'My Father' (John v. 17), and 'I from the Father' (John xvi. 28)? If the Father is the common Father of all, he is not his Father only, and he is not the only one who 'has come forth from the Father' (John xvi. 28; cf. viii. 48). The Father is sometimes called 'our Father', because he has himself become partaker of our flesh. This is the reason why 'the Logos became flesh' (John i. 14), that since the Logos is Son, and because of the Son dwelling in us (cf. Col. iii. 16), he may be called our Father also, for 'He sent forth the Spirit of his Son into our hearts crying, Abba, Father' (Gal. iv. 6). 'Therefore, the Son in us, calling upon his own Father, causes him to be named "our Father" also. Surely God cannot be called Father of those who do not have the Son in their hearts?'[2]

Turning to his third question, Ps.-Athanasius argues that if neither the Logos nor the flesh is Son, but the conjunction of the two, the cause which brings the Son into existence will precede the union which constitutes the Son. Therefore, in this way too, the Son was before the flesh. In the face of this argument, he says, his opponents will take refuge in yet another pretext; this leads him to discuss what we have already seen to be one of the central doctrines of Marcellus; he states it in these words:

(c) *Neither the Man is Son, nor both together, but the Logos was simply Logos in the beginning, but when he became man, then he was named Son; for before his appearing, he was not Son, but Logos only; and as 'the Logos became flesh' (John i. 14), not being flesh before, so the Logos became Son, not being Son before.*[3]

If the Logos became Son when he became incarnate, says Ps.-Athanasius, then the incarnation was the cause of his becoming Son; if, however, the Man is the cause of his being

---

[1] *Ibid.* 21 (*PG*, XXVI, 500).   [2] *Ibid.* 22 (*PG*, XXVI, 500 ff.).
[3] *Idem.*

Son, or both together, then the same absurdities result as before. If, on the other hand, he is first Logos, then Son, it will be evident that he knew the Father after the incarnation but not before it, for it is not as Logos, but as Son, that he knows the Father, for 'no one knows the Father but the Son' (Matt. xi. 27). So, also, it is after the incarnation that he comes to be in the bosom of the Father (John i. 18), and that he and the Father become one (John x. 30), and that 'He that hath seen me hath seen the Father' (John xiv. 9), for it is the Son who says these things. They will be forced then to say that the *Logos* was nothing but a name, for it is not he who is in us with the Father (John xvii. 21), nor has he who has seen the Logos seen the Father (John xiv. 9), and the Father was known to no one at all before the incarnation—for it was said, 'And he to whom the Son will reveal him' (Matt. xi. 27)—for if the Logos was not yet Son, he did not yet know the Father.[1]

Continuing his exegesis of Matt. xi. 27, Ps.-Athanasius argues that God's self-revelation to Moses, the patriarchs and the prophets was 'through the Son'. 'If God was revealed, there must have been a Son to reveal (him).' It is nonsense to say that the Logos is one being and the Son another; if we ask them where they derived this notion from, they will say, 'because there is no mention of the Son in the Old Testament, but only mention of the Logos'. Thus they make a division between the Old Testament and the New, saying that they disagree with each other, which is what the Jews and the Manichees say; the former oppose the New Testament and the latter oppose the Old. If what is contained in the Old Testament is older than what is in the New, then John x. 30; i. 18; xiv. 9 are later, and refer, not to the Logos, but to the Son.[2]

This argument of theirs is completely false, says Ps.-Athanasius, for much is said about the Son in the Old Testament. He quotes Ps. ii. 7; Ps. ix (title—LXX); Ps. xliv (title—LXX); Isa. v. 1—'Who is this "well-beloved" but the only-begotten Son?';[3] Ps. cx. 3 (LXX);[4] Prov. viii. 25 (LXX), and Dan. iii. 25. Marcellus would say that these are meant to be understood as prophecies.[5] If this is so, answers Ps.-Athanasius, then the

---

[1] *Ibid.* 23 (*PG*, XXVI, 501).

[2] *Idem* (*PG*, XXVI, 504).

[3] *Ibid.* 29 (*PG*, XXVI, 513).

[4] *Ibid.* 27 f. (*PG*, XXVI, 509 f.).

[5] Marcellus, Fr. 42; 111.

Logos must also be spoken of prophetically. If 'Thou art my Son' (Ps. ii. 7) refers to the future, so also does 'By the Logos of the Lord were the heavens established' (Ps. xxxiii. 6—LXX, xxxii. 6). If the title of Ps. xlv (LXX, xliv), 'For my well-beloved' (ὑπὲρ τοῦ ἀγαπητοῦ), refers to the future, so also does the first verse of the same Psalm, 'My heart has uttered a good Logos'. If 'the only-begotten' is 'in the bosom', then the 'well-beloved' is 'in the bosom', for μονογενής is the equivalent of ἀγαπητός.[1] When Abraham is commanded, 'Offer thy son, thy well-beloved' (Gen. xxii. 2), it means 'only' son, for Isaac was the only son of Abraham from Sarah. From this argument, Ps.-Athanasius draws the conclusion:

The Logos, then, is the Son, not recently come into existence, or named Son, but always Son. For if he is not Son, neither is he Logos, and if he is not Logos, neither is he Son. For that which is from the Father is Son; and what is from the Father but the Logos which went forth from the heart (Ps. xlv. 1—LXX, xliv. 1), and was born from the womb (Ps. cx. 3—LXX, cix. 3)? For the Father is not the Logos, nor the Logos Father, but one is Father and the other Son; and one begets and the other is begotten.[2]

Having demonstrated against Marcellus the pre-existence of the Son, Ps.-Athanasius proceeds to the question of his eternity. St John, he says, proves that the Son has no beginning of being, but was ever with the Father before the incarnation, when he writes, 'That which was from the beginning, which we have heard, which we have seen with our eyes, which we have looked upon, and touched with our hands, concerning the Logos of life—the life was made manifest, and we saw it, and testify to it, and proclaim to you that eternal life which was with the Father and was made manifest to us' (I John i. 1, 2). Here St John says that 'the Life' was 'with the Father', but at the end of the epistle he says that the Son is the Life: 'And we are in him that is true, even in his Son, Jesus Christ; this is the true God and eternal life' (I John v. 20). Ps.-Athanasius comments: 'But if the Son is the Life and the Life was with the Father, and the same evangelist says, "And the Logos was with God" (John i. 1 b), the Son must be the Logos, which is ever with the Father. And as the "Son" is "Logos", so "God" must be "the

[1] See below, pp. 313 f. [2] *Or. c. Ar.* IV, 24 (*PG*, XXVI, 505).

Father".[1] Moreover, St John says that the Son is not merely God, but 'true God', for he says, 'The Logos was God' (John i. 1c), and the Son says, 'I am the Life' (John xiv. 6). Thus the Son is the Logos and the Life which is with the Father. Similarly John i. 18 shows that the Son always existed, being in the bosom of the Father.

There are plenty of references to the Son in the Old Testament, then, says Ps.-Athanasius, who goes on to ask his opponents where in the Old Testament there is any mention of the Holy Spirit as 'Paraclete'. The Holy Spirit is mentioned, but not the Paraclete. Is the Paraclete different from the Holy Spirit, then? 'No! For the Spirit is one and the same, then and now sanctifying and comforting those who receive him, just as one and the same Logos and Son even then led those who were worthy to the adoption of sons. For under the Old (Covenant) sons were made such through no other than the Son.'[2] Just as St John says concerning the Holy Spirit, 'But the Paraclete which is the Holy Spirit, whom the Father will send in my name' (John xiv. 26), identifying them and drawing no distinction between them, so also when he says, 'And the Logos became flesh and dwelt among us, and we beheld his glory, glory as of an only-begotten from the Father' (John i. 14), he is affirming the identity of the Logos and the Son, and not a distinction between them; the Logos, then, is the only-begotten Son.[3]

As he concludes this argument Ps.-Athanasius returns to the designation 'Well-beloved' (ἀγαπητός) (Ps. xlv, title—LXX, Ps. xliv; Isa. v. 1; Matt. iii. 17), which, he says, the Greeks knew to be the equivalent of 'only-begotten' (μονογενής):

For Homer speaks thus of Telemachus, who was the only-begotten of Ulysses, in the second book of the Odyssey (lines 363–6):

O'er the wise earth, dear youth, why seek to run,
An only child, a well-beloved son?
He whom you mourn, divine Ulysses, fell
Far from his country, where the strangers dwell.

Therefore, he who is the only son of his father is called 'well-beloved'.[4]

---

[1] *Ibid.* 26 (*PG*, xxvi, 508).   [2] *Ibid.* 29 (*PG*, xxvi, 513).
[3] *Idem* (*PG*, xxvi, 513).
[4] *Idem* (*PG*, xxvi, 513). Cf. Paul Winter, 'Μονογενὴς παρὰ πατρός', *ZRGG*, v (1953), 335 ff., and C. H. Turner, 'ὁ υἱός μου ὁ ἀγαπητός', *JTS*, xxvii (1926), 113 ff.

With chapter 29, Ps.-Athanasius' refutation of Marcellus ends; he then turns his attention to 'some of the followers of the Samosatene' who hold yet another view of the relation of the Logos to Jesus Christ the Son. They say that the Son is Christ, but that the Logos is another, basing this view on Peter's words in Acts x. 36, 'The Word (Logos) he sent to the children of Israel, preaching peace by Jesus Christ; he is Lord of all'. These Samosatenes say that since the Logos spoke through Jesus Christ as he did through the prophets, and the prophet was one and the Lord another, therefore Christ was one and the Logos another. Ps.-Athanasius refutes their interpretation of Acts x. 36 by referring to I Cor. i. 7, 8 and John i. 14. He says:

The Father sent the Logos made flesh (σαρκὰ γενόμενον), so that being made man, he might preach by means of himself. Therefore Peter straightway adds, 'This is the Lord of all', but the Lord of all is the Logos.[1]

Therefore it is not necessary to think that the Logos is one and Christ another, but that they were identical because of the union which took place in his divine and loving condescension and incarnation.[2]

He refers to one of the rules of exegesis which Athanasius had laid down in his refutation of the Arians, namely that we must pay attention to the scope of the teaching of scripture, which is that 'it contains a double account of the Saviour; that he was ever God, and is the Son...and that afterwards for us he took flesh of a Virgin...and was made man'.[3] Ps.-Athanasius says:

Even if he be considered in two ways, still it is without any division of the Logos, as when the inspired John says, 'And the Logos was made flesh and dwelt among us' (John i. 14). Peter's saying (Acts x. 36) means, then, that the Logos incarnate has appeared to the children of Israel, so that it may correspond to 'And the Logos became flesh'.[4]

The Samosatenes, by separating the divine Logos from the divine incarnation 'have a degraded notion of his having become flesh, and, thinking as they do, they think the thoughts of the Greeks concerning the incarnation, that it is an alteration of the divine Logos'.[5]

---

[1] *Or. c. Ar.* IV, 30 (*PG*, XXVI, 516).   [2] *Ibid.* 31 (*PG*, XXVI, 516).
[3] *Ibid.* III, 29 (*PG*, XXVI, 386).   [4] *Ibid.* IV, 31 (*PG*, XXVI, 517).
[5] *Idem.*

Ps.-Athanasius appeals to another exegetical rule which Athanasius had emphasised against the Arians, namely that we should pay attention to the 'custom' of scripture,[1] which expresses itself by 'inartificial and simple phrases':

If the Logos of God is called Wisdom and Power, etc...and if in his love for men he has become one with us, putting on our first-fruit and being blended with it, then the Logos himself has taken, as was natural, the rest of the names. For the fact that John has said that 'in the beginning was the Logos' and he with God and himself God (John i. 1), and all things through him and without him nothing made (John i. 3), shows clearly that even man is a formation of God the Logos (πλάσμα τοῦ θεοῦ λόγου).[2]

If then after he has taken to himself corrupted humanity he renews it, we cannot think of him as a prophet like the rest and say that he is a 'mere man'.[3]

As the treatise closes, Ps.-Athanasius appeals to the reader to 'consider Christ in both ways, the divine Logos, made one in Mary with him who is from Mary'.[4] Scripture often calls even the body by the name of Christ (e.g. Acts x. 38; ii. 22; xvii. 31), and the sacred writers give many names to the union of the Logos with the Man—anointing, mission, appointment. After his resurrection, the Lord said to Thomas, 'Reach hither thy hand and thrust it into my side, and reach hither thy finger and behold my hands' (John xx. 27):

Thus speaks God the Logos, speaking of his own side and hands, and of himself as at once whole man (ὅλον ἄνθρωπον) and God.[5]

He concludes the treatise with the words:

Therefore God the Logos himself is Christ from Mary, the God-Man (θεὸς ἄνθρωπος)...To him be the adoration and the worship, who was before, and now is, and ever shall be, even to all ages. Amen.[6]

It is evident from the arguments and exegesis of this treatise that the writer, like Athanasius, has grasped the significance of the two Johannine paradoxes, the unity and distinction of the Son from the Father, and the completeness of the divinity and the humanity in the incarnate Saviour. The cosmological

---

[1] *Ibid.* II, 53; III, 18, 30.
[3] *Idem.*
[5] *Ibid.* 35 (*PG*, XXVI, 521).
[2] *Ibid.* IV, 33 (*PG*, XXVI, 517 f.).
[4] *Ibid.* 34 (*PG*, XXVI, 520).
[6] *Ibid.* 36 (*PG*, XXVI, 524).

interest is overshadowed, as it is in the gospel, by the emphasis on the reality of the self-revelation of God in Jesus Christ and on the saving purpose of the incarnation. Just as Athanasius had refuted the Arians by setting forth a theology which safeguarded the two paradoxes and the faith of the church in Jesus Christ as the bearer of God's self-revelation for the salvation of men, so also Ps.-Athanasius refutes Marcellus on the basis of a Johannine theology and by Johannine exegesis. Both writers, if indeed they are two and not one, understand the mind and intention of St John in a way far superior to that of their opponents.

D. CONCLUSIONS

1. The Marcellan Controversy is the arena in which four different theological traditions come into conflict, and at the same time the meeting-place of four different methods of interpreting the Fourth Gospel:

(a) The Arians set forth a novel theology which, it appears, is the result of a fusion of elements drawn from the Alexandrian and Antiochene traditions, a theology whose starting-point is a metaphysical monotheism, in the light of which the Logos is interpreted as an attribute of God, and the Son of God is considered to be a creature, demi-god and demi-man, subordinate to the unoriginate God as being inferior, posterior and exterior to him. For them, cosmology is everything; they neglect the central Christian doctrine of salvation, while they explicitly deny the possibility of a genuine self-revelation of God in Jesus Christ. While there is little evidence on which to base a judgment on their use of St John's Gospel, the selective use of scripture as a whole points to the certainty that they selected Johannine texts which emphasised the distinction of the Son from the Father and either completely ignored or explained away those which emphasised the oneness of the Son with the Father, just as the Patripassians had selected those which had emphasised the oneness at the expense of those which emphasised the distinction, and the opponents of Novatian had emphasised those which assert the humanity of Jesus Christ at the expense of those which testify to his divinity.

(b) In opposition to the complete distinction and separation of the Son from the Father, taught by the Arians, Marcellus proclaims a doctrine which has its roots deep in biblical monotheism. Basically he interprets the Logos of the Prologue of the Fourth Gospel as the Old Testament *Word* of creation and revelation, which he makes regulative for his interpretation of the gospel as a whole and the foundation of his theological system. In this respect he stands in the old Antiochene tradition, but somehow, it seems, elements of the old Alexandrian tradition have entered his system and exert an influence on his view of the incarnation. Fundamentally, however, his system, with its strong emphasis on *Heilsgeschichte* and on the self-revelation of God, is biblical. By making the Hebraic Word-concept regulative, however, he has failed to do justice to the Johannine witness to the distinction of the Son from the Father.

(*c*) Like the Arians, whom he supported against Marcellus and the Nicene theologians, Eusebius of Caesarea emphasises the distinction of the Son from the Father and his subordination to him. In opposition both to the Arians and to Marcellus, he strives to maintain the identity of the Logos with the only-begotten Son, but like the Arians he transfers the content of the cosmological Logos-concept of the Alexandrian tradition to the Son-concept. His conception of God is fundamentally Greek; therefore, for him, the Son is a second God, a demigod, the intermediary between God and the universe for its creation, preservation and government. The function of the Son is cosmological, and in the light of this cosmological function, derived by reading into the Prologue of St John presuppositions which have come from extra-biblical sources, he interprets the Fourth Gospel as a collection of eternal truths, and not as the history of God's intervention in human history in Jesus Christ, the divine Logos who has become flesh for the salvation of men. The incarnation loses its centrality, and 'soteriology is an appendix to the doctrine of creation'.[1]

(*d*) Ps.-Athanasius, a genuine disciple of Athanasius (if he is not Athanasius himself) concentrates his attention on soteriology. The biblical Son-concept is regulative; the Logos is God from God, the Logos is the only-begotten Son of God, and Jesus Christ is the Logos. The subject of the Prologue of St John is the same as the subject of the rest of the gospel: Jesus Christ, the Son of God. He emphasises equally the unity of the Son with

---

[1] Berkhof, *Eusebius von Caesarea*, p. 79.

the Father and his distinction from him, and at the same time the completeness of both the divinity and the humanity of Jesus Christ. By emphasising the unity of Father and Son he avoids the errors of Arianism and extreme Origenism; by emphasising the distinction of the Son from the Father within the one godhead, he avoids the errors of Sabellianism and Marcellanism. By emphasising the divinity of Jesus Christ, he avoids the errors of humanitarian monarchianism and adoptionism; by emphasising the completeness of the humanity, he avoids the errors of docetism and Apollinarianism. In the theology of Ps.-Athanasius, as in that of Athanasius himself, the common faith of the church finds its theological expression, a faith in which the knowledge that God has acted in Jesus Christ for the salvation of mankind is central and regulative for every thought concerning his relation to the godhead on the one hand, and to humanity on the other. In Ps.-Athanasius, and in Athanasius, the common faith of the Christian church of Alexandria meets the common faith of the church in the West, which had already, a century before, found its theological expression in the writings of Tertullian and Novatian. The Nicene Creed is the meeting-place of the common faith of Christians in the churches of East and West, a faith which finds its clearest scriptural expression in the Johannine portrait of Jesus Christ, the only-begotten Son of God.

2. In the Arian and Marcellan controversies, the inadequacy of the Logos-concept, however it be interpreted, as the basis for Christian thinking about Jesus Christ is revealed. To the Antiochene tradition which, in Marcellus of Ancyra, made the Word-concept regulative, Eusebius of Caesarea opposes the Greek philosophical Logos-concept, which he had inherited from the Alexandrian tradition of Clement and Origen, a concept which leads him ultimately very close to tritheism. Neither concept is adequate as a theological expression of Christian faith in God the Father and in Jesus Christ his Son our Saviour. Jesus Christ is the focal point of Christian thinking about God, and it is in the light of the historical fact of Christ that monotheism must be interpreted, not in the light of a Hebraic Word-concept or a Greek Logos-concept. Christianity may be 'debtor both to Greeks and to Jews' (Rom. i. 14), but its centre is 'Christ crucified, a stumbling-block to Jews and folly to Gen-

tiles' (I Cor. i. 23). Thus the Marcellan controversy is the battleground between a soteriological theology on the one hand, and attempts to interpret Jesus Christ according to the categories of late-Hellenistic philosophy and ancient Hebraic theology on the other.

3. In the Marcellan controversy the inadequacy of the old christological *schemata*, *Logos–sarx* and *Word–Man*, is made manifest; in opposition to both, Ps.-Athanasius, perhaps more clearly than Athanasius himself, puts forward a *God–Man* schema which was to be enshrined in the christological formula of the Council of Chalcedon in A.D. 451.

4. It was St John's Gospel, with the Logos-concept of the Prologue, which opened the way for the misinterpretations of the Christian message as a Word-theology and as a Logos-theology. It was, however, the same gospel that also provided the basis for the refutation of both these misinterpretations and for the establishment of a theology in which Jesus Christ is central as the Son of God who became man for us men and our salvation.

5. The question at stake in the Marcellan controversy, as well as in the Arian controversy, was which of the three mediatorial functions emphasised in St John's Gospel—creative, revelational or soteriological—is the key to understanding the person of Jesus Christ, and therewith his relation to God the Father on the one hand, and to mankind on the other. Both revelation and creation are proved to be false perspectives which give only a partial and distorted view of the truth about Jesus Christ; only from the perspective of salvation can the church's faith in and the New Testament's witness to Jesus Christ as the Lord and Saviour of men be comprehended. When Jesus Christ is approached from this point of view, the other functions of the Son of God—revelation and creation—are seen in their proper perspective, the perspective in which St John intended them to be seen in his Gospel:

THESE THINGS ARE WRITTEN THAT YOU MAY BELIEVE THAT JESUS IS THE CHRIST, THE SON OF GOD, AND THAT BELIEVING, YOU MAY HAVE LIFE IN HIS NAME.

APPENDIX

The word Homoousios

The history of the word ὁμοούσιος has been set out by J. F. Bethune-Baker, G. L. Prestige, J. N. D. Kelly, and A. d'Alès, among others.[1] It is certain that at the Nicene Council itself, some, notably Eusebius of Caesarea, hesitated to accept this word, and that after the Council a reaction set in against it. It has been widely assumed that one of the main reasons for the reaction was the word's connection with Sabellianism. R. L. Ottley, for example, says that 'one consideration which caused the *Homoousion* to be accepted with great reluctance was the fact that it had been condemned at Antioch (269), as a phrase capable of Sabellian connotation'.[2] This view ignores two important facts:

(*a*) the condemnation of the term ὁμοούσιος by the Origenist bishops at Antioch in 269 was completely forgotten until 358 when Basil of Caesarea and the Homoiousians raised it as an objection to the Nicene formula. Eusebius of Caesarea, who had every reason to object to this term, knows nothing of its rejection at Antioch, or he would most certainly have used it as an objection. In the ante-Nicene stage of the controversy Arius objected to the term, not because of its association with Sabellius or Paul of Samosata, but because of its use by the Manichees who asserted that 'the offspring was a co-essential part of the Father' (μέρος ὁμοούσιον τοῦ πατρὸς τὸ γέννημα (*Urk*. 6); Eusebius of Nicomedia denied that the Son is 'derived from the essence of the Father' (ἐκ τῆς οὐσίας αὐτοῦ γεγονός, *Urk*. 8), and scorned the word ὁμοούσιος 'in the memorandum, now lost, which (if we are justified in linking together a reminiscence of Eustathius of Antioch and a story told by St Ambrose) was read out and torn to shreds at the Council. His actual words are reported to have been, "If we describe him as true Son of God and increate, we are beginning to say he is homoousios with the Father".[3] Before the Council met at Nicaea the Arians had made known their objection to the word, but never do they associate it with Sabellianism which was, for them, the heresy *par excellence*.

[1] Bethune-Baker, *The Meaning of Homoousios in the Constantinopolitan Creed* (*TS*, O.S. VII, 1); Prestige, *God in Patristic Thought*, ch. x; Kelly, *Early Christian Creeds*, pp. 242 ff.; d'Alès, *Le dogme de Nicée*, ch. I.

[2] *Doctrine of the Incarnation*, p. 327.

[3] Kelly, *Early Christian Creeds*, p. 249.

Eusebius of Caesarea was afraid of the term because of the suggestion which it bore that the essence of the Father was divisible, an idea which has no connection with Sabellianism.

(b) The term ὁμοούσιος and its Latin equivalent, *consubstantialis*, were in orthodox use in the Western Church before it was associated with the name of Paul of Samosata by the Synod of Antioch (269). Several years before Paul's use of the word was condemned, Dionysius of Alexandria was taken to task by his Roman namesake for not using it. He replied that his hesitation concerning the word was due to the fact that it was unscriptural, but that he accepted the doctrine implied by the word (*apud* Athanasius, *de Sent. Dion.* 18). The memory of the correspondence between the two Dionysii 'remained at Alexandria during the following fifty years and prepared the way for the acceptance of the Western doctrine at Nicaea'.[1] Some opponent of Arius must have used the term against him in the early stages of the controversy; otherwise Arius would have no reason to express his objection to it as savouring of Manichaean teaching. It is unlikely that this opponent was from the West, and up to the time when Arius raised this objection the controversy had, as far as we know, been confined to the quarrel between Alexander and Arius, and to the letters which Collucianists had written to each other in support of Arius' opinions. It seems then that the term had already been used by an opponent at this early stage. Dionysius 'the Great' when pressed, had been willing to use the term;[2] it must be remembered that he was combating Sabellianism, and if the word had any Sabellian associations he would surely have mentioned the fact, which he does not.

The myth of the Sabellian associations of the word ὁμοούσιος probably arose from the fact that the most common charge levelled against the defenders of the Nicene definition by their Arian opponents was that of Sabellianism. Both Eustathius of Antioch and Marcellus of Ancyra were deposed on the grounds that they were Sabellian, and it is possible that their opponents argued that the term ὁμοούσιος, interpreted as they had interpreted it, smacked of Sabellianism.[3] Yet Athanasius asserted the identity of the Son's

---

[1] Bethune-Baker, *The Meaning of Homoousios*, p. 24.

[2] Kelly (*Early Christian Doctrines*, p. 130) draws attention to one 'trinitarian' occurrence of the word in a Latin translation of Origen (*Frag. in Hebr.* (*PG*, XIV, 1308)), where the Greek word is left untranslated. Kelly comments, 'Whether or not the term ὁμοούσιος is original in this passage (there seems to be no cogent reason why it should not be), the idea expressed is authentically Origenist'.

[3] Socrates (*Hist. Eccl.* i. 23): 'Those who objected to the word ὁμοούσιος, conceived that those who approved it favoured the opinion of Sabellius

essence with that of the Father just as strongly as Marcellus did, and Sabellianism was one of the few things of which he was never accused. The fact that Athanasius uses the word only once in his *Orations against the Arians* (i, 9) does not point to any dislike for the word on the part of Athanasius, but rather to his diplomacy in avoiding the word which was suspected by some, while strongly maintaining the doctrine which the term was introduced to safeguard.

The objection to the word in the church after the Council of Nicaea was not due to its association with Sabellianism. The only objection of which there is any evidence at all during the thirty-three years between the Council of Nicaea and the rediscovery of the fact that the Synod of Antioch (269) had condemned the word, the fact that it was unscriptural,[1] and the whole tenor of Athanasius' refutation of the Arians in the *Orations* show that he is attempting to prove that the doctrine which the word testifies is scriptural even if the word itself is not.

and Montanus.' Against this general statement of Socrates, however, may be cited the fact that in his lengthy refutation of Marcellus (*contra Marcellum* and *de Ecclesiastica Theologia*) Eusebius, while accusing Marcellus of Sabellianism, never quotes any passage where Marcellus uses the word, nor himself argues against the word.

[1] But see preceding note.

BIBLIOGRAPHY

A. ANCIENT TEXTS AND TRANSLATIONS

NOTE. The translations listed have been referred to but not strictly followed in quotations.

Ignatius of Antioch
Text: *Ignace d'Antioche: Lettres*, ed. T. Camelot (*SC*, 10).
Translation: *Early Christian Fathers*, tr. C. C. Richardson (*LCC*, 1).

Odes of Solomon
Translation: J. R. Harris & A. Mingana, *The Odes and Psalms of Solomon*, Manchester, 1920.

Melito of Sardis
Text and translation: C. Bonner, *The Homily on the Passion of Melito of Sardis* (*SD*, 13), 1940.

Theophilus of Antioch
Text: G. Bardy, *Théophile: Trois livres à Autolycus* (*SC*, 20).
Translation: M. Dods, *ANCL*, 3.

Justin Martyr
Text: Migne, *PG*, VI.
Translation: *Apology I*: E. R. Hardy, *Early Christian Fathers* (*LCC*, 1).
 Apology II: M. Dods, *ANCL*, 2.
 Dialogue with Trypho: G. Reith, *ANCL*, 2.

Irenaeus of Lyons
adversus Haereses: Text: W. Harvey, 2 vols.
 Translation: A. Roberts & W. H. Rambaut, *ANCL*, 5 & 9.
Demonstration of the Apostolic Preaching:
Translations: J. A. Robinson, *TCL*, 38; L. M. Froidevaux, *SC*, 62 (French); J. P. Smith, *ACW*.

Hippolytus of Rome
Text: P. A. Lagarde, *Hippolyti Romani quae feruntur omnia graece*, 1858.
 P. Nautin, *Hippolyte: Contre les Hérésies*, Paris, 1949.
Translation: J. H. Macmahon, *ANCL*, 6 & 9.

Tertullian
Text and translation: E. Evans, *Tertullian's Treatise against Praxeas*, London, 1948.

Novatian
Text: W. Yorke Fausset (*CPT*), 1909.
Translation: H. Moore, *TCL*, 1919.
Clement of Alexandria
Text: O. Stählin, *Clemens Alexandrinus Werke*, 4 vols, *GCS*.
Text and translation: *Protrepticus* and *Quis dives salvetur?*, G. W.
Butterworth, *LCL*.
        Stromateis, VII, F. J. A. Hort and J. B.
Mayor, 1902.
        Excerpta ex Theodoto, R. P. Casey, *SD*, 1934;
F. M. Sagnard, *SC*, 23. (with French tr.)
Translation: *Protrepticus, Paedagogus* and *Stromateis*, W. Wilson,
ANCL, 2 vols. 1909.
Origen
contra Celsum: Text: P. Koetschau, *GCS*, I–II.
        Translation, H. Chadwick, Cambridge, 1955.
Commentary on St John: Text: E. Preuschen, *GCS*, IV.
        Translation: Books I–X, A. Menzies, *ANCL*,
additional volume.
de Principiis: Text: P. Koetschau, *GCS*, V.
        Translation: H. Butterworth, *Origen on First Principles*, London, 1936.
Dialogue with Heraclides: Text: J. Scherer, *SC*, 67.
        Translation: H. Chadwick, *Alexandrian
Christianity* (*LCC*, 2).
Dionysius of Alexandria
Text: C. L. Feltoe, *The Letters and other Remains of Dionysius of
Alexandria* (*CPT*), 1904.
Translation: C. L. Feltoe, *Selection from the Writings of Dionysius of
Alexandria* (*TCL*), 1918.
Theognostus
Text: Routh, *Reliquiae Sacrae*, III, 407–14.
Pierius
Text: Routh, *Reliquiae Sacrae*, III, 425–31.
Peter of Alexandria
Text: Routh, *Reliquiae Sacrae*, IV, 21–51.
Eusebius of Caesarea
Historia Ecclesiastica: Text and translation: K. Lake and J. E. L.
Oulton, *LCL*, 2 vols.
Preparatio Evangelica: Text: K. Mras, *GCS*, VIII.
        Translation: E. H. Gifford, 2 vols, Oxford,
1903.
Demonstratio Evangelica: Text: I. A. Heikel, *GCS*, VI.
        Translation: W. J. Ferrar, *TCL*, 2 vols.

contra Marcellum and *de Ecclesiastica Theologia*: Text: E. Klostermann, *GCS*, IV.

Theophaneia: Translation: S. Lee, London, 1832.

Documents from the Early Stages of the Arian Controversy

H. G. Opitz, *Athanasius Werke*, Band III, Teil 2: *Urkunde zur Geschichte des arianischen Streites*.

Athanasius

Text: Migne, *PG*, XXVI.

Translation: A. Robertson, *St Athanasius* (*NPNF*, 4).

    C. R. B. Shapland, *The Letters of Athanasius concerning the Holy Spirit*, London, 1951.

B. BOOKS

Altaner, B. *Patrologie: Leben, Schriften und Lehre der Kirchenväter*, 3rd edn. Freiburg, 1951.

Armstrong, A. H. (ed.) *The Cambridge History of Later Greek and Early Medieval Philosophy*, Cambridge, 1967.

Armstrong, A. H. & Markus, R. A. *Christian Faith and Greek Philosophy*, London, 1960.

Barbel, J. *Christos Angelos*, Bonn, 1941.

Bardy, G. *Saint Athanase*, Paris, 1916.

Paul de Samosate (*Spicilegium Sacrum Lovaniense: Études et Documents*, Fasc. 4), Louvain, 1923.

Recherches sur saint Lucien d'Antioche et son école, Paris, 1936.

Trois Livres à Autolycus (*SC*, xx), Paris, 1948.

Barnard, K. W. *Studies in the Apostolic Fathers and their Background*, Oxford, 1966.

Justin Martyr: his Life and Thought, Cambridge, 1967.

Barrett, C. K. *The Gospel according to St John*, London, 1955.

Bell, H. I. *Jews and Christians in Egypt*, London, 1924.

Cults and Creeds in Graeco-Roman Egypt, Liverpool, 1953.

Benoit, A. *Saint Irénée. Introduction à l'étude de sa théologie*, Paris, 1960.

Berkhof, H. *Die Theologie des Eusebius von Caesarea*, Amsterdam, 1939.

Bernard, R. *L'image de Dieu d'après saint Athanase*, Paris, 1952.

Bethune-Baker, J. F. *An Introduction to the Early History of Christian Doctrine*, London, 1903.

The Meaning of Homoousios in the Constantinopolitan Creed, (*TS*), Cambridge, 1901.

Bianchi, U. *Le Origini dello Gnosticismo* (*Studies in the History of Religions*, *Numen* Supplement XII), Leiden, 1967.

Bigg, C. *The Christian Platonists of Alexandria*, Oxford, 1913.

Boismard, M. E. *St John's Prologue*, London, 1957.

Boman, T. *Hebrew Thought compared with Greek*, London, 1960.

Bonnard, P. *La Sagesse en Personne, annoncée et venue: Jésus-Christ*, Paris, 1966.

Bouyer, L. *L'incarnation et l'église-corps du Christ dans la théologie de saint Athanase*, Paris, 1943.

Braun, F. M. *Jean le théologien*. Vol. I. *Son évangile dans l'église ancienne*, Paris, 1959. Vol. II. *Les grandes traditions d'Israël: l'accord des Écritures d'après le quatrième évangile*, Paris, 1964. Vol. III. *Sa Théologie: le mystère de Jésus-Christ*, Paris, 1966.

Bright, W. *The Canons of the First Four General Councils*, 2nd edn, Oxford, 1892.

Brown, R. E. *New Testament Essays*, London, 1965.
The Gospel according to St John (Anchor Bible), vol. I, New York, 1966.

Bultmann, R. *Theology of the New Testament*, 2 vols. (E. Tr.), London, 1952–5.
Das Evangelium des Johannes, Göttingen, 1941.

Burn, A. E. *The Council of Nicaea*, London, 1925.

Burney, C. F. *The Aramaic Origin of the Fourth Gospel*, Oxford, 1922.

Burrows, M. *The Dead Sea Scrolls*, London, 1955.
More Light on the Dead Sea Scrolls, London, 1958.

Campenhausen, H. von. *The Fathers of the Greek Church* (E. Tr.), New York, 1959.
The Fathers of the Latin Church (E. Tr.), New York, 1964.

Cadiou, R. *La jeunesse d'Origène: Histoire de l'école d'Alexandrie au début du IIIᵉ siècle*, Paris, 1935.

Cavallera, F. *Saint Athanase*, Paris, 1908.

Chadwick, H. *Early Christian Thought and the Classical Tradition*, Oxford, 1966.
The Early Church, London, 1967.

Cornford, F. M. *Plato's Cosmology*, London, 1937.

Corwin, V. *St Ignatius and Christianity in Antioch*, Yale, 1960.

Cross, F. L. *The Study of St Athanasius*, Oxford, 1945.
The Early Christian Fathers, London, 1960.
(ed.) *The Jung Codex*, London, 1955.

Crouzel, H. *Théologie de l'image de Dieu chez Origène*, Paris, 1956.

Cullmann, O. *Christology of the New Testament*, London, 1959.

D'Alès, A. *Le dogme de Nicée*, Paris, 1926.
Novatien. Étude sur la théologie romain au milieu du IIIᵉ siècle, Paris, 1925.

Daniélou, J. *Origène*, Paris, 1948 (E. Tr.), London, 1955.
The Theology of Jewish Christianity, London, 1964.
Message évangelique et culture hellénistique aux IIᵉ et IIIᵉ siècles, Paris, 1961.

Davey, J. E. *The Jesus of St John*, London, 1958.
Davies, W. D. & Daube, D. (eds.). *The Background of the New Testament and its Eschatology*, Cambridge, 1956.
Dodd, C. H. *The Interpretation of the Fourth Gospel*, Cambridge, 1953.
Historical Tradition and the Fourth Gospel, Cambridge, 1963.
New Testament Studies, Manchester, 1953.
Doresse, J. *The Secret Books of the Egyptian Gnostics* (E. Tr.), London, 1960.
Dorner, J. A. *History of the Development of the Doctrine of the Person of Christ* (E. Tr.), 5 vols. Edinburgh, 1878.
Drummond, J. *Philo Judaeus: or the Jewish Alexandrian Philosophy in its Development and Completion*, 2 vols. London, 1888.
Eynde, D. van den. *Les normes de l'enseignement chrétien dans la littérature patristique des trois premiers siècles*, Gembloux, 1933.
Farrar, F. W. *History of Interpretation*, London, 1886.
Faye, E. de. *Clément d'Alexandrie: Étude sur les rapports du christianisme et de la philosophie grecque au IIe siècle*, Paris, 1898.
Esquisse de la pensée d'Origène, Paris, 1925.
Origène: sa vie, son œuvre, sa pensée, 3 vols. Paris, 1923–8.
Fleeseman-Van Leer, E. *Tradition and Scripture in the Early Church*, Leiden, 1953.
Gericke, W. *Marcell von Ancyra, der Logos-Christologe und Biblizist: sein Verhältnis zur antiochenischen Theologie und zum Neuen Testament*, Halle, 1940.
Grillmeier, A. *Christ in Christian Tradition*, London, 1965.
Grillmeier, A. & Bacht, H. *Das Konzil von Chalkedon*, 3 vols. Würzburg, 1951–4.
Grobel, K. *The Gospel of Truth*, London, 1960.
Gwatkin, H. M. *Studies in Arianism*, 2nd edn, Cambridge, 1900.
Hanson, R. P. C. *Origen's Doctrine of Tradition*, London, 1954.
Allegory and Event. A Study of the Sources and Significance of Origen's Interpretation of Scripture, London, 1959.
Tradition in the Early Church, London, 1962.
Hardy, E. R. *Christian Egypt*, New York, 1952.
Harris, J. Rendell. *The Origin of the Prologue to St John's Gospel*, Cambridge, 1917.
Hautsch, E. *Die Evangelienzitate des Origenes* (*TU*, 34), Leipzig, 1910.
Hort, F. J. A. *Two Dissertations*, London, 1876.
Hoskyns, E. *The Fourth Gospel*, London, 1956.
Houssiau, A. *La christologie de saint Irénée*, Louvain, 1955.
Howard, W. F. *The Fourth Gospel in Recent Criticism* (4th edn, revised by C. K. Barrett), London, 1955.
Ivanka, E. von. *Hellenisches und christliches im frühbyzantinischen Geistesleben*, Vienna, 1948.

Kaye, J. *Clement of Alexandria*, London, n.d.

Kelly, J. N. D. *Early Christian Creeds*, London, 1940.

Early Christian Doctrines, 4th edn, London, 1968.

Kennedy, H. A. A. *Philo's Contribution to Religion*, London, 1919.

Klassen, W. & Snyder, G. F. (eds.). *Current Issues in New Testament Interpretation*, London, 1962.

Knight, G. A. F. *A Biblical Approach to the Doctrine of the Trinity*, (*SJT* Occasional Paper 1), Edinburgh, 1953.

Knox, J. *The Humanity and Divinity of Christ*, Cambridge, 1967.

Laeuchli, S. *The Language of Faith*, New York, 1962.

The Serpent and the Dove, New York, 1966.

Lawson, J. *The Biblical Theology of St Irenaeus*, London, 1948.

Liébaert, J. *L'incarnation*. 1. *Dès origines au Concile de Chalcédoine*, Paris, 1966.

Little, V. A. S. *The Christology of the Apologists*, London, 1934.

Loewenich, W. von. *Das Johannesverständnis im zweiten Jahrhunderte*, (*ZNTW*, Beiheft 13), Giessen, 1932.

Lofthouse, W. F. *The Father and the Son: A Study in Johannine Thought*, London, 1934.

Loofs, F. *Leitfaden zum Studium der Dogmengeschichte* (5th edn, revised by Kurt Aland), Halle, 1951.

Paulus von Samosata (*TU*, 44, 5), Leipzig, 1924.

Theophilus von Antiochien adversus Marcionem (*TU*, 46, 2), 1930.

Luneau, A. *L'histoire du salut chez les Pères de l'Église*, Paris, 1964.

Manson, T. W. *Studies in the Gospels and Epistles*, Manchester, 1962.

On Paul and John (*SBT*), London, 1963.

Manson, W. *The Incarnate Glory*, Edinburgh, 1923.

Marsh, H. *Criticism and Interpretation of the Bible*, London, 1838.

Menoud, P. H. *L'évangile de Jean d'après recherches récentes*, Neuchâtel and Paris, 1947.

Milburn, R. L. P. *Early Christian Interpretations of History*, London, 1954.

Molland, E. *The Conception of the Gospel in the Alexandrian Theology*, Oslo, 1938.

Mondésert, C. *Clément d'Alexandrie: Introduction à l'étude de sa pensée religieuse à partir de l'écriture*, Paris, 1944.

Mussner, F. *The Historical Jesus in the Gospel of St John*, London, 1967.

Nautin, P. *Hippolyte: Contre les Hérésies, Fragment, étude et édition critique*, Paris, 1949.

Le dossier d'Hippolyte et de Méliton dans les florilèges dogmatiques et chez les historiens modernes, Paris, 1953.

Lettres et écrivains chrétiens des IIe et IIIe siècles, Paris, 1961.

Newman, J. H. *The Arians of the Fourth Century*, 6th edn, London, 1890.

Opitz, G. H. *Untersuchungen zur Überlieferung der Schriften des Athanasius*, Berlin, 1935.

Orbe, A. *En los albores de la exegesis Iohannea (Ioh. i. 3) (Estudios Valentinianios*, II), Rome, 1955.

Patterson, L. G. *God and History in Early Christian Thought*, London, 1967.

Prat, F. *Origène: le théologien et l'exégète*, Paris, 1907.

Prestige, G. L. *God in Patristic Thought*, London, 1952.

Fathers and Heretics, London, 1940.

Puech, A. *Histoire de la littérature grecque chrétienne depuis les origines jusqu'à fin du IVe siècle*, 3 vols. Paris, 1930.

Quasten, J. *Patrology*, 3 vols, Utrecht and Brussels, 1951–60.

Radford, L. B. *Three Teachers of Alexandria: Theognostus, Pierius and Peter*, Cambridge, 1908.

Raven, C. E. *Apollinarianism*, Cambridge, 1923.

Rawlinson, A. E. J. (ed.). *Essays on the Trinity and Incarnation*, London, 1933.

Riedmatten, H. de. *Les actes du procès de Paul de Samosate: étude sur la christologie du IIIe au IVe siècle*, Freiburg, 1952.

Ritschl, D. *Athanasius: Versuch einer Interpretation*, Zürich, 1964.

Robinson, J. A. T. *Twelve New Testament Studies (SBT)*, London, 1962.

Sanders, J. N. *The Fourth Gospel in the Early Church*, Cambridge, 1943.

Schwartz, E. *Zur Geschichte des Athanasius (Gesammelte Schriften*, vol. III), Berlin, 1959.

Sellers, R. V. *Eustathius of Antioch and his Place in the Early History of Christian Doctrine*, Cambridge, 1928.

Two Ancient Christologies, London, 1940.

Simon, M. *Verus Israel: étude sur les relations entre Chrétiens et Juifs dans l'Empire Romain (135–425)*, Paris, 1948.

Simonetti, M. *Studi sull'Arianesimo*, Rome, 1965.

Smulders, P. *La doctrine trinitaire de saint Hilaire de Poitiers*, Rome, 1944.

Spanneut, M. *Recherches sur les écrits d'Eustathe d'Antioche*, Lille, 1948.

Stendahl, K. (ed.). *The Scrolls and the New Testament*, New York, 1957.

Stevenson, J. *Studies in Eusebius*, Cambridge, 1929.

Tixeront, J. *Mélanges de patrologie et d'histoire des dogmes*, Paris, 1921.

Tollinton, R. B. *Selections from the Commentaries and Homilies of Origen (TCL)*, London, 1929.

Clement of Alexandria, 2 vols. London, 1914.

Turner, H. E. W. *The Patristic Doctrine of Redemption*, London, 1952.

The Pattern of Christian Truth, London, 1954.

Vermes, G. *The Dead Sea Scrolls in English*, London, 1962.

Warfield, B. B. *Studies in Tertullian and Augustine*, New York, 1930.

Weber, A. APXH: *ein Beitrag zur Christologie des Eusebius von Cäsarea*, Rome, 1965.

Wiles, M. F. *The Spiritual Gospel: the Interpretation of the Fourth Gospel in the Early Church*, Cambridge, 1960.

The Christian Fathers, London, 1966.

The Making of Christian Doctrine, Cambridge, 1967.

The Divine Apostle: the Interpretation of St Paul's Epistles in the Early Church, Cambridge, 1967.

Wilson, R. McL. *The Gnostic Problem*, Oxford, 1958.

Gnosis and the New Testament, London, 1968.

Wingren, G. *Man and the Incarnation: a Study in the Biblical Theology of Irenaeus*, Edinburgh and London. 1959.

Wolfson, H. A. *Philo: Foundations of Religious Philosophy in Judaism, Christianity and Islam*, 2 vols. Harvard, 1947.

The Philosophy of the Church Fathers, 2nd edn, Harvard, 1964.

C. ARTICLES

Albright, W. F. 'Recent Discoveries in Palestine and the Gospel of John', *The Background of the New Testament and its Eschatology* (ed. W. D. Davies & D. Daube), Cambridge, 1956, pp. 153 ff.

Andresen, C. 'Justin und die mittlere Platonismus', *ZNTW*, XLIV (1952–3), 157 ff.

Arnou, R. 'Arius et la doctrine des relations trinitaires', *Greg*, XIV (1938), 270 ff.

'Unité numérique et unité de nature chez les Pères après le Concile de Nicée', *Greg*, XV (1934), 242 ff.

Bardy, G. 'Pour l'histoire de l'école d'Alexandrie', *Vivre et Penser* (*RB*), 2nd series (1942), pp. 86 ff.

'Interprétation chez les Pères', *DB* (Supp.), IV, cols. 569 ff.

'La Thalie d'Arius', *RPh*, LIII (1927), 211 ff.

'Asterius le sophiste', *RHE*, XXII (1926), 221 ff.

'Origène', *DTC*, XI, cols. 1489 ff.

'La théologie d'Eusèbe de Césarée d'après l'Histoire Ecclésiastique', *RHE*, L (1955), 5 ff.

Barnes, W. 'Arius and Arianism', *ExpT*, XLVI (1934), 18 ff.

'Athanasius', *ERE*, II.

Behm, J. 'Der gegenwärtige Stand der Erforschung des Johannesevangeliums', *TLZ*, LXXIII (1948), 22 ff.

Berchem, J. B. 'Le rôle du Verbe dans l'œuvre de la création et de la sanctification d'après saint Athanase', *Ang*, XV (1938), 201 ff.

'Le Christ Sanctificateur d'après saint Athanase', *Ang*, XV (1938), 515 ff.

Black, M. 'Theological Conceptions in the Dead Sea Scrolls', *SEÅ*, xvii–xix (1953–4), 80 ff.

Boer, W. den. 'Hermeneutic Problems in Early Christian Literature', *VC*, i (1947), 150 ff.

Bouyer, L. 'The Fathers of the Church on Tradition and Scripture', *ECQ*, vii (Supp.) (1947), i ff.

Braun, F. M. 'L'arrière-fond judaïque du quatrième évangile et la Communauté d'Alliance', *RB*, lxi (1955), 5 ff.

Bright, W. 'Alexander of Alexandria', *DCB*, i, 79–82.

'Athanasius', *DCB*, i, 179–203.

Brown, R. E. 'After Bultmann, What?', *CBQ*, xxvi (1964), 1–30.

'The Problem of Historicity in John', *CBQ* xxiv (1962), 1–14 (= *New Testament Essays*, London, 1965, ch. ix).

'How much did Jesus know?', *CBQ*, xxix (1967), 315–45.

'The Qumran Scrolls and the Johannine Gospel and Epistles', *CBQ*, xvii (1955), 559 ff. (= *The Scrolls and the New Testament*, (ed. K. Stendahl), New York, 1957, pp. 183 ff.).

'Second Thoughts: the Dead Sea Scrolls and the New Testament', *ExpT*, lxxviii (1966–7), 21 ff.

'Does the New Testament call Jesus God?', *ThS*, xxvi (1965), 545 ff.

Brownlee, W. H. 'A Comparison of the Covenanters of the Dead Sea Scrolls with pre-Christian Jewish Sects', *BA*, xiii (1950), 71ff.

Casey, R. P. 'Clement and the Two Divine Logoi', *JTS*, xxv (1923), 43 ff.

Clavier, H. 'Mediation in the Fourth Gospel', *BullSNTS*, i (1950), 11 ff.

Conybeare, F. C. 'The Authorship of the *contra Marcellum*', *ZNTW*, iv (1903), 330 ff; vi (1905), 250 ff.

Cross, F. L. 'The Council of Antioch in 325 A.D.', *CQR*, cxxviii (1939), 49 ff.

Crouzel, H. 'L'anthropologie d'Origène dans la perspective du combat spirituel', *RAM*, xxxi (1955), pp. i ff.

Cullmann, O. 'The Significance of the Qumran Texts for Research into the Beginnings of Christianity', *JBL*, lxxiv (1955), 213 ff.(= *The Scrolls and the New Testament* (ed. K. Stendahl), New York, 1957, ch. ii).

Daniélou, J. 'Les divers sens de l'Écriture dans la tradition chrétienne primitive', *Analecta Lovaniensa Biblica et Orientalia*, ii, fasc. 6.

'The Fathers and the Scriptures', *Theology*, March 1954.

Davies, W. D. ' "Knowledge" in the Dead Sea Scrolls and Matt. xi. 25–30', *HTR*, xlvi (1953), 113 ff.

Dodd, C. H. 'A New Gospel', *BJRL*, xx (1936), 56 ff. (= *New Testament Studies*, Manchester, 1953, ch. 2).

Dodd, C .H. (*cont.*)
'The Background of the Fourth Gospel', *BJRL*, xix (1935), 329 ff.

Dupont-Somner, J. 'Le problème des influences étrangères sur la secte juive à Qumran', *RHPR*, xxxv (1955), 75 ff.

Filson, F. V. 'The Gospel of Life', *Current Issues in New Testament Interpretation* (ed. W. Klassen & G. N. Snyder), London, 1962, pp. 111 ff.

Foakes-Jackson, F. J. 'Arianism', *ERE*, i, 775 ff.

Fritz, G. 'Nicée', *DTC*, xi.
'Origènisme', *DTC*, xi.

Gaudel, A. 'La théologie du Logos chez saint Athanase', *RevSR*, ix (1929), 524–39, and xi (1931), 1–26.

Grant, R. M. 'The Odes of Solomon and the Church of Antioch', *JBL*, lxiii (1944), 363 ff.

Grossouw, W. 'The Dead Sea Scrolls and the New Testament: a Preliminary Survey', *StC*, xxvi (1951), 289 ff.; xxvii (1952), 1 ff.

Guillet, J. 'Les exégèses d'Alexandrie et d'Antioche, conflit ou malentendu?', *RechSR*, xxxiv (1947), 257 ff.

Hall, S. G. 'Melito's Paschal Homily and the *Acts of John*', *JTS*, N.S. xvii (1966), 95 ff.

Holte, R. 'Logos Spermatikos: Christianity and Ancient Philosophy in St Justin's Apologies', *ST*, xii (1958), 109–68.

Hunter, A. M. 'Recent Trends in Johanine Studies', *ExpT*, lxxi (1959–60), 164 ff.

Kannengiesser, C. 'Le témoinage des *Lettres Festales* de saint Athanase sur la date de l'Apologie *contre les Paiens, sur l'Incarnation du Verbe*', *RechSR* lii (1964), 91 ff.

Kraeling, C. J. 'The Jewish Community in Antioch', *JBL*, liv (1932), 138 ff.

Kuhn, K. G. 'Johannesevangelium und Qumrantexte', *Neotestamentica et Patristica* (Supp. to *NovT*, vi), 111 ff.
'Die in Palästina gefundenen hebräischen Texte und das Neue Testament', *ZTK*, xlvii (1950), 192 ff.

Laeuchli, S. 'The Polarity of the Gospels in the Exegesis of Origen', *CH*, xxi (1952), 215 ff.
'The Case of Athanasius against Arius', *CTM*, xxx (1959), 416 ff.

Lamarche, P. 'Le prologue de Jean', *RechSR*, lii (1964), 497 ff.

Lawlor, H. J. 'The Sayings of Paul of Samosata', *JTS*, xix (1918), 20 ff., 115 ff.

Lebreton, J. 'Le désaccord de la foi populaire et de théologie savante dans l'église chrétienne du IIIe siècle', *RHE*, xix (1923), 481 ff.

Leenhardt, F. L. 'La signification de la notion de Parole dans la pensée chrétienne', *RHPR*, xxxv (1955), 263 ff.

Loofs, F. 'Die Trinitätslehre von Marcellus von Ancyre und ihr Verhältniss zur älteren Tradition', *SAB*, 1902, 764 ff.

'Marcellus von Ancyre', *RE*, xxvi, 64 ff.

'Eustathius von Antioche', *RE*, xxiii, 437 f.

'Arianismus', *RE*, xxiii, 113 ff.

'Athanasius', *RE*, xxiii, 126 ff.

Lowry, C. W. 'Origen as Trinitarian', *JTS*, xxxvii (1936), 225 ff.

'Did Origen style the Son a Ktisma?', *JTS*, xxxix (1938), 39 ff.

Macnicol, J. D. A. 'Word and Deed in the New Testament', *SJT*, v (1952), 237 ff.

Manson, T. W. 'The Life of Jesus: A Survey of the Available Materials. (5) The Fourth Gospel', *BJRL*, xxx (1946–7) (= *Studies in the Gospels and Epistles*, Manchester, 1962, ch. 6).

Markus, R. A. 'Trinitarian Theology and the Economy', *JTS*, N.S. ix (1958), 89 ff.

Moody, D. ' "God's Only Son": the Translation of John iii. 16 in the R.S.V.', *JBL*, lxxii (1953), 213 ff.

Mowry, L. 'The Dead Sea Scrolls and the Background for the Gospel of John', *BA*, xvii (1954), 78 ff.

Murphy, R. E. 'Assumptions and Problems in Old Testament Wisdom Research', *CBQ*, xxix (1967), 109 ff.

Nash, H. S. 'The Exegesis of the School of Antioch', *JBL*, xi (1892), pt. 1, pp. 32 ff.

Nordberg, H. 'A Reconsideration of the Date of St Athanasius' *contra Gentes and de Incarnatione*', *SP*, iii, 262 ff.

Opitz, H. G. 'Euseb von Caesarea als Theologe', *ZNTW*, xxxiv (1935), 131 ff.

Otis, B. 'Cappadocian Thought as a Coherent System', *DOP*, xii (1958), 95 ff.

Perry, A. M. 'Is John an Alexandrian Gospel?', *JBL*, lxiii (1944), 99 ff.

Pollard, T. E. 'The Fourth Gospel: its Background and Early Interpretation', *ABR*, vii (1959), 41 ff.

'The Exegesis of John x. 30 in the Early Trinitarian Controversies', *NTS*, iii (1956–7), 334 ff.

'The Origins of Arianism', *JTS*, N.S. ix (1958), 103 ff.

' "That they all may be one" (John xvii. 21)—and the Unity of the Church', *ExpT*, lxx (1959), 149 ff.

'The Impassibility of God', *SJT*, viii (1955), 353 ff.

'The Origins of Christian Exegesis', *JRH*, i (1961), 138 ff.

'The Exegesis of Scripture and the Arian Controversy', *BJRL*, xli (1959), 414 ff.

Pollard, T. E. (*cont.*)

'Cosmology and the Prologue of the Fourth Gospel', *VC*, XII (1958), 147 ff.

'Logos and Son in Origen, Arius and Athanasius', *SP*, II (*TU*, 64), 1957, 282 ff.

'The Creeds of A.D. 325: Antioch, Caesarea, Nicaea', *SJT*, XIII (1960), 278 ff.

Prestige, G. L. "'Αγέν[v]ητος and γεν[v]ητός and Kindred Words in Eusebius and the Early Arians', *JTS*, XXIV (1923), 486 ff.

Quispel, G. 'Gnosticism and the New Testament', *VC*, XIX (1965), 65 ff.

Reicke, B. 'Traces of Gnosticism in the Dead Sea Scrolls?', *NTS*, I (1954–5), 137 ff.

Richard, M. 'L'introduction du mot "hypostase" dans la théologie de l'incarnation', *MSR*, II (1945), 5 ff., 243 ff.

'Saint Athanase et la psychologie du Christ selon les Ariens', *MSR*, IV (1947), 5 ff.

Ritschl, D. 'Athanasius, Source of New Questions', *JES*, I (1964), 319 ff.

Robinson, J. A. T. 'The New Look on the Fourth Gospel', *SE*, I (1959), 338 ff. (= *Twelve New Testament Studies*, London, 1962, p. 94 ff.).

Schneemelcher, W. 'Zur Chronologie des arianischen Streites', *TLZ*, LXXIX (1954), 393 ff.

Simonetti, M. 'Alcune considerazioni sul contributo di Atanasio alla Lotta controgli Ariani', *Studi e Materiali di Storia delle Religioni*, XXXVIII (1967), 513 ff.

'S. Agostino e gli Ariani', *Revue des Études Augustiniennes*, XIII (1967), pp. 55 ff.

'L'esegesi ilariana di Col. i. 15 a', *Vetera Christianorum*, II (1965), 165 ff.

Skard, E. 'Asterios von Amaseia und Asterios der Sophist', *SO*, fasc. 20 (1940), pp. 86 ff.

Snape, H. C. 'The Fourth Gospel, Ephesus and Alexandria', *HTR*, XLVII (1954), 1 ff.

Spanneut, M. 'La position théologique d'Eustathe d'Antioche', *JTS*, N.S. V (1954), 220 ff.

Stead, G. C. 'Divine Substance in Tertullian', *JTS*, N.S. XIV (1963), 46 ff.

'The Platonism of Arius', *JTS*, N.S. XV (1964), 16 ff.

'The Significance of the *Homoousios*', *SP*, III, 397 ff.

Strong, T. B. 'The History of the Theological Term Substance', *JTS*, II (1901), 224 ff.; III (1902), 22 ff., 291 ff.; IV (1903), 28 ff.

Testuz, M. 'Un nouveau manuscrit de l'homélie "Peri Pascha" de Méliton', *SP*, III, 139 ff.

Tetz, M. 'Zur Theologie des Markell von Ankyra I. Eine Markell-ische Schrift *de Incarnatione et contra Arianos*', $\mathcal{Z}KG$, LXXV (1964), 217 ff.

'Zur Theologie des Markell von Ankyra II. Markells Lehre von der Adamssohnschaft Christi und eine pseudoklementinische Tradition über die wahren Lehrer und Propheten', $\mathcal{Z}KG$, LXXIX (1968), 3 ff.

Tuilier, A. 'Le sens du terme ὁμοούσιος dans le vocabulaire théologique d'Arius et de l'école d'Antioche', *SP*, III, 421 ff.

Turner, C. H. 'ὁ υἱός μου ὁ ἀγαπητός', *JTS*, XXVII (1926), 113 ff.

White, R. C. 'Melito of Sardis: Earliest Christian Orator', *LTQ*, II (1967), 82 ff.

Wiles, M. F. 'Some Reflections on the Origins of the Doctrine of the Trinity', *JTS*, N.S. VIII (1957), 92 ff.

'Eternal Generation', *JTS*, N.S. XII (1961), 284 ff.

'In Defence of Arius', *JTS*, N.S. XIII (1962), 339 ff.

Wilken, R. L. 'Tradition, Exegesis and the Christological Controversies', *CH*, XXIV (1955), 123 ff.

Williams, G. H. 'Christology and Church–State Relations in the Fourth Century', *CH*, XX (1951), no. 3, pp. 3–33; no. 4, pp. 3–26.

Wilson, R. McL. 'Gnostic Origins', *VC*, IX (1955), 193 ff.

'Philo and the Fourth Gospel', *ExpT*, LXV (1953–4), 47 ff.

Winter, P. 'Μονογενὴς παρὰ πατρός', $\mathcal{Z}RGG$, V (1953), 335 ff.

Wolfson, H. A. 'Philosophical Implications of Arianism and Apollinarianism', *DOP*, XII (1958), 3 ff.

I. INDEX OF PASSAGES CITED

I. INDEX OF PASSAGES CITED

A. OLD TESTAMENT

John (*cont.*)

i. 12	16, 21(2), 179 n.
i. 13	133, 179 n.
i. 14	9, 13, 15, 16, 19, 66, 69 f., 72(2), 73, 81, 82, 83, 84, 85, 112, 128, 129, 133, 168, 175, 177 n., 179 n., 186, 197, 210, 216, 235, 242, 258, 269, 275, 291, 310(2), 313, 314(2)
i. 15	16, 72, 269, 271
i. 16	15, 16, 269, 371
i. 17	16, 21, 35, 217, 274, 285
i. 18	14, 15, 16, 21, 66, 81, 147, 148, 149, 149 n., 151, 157, 158, 168, 177 n., 197, 212, 213, 259, 271, 286, 305, 308(2), 311(2)
i. 29	16 n., 21, 66
i. 30	16, 19
i. 36	16 n., 66
i. 41	16 n.
i. 49	16 n., 66
i. 50	66
ii. 16	66
ii. 19	73
iii. 2	16 n.
iii. 3	136
iii. 5	237
iii. 6	285
iii. 13	54
iii. 16	16, 16n., 21, 158, 158 n., 168, 177 n., 197, 215, 286
iii. 16–19	307
iii. 16–18	259, 272
iii. 16 f.	21, 66
iii. 17	17, 21, 177 n., 187, 197, 210, 308
iii. 18	158, 168, 177 n., 286, 307
iii. 19	270
iii. 31 f.	72, 73, 272
iii. 31	270
iii. 32	270, 272
iii. 34	17, 100
iii. 35 f.	234, 240
iii. 35	66, 270, 272, 280
iii. 36	309
iv. 19	16 n.
iv. 22	177 n.
iv. 25	66
iv. 29	19
iv. 34	17, 66
iv. 47	21
v. 7	177 n.
v. 17	66, 204, 205, 206, 260, 310
v. 18	66, 177 n., 201
v. 19 ff.	66
v. 19 f.	17(2)
v. 19	27 n., 72, 204, 205(3), 209, 228
v. 22 f.	278
v. 22	234, 238, 240
v. 23	17, 147, 153, 190, 225, 226, 278
v. 24	17
v. 26	72, 239, 240, 270, 272, 277
v. 30	17, 262, 277
v. 36	17, 66, 208, 214
v. 37–8	229
v. 37	17, 66
v. 43	16, 66
vi. 6	240
vi. 14	16
vi. 29	17, 66
vi. 32	177 n.
vi. 35	307
vi. 37	234, 238, 240, 270
vi. 38–40	210
vi. 38	17, 73(2), 177 n., 226, 277(2)
vi. 39	17
vi. 40	17, 21
vi. 41	177 n.
vi. 42	177 n.
vi. 44	17, 67, 147
vi. 46	17, 72, 205
vi. 48	270
vi. 50	177 n.
vi. 51	72, 177 n., 270
vi. 57	17, 277
vi. 58	177 n., 272
vi. 62	72
vi. 63	197, 257, 265, 294
vi. 65	170 n.
vi. 69	16 n., 66
vii. 15 f.	66
vii. 16	17
vii. 18	17
vii. 26–9	66
vii. 28	16
vii. 29	17
vii. 32 f.	66
vii. 38	307
vii. 40	16 n.
viii. 12	21, 98, 177 n., 198, 210, 270
viii. 14 f.	72
viii. 16	17, 66
viii. 17 f.	73, 274
viii. 18	17, 66

D. PATRISTIC WRITINGS

D. PATRISTIC WRITINGS

II. INDEX OF PROPER NAMES

351

B. MODERN AUTHORS

III. INDEX OF WORDS

A. GREEK

B. LATIN

IV. INDEX OF SUBJECTS